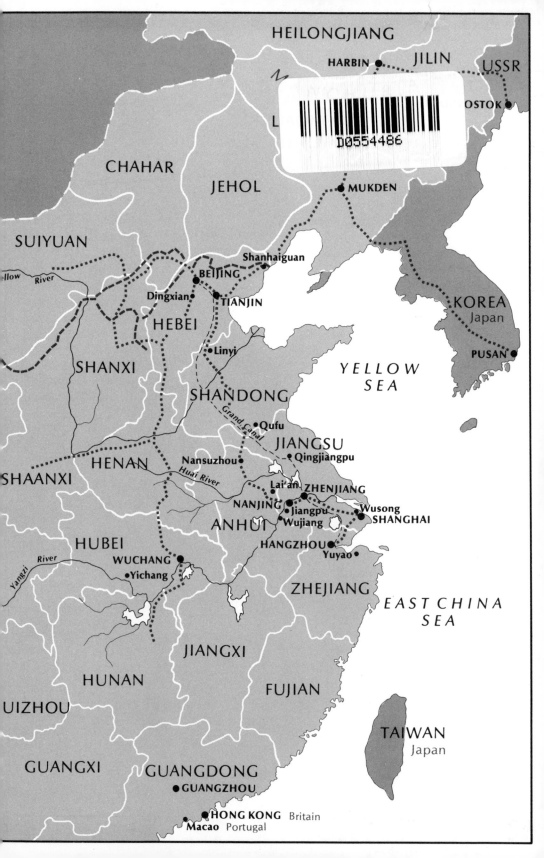

go cloth

12⁵⁶

THE
STUBBORN
EARTH

THE

STUBBORN

EARTH

American Agriculturalists on Chinese Soil, 1898–1937

RANDALL E. STROSS

University of California Press
Berkeley   Los Angeles   London

University of California Press
Berkeley and Los Angeles, California

University of California Press, Ltd.
London, England

Library of Congress Cataloging in Publication Data

Stross, Randall E.
  The stubborn earth.

  Bibliography:
  Includes index.
    1. Agriculture—China—History.   2. Agriculturists—
United States—History.   3. Agriculture—United States—
History.   4. Agriculture—China—Technology transfer—
History.   5. Agriculture—United States—Technology
transfer—History.   I. Title.
S471.C6S78   1986   630'.951   86-5547
ISBN 0-520-05700-0 (alk. paper)

Printed in the United States of America

1   2   3   4   5   6   7   8   9

To Maureen

CONTENTS

ACKNOWLEDGMENTS

I am indebted to many individuals and institutions for their help, and I am afraid that brief acknowledgment here will convey most inadequately the generous spirit that I found so often in the course of seeking assistance.

The research for the Chinese side of the story told in this book began with graduate work at Stanford University. Hal Kahn and Lyman Van Slyke were ideal advisers—always insistent upon high standards, yet unceasingly encouraging and caring. The cooperative and familial spirit in which they nurtured their students produced a closely knit brood, and I learned much from the others in the nest: Gail Hershatter, Emily Honig, and Helen Chauncey. Since leaving Stanford, I have continued to rely heavily on guidance provided by the members of the old group. Hal, Van, Gail, Emily, and Helen all read this book in draft form and offered copious editorial suggestions.

I owe a special debt to Larry Schneider, who helped me start the postdoctoral research in American archives and who critiqued the draft manuscript. I also obtained suggestions from a number of other gracious individuals who read the manuscript and contributed numerous improvements: Dan Bromley, Gould Colman, John Dixon, Chris Gibbs, Bill Haas, Chuck Hayford, Emily and Norm Rosenberg, Vikram Seth, and Barry Shank.

Many institutions were unstinting in their support. On the American side, I received the assistance of library and archival staff at Stanford and the East Asian Collection of the Hoover Institution; the University of California at Berkeley and the Bancroft Library; the Rockefeller Archive Center; Yale University Divinity School; Cornell University; the Library of Congress, the National Archives, and the National Agricultural Library; Pennsylvania State University; International Harvester Company; the University of Minnesota; the Midwest China Center; Claremont College; and the University of Hawaii at Manoa.

On the Chinese side, I am most grateful to the helpful staff and officials of Nanjing University, who cheerfully hosted a two-year stay. I would also like to thank particularly those individual members of various library staffs who assisted me at Nanjing University, Beijing University, the Nanjing Library, the Shanghai Library, and the Beijing Library. Because I found that many libraries in China did not welcome Chinese patrons, and welcomed foreign patrons even less, the assistance I received at these institutions was doubly appreciated.

Funding to support the research in China was provided by Stanford University and the National Academy of Sciences' Committee on Scholarly Communication with the People's Republic of China. In the United States, Rockefeller University awarded a travel grant that permitted me to use the materials at the Rockefeller Archive Center.

Two institutions helped me put the results of my research into book form. The East-West Center, in Honolulu, awarded a postdoctoral fellowship that permitted me to spend the 1984–85 academic year at the center, free to devote myself to the task of writing. I was helped by many individuals there, and would like to thank Katina Clark and Sheryl Bryson in particular for their excellent editorial assistance during the year. The center also commissioned Pat Pennywell, at the University of Hawaii, to prepare the endpaper map. For the stay in Hawaii, the Colorado School of Mines provided financial assistance and a leave of absence, a package that gave me a sabbatical long before a junior faculty member should have been eligible for one.

At the University of California Press, Victoria Scott and Stanley Holwitz deserve special thanks for the tender care they gave the book.

Golden, Colorado   R. S.
January 1986

A NOTE ABOUT TERMS AND ROMANIZATION

For readers who may not be familiar with modern Chinese history, I have provided some background material in the introduction and in the body of the text.

A few preliminary words about terms may be helpful. The standard measure of land in China is the *mou*, about one-sixth of an acre; the standard unit of currency is the *yuan*, the exchange value of which fluctuated in the early twentieth century between US $0.50 (1900) and $0.30 (1937). United States equivalents are provided in parentheses whenever *mou* and *yuan* appear in the text.

I used *pinyin* for most Chinese names and terms, but changed neither the names of Chinese who adopted their own spelling scheme nor those of figures such as Sun Yat-sen and Chiang Kai-shek, who were well-known to Americans. I also left untouched the idiosyncratic romanization of Chinese phrases, places, and persons that occur in the directly quoted writings of Americans who were resident in China. The reader who is familiar with Mandarin may be irritated by these inconsistencies, but is unlikely to be led astray. One brief word of caution is needed to point out a distinction between "Nanking" and "Nanjing," however. Both spellings recur throughout the book, but "Nanjing" refers exclusively to the city, while "Nanking" is reserved for the University of Nanking (*Jinling daxue*), just as it was used in the shorthand of the university staff fifty years ago.

I have not continued another convention—namely, that of referring to Chinese who lived in the countryside as "peasants," a quaint taxonomic term that Americans usually employed and that served to keep the Chinese apart—and ranked vaguely below—the "farmers" at home. Later, American social scientists perpetuated the separation, giving rise to journals and conferences devoted to "peasant studies." This book favors a consistent use of the term "farmers," applied to Chinese and Americans alike (as the Chinese term *nong min* conveys). Their lives in the two countries were different in important respects, but those differences need not be linguistically loaded.

INTRODUCTION

George Washington and the Qianlong emperor of China were contemporaries—the one, ruler of a country small and new; the other, of a country large and not so new. During their simultaneous reigns, both countries were overwhelmingly agricultural; the mechanization and scientific support of agriculture had yet to take hold widely in either one. Both men died in 1799, and in the hundred years that followed, agriculture in the United States was rapidly revolutionized; in China, it remained largely unchanged. The reasons for the difference were many, but the widely differing personal interests of Washington and Qianlong augured divergent paths for the two countries.

Each man, as sovereign of an agricultural country, was aware of the importance of agriculture to his nation's interests. And each was a large landholder himself: Washington at one time held close to 70,000 acres scattered in thirty-seven localities; Qianlong was one of the largest landlords in the world, since the "royal banner" holdings (as well as all land in the Chinese Empire) were legally his. But Washington, unlike Qianlong, liked nothing better than to farm the land himself (he was also the only one of the American founders who freed his slaves). He tinkered with new tools, tried out new seeds and manures, and ran his five holdings at Mount Vernon as a kind of experiment station. To Washington, farming was more than a passing hobby—it was his primary intellectual interest, his favorite topic of conversation, and the focus of his private correspondence. His friends knew that the way to please him was to send him new seeds or animal breeds, and Noah Webster said that at the time of his visit to Mount Vernon, when Washington was experimenting with using muck dredged from the Potomac as a fertilizer, the standing toast was, "Success to the mud!" [1]

In stark contrast to the muck at Mount Vernon was the rarefied atmosphere of the court of Qianlong, at the apogee of the Qing dynasty and the center of what many historians regard as one of the most luxurious reigns in Chinese history. When Britain's Lord George Macartney led a mission to China in 1793, he took the best gifts George III had to offer: Vulliamy clocks, Wedgwood porcelains, globes, orreries, and an entire planetarium. But these could not match the Chinese treasures that casually adorned the palace. It was the great age of decorative art in China, and Qianlong was a sophisticated patron, better trained in the arts, in literature, and in history than the graduates of most European universities of the time. The Qianlong court was physically and intellectually far removed from agriculture; in the hermetic inner sanctum of the imperial compound, mud was not the subject of toasts.[2]

Washington and Qianlong never corresponded; if they had, Washington would have found himself hopelessly outclassed. Qianlong was an accomplished and prolific writer who bequeathed to posterity more than forty-three thousand poems. Washington left more prosaic writings, such as a diary filled with recipes for composts and notes on improved farm tools. It would be hard to picture the Qianlong emperor, in all his regal glory, noting as Washington did in a typical diary entry: "Spent the greater part of the day in making a new plow of my own Invention. She answered very well."[3]

A provincial bumpkin compared to Qianlong, Washington was able to see what Qianlong—and Qianlong's successors—could not: the need for direct governmental support of agricultural improvement. In a number of addresses to Congress, Washington raised the topic, and in his last annual message, in 1796, he urged the creation of a federal board of agriculture, "charged with collecting and diffusing information, and enabled by premiums and small pecuniary aids to encourage and assist a spirit of discovery and improvement." The board would stimulate advancement by "drawing to a common center the results everywhere of individual skill and observation and spreading them thence over the whole nation. Experience accordingly has shewn [sic] that they are very cheap instruments of immense national benefits."[4]

While China in 1790 had a population of well over 275 million, the United States had only 4 million; it was a nation too small and inexperienced to afford the luxury of being indifferent to other countries. Washington and other Americans looked abroad for examples of improved agricultural practices or products worthy of import, and much early attention was directed toward Europe. Washington corresponded with Arthur Young and other leading agriculturalists in England. Jefferson was more aggressive; while traveling in Italy he discovered a new variety of rice that the Italians did not want to share—its export was prohibited, he was told, "on pain of death"—and smuggled out a packet of the seed for testing in South Carolina and Georgia.[5]

Chinese agriculture was largely ignored except by Benjamin Franklin, who loved reading about things Chinese and had the impression that China "clothes its Inhabitants with Silk, while it feeds them plentifully and has besides a vast Quantity both of raw and manufactured [silk] to spare for Exportation." He carefully noted any enlightening materials that he happened across about Chinese agriculture and sericulture, and gave thought to what practices might be suitable for

American adoption. After reading that Chinese farmers in Zhejiang Province collected two crops of mulberry leaves a year for silkworm feeding, Franklin wrote that this "may account for the great Plenty of Silk there," but "perhaps this would not answer with us, since it is not practis'd in Italy, tho' it might be try'd." He never visited China himself, but when in Europe he sent back to America silkworm eggs and mulberry cuttings in an effort to start a silk industry like that of "the most populous of all Countries," which appeared to Franklin to provide so well for its people.[6]

Early American curiosity about Chinese agricultural practices did not lead to direct contacts, however, and the Chinese could scarcely have been less curious about the Americans. In the nineteenth century, agriculture in the two countries took separate courses that were not influenced by each other, and the more dramatic events took place in the United States. Even before the Civil War, the period customarily said to mark the beginning of mechanized agriculture in the United States, a spectacular technological revolution was under way.

Colonial American farming, an amalgam of practices from extensive European agriculture and intensive native American and African farming, used plows, hoes, axes, scythes, and other tools whose inefficiency imposed a tight limit on the area a single family could cultivate. But in the 1830s, new designs and new machines began to appear. John Lane, an Illinois blacksmith, made prairie sodbusting possible when he fashioned a plow with a shiny moldboard that scoured well and let the sticky soil slide off. John Deere added a steel share and new features; the resulting design scoured so well that it was called "the singing plow." The new plows actually ran through the soil too fast and had to be put into gangs, with as many as twelve or fourteen plows pulled by a large team of horses; the jump in productivity was tremendous. At the same time, new horse-drawn drills and seeders proved most profitable on larger acreages, further encouraging the expansion of tilled land.[7]

The mechanical reaper was perhaps the single invention most responsible for the revolution in American farming during the nineteenth century. Although many American inventors offered these horse-drawn machines, which were vastly more efficient than hand tools such as the cradle, it was Cyrus McCormick, a master of both self-promotion and mechanical invention, who garnered the most public attention. McCormick patented his design in 1831 and in 1851 sent his machine to the London Exhibition, where European observers laughed at its appearance: it was huge, unwieldy, an "ugly duckling." But in a practical demonstration in a wheat field a few miles outside of London, the machine went through the wheat, which was still green and heavy, without difficulty, cutting a swath 74 yards long in 70 seconds. An American observer noted that the McCormick reaper not only cut down the grain but also "mowed down British prejudice and opened the way for the bringing of our countrymen and their contributions before the public in a proper light." When the machine was returned to the exhibition hall, it was awarded the Grand Medal and attracted more visitors than the famed Koh-i-noor diamond.[8]

With the new plows and machines, white Americans pressed westward at an accelerating pace before the Civil War. In Minnesota, for example, only 1,900 acres were plowed in 1850, but by 1860 more than 5 million acres were in crops. National grain statistics also reflected this trend: during the same decade, annual corn production for the United States doubled and, even more dramatic, annual wheat production rose from 44 million bushels to almost 200 million. Such increases fed a nascent boastfulness and a cult of the machine. In the 1850s, many Americans (including Abraham Lincoln) prematurely hailed steam-powered plows as an earthshaking advance. Though earthshaking in a strictly literal sense, the engine proved too cumbersome to be hauled over the fields and too expensive for individual farmers to own. Inventor J. W. Fawkes, whose name the *Wisconsin Farmer* had declared would be "immortal," was soon forgotten.[9]

In congratulating themselves on their mechanical ingenuity, Americans at the time did not fully credit the foreign or nonmechanical contributions to their agricultural successes. In 1841, an English translation of German chemist Justus von Liebig's *Chemistry and Its Applications* was published. A classic in agricultural chemistry, it was widely influential and explained the need to replenish the nutrients in the soil. Until Liebig's work became known, the prevailing understanding had been that plants received most of their nourishment from the air.[10]

More important still, yet largely unappreciated, were the newly devised means of transmitting agricultural information to farmers. An early farm organization was the agricultural society. Established in the 1780s, it imitated earlier English organizations dedicated to seeking out and encouraging more productive ways of farming. After serving as President, Thomas Jefferson helped write the constitution of a Virginian agricultural society, proposing that accounts of good and bad farming be assembled so "the choicest processes" could be culled from each farm. In 1807, an exhibition of Merino sheep in Pennsylvania launched the first livestock and agricultural fair, where farmers could show the fruits of their labor and learn from others.[11]

American farmers were also readers. More than four hundred farm periodicals were begun before the Civil War. With the increased interest in agricultural science (Ralph Waldo Emerson predicted that "the chemist with a teaspoonful of guano could turn a sand bank into a corn hill") came the establishment of the first agricultural schools. In 1855, the Farmers High School was founded, later to become Pennsylvania State University. Michigan State Agricultural College was established two years later. And a one-man college of agriculture, the Sheffield Scientific School at Yale, earned the praise of *Scientific American*, which said, "To see Yale College stepping out from among the mists of antiquity and the groves of dead languages and taking up the shovel and the hoe is certainly one of the signs of the times."[12]

These changes in American agriculture went largely unnoticed in China. One exception was the American steam-powered plow, which Feng Guifen, a scholar and official, heard about and assumed was a machine widely used in the United States; apparently he was unaware of the exaggerated and premature nature of American claims. Feng wrote several essays extolling the benefits of the fire-wheeled machine (*huo lun ji*) in opening new land for cultivation. He reported, "They require little effort and are quite successful." Little notice was taken of Feng's recommendation.[13]

China was preoccupied with problems that were more serious and pressing than anything the United States had confronted. Widespread corruption during Qianlong's reign had depleted the imperial treasury; the monarchy had difficulty suppressing a stubborn millenarian rebellion, which depleted the treasury further; and Western powers, led by Britain but including the United States, insistently claimed the right to sell the Chinese any and all goods, including opium (though the same powers did not permit opium to be sold freely within their own countries). China refused to acquiesce, and the issue led to a war with Britain. China was completely unprepared, partly because military academies were as unknown in China at the time as were agricultural schools. Unlike Yale, but just like Harvard and other elite American institutions, China's finest academies continued to dwell in the "mists of antiquity." Defeat brought major legal concessions in the "Unequal Treaties," as well as increased opium imports, and in the wake of these embarrassments, the monarchy found that its legitimacy was questioned by the populace.

Then, in the middle of the nineteenth century, the separate histories of China and the United States turned along parallel and horrible paths: each was torn by the bloodiest civil war in its history. While the Union sought to counter the secession of the South and preserve the United States, the Qing dynasty was desperately fighting to contain the Taiping Revolution; the fighting and disruption of the latter claimed thirty million lives, many of the casualties being victims of starvation. Agriculture was devastated, as a gentryman in Anhui described: "From 1860 to 1864, for five years, people could not grow food. Toward the end all roots and herbs in the hills were exhausted and cannibalism occurred. Consequently epidemics struck. At that time corpses and human skeletons piled up and thorns and weeds choked the roads. Within a radius of several tens of *li* there was no vestige of humanity. The county's original population was over 300,000. By the time the rebels were cleared only a little over 6,000 survived." In the midst of such devastation, Chinese agriculture could hardly advance.[14]

In the United States, the worst destruction was restricted to the South, and the departure of Southern politicians from Washington permitted Lincoln and the Republican party to launch new federal government programs dear to the heart of "free-soil" agricultural interests. In 1862, legislation was approved to establish a Department of Agriculture and to provide federal aid through large land grants for a system of state agricultural colleges. Similar proposals had been introduced several times before but had failed to pass. That China did not adopt such measures during its civil war is perfectly understandable; so too is the prior reluctance of American congresses and presidents to approve similar proposals and enlarge the traditional responsibility of the federal government.

The new Department of Agriculture grew out of George Washington's original proposal. The usefulness of a federal department devoted solely to agriculture had been suggested through the years by activities of the Patent Office, which in the 1830s had begun to distribute seeds obtained from abroad to American farmers. The seeds (30,000 packages were distributed in 1840 alone) led to the collection of farm statistics and an interest in agricultural experimentation; by the 1850s, the Patent Office employed its own chemist, botanist, and entomologist to conduct research. These ad hoc arrangements seemed inadequate; Henry Ellsworth, the commissioner of patents who began the seed distribution, had appealed early for a more suitable government agency to conduct the work. He wrote in 1837: "Our citizens who are led by business or pleasure into foreign countries, and especially the officers of our navy and others in public employment abroad, would feel a pride in making collections of valuable plants and seeds, if they could be sure of seeing the fruits of their labors accrue to the benefit of the nation at large." Many of the seeds, however, had "perished on their hands, for want of some means of imparting to the public the benefit they had designed to confer." [15]

The legislation that finally established a Department of Agriculture in 1862 charged the department "to acquire and to diffuse among the people of the United States useful information on subjects connected with agriculture in the most general and comprehensive sense of that word, and to procure, propagate, and distribute among the people new and valuable seeds and plants." The first commissioner of agriculture, Isaac Newton, used China as an example of a place from which the United States had much to learn. "While Americans are ever disposed to boast of their inventive skill and teachable disposition," Newton wrote in his first report in 1862, "the elder nations, which we affect to despise, offer us some valuable lessons in agriculture. The Chinese, by minute and careful culture, by rotation of crops, and by the use of *every possible kind* of manure, have made their lands yield undiminished products for thousands of years." In pursuit of a better variety of sorghum as a sugar source, Newton dispatched "an educated, intelligent, and reliable person to China, with directions to purchase seed, and ascertain minutely the method of making the sugar as practiced by the natives of that country." No record was made of the mission's return. [16]

In the United States, labor shortages during the Civil War accelerated agricultural mechanization, a process that Newton described as one of the "compensations" for the war's "wide-spread evils." Unlike the men in the Revolutionary War, Union soldiers did not have to desert and go home to harvest their crops—machines took their place. Secretary of War Stanton, as well as others, went so far as to credit the McCormick reaper with "winning" the war, and to claim that

McCormick had done more for the cause of abolition than William Lloyd Garrison or Wendell Phillips.[17]

A succession of new machines and other equipment speeded farm mechanization in the United States after the war. Sulky gang plows doubled the amount of land a farmer could handle; new disk harrows broke up heavy soils; spring-tooth harrows were devised for rocky and lighter soils; and improved seed drills permitted economic seeding for large wheat operations. Coupling reapers and threshers, giant combines appeared in the 1880s and were pulled by twenty or more horses in two ranks. A brief period of steam-powered combines preceded the gasoline tractor, which began to be mass-produced around the turn of the century. The early tractors were not sleek. In 1892, John Froelich, an Iowa farmer, improvised a functioning tractor that weighed 9,000 pounds and produced about 30 horsepower. Still, it was an advance over the heavier and more expensive steam machines, and a large advance in efficiency over horses and other draft animals. Federal support of agriculture expanded at an equal pace, with establishment of agricultural experiment stations in every state—the first such system in the world. And in 1889, the Department of Agriculture was raised to cabinet-level rank, signaling formal recognition of its importance.[18]

Agricultural mechanization, in tandem with the industrialization of the urban economy, gave many nineteenth-century Americans an exalted sense of accomplishment and exceptionalism. Joseph C. G. Kennedy, a superintendent of the census, wrote with pride:

> With us but few of the prejudices have to be overcome which in older countries attach to the use of improved agricultural implements, and to a system of culture obsolete where intelligence prevails. Here we have no dull, lethargic confidence in the perfection of anything connected with agriculture, because we cannot move without realizing the rapid, ever-varying improvement, such as must convince even a man blind from his youth that nearly all the operations of the farm are conducted in a manner different from what they were formerly.[19]

✧ ✧ ✧ ✧ ✧

Extreme pride, however, often led to extreme condescension toward those who appeared to lag behind. No one better illustrates this problem than Charles Denby, the American minister to China for thirteen years, under the administrations of Cleveland, Harrison, and McKinley. When Denby first took the post in 1885, he was a diplomatic innocent who had earned the appointment by virtue of his many years of labor in Indiana state politics. He not only knew little about China but was uninterested in learning, and was content to spend his many years there cloistered in the community of foreign residents. This did not prevent him from assuming the air of an authority and lecturing Americans on all aspects of China, drawn from what he implied was his own vast storehouse of knowledge.[20]

Denby took a particular interest in Chinese agriculture. He told American readers, "In a country like China, from whose broad plains 400,000,000 of our

fellow-men obtain their sustenance, no subject is of such interest as agriculture."
Unlike Isaac Newton, who had urged Americans to learn from China, Denby
credited the Chinese only with early development of agricultural methods, and
granted little else: "Notwithstanding the great antiquity of agriculture among
them, the Chinese have failed to make any great progress in it. Their system of
cultivation is very careful and marked by attention to details; but it shows ignorance of the principles of rotation of crops and of adaptation of soils to particular
grains, and an extremely primitive knowledge of agricultural implements." In
irrigation and the skilled terracing of steep slopes, as everything else, "the Chinese
seem to have early learned its value and developed it practically to a certain degree
of efficiency, and then stopped." Chinese fields might look impressively like gardens, but, Denby warned the unwary, "they have made no improvements in this
line for a thousand years, just as they have stood still in every other art of
civilization." [21]

Based upon what he had observed when spending summers in the Western
Hills outside of Beijing, Denby declared that the arrival of Americans was pro-
vidential. Echoing the conventional judgment of other resident foreigners, Denby
wrote that agriculture in China was "what it was millenniums ago, and what it
would always have remained had the foreigner not come with his strange
inventions." [22]

In the latter part of the nineteenth century, the China that Denby observed
was still recovering from the Taiping Revolution, and had fresh diplomatic and
military setbacks as Western powers imposed new demands on the weakened
monarchy. In more tranquil, earlier periods, China had developed the most sophisticated agriculture in the world and had given Europe the moldboard plow,
one of the fundamental elements in the transformation of North European agriculture (though the gift remained unacknowledged). Before Denby's era, Chinese
agricultural development had been anything but stagnant. Between the eighth and
twelfth centuries in central and south China, mastery of wet-rice cultivation made
possible the settlement of what was then largely a frontier. In the sixteenth
century, three major food crops were introduced into China: sweet potatoes, corn,
and peanuts. An agricultural revolution followed on unirrigated upland fields that
had not been cultivated previously. New cultivation techniques and seed varieties
further increased productivity, and despite few improvements in farm tools,
Chinese crop yields climbed steadily, doubling between the fourteenth and
nineteenth centuries. [23]

Charles Denby had looked at the simple tools used in fields near his favorite
summer resort in north China and had jumped to the sweeping conclusion that
nothing had changed for "millenniums." The plows in use on the north China plain
had indeed changed little over time, just as many tools in use on most American
farms had resembled those of biblical times until just a few years before. But north
China, situated outside the rice belt, had not kept pace with the rest of the country

in the revolutionary advances made in soil preparation, water control, selection of superior rice varieties, introduction of new upland crops, and publication of agricultural treatises. The action had taken place in central and south China, which Denby had not visited.

China also pioneered in the widespread distribution of agricultural handbooks written in understandable terms for the literate gentry. In the Qing dynasty (1644–1911), however, publication of the handbooks was infrequent; among scholars, intramural scholasticism had supplanted earlier intellectual interest in agricultural affairs. A lone dissenting voice of the early nineteenth century was that of Bao Shichen, who blamed fellow scholars for the recent failure to increase agricultural productivity: "They despise anything to do with farming, and do not research into it." Thus the problem belonged to a specific period and was not a symptom of suprahistorical inertia. China had achieved agricultural supremacy in an earlier period, between the eighth and the twelfth centuries, when massive migration to south China—then an open frontier—stimulated technological innovation. The United States was witnessing a similar phenomenon in its own history.[24]

Although the Chinese government had a long history of actively encouraging agricultural innovation, the Qing emperors failed to continue that tradition; early monarchs, like Qianlong, stood aloof from agriculture, and later ones were preoccupied with military affairs and national "self-strengthening." Traditional isolation and ethnocentrism also restricted the vision of Chinese leaders. The only examples of foreign accomplishments that were entertained for adoption in China were those that contributed to military prowess—Western-style armaments and armies were to be used to repel the Western powers—and even their adoption was steadfastly opposed by conservatives.

China's first major effort to seek information about the West was the Chinese Educational Mission, which in the early 1870s dispatched 120 young men, mostly between the ages of twelve and fifteen, to Hartford, Connecticut. The students, whose parents were required to sign an unconditional release allowing them to remain abroad for fifteen years, were expected to retain their Chinese identity (a staff of Chinese teachers accompanied them) while becoming thoroughly knowledgeable about the United States and eventually graduating from American colleges and universities.[25]

Sending boys abroad at a formative age for such a period of time fostered a rapid accumulation of knowledge but also led to a worrisome attachment to things American. The boys were required by their Chinese chaperons to wear long gowns, the traditional garment of the Chinese scholar, and to keep their hair plaited in a long queue. Their American schoolmates in Hartford taunted them, saying they looked like girls. The Chinese students pleaded to be allowed to look like the Americans, and the Chinese authorities granted a compromise: the queues must stay, but American trousers and coats would be permitted. More concessions to American ways were demanded over time, the Chinese lessons lapsed, and the students became passionately attached to baseball (their nicknames attest to their Americanization: Breezy Jack, Sitting Bull, Yankee Kwong). Sponsors in the government at home, tentative in their support of the experiment from the first, became alarmed at the students' deracination, as well as angry that the United States did not permit foreigners to enroll in the academies at West Point and Annapolis. The mission was recalled to China in 1882, prematurely ending the college educations of the students (about a dozen of whom refused to return).[26]

✢ ✢ ✢ ✢ ✢

In contrast to China, Japan was eager to assimilate Western knowledge. While China was besieged by foreign military threats and was forced to think of little but defense, the Meiji Restoration in Japan was immune to foreign intrusion precisely because the much larger plum of China was conveniently located next door, and thus embarked on a wide-ranging reform program. An important component of the program was agricultural improvement based on foreign models, particularly that of the United States. At first, in the early 1870s, Japanese officials assumed that the pattern of agriculture they admired in America could be transplanted easily to home. American tools were purchased; American fruit and vegetable seeds were imported; American textbooks, such as *Harris on the Pig* and *Parsons on the Rose*, were translated into Japanese. The Japanese also hired General Horace Capron, then commissioner of the U.S. Department of Agriculture, to serve as adviser for colonization of Hokkaido, the large northern island whose unsettled land seemed to resemble the northern territories of the American frontier. Capron stayed four years, and William Smith Clark, president of Massachusetts Agricultural College, came for one year to launch a new agricultural school (his parting words to the students were, "Boys, be ambitious"). After a decade of indiscriminate trials, however, the Japanese government realized that there were fundamental differences in agricultural conditions in the two countries and decided to emphasize agricultural improvement along more traditional Japanese lines.[27]

In this same period, when Japan had not only begun but also completed the process of obtaining what seemed useful from American agricultural experiences, China was just beginning to consider learning something about foreign agriculture. During the 1880s and early 1890s, new voices were heard among Chinese leaders calling for the government to help "enrich the people" (*fumin* or *limin*). Writing in 1890, Ma Jianzhong, a French-educated protégé of senior official Li Hongzhang, argued that China had to increase its exports and reduce its imports, which required agricultural modernization if Chinese goods were to be competitive in foreign markets. Chen Zhi, a secretary in the central government, noted that in Western countries development of industry did not mean neglect of agriculture, and urged that China set up a government office charged with the responsibility of promoting the country's agricultural improvement through proper measures.[28]

In 1895, Kang Youwei, the leading proponent of reform, carried an appeal for agricultural improvement directly to the Guangxu emperor. Kang was rhapsodic about Western achievements: in the West, "every kind of machine and vehicle is available to farmers; bird droppings are used for fertilizer; electricity is used to hasten growth; scalding can defrost the earth; glass covers can keep out winter air; with a mechanical reaper one person can equal the labor of several hundred; with a seed drill, 300 *mou* (50 acres) can be planted in one day; by selective planting, one kernel can produce 10,800; 1,000 kernels can feed one person for one year; two *mou* [less than 0.5 acre] can support one family; poor soil can be transformed into fertile." Kang had never visited the United States, and some of his impressions were quite remarkable—somewhere he had been told that the income to be earned from beekeeping was equal to that of "the gold mines of San Francisco" (which, strictly speaking, was probably true). But the most important lesson he drew from the American example was astute—namely, the critical role of government assistance. If "the nation," as Kang put it, provided Chinese farmers with some support, distributing agricultural information, encouraging agricultural societies, and providing agricultural specialists for consultation, then the country's agriculture would prosper as farmers made comparisons between old practices and new recommendations and discovered for themselves what methods should be discarded.[29]

Kang and others who urged the government to take initiative in supporting agricultural development were nationalists who felt deeply the humiliation of China's military defeats—first at the hands of the Western powers, then, in 1895, at the hands of the Japanese, whom the Chinese had traditionally regarded as an inferior race of "dwarfs." Clearly, something had to be done to strengthen the country, and the earlier fumbling with arsenals and military defenses was not sufficient. By the late 1890s, many Chinese intellectuals were calling for broad reforms based upon foreign examples. For agricultural development on a giant scale, China understandably would look closely at the United States, the world's most successful agricultural producer, even though differences in crops, conditions, and cultures made the match less than ideal.

✣ ✣ ✣ ✣ ✣

How transferable was American agriculture? James Bryce, a British observer, wrote in the late nineteenth century that western America was "one of the most interesting subjects the modern world has seen." With its good climate, fertile soil, and abundant resources, "the whole of this virtually unoccupied territory [was] thrown open to an energetic race, with all the appliances and contrivances of modern science at its command—these are phenomena absolutely without precedent in history, which cannot occur elsewhere, because our planet contains no such other favored tract of country."[30] China, crowded with a population of more than 400 million by the late nineteenth century, was certainly less "favored" than the United States had been when European-American settlers subjugated western North America. Nevertheless, some Chinese—and, when their attention was drawn to China, many Americans—believed that American agricultural expertise could be usefully applied to Chinese problems. A stream of Americans—senior agricultural specialists and inexperienced college graduates, agricultural missionaries and agricultural economists, seasoned farmers and well-meaning amateurs—made their way to China in the early twentieth century in search of adventure and an opportunity to help Chinese farming.

Some of these Americans were invited by the Chinese, and some invited themselves. In either case, no central agency dispatched them or received them, and they were scattered in different parts of China. The stories that follow are snapshots of the most prominent figures, the ones who wrote about their experiences and left behind evidence of their presence. Together they comprise most of the American corps of agricultural experts who went to China, but the experiences of their less literary agricultural colleagues are, of course, missing.

This album is an assembly of stories in which varying temperaments and circumstances yielded a range of encounters between orderly American ideals and disorderly Chinese realities. For the most part, I have let the participants tell the stories in their own words. As the reader becomes familiar with the major figures, some of the Americans may seem more likable than others, but one thing is certain: the group portrait does not fit tidily into the usual stereotypes—good or bad—of American reformers abroad.

Without sanding and smoothing the distinctive details of the individual stories, we can nevertheless discern several patterns that the participants themselves could not see. The reader will notice an evolution in American attitudes over time. In the 1890s and early 1900s, when China began to take an interest in American agriculture and hired the first Americans to serve as advisers, the United States seemed little interested in exporting American models of development to the Pacific. The principal U.S. Department of Agriculture representative stationed in China during this early period was interested only in what China had to offer the United States. But during the 1920s and 1930s, American power in the interwar period grew, and so too did Americans' self-confidence in their own expertise and "know-how"; accordingly, Americans went to China to show the Chinese how to reform their agricultural practices, establish agricultural schools, and administer government agricultural programs, all along American lines. By the mid-1930s, this assertiveness had grown to elephantine proportions, as in the ambitious plans of the Rockefeller Foundation to uplift the face of rural China—plans that went far beyond the foundation's mild expression of interest a decade before. The narrative of this book ends in 1937, when the Japanese invasion of China closed the era of peacetime experimentation there.

American self-confidence (some might call it hubris) was not simply a reflection of the United States' increasingly important position in world affairs, especially after World War I. It was also the outgrowth of American technological progress during the nineteenth century. Despite their different backgrounds and personalities, the Americans in China seem to have been united by an implicit faith in technology as China's salvation. The remarkable agricultural advances that America had recently achieved were fresh in the minds of early-twentieth-century Americans, who were eager to help China accomplish an equally spectacular success. The beneficent power of technology seemed unlimited, and Americans regarded themselves as the rightful tutors to the rest of the world. Thus the expansion of American influence abroad sprang partly from a national tendency toward technological conceit, which started strongly at the beginning of this century and became more pronounced over time.

One final and related pattern was the American tendency to assume that technological improvements would, in and of themselves, solve China's rural problems. The Americans saw themselves as technical experts who were traveling to China to impart universal truths of agronomy, soil science, and agricultural economics. They conceived of their mission narrowly, and rarely understood how social, political, cultural, and other conditions could affect their technical prescriptions for China. The reader will soon gain a sense of the segregated lives that the expatriate Americans led in China. Unable to speak the language, insulated physically as well as mentally from the Chinese world that surrounded them, and caught up in the intramural affairs of the expatriate community, Americans generally dwelt in protective bubbles. The stories that follow, based on their own accounts of their experiences, faithfully register the degree of their isolation. Unfortunately, they often leave the Chinese side of the picture poorly lighted.

The Americans in China were only dimly aware of the larger political turbulence that chronically engulfed them. The forty years between 1898 and 1937 encompassed three separate political eras in China: monarchical rule (1898–1911); warlord rule, administered by frequently changing generals (1912–1927); and Nationalist rule, under the direction of Chiang Kai-shek (1927–1937). Throughout all three eras, the national leader was only in nominal control of the country; national tax revenues were mostly diverted to military expenditures and were rarely available for economic programs; and official rhetoric denouncing "barbarians" and "imperialists" meant that resident foreigners were not always welcomed. Americans who went to China in the early twentieth century often knew little about nineteenth-century Chinese history. The political and financial problems that Western powers had created in the process of forcing China to open its doors meant that many Chinese, high and low, held a strong animus against Western foreigners. The Americans in China of course wanted to dissociate themselves from any earlier unfortunate episodes; they wanted to be judged as helpful individuals. But although circumstances forced the Chinese to look to the West for assistance in strengthening their economy, many individual Chinese regarded individual foreigners—including Americans—as China's scourge.

With political power in China shifting again and again, seemingly without end, and with their own status in China frequently placed in question, the Americans usually abandoned hope of large-scale agricultural programs that required the cooperation of the national government. Instead, they sought to build small research and field demonstration projects that they hoped would be copied sometime in the future, when China entered a politically more stable period. But even Americans with modest expectations found that Chinese soil was unyielding, both literally and figuratively. Experimental sanctuaries, they discovered painfully, could not remain isolated from the inhospitable political and social conditions that plagued rural China.

The present book closes with the account of an American-trained Chinese agronomist, Shen Zonghan, and his attempt to apply the lessons that he had learned in the United States. Like his American mentors, Shen subscribed to the belief that scientific and technological work could stand apart from—and be immune to—political, economic, social, and cultural difficulties. And like the Americans, Shen was stymied not by technical obstacles but by hindrances in the wider environment of human affairs. The stories in this book are of pioneers who were intrepid but who could not keep nontechnical problems from intruding into their domains of expertise. Their experiences make concrete the commonly repeated but perhaps still poorly appreciated maxim that technology and society are interdependent.

1

CURIOSITY

The U.S. Department of Agriculture Looks Abroad, 1890s–1910s

The Wisconsin historian Frederick Jackson Turner was not the first to announce the closing of the American frontier. Among others, the superintendent of the U.S. Census had sounded an alarm several years before Turner delivered his 1893 paper on the frontier, which earned his name a secure place in the minds of the reading public at the time, as well as in the lesson books of future schoolchildren. It was Turner, however, who articulately explained the disturbing implications of the news. Gone, he said, was the "gate of escape" that had allowed society to break with old customs and conventions. Gone too was opportunity for American political institutions to be constantly renewed by the down-to-earth way of life of the frontier. The American continent suddenly seemed cramped.[1]

In truth, the "frontier" of the American West was still largely uninhabited, but the idea that America was overcrowded captured the public imagination. The Panic of 1893, which ushered in the third major recession in as many decades, paralyzed the American economy; the cities were indeed crowded with unemployed people and unpurchased goods. Since America seemed no longer to have the capacity to absorb surpluses domestically, increased attention was directed toward finding markets abroad. A later historian, Walter LaFeber, has called the 1890s a time when America was in quest of "New Empire," not of colonial holdings but of commercial dominion and the strategic possessions needed to maintain and protect it.[2]

The United States in the 1890s looked primarily to Asia for opportunities to expand its influence. Josiah Strong, a fiery evangelist, had recently called for the Christianization of the East, and Alfred Thayer Mahan had proposed a large navy to protect American trade routes to the Pacific. At the end of the Spanish-American War, the United States gained control of the Philippines, Hawaii, Wake, and Guam, possessions that were considered important not for intrinsic benefits, but as stepping-stones to the real commercial prize: China.[3]

The commercial conquest of the fabled "China market" occupied the thoughts of many American business leaders during the late 1890s and early 1900s, and the

U.S. government seemed to be no less transfixed by the possibilities of trade. Given the expansionist temper of the times and the particular interest in China, it is hardly surprising that the U.S. Department of Agriculture (USDA) established a special section devoted to foreign agricultural work, with considerable emphasis placed on China.

The official apparatus of the state did not operate with the consensus or coordination suggested by appearances, however. Some members of the government regarded Chinese agricultural practices with contempt and worked toward promoting American agricultural exports to China. Others considered China's agriculture to be more advanced than America's in important respects and sought to import Chinese crops and methods. What might appear to have been a powerful state pursuing clearly defined objectives that meshed neatly with the expansionism of the times was actually nothing of the kind.

To Charles Denby, the self-appointed agricultural expert in residence in China, the need for American tools was clear, although he wavered between optimistic and pessimistic estimations of the future Chinese market for American agricultural technology. When discussing the ineffectiveness of the foot-driven Chinese irrigation pump, Denby predicted that "some time American windmill pumps will change all that, and it may not be very long in the future, either."[4] On another occasion he observed that even though American implements, especially plows, would greatly improve productivity, their "price will always operate against such introduction." Chinese tools were made cheaply by a local blacksmith or by the farmer himself; in contrast to rural America, "there are no great stores devoted to the sale of agricultural implements."[5]

Denby's subordinates, the staff in the consulates scattered in the Chinese hinterland, had a much better understanding of Chinese agriculture; they were not as contemptuous of Chinese techniques and saw much less of a market for American technology than did Denby. The representatives of the American state pushed expansion into the rural China market in inverse proportion to their physical proximity to China: Washington was the most active scene of promotion; the Beijing legation was distinctly less active; and the official representatives stationed at outposts in the Chinese provinces were the least supportive, because they could not help but see that the Chinese market was a phantom.

They had difficulty dissuading U.S. manufacturers from launching impractical campaigns to market American machinery in China, however. In 1900, for example, William Martin, an American consul stationed in Zhenjiang, Jiangsu, received a letter from American manufacturers requesting a list of local dealers in agricultural implements, "with a view to the introduction of these articles into this portion of China." Martin had to explain to them that such dealers did not exist, "the agricultural conditions not warranting such." To "save our manufacturers of agricultural machines and implements a good deal of useless expense and labor,"

Martin asked that the State Department publish his description of local agricultural conditions and the inappropriateness of American machines.[6]

Martin explained that "farming is not carried on in a large way here. Farms ranging from half an acre to five acres constitute the large and small holdings; it is clear they do not require reapers, mowers, thrashing machines, or steam plows." Chinese farmers in the area were occupied mostly with tending rice crops, which meant a possible market only for the smallest of American tools—hoes, rakes, shovels, and inexpensive rice hullers. Yet Martin shared Denby's confidence in the superiority of American implements, which were "as far ahead of what [the Chinese] use as a diamond is superior to a sandstone."[7]

The Hong Kong consulate also did its best to trim the inflated hopes of American farm machinery interests seeking to open a market in China. Rounsevelle Wildman, the consul general, complained in 1901 that his office was deluged with brochures extolling the merits of American harvesters and other machines. And since the close of a recent exposition in Paris, "almost every firm of this nature in the United States which was represented at that exposition has sent me letters and marked newspapers proclaiming the awards their particular companies received at Paris." Wildman explained, "While these statements are all very interesting to me as an American, they are of absolutely no value to the sender, as I can make no use of them to their advantage."[8]

The fact was that no market existed in southern China for the reapers, mowers, horse rakes, steam and gang plows, seed drills and harrows that American manufacturers tried to enlist Wildman in promoting. He had to explain, as his associate in Zhenjiang had (and as Denby in Beijing had not), that Chinese farmers tilled very small holdings. Wildman pointed out that the farmers subsisted on a few cents a day; "even if they could afford to purchase modern American farming machinery there would be no room to use it." Steam-powered machines were especially inappropriate, since fuel was so expensive. He concluded, "As long as labor has almost no value and flesh and blood is the cheapest thing on the market, I can not recommend American manufacturers to waste good printed matter and postage stamps on so impossible a field."[9]

George Anderson, the consul stationed in Hangzhou, was a little more encouraging. He predicted in 1904 that "it is probable that modern American garden implements will soon be welcomed and that there will be a wide field for enterprise in this line." He reported that "Chinese farmers are commencing to consider foreign ideas and methods, and there will soon be a breaking up of present methods and a turning to new tools." But the tools, Anderson added, had to suit the intensive methods of farming; he suggested inexpensive American rakes and hoes for sale to Chinese farmers. In a variation of the standard arithmetic used in calculating the fabulous profits that could be made in the China market, Anderson wrote encouragingly about the rakes and hoes: "It is well to bear in mind that the general introduction of a single one of these articles in China would mean the sale of an immense number." Still, Anderson made it clear that in the case of large machines—the item that American manufacturers were most eager to sell to rural China—there was no foreseeable demand.[10]

American consular officials were no more encouraging about American grain and fruit exports to China than they were about American farm machinery prospects. Henry Miller, the American consul stationed at Chongqing, was asked by the Oregon State Board of Agriculture about the market for American fruit in China. He was bluntly pessimistic: "There will never be a very large market here for [American fruit], until some plan is devised to get them into the hands of the consumers at a much less cost than at present." Oregon's neighbor, Washington State, had already tried to enter the China market and was exporting about a thousand cases of apples a year. But they arrived in poor condition and at high cost, and only foreign residents could afford them. A mass market for them was unlikely. American consuls were simply the bearers of the unwelcome tidings.[11]

＋ ＋ ＋ ＋ ＋

China was discussed not only as a market that the U.S. government was expected to open but also as a backward country whose government should model itself along American lines. Chinese development of agriculture, Americans felt, would be hastened if China set up its own department modeled on the U.S. Department of Agriculture. William Preston Bentley, an American missionary of long residence in China, took the arguments for an American model directly to literate Chinese in a 1903 pamphlet, *Guojia zhuanshe nongbu yi* (A suggestion for a national department of agriculture).[12]

Bentley's "suggestion" was actually a detailed agenda, advising the establishment of a comprehensive department that included no less than twenty separate bureaus. From livestock to grasses, statistics to soils, roads to reading rooms, programs within the department would guide almost every aspect of agricultural production and rural life. Some elements of Bentley's outline seem quite ahead of their time. A soil survey would map the soils of each area in China and then indicate crops that were most appropriate for each type. Another section of the plan proposed a bureau for studying rural ecology, again mapping all living things in a given area and studying mutually protective and destructive relationships in the ecosystem.

Aside from suggesting money-saving services, such as timely weather predictions, that a Chinese department of agriculture could provide, Bentley subtly criticized the Chinese government. Chinese officials who had been responsible for agriculture had done little, he argued; the solution was to put agricultural experts in charge and, he implied, not allow appointments to be sinecures for the unqualified. Bentley also lectured the Chinese on the need for a meat inspection bureau to check for diseased meat, including daily inspection of meat samples with a microscope. (He did not tell his readers that the battle for federal inspection of meat in his own United States had yet to be won—Upton Sinclair's *The Jungle* and the passage of the Clean Food and Drug Act were still several years in the future.)

Bentley's recommendations extended far beyond the likely capabilities of the Qing monarchy. His assumption that America's flourishing agriculture relied upon the presence of agricultural schools "as numerous as trees in a forest" was a slight exaggeration at the time (though it would hold true in the succeeding decades), and he provided no suggestion as to how China might finance its own system. He assumed that the imperial government would have vast financial resources to provide for the network of agricultural colleges that he recommended, with one college for each province, just as each state in the U.S. had one. Even the weather bureau recommendations assumed financial resources that did not exist: to notify the hundreds of millions of Chinese farmers of imminent weather dangers, Bentley proposed a dense network of weather stations, each flying a warning flag if a particular danger approached, and apparently so numerous as to be within visual range of every Chinese village. Bentley also assumed a more literate countryside than existed at the time. He wanted the soil survey maps to be bound and published as a book for "public" consultation. He also wanted China to establish numerous reading rooms throughout the countryside, for "the convenience of the farmers."

Reflecting American interests at the time, Bentley also emphasized the twin importance of technology and exports in framing recommendations for a Chinese department of agriculture. He believed that flat roads were of the utmost importance for helping farmers transport their produce to markets, and he included a picture of a massive American steamroller to show the proper machine for the task. He proposed that the Department of Agriculture construct a few roads to serve as a pattern, "then the farmers can extend the pattern and construct roads near and far."

A Chinese department of agriculture organized along American lines would also help China compete in world markets. Bentley advised China to ask all of its diplomatic personnel stationed abroad to collect information about their host countries' agriculture, livestock, and manufactured goods, and all agricultural imports and exports. A separate bureau of foreign markets was to keep track of the necessary data and to publish notices advising Chinese farmers of market opportunities abroad. Bentley also advised constructing maps to represent consumption of particular agricultural commodities in foreign markets and possible openings for Chinese exports.

This kind of advice, and its meticulous attention to such details as how to pack agricultural products for safe oceanic transport, was received by a monarchy that was fighting for its own survival and only beginning to collect foreign experiences in agricultural promotion. But Bentley's advice was kindhearted, for it encouraged China to join the world market and fight for its own interests, rather than remain a passive market for the exports of others. Bentley's program for

China was one example of American advice that was not prompted by self-serving commercial interests.

✢ ✢ ✢ ✢ ✢

Although Bentley and others regarded the USDA as a model, the department did not actively promote itself abroad. Its initial interest overseas simply concerned American farm exports. When the USDA was promoted to cabinet rank in 1889, part of its growing budget (the department grew from 488 employees in 1889 to 1,870 in 1893) was devoted to securing wider foreign markets for American farm products. Secretary Julius Sterling Morton, who took office just as the 1893 depression started, practiced administrative economies by lowering the salaries of women employees and by restricting installation of the new telephone system to hallways to discourage unnecessary and expensive conversations. But he still found money to establish a new office within the department, the Section of Foreign Markets.[13]

The foreign agricultural program that eventually earned the USDA world fame was the Section of Seed and Plant Introduction, which opened in 1898. It was to serve as the department's primary foreign program for the next half century and was to play an important role in China. But the timing of the office's establishment, at the peak of national talk of expansion abroad, creates a misleading impression that the USDA was in step with the Department of State and other government agencies. Its establishment actually owed less to the expansionist times than to the interests of one young USDA scientist, David Fairchild, who happened to secure an eccentric millionaire as a patron to begin a foreign agriculture program.

Fairchild had grown up on the campus of Kansas Agricultural College, where his father was president, and had graduated from the school at the age of nineteen, with a major in plant pathology, a special interest in fungi, and a seemingly bright future in laboratory work. After being hired by the USDA and going to Washington, however, he found his future redirected when he was dispatched by the USDA to set up an exhibit at the Chicago World's Fair in 1893. In his memoirs, he later described the fair as "the greatest dream-city man had ever built." He wrote, "It burst upon the consciousness of Middle Westerners with a force which it is impossible for the generation of today to understand."[14]

His curiosity about the wider world whetted, Fairchild searched for a means to support a trip abroad and was offered a Smithsonian research appointment in Italy at the Naples Zoological Station. His superiors at the USDA advised him to decline and warned him of other "young men who had gone to Europe and returned filled with newfangled scientific notions which were of little use in practical American life." But Fairchild decided to make use of the opportunity and sailed for Europe in November 1893. During the voyage, Fairchild met Barbour Lathrop, "the man who was to 'direct my destiny,'" and who financed Fairchild's future trips around the world, including travel to China.[15]

Lathrop was a wealthy American whose inheritance had allowed him to make world travel his full-time occupation; when he met Fairchild in 1893, he had already been around the globe eighteen times. He was a society figure, self-assured, used to getting his way in all things, and was regarded by young Fairchild as "the wittiest man I had ever heard." Lathrop decided to be Fairchild's patron and gave him $1,000 to travel from Europe to Asia to collect plants, a pursuit that Lathrop found amusing.[16]

This first circumnavigation took Fairchild through Southeast Asia and Oceania. He returned to Washington in 1897, four years after he had left, convinced of the need to systematically collect foreign plants for introduction to America. With Walter T. Swingle, an old friend and classmate from Kansas who had also gone to work in the USDA, Fairchild drew up a plan for a plant introduction program in the department. The idea of a formal, funded program for bringing foreign plants into the United States was so novel that Fairchild had to tuck the proposal into an existing program, the Congressional Seed Distribution, which gave congressmen several thousand packages of seed for distribution to constituents. With trepidation, Fairchild presented his plan to the Secretary of Agriculture, James Wilson.

Years later, Wilson would be credited for his foresight in organizing a Seed and Plant Introduction program, but when Fairchild walked into his office to first tell him about the proposal, Wilson did not leap to embrace it. Fairchild later recalled, "Secretary Wilson was a tall, gaunt man with gray beard and deep-set eyes. He sat listening to us with his eyes half closed and at intervals made use of the near-by spittoon.... When we finished talking, the Secretary seemed deep in thought." After a long interval, Wilson announced his approval, although the language of the proposal was reworked to make it more palatable to a Congress that would resist sharing its cherished seed distribution budget.[17]

Money was found to begin work before appropriations were secured from Congress, and Fairchild was appointed as head. The office was set up in the attic of the department's old building on Pennsylvania Avenue, and almost as soon as Fairchild had begun work, his patron, Barbour Lathrop, reappeared. Lathrop scolded his adopted charge: "You're no more fit to build up a government office of plant introduction than I am to run a chicken farm—and I don't know a thing about chickens. You have no contacts with the rest of the world." Lathrop offered to pay Fairchild's expenses for a "quick reconnaissance of the world" to give Fairchild ideas about how he should organize the office.[18]

Fairchild leapt at the opportunity, but it took an uncomfortable hour-long audience with Secretary Wilson, who regarded Fairchild's travel as "running away" from duties, before Fairchild was able to secure appointment as a Special Agent of the USDA's new Section of Seed and Plant Introduction. He was also equipped with letters of introduction and enormous certificates of identification. "The papers," Fairchild recalled, "were wonderful creations, hand-printed on parchment, bedecked with ribbons, and emblazoned with the gold seal of the Department of

Agriculture. Nothing the Department of State ever produced could compare with them, and they soon became affectionately known as 'Dago Dazzlers.'"[19]

Fairchild and Lathrop left in 1898, touring Central and South America, Europe and North Africa, Southeast Asia, then Hong Kong and China. Of the hundreds of places he visited, Fairchild cited China as particularly fascinating and unforgettable. He noted approvingly that there was "a discipline and an orderliness about the Chinese life in strong contrast to the careless, happy-go-lucky existence of the Malays." But when he arrived in Guangzhou and tried muscling his way through the streets packed with people, he became conscious of an overpowering stench. He soon realized that "I was being crowded by a coolie bearing a bamboo pole over his shoulder at each end of which hung an earthenware pot. During the moments necessary for him to pass me I felt that I was actually smelling the entire sewage system of China." He credited Chinese night soil as an important fertilizer, but could not understand why the Chinese had not developed "other and less obnoxious methods of sewage disposal," and why modern chemistry was not used to replace an ancient method "which condemns many people to lives of disgusting drudgery."[20]

Fairchild's introduction to Chinese agriculture was a brief one, taking him no farther than Guangzhou before he returned to Hong Kong in March of 1900. Before leaving, however, Fairchild did gather water chestnuts and send them back to the United States. He also collected as many different kinds of rice as he could, although he initially felt that "rice was one agricultural crop in which America could never compete with the Orient." Seeing the enormous opportunities for plant collection in China, Fairchild wondered how to arrange for Chinese to send samples to Washington. When he mentioned the problem to Augustine Henry, an Irish botanist who had done plant collecting in Sichuan, Henry told him: "Don't waste money on postage—send a man."[21]

Leaving Guangzhou, Fairchild felt he was leaving an entirely different world: "I returned to Hongkong with the feeling that I had been living in a dream. Surely only a nightmare could fill my brain with such fantastic people, practices, and customs. Everything which I had experienced during my days in [Guangzhou] seemed utterly unbelievable." His odyssey with Lathrop continued with another year of travel in Europe. As soon as they returned to the United States, Lathrop suggested starting another trip, which would include India and a return to East Asia and the fantastic world of China. Since Lathrop was again willing to pay the expenses, the USDA approved the extension on what had originally been planned as Fairchild's "quick reconnaissance."[22]

Oblivious to international politics, the "Open Door," and the Boxers and their recent suppression by foreign powers, including the United States, Fairchild returned to Hong Kong and Guangzhou in November 1901, interested only in botany and agriculture. He remained fascinated by what he saw. Chinese truck gardens "did not contain a single vegetable with which we are familiar in America.

The people, apparently well nourished, live on an entirely different diet from that which we consider necessary for health and happiness." Fairchild was particularly impressed by Chinese "marsh plants," such as the water chestnut that had interested him during his first visit, stating that "we have much to learn from them [the Chinese] regarding methods of handling our swamp lands."[23]

Fairchild also viewed China as a possible market for American exports. Writing a public report of his impressions in 1902, he noted that "already American flour is being imported in large quantities into China, and is sold cheaper there than the native wheat can be grown and ground." He went on to predict that "the growth of our agricultural as well as other exports to China will, I believe, be a phenomenal one, and will include many classes of canned and dried goods from our orchards, and preserved meats and dairy products from our farms and ranches." He even speculated about introducing unfamiliar Chinese products to America, not for American consumption but for profitable export back to China: "Red watermelon seeds, of which the consumption must be enormous; the 'Chinese olives,' of equal importance; the wood oil tree ... ginger, water chestnuts, dried persimmons, and a host of other products."[24]

More Americans needed to become aware of the agricultural importance of China, and Fairchild reported encouragingly to American readers that in China "there are everywhere the most unmistakable signs of progress." The body of Chinese farmers, he declared, was "more intelligent about its own affairs, quicker, and vastly more industrious than the peasant class of Europe. These Chinese peasants are not as a rule unwilling to learn, and are quick to appreciate the value of tools which are really improvements over their own. The delight which a Chinese mulberry grower showed at the sight of a pair of modern pruning shears which I was using, could hardly have been equaled by a peasant in southern Europe."[25]

Fairchild was most eager to bring home the Chinese plants that could be introduced to the United States and perhaps create "new industries," but he could see from his visit that Henry was correct that he would need to keep trained USDA representatives on the scene to carry out the selection and shipping. He thought it would be best if they were "not stationed so long in the provinces as to lose touch with American conditions, but remain long enough to thoroughly master the methods of cultivation of the crops and secure the necessary seeds and plants for introduction."[26]

✣ ✣ ✣ ✣ ✣

The world tour continued to the Middle East, then returned through Asia, but as soon as Fairchild arrived in San Francisco, preparing to return to Washington, Lathrop proposed still another trip, to Africa. Thus two more years passed before Fairchild returned to Washington and searched for a USDA representative for China. In the meantime, the department had taken an interest in Asia, sending Seaman A. Knapp on two exploration trips, in 1898 and 1901. Knapp had already

become a giant on the contemporary agricultural scene by using improved techniques on his farm at Vinton, Iowa; teaching and serving as president at Iowa State
College of Agriculture and Mechanic Arts; drafting the bill that became known as
the Hatch Act, which provided federal aid for agricultural experiment stations; and
taking successful charge of a large colonization experiment in Louisiana. While
working in the South, he had actively promoted expansion of rice production, and
thus was a natural choice (as well as a long-standing personal friend of the
secretary of agriculture, also from Iowa) to be sent by the USDA to Japan, China,
and other countries in East Asia.

The goals assigned to Knapp's two trips stand as early examples, albeit
singular ones, of the United States asking Asia for help on specific agricultural
problems. American rice growers had found that new milling technology had
brought unforeseen problems: recently installed power mills cracked 60 to 90
percent of the grain during hulling and cleaning. Broken grain was worth only a
half or a third of unbroken whole kernels on the market, so the new milling
machinery (aside from being a large capital investment) cost the growers millions
in lowered market prices for the processed rice. Knapp, who was founder and
president of the American Rice Association and editor of the *Rice Journal*, thought
that Asia might have rice varieties that were tougher and more resistant to
breakage.[27]

On the 1898 trip, Knapp went to Japan and selected a Kyushu rice. When
brought back and tested the next year, it proved superior in all aspects: yields
were 25 percent higher than local varieties and, best of all, breakage was reduced
to a fraction of what it had been. Several hundred tons of seed were imported for
the following year, and the rice quickly became the leading variety in Louisiana.[28]
Encouraged by this success, Knapp proposed a second trip to search for early-,
medium-, and late-maturing varieties of rice and to look for other plants, such as
fruit trees and shrubs, that could be used in the reclamation of cutover lands in the
South which had been stripped of timber. At the age of almost seventy, Knapp
returned in 1901 to Japan, and also visited China.

"In scholarship, energy, and business qualities," Knapp reported, "the Chinese
take very high rank among the nations of the earth. They are bright, apt, of
indefatigable perseverance, and instinctively grasp the financial bearings of business transactions." Yet this praise, which may have owed more to positive
stereotypes than to personal observation, was not followed by an encouraging
report about Chinese agriculture. Knapp had not found the information he had
sought: "It is difficult to deal with the agricultural conditions in China in a comprehensive way, because there are no reliable statistics published, and the traveler is
limited to his observations and the very meager information to be obtained from
Chinese farmers." Even more frustrating, Knapp had found that the farmers were
"not disposed to give information to a stranger, thinking that some advantage will
be taken of it."[29]

Knapp explained that he was quite surprised to discover "the almost entire absence of timber or woodlands in eastern China." The highlands and mountains were denuded, with the result, he observed, of alternating periods of severe drought and excessive runoff. Knapp was familiar enough with the problem, for his visit was a search to find ways to re-cover similarly denuded land in the American South. China did not offer promising solutions, and Knapp was amazed to find so much land there that seemed unused and abandoned. He learned that thousands of acres of land in the vicinity of large cities lay fallow, and "even in the vicinity of Nanking, the old capital of the Ming Dynasty, there are thousands of acres of land, evidently fertile if properly tilled, which lie neglected as commons."[30]

Knapp brought back to the United States new rice varieties and much new information about Asia. Upon his return to the South, he began remarkable new programs in agricultural extension work, developing demonstration farms, dispatching "lecture trains," and organizing boys' and girls' clubs that were forerunners of the 4-H movement. This work, vigorously organized by a man in his seventies, earned Knapp even more public recognition than he had previously received, and stands in curious relation to his contact with China. Knapp never wrote an autobiography, so whether his trip to China (where there was a glaring need for agricultural extension programs) had any part in prompting the innovative work he began in the South upon his return remains a matter of speculation. Knapp died in 1911. In later years other Americans would take some of Knapp's extension programs back to China for trial, replacing America's original role as curious student with that of instructor.

✢ ✢ ✢ ✢ ✢

Knapp's short trips to Asia were too limited to fulfill what David Fairchild had in mind for long-term plant collection. When Fairchild finally returned in 1903 from his journeys with Lathrop and resumed office work at the USDA in Washington, he still did not know whom he could send to carry out extensive plant collection in China. He tried to forge a cooperative agreement with Harvard's Arnold Arboretum, which had hired the famed British plant collector, E. H. Wilson, for explorations in China. But the USDA was interested in cultivated crops that had potential economic value, while the Arnold Arboretum sought plants that were wild or ornamental and that expressly lacked economic value. Personal conflicts between Fairchild and the arboretum's director, which Fairchild politely ascribed to "different temperaments," did not help, and the USDA efforts to join forces with the arboretum failed.[31]

Fairchild then launched an intensive search for a suitable candidate to send to China as the USDA's representative, and the name of Frank Meyer was brought to his attention by a colleague. Meyer, then twenty-nine, was originally from Holland and had come to the United States a few years before. While beginning naturalization, he had worked in the USDA greenhouses in Washington and had gained a reputation in the department not only as a devoted gardener but also as an indefatigable hiker. (A story that made the rounds of the office told of Meyer, raised on the novels of James Fenimore Cooper and recently arrived in America, hiking near Mt. Vernon and wondering why he "did not see any redskins during the whole trip.") Fairchild called him in for an interview and was impressed with his direct manner, evident passion for plants, and willingness to work for virtually any sum. Meyer was hired.[32]

Meyer sailed for China in 1905, at the beginning of what would turn out to be thirteen years of explorations for the USDA. He was designated as "Agricultural Explorer," since Fairchild had learned from his own experience that the older term, "Special Agent," conjured up suspicions of espionage. Meyer also was equipped with an impressive document of authorization, complete with an ornate "Be it known that . . ." and engraved figures of an American eagle, flanked by the head of a horse on one side, and that of a cow on the other, which was to serve notice even to the non-English-speaker that the bearer of this document was from the United States Department of Agriculture, not the Department of War.[33]

The USDA wanted extensive explorations of China because, in Meyer's words, "when we turn to other countries, particularly toward Asia, we find that in China, especially, climatic and soil conditions are in the main very similar to those in the United States." In fact, Meyer declared, vegetation in China in some parts so resembled that of the eastern United States that "a person suddenly transported from either region to the other would not always exactly realize where he was." Since China had been settled long before "Caucasian races" had appeared on American soil, Meyer observed, its people had developed many improved plant varieties over time which, given the similarity in climate, would permit successful transplantation to the United States.[34]

Meyer arrived in Shanghai, then moved north to Tianjin and Beijing, observing local markets and trying to discover where products originated. He took an early interest in Chinese fruits, but soon discovered that hikes in the immediate vicinity of the cities failed to lead him to any worthwhile items. He quickly pieced together an understanding of the extensive distribution network that brought goods to urban markets and learned that most of the fruit grew in far distant locales. Wild vegetation closer to cities had been destroyed by Chinese farmers who, Meyer complained, "cut down and grub out every wild woody plant in their perpetual search for fuel." The result was that "one therefore finds it exceedingly hard to discover anything of importance near centers of population, and a man is obliged to go into the real interior, often many weeks' march away from any large center."[35]

A man who enjoyed nothing more than being outdoors, Meyer did not mind the hikes of weeks and months through north China and Central Asia, but he did mind the bulky paraphernalia that he had to bring along: canned food, cooking utensils, bedding, packing material for his plants, a large camera, and hundreds of photographic plates. At least one cart and often several were required, along with drivers and donkeys and an interpreter. The party would stop at inns, if they could be found, but Meyer found the filth appalling. He wrote indignantly to a USDA colleague in Washington: "When I tell you that chamber pots and water closets are unknown, you may imagine the rest." [36]

Meyer's colleagues and family worried about his personal safety while traveling in a country where antiforeign feeling resulted in violent attacks on Westerners. On one occasion, Meyer encountered a group of unfriendly soldiers who at first barred him from stepping into a country inn; later, as Meyer tried to eat, they stared menacingly at him—until he offered them food, "of which they made liberal use." Another time, Meyer was on the periphery of trouble in Shanhaiguan, where he helped dress the wounds of a foreigner who had been beaten by a mob (the wounded man had been the first to use violence, drawing the town's wrath because he had beaten a Chinese man with his cane for a perceived insult). But Meyer seemed immune from trouble, at least in the early years, and wrote home, "Sometimes I am surprised at myself because I get so easily through so many difficulties." [37]

The popular press in America regarded Meyer's trips as romantically dangerous ("nerve-wracking" and "health-shattering") and as comparable to the early explorations of the American continent—work "that calls for the same kind of grit possessed by the old heroes and which exacts just as big a toll of risk and danger and self-sacrifice." Based on his letters written to the USDA, *Outing* magazine portrayed Meyer as a gun-toting tough guy, who once awoke to find two Chinese standing over him armed with a sword and club; he sent his would-be assailants retreating in fear when he flashed his gun. (The article explained, "Meyer did not even fire his pistol; for Americans have a world-wide reputation for shooting to hit.") [38]

In truth, the worst part of being in China for Meyer was the loneliness. Among Chinese, he felt like an animal in a zoo, a curiosity constantly under inspection. He was also isolated from Chinese people by the language barrier; even though Meyer could speak English, German, and Dutch fluently, and knew some French, Italian, Spanish, and Russian, he never learned much Chinese. And he had difficulty finding companionship among the Westerners he met in China. The foreigners who had come to live in China's cities were men who "lead fast lives and go to the dogs." He shunned them and came to accept his fate philosophically: "Loneliness hangs always around the man who leaves his own race and moves among an alien population." [39]

Meyer found rewards for the difficulties, however, "for there are glorious blue mountains in China and lovely valleys and ravines"; and when he found rare and promising vegetation, "one feels fully compensated for the trials gone through." Plant collection was his purpose, and he devoted himself to it with singular energy. He was not interested in "ordinary" botany; he sought plants that would have the most economic importance to his adopted country. He wrote the

USDA: "I hope to do my very best to enrich the United States of America with things good for her people and their households." But he did not know at first what kinds of items he should send. Would lotus roots, bamboo and alfalfa shoots, and water chestnuts be welcomed on American tables? Wanting to avoid foods that might be regarded by Americans as "rubbish," he wrote to Fairchild for guidance.[40]

Meyer also had to master the art of packing specimens for shipment. He learned by trial and error which techniques worked best, and settled upon packing perishable seeds in powdered charcoal or dampened sphagnum moss. Cuttings required more trouble and care, since they had to be collected when the plants were resting, usually in winter, and needed to be wrapped in dampened moss immediately after being cut. Meyer reported, "In severe winter weather we often had to heat water to prevent it from freezing, in order to moisten the sphagnum moss, and sometimes a few minutes after the cuttings were wrapped the parcel was frozen hard, for in the rooms of a North China inn there are no stoves, the paper windows are often broken and torn, and the temperature inside is but little higher than that outside." He kept the packages for several weeks until he next reached a Chinese post office that was willing to accept them for mailing (small offices often refused), either to the United States, or to the United States consulate in Shanghai, which forwarded the plants or seeds in the diplomatic pouch.[41]

Meyer's mandate for plant collection was left virtually unrestricted, and over the years he sent some twenty-five hundred different plant introductions. The inventory of an early shipment of materials set a pattern of diverse variety: seeds of asparagus, clover, oats, hemp, and cotton, as well as eighteen varieties of soybeans; thirty kinds of bamboo; shrubs, flowers, and ornamental trees; and two live monkeys. Once the introductions arrived in the United States, they faced stringent fumigation that often killed them. (Plant collectors of the USDA were chronically angry with their own department colleagues, the plant pathologists and entomologists, who were responsible for what the collectors felt were unnecessarily strict quarantine measures.) Then the materials were distributed to plant introduction gardens operated by the USDA, where they faced new dangers, such as neglectful mismanagement at the Chico Garden in California or Gulf hurricanes at Galveston. The survival rate of Meyer's scions and plants was a remarkably high percentage of about 50 percent.[42]

The official Chinese reaction to this outflow of plant material to the United States was not known, since the Chinese had never been consulted about it. But David Fairchild speculated that Meyer's work was probably misunderstood by Chinese farmers. "What a picture of America Meyer must have left on the minds of the villagers!" Fairchild wrote. "How was it possible that a man who was not crazy could leave a comfortable home on the other side of the world, come to a Chinese farmhouse and find the common plants of the little garden so wonderful that he would pack some of them up in boxes or bags and take them away with him?"[43]

Usually Meyer had no trouble simply taking, or, when necessary, purchasing, the cuttings and seeds he wanted. But when he sought the famed peaches of Feicheng, which often weighed a pound each and were regarded as the best in China, Meyer encountered difficulties. He found, "naturally enough, a fear in the minds of the owners of the Fei peach lest this foreigner would take away their monopoly in the growing of it." Actually, the local residents were willing to allow Meyer to collect scions, but they refused to sell entire trees for less than $40 or $50 per tree, a price Meyer regarded as exorbitant. Meyer's interpreter devised a ruse and talked a farmer into selling a small plot of land that contained eight peach trees for $40. Meyer removed the trees immediately and hurried off, because the farmer's relatives wanted the trees returned. Fairchild was pleased by the acquisition and amused by the story. He wrote at the time, "The Fei peach promises much as a late peach for our Southwest, and the orchardists need have no fear that its cultivation in America will in any way interfere with their business in Shantung." [44]

Meyer did not care whether the Chinese resented his taking cuttings or seeds, for he regarded Chinese farmers more as adversaries than as friends. Especially as his years in China mounted, Meyer saw the country and its people in a negative light. In an article reporting his opinions that appeared in 1916 in the widely read farm journal, *Wallace's Farmer*, Meyer credited the Chinese with mastering cultivation of aquatic food products, from which the United States had much to learn (if the American farmer would ever be willing "to grow crops which call for cultivation in water waist deep"), but he regarded Chinese agriculture overall to be retrograde. The absence of seed stores and extension mechanisms meant that "superior varieties grown on one farm often are not used on adjoining farms, and are unheard of ten miles away. The farmer who develops an improved variety guards it jealously, and gives seeds or cuttings or scions only to his immediate relatives." The result, Meyer wrote, was the disappearance of excellent varieties that had been traditionally known or that were mentioned in earlier Chinese literature. [45]

The Chinese, he felt, were guilty of even worse—namely, of "destroying the balance of nature." He wrote to Fairchild that he was observing the "last vestiges of a once grand vegetation." He listed the crimes the Chinese had committed: "Every wild tree or shrub is mercilessly cut down; every edible bird is trapped and eaten. Their mountains are barren wastes which let the rains rush off with great velocity, bearing with them arable soil and covering valleys with stony and sandy matter. Their climate gets drier year after year and famines result." [46]

The only Chinese with whom he liked to spend time were Buddhist and Taoist priests, whom he credited with protecting plants around temples. "If it were not for them," Meyer reported to Americans, "many a species or variety of plant which now adorns our gardens and parks would have been exterminated." [47] But Meyer had little patience to spare for other Chinese. He grew tired of being stared at by groups and became cranky from the intellectual isolation; as he wrote to Fairchild, "Too long in China kills one's brain." He became outraged when he was abandoned in remote places by his Chinese interpreters, upon whom he was utterly dependent and whose replacement out in the field was virtually impossible. When his "cowardly" interpreter deserted him on the border of Tibet, Meyer thought the act was the height of ingratitude to the United States, since the man had been educated by American missionaries in Beijing, his family had been protected by Americans during the Boxer Rebellion, and his brother had been sent "by charitable American people" to take his Ph.D. at Columbia University. Meyer wanted to retaliate with that most American instrument, the legal suit seeking damages.[48]

By coincidence, an English plant hunter, Reginald Farrer, crossed paths with Meyer's expedition just as Meyer faced the mutiny of his crew. Farrer, who confessed that news of another plant collector's arrival was a surprise and "by no means wholly pleasurable," nevertheless reveled in Meyer's difficulties. He wrote to readers of Gardener's Chronicle in England: "Mr. Meyer had been ill-advised enough to bring up-country with him a very expensive fine gentleman of an 'interpreter' from the coast, of lily hand and liver to match." When the interpreter had refused to budge from the town, a fight with Meyer ensued, followed by "a rapid descent of the stairs by the interpreter." Farrer could not resist gloating, "There is poor Mr. Meyer, perfectly helpless ... as many years in China have not led him to like the Chinese well enough to learn their language."[49] The interpreter's defection and the lack of assistance provided by his opium-addicted replacement (found by Farrer) soon forced Meyer to head back toward the capital. On the road near the Gansu-Shaanxi border, a patrol of four soldiers stopped Meyer's party and attempted to search them for contraband. When Meyer objected, a soldier spat on him; Meyer's assistant on this trip, a young countryman from Holland, responded by "giving the soldier a few kicks" with the butt of his rifle. The other soldiers jumped into the fight, and Meyer and his assistant returned the blows "with our fists, a walking-stick, and the above-mentioned rifle." Meyer dryly recorded, "After the fight was finished, we left."[50]

The incident was hardly over. Meyer had been detained by, and had severely beaten, a patrol looking for opium smugglers, and Meyer's own train of carts loaded with plant materials and seeds had naturally appeared suspicious. After the fight, a much larger contingent of soldiers soon caught up with Meyer's party, and marched them to a nearby city for questioning. The customs director delivered what Meyer regarded as a "haughty and disrespectful lecture" about Meyer's treatment of the border patrol. Then Meyer was asked about carrying opium, poppy heads, or poppy seeds, which he denied. Finally Meyer and his crew were released.[51]

Not content with mere release, Meyer filed with Paul Reinsch, the American minister in Beijing, a strong protest about what he regarded as maltreatment in the incident. He demanded an apology from the "haughty" officer and from the soldier who had spat upon him. Later, the Chinese Foreign Ministry reported that the soldiers involved had been severely punished. But the indignation of Meyer and his uninformed proxy, Paul Reinsch, obscured the fact that the Chinese suspicions were not wholly unfounded. The year before, Meyer had sent upon Fairchild's request twenty pounds of seeds "of the variety of hemp from which hashish is made." (Meyer had wondered "what use the American public can make of this hashish.") The year after Meyer's fight with the border patrol, Fairchild again asked Meyer to "ship immediately 100 pounds viable poppy seed." Having learned that such matters could not be treated casually, Meyer wrote back and lectured Fairchild that Chinese farmers who raised poppies were beheaded, he himself had barely escaped execution when suspected of smuggling, and the requested amount was "enough to sow half a province." Fairchild apologized, explaining that he had made his request without thinking of such matters and had only wanted to alleviate the shortage of opium then experienced by American hospitals.[52]

Meyer returned to the United States in the fall of 1915 and spent the winter visiting plant introduction gardens and lecturing on his China explorations, illustrating his talks with hand-colored lantern slides. The next year, on the eve of returning to China for another expedition, Meyer showed signs of reluctance. He wrote the USDA that he hoped it would not be a long trip because he wanted to live "among my own race before I get too old." When Meyer arrived back in China, he resumed his energetic collections and traveled in central China for two years, but he was frequently depressed. On an envelope he scribbled: "It may seem strange that a person of my age, 41, should already become weary, but my long travels in so many uncongenial parts of the world, the fact that I have so much absolutely unnecessary indoor work to do [attending to government paperwork], and that one is unable to associate himself permanently in this sort of life with congenial people—all these slowly but surely have been molding my mind in this state." He repeatedly lamented, "I have so much to do, and China is *so* awfully large."[53]

Boarding a Yangzi riverboat at Yichang, Hubei, Meyer headed for Shanghai in May 1918. One night, he left his cabin presumably to go to the water closet, and did not return. His Chinese servant notified the captain and the small steamer was searched, but Meyer was not found. Several days later his swollen body was pulled from the river.[54]

Many debated whether Meyer's death was a suicide or a murder; Fairchild concluded that it would always remain a mystery. The USDA program in China never resumed the ambitious explorations that Meyer had pursued. In 1920, Fairchild hired a new "agricultural explorer," Joseph Rock, who was sent first to Southeast Asia and entered China overland from Burma only in 1922. Rock was less hardy than Meyer and insisted on enjoying in the field the amenities of home. He had servants set up a table with linen at dinnertime and commanded his cook to serve elaborate dishes; he insisted on daily baths in an Abercrombie and Fitch folding bathtub and always dressed fastidiously in a white shirt, necktie, and jacket. The USDA funded Rock only for a year. (The National Geographic Society then agreed to hire him, and Rock spent most of the next twenty-seven years in the mountains near Tibet.) Later USDA-sponsored expeditions to Asia, specializing in chestnuts and soybeans, included China in their itineraries, but the era of extensive plant collecting in China had come to an end.[55]

✛ ✛ ✛ ✛ ✛

The era did not end, however, before Fairchild had gained more appreciation for agricultural expertise in China and Japan. He became alarmed, in fact, when he observed that hundreds of thousands of Asians were studying English yet virtually no Americans were studying the Chinese or Japanese languages. Fairchild warned the American public:

> These Orientals are developing institutions of research. They are publishing magazines and books of great scientific importance—in their own languages—and we have no way of reading them. It is time we saw clearly the situation and stated it strongly. Hundreds of millions of intelligent human beings looking toward America and American institutions for models, learning to read our language, gathering together our books into their libraries, assimilating the good in our civilization, sending hundreds of their brightest young people to learn about us, and we, in the conceit of our greatness, not recognizing in any practical way the astonishing fact that we cannot read their newspapers or magazines, or understand, so to speak, a single word of the great new literature that is being built up by these peoples.

The Chinese and Japanese had achieved notable scientific advances related to agriculture, he said, but little had been published about them in English. Fairchild proposed that the U.S. government establish an American Bureau of Oriental Publicity, staffed with bilingual translators who could keep Americans abreast of the growing scientific literature published in Asia.[56]

The proposed bureau was never established, but in 1917, the USDA briefly expanded the scope of its program to learn from China, and established an interesting—if only briefly meaningful—precedent: hiring a Chinese person to serve as an agricultural adviser to the United States. Dr. Kin Yamei, who claimed to be the only Chinese woman to have graduated from an American medical school, was hired to return to China and study the Chinese soybean on behalf of the USDA. The *New York Times* hailed the appointment as "the first time the United States Government has given so much authority to a Chinese."[57]

China, the newspaper pointed out to skeptics, already had given the world many things: paper, gunpowder, porcelain, chess, playing cards, and silk embroideries. Now Dr. Kin was "going to see if her native land can teach the United States how to develop a taste for the soy bean in its numerous disguises." On the eve of her departure for China, Kin explained that "Americans do not know how to use the soy bean. It must be made attractive or they will not take to it. It must taste good." But that could be done, and she described delicious dishes, from soup noodles to a "delightful chocolate pudding" that could be easily made. Kin told American readers, "Human nature is about the same everywhere, and the Chinese don't care for a monotonous bean diet any more than other people."[58]

Kin's case for the soybean anticipated many of the arguments that Americans would use to promote vegetarianism in the United States fifty years later. The world could not afford, Kin said, to rely upon animals as a protein source. "A terribly high percentage of the energy is lost in transit from grain to cow to a human being. Roughly speaking, the process is not unlike the loss of heat units in coal burned in a locomotive before the wheels go round." The Chinese had a better method: "Instead of taking the long and expensive method of feeding grain to an animal until the animal is ready to be killed and eaten, in China we take a short cut by eating the soy bean, which is protein, meat, and milk in itself."[59]

A common stereotype of Chinese being "coolies" and eating a monotonous diet, Kin feared, stood in the way of American acceptance of the Chinese soybean. She drew an analogy: "It would not be fair for intelligent persons in China to believe that America's bill of fare was made up exclusively of the dishes set before the mountaineers of Eastern Kentucky." If Americans could appreciate the fact that "Chinese are fond of eating, and devote much attention to doing it well," then China and the United States could enjoy a balanced, reciprocal exchange of agricultural expertise. Kin said, "America can help China in teaching her the use of machinery, and we can help America by teaching her the value of the ground that your splendidly efficient farming implements cultivate."[60]

When Kin left for China in the summer of 1917, she was supposed to study the soybean exclusively and to return to the United States in the fall to present her report. But things did not go as planned. The USDA apparently did not receive any report on soybeans; what it did receive were cables from State Department representatives in Beijing, reporting that Kin had claimed USDA endorsement for a huge cotton-growing scheme, involving large tracts of land, which she was trying to launch with private capital in Shandong, Henan, and Zhili. The USDA explained to the State Department that it knew nothing about the scheme. Kin disappeared from view, and her plans to put soy products on American tables were lost for the moment. Eventually, in the 1930s, soybean production took off in the United States, and by 1942 exceeded the production of Manchuria, but Americans continued to disdain eating the bean directly.[61]

✣ ✣ ✣ ✣ ✣

The idea that the United States had much to learn from Chinese agriculture was an important one in the early twentieth century, before it gave way to the belief that the Chinese had more to learn from American agriculture. While Frank Meyer was tramping the remote mountain reaches of China, a retired USDA employee, Franklin Hiram King, was most responsible for convincing some USDA staff in Washington and the wider community of American agricultural specialists that China, not America, should occupy the tutorial role in the exchange of agricultural information between the two countries.

King was born in 1848 and had grown up on a Wisconsin farm when the area was still sparsely settled frontier land. He had studied at Cornell and been appointed to the Wisconsin College of Agriculture to occupy the first chair in "agricultural physics" (King is credited with encouraging the adoption of that now most familiar of sights, the round silo). After a distinguished teaching and publishing career, King served as chief of soil management for the USDA, retiring in 1904 to write and travel. A five-month trip to China, Korea, and Japan inspired him to write an account of his observations, and the resulting manuscript was almost completed when he died in 1911. Published posthumously, *Farmers of Forty Centuries* exerted a tremendous influence in shaping American images of Asian agriculture, particularly Chinese agriculture, and served briefly to counteract the attitude (which, in the end, prevailed) that America knew more about agriculture than did China.

King's trip to Asia was prompted by his long-standing desire "to learn how it is possible, after twenty and perhaps thirty or even forty centuries, for their soils to be made to produce sufficiently for the maintenance of such dense populations." Once he arrived, King found that "almost every day we were instructed, surprised and amazed at the conditions and practices which confronted us whichever way we turned." China was his favorite country in Asia, and no sight that he found there failed to charm him. Even the desire of people to touch his person and scrutinize him like "a caged chimpanzee" (which, during long years of residence, had irritated Meyer almost beyond endurance) did not diminish King's enjoyment of the experience.[62]

The central lesson that King learned and sought to impress upon his readers was that the Chinese returned human and other wastes to the soil, while Americans disposed of wastes in the sea. King regarded Western man as "the most extravagant accelerator of waste the world has ever endured. His withering blight has fallen upon every living thing within his reach, himself not excepted; and his bosom of destruction in the uncontrolled hands of a generation has swept into the sea soil fertility which only centuries of life could accumulate." Only the use of enormous amounts of mineral fertilizers had permitted Americans to indulge in such wasteful practices, and King predicted that it could not be continued indefinitely. Americans should look, then, to the Chinese, who held human wastes, "both urban and rural, and many others which we ignore, sacred to agriculture, applying them to their fields."[63]

King sought to destroy derogatory stereotypes of Chinese farmers which were common among white Americans. "The foreigner accuses the Chinaman of being always long on time, never in a fret, never in a hurry," but King noted that this observation neglected how the Chinese "set their faces toward the future and lead time by the forelock," having realized long before that much time is required to transform organic matter into forms available for plant food. King credited their labor with the results of a much longer growing season and an ingenious system of multiple cropping. Moreover, the use of legumes as nitrogen fixers had been confirmed in Europe only in 1888, while in China "these old world farmers whom we regard as ignorant, perhaps because they do not ride sulky plows as we do, have long included legumes in their crop rotation, regarding them as indispensable."[64]

After describing how farmers in south China completely reshaped their fields between crops, throwing up high ridges for vegetables, then leveling the beds for rice, King challenged the assertions of Charles Denby and others: "The statement so often made, that these people only barely scratch the surface of their fields with the crudest of tools is very far from the truth, for their soils are worked deeply and often, notwithstanding the fact that their plowing, as such, may be shallow." The Chinese practice of building elaborate compost piles, King said, was "a very old, intensive application of an important fundamental principle only recently understood and added to the science of agriculture." Again, King took the opportunity to correct prevailing stereotypes: "It would be a great mistake to say that these laborious practices are the result of ignorance, or a lack of capacity for accurate thinking or of power to grasp and utilize. If the agricultural lands of the United States are ever called upon to feed even 1200 millions of people, a number proportionately less than one-half that being fed in Japan today, very different practices from those we are now following will have been adopted."[65]

In a period when immigration laws in the United States excluded Chinese and racist attitudes deprecated Chinese achievements, King gave American readers a new picture of the Chinese people as "a virile race of some five hundred millions of people who have an unimpaired inheritance moving with the momentum acquired through four thousand years; a people morally and intellectually strong, mechanically capable, who are awakening to a utilization of all the possibilities which science and invention during recent years have brought to western nations." Trying to reverse negative impressions in the United States, King painted a picture that was bucolically unreal: "Everywhere we went in China," the people were "happy and contented" and "well-nourished." Nowhere in his travels did he observe anyone intoxicated (aside from many Americans and Europeans). The only fight that he observed during five months was between two children in a quarrel. Physically disabled people, he granted, were seen begging, but "in proportion to the total population these appear to be fewer than in America or Europe." The only criticism that King would permit of the Chinese was the increasing addiction "to the western tobacco habit, selfish beyond excuse, filthy beyond measure, and unsanitary in its polluting and oxygen-destroying effect upon the air all are compelled to breathe. It has already become a greater and more inexcusable burden upon mankind than opium ever was." But this misfortune was largely the responsibility not of the Chinese but of "the pitiless efforts of the British-American Tobacco Company."[66]

King had planned to write a final chapter on the "Message of China and Japan to the World," but he died before it was completed. His recommendations, however, were interspersed throughout the body of his book, and have a modern ring. King warned: "If the United States is to endure; if we shall project our history, even through four or five thousand years as the Mongolian nations have done, and if that history shall be written in continuous peace, free from periods of widespread famine or pestilence, this nation must orient itself; it must square its practices with a conservation of resources which can make endurance possible." China, as well as Japan and Korea, had instituted what King termed "permanent agriculture." Their system was not perfect, and they could, and would, make improvements. But "it remains for us and other nations to profit by their experience, to adopt and adapt what is good in their practice and help in a world movement for the introduction of new and improved methods."[67]

"It is high time," King wrote, "for each nation to study the others." He called for colleges of all nations, "instead of exchanging courtesies through their baseball teams," to send selected students as investigation teams, "by international agreement, both east and west," to study "specifically set problems." Such an international program could be paid for "by diverting so much as is needful from the large sums set aside for the expansion of navies, for such steps as these, taken in the interests of world uplift and world peace, could not fail to be more efficacious and less expensive than increase in fighting equipment." In American contacts with countries such as China, King wanted to see more of "the spirit of pulling together and of a square deal rather than one of holding aloof and of striving to gain unneighborly advantage."[68]

King's book drew wide praise. Liberty Hyde Bailey, America's most eminent agriculturalist, contributed a preface and declared, "We in North America are wont to think that we may instruct all the world in agriculture, because our agricultural wealth is great and our exports to less favored peoples have been heavy; but this wealth is great because our soil is fertile and new, and in large acreage for every person." Over time, Bailey predicted, America would confront the problem of maintaining the soil's fertility, a problem that "the oriental peoples have met." Bailey suggested, "We may never adopt [their] particular methods, but we can profit vastly by their experience."[69] Favorable reviews in the scholarly and popular press in the United States helped make the title, *Farmers of Forty Centuries*, a phrase that later writers would routinely use when describing Chinese agriculture.

✧ ✧ ✧ ✧ ✧

The program that most reflected King's injunction to learn from the Chinese was the USDA's ongoing plant-collection program (though its primary representative in China, Frank Meyer, was interested merely in Chinese plants, not Chinese agricultural knowledge). To the public, plant collection was presented in the 1920s as an example of America's internationalist spirit. *Scientific American*, in an article celebrating the twenty-fifth anniversary of the USDA's Seed and Plant Introduction Office, told "How Modern Science Combs the World for New Things to Eat, Picking and Choosing for the Menu of the Future." The illustration showed an American with a bow tie, hat, and amazed expression, holding an enormous object the size of a watermelon. The caption explained: "A radish from Chinese seed." [70]

The USDA had much to celebrate. Date palms from the Middle East had become a major industry in California; long-staple cotton, imported from Egypt, had become important in the Southwest; and durum wheat, introduced from Russia, made possible annual production of 25 to 45 million bushels in areas in the Northwest that formerly could not grow any crops at all. Frank Meyer was heralded as the man who had walked "10,000 miles" through China on behalf of Americans, earning David Fairchild's tender posthumous tribute: "His hardy yellow rose peers in upon me through my study window, and up in the border his scarlet lily is in bud, while the perfume of his lilac has barely passed away. His white-barked pine is dusting its pollen into the air, his Euonymous and his hardy bamboo are growing at the corners of the house, and his dry-land elm with its delicate branches shades the entrance. So much of China has he successfully transplanted to this country." [71]

Walter Swingle, Fairchild's colleague at the USDA and a fellow enthusiast about China's agricultural contributions, once declared that China was America's "chief agricultural creditor." But the claim was overstated. Inventories of Chinese introductions that were successful in the United States tend to list ornamentals or economically insignificant lines (such as can be seen in Fairchild's tribute to Meyer). The most important contributions were soybeans, which have become a major agricultural crop, and the Siberian elm, which was planted in the late 1930s in extensive windbreaks from Canada to Texas and, fortunately, was relatively undamaged by the ravages of Dutch elm disease. However, the Feicheng peach, which the USDA obtained only through skulduggery, did not turn out to be useful in subsequent breeding for improved fruit. When the Chico Plant Introduction Garden in California was taken over by another government agency in the early 1970s, bulldozers removed the Feicheng peach trees that had been grown from Meyer's scions. [72]

Americans proved slow to show interest in unfamiliar Chinese products, such as the jujube, lichee, and edible bamboos, which Fairchild erroneously predicted would be "adapted by Yankee ingenuity and accepted by the open-minded taste of the American." Even the "odorless cabbage," imported from China but largely ignored, did not fulfill one reporter's early prediction that it "would abolish all memory of the old familiar cooking recipe that cabbage should be boiled four hours and four miles from any human habitation,' since the Chinese cabbage does not betray its presence in the kitchen." [73]

Another legacy of early USDA interest in China is found in the department's assiduous collection of books on the country. When David Fairchild left his position at the Seed and Plant Introduction Office in 1924, it fell to Walter Swingle to pursue studies of China's agriculture. Building upon the libraries that several American ministers to China had donated to the Library of Congress, Swingle directed his energy to commissioning additional purchases of books in China. One of his major finds was a collection of one thousand local histories, which he secured "at remarkably low prices." The collection that he helped expand became the largest Chinese collection outside of China and Japan.[74]

The collection of Chinese plants and books, although a seemingly commendable (and rare) instance of American willingness to learn from others, did raise some troubling questions. What Fairchild called China's "sharing the wealth of its flora" could, in another light, be regarded as theft for which China received no or little compensation. A Chinese university raised the point in 1925, noting that the United States had sent four plant collecting expeditions to China, all conducted unilaterally, without sharing duplicate specimens with Chinese institutions: "It seems to us very unfortunate, though readily understood, that of all the botanical collections made in China by Americans and other nationals, none has ever come back to China where it would have very great scientific and practical value. There are far better collections of Chinese plants in America, England, and other countries than there are in China at the present time, a situation we are trying to change."[75]

Instead of expanding the scope of its earlier agricultural explorations in China and making Chinese institutions participating partners and beneficiaries of the program, the USDA cut back the scope of its foreign explorations, and China never had an opportunity to participate actively. The next time that the USDA took active interest in the agriculture of others was on the eve of the Second World War, and then in the war's aftermath. But that era was noticeably different from the earlier one that had brought the USDA to China. By 1938, when the first American technical assistance program in agriculture was launched overseas (Liberia and the Philippines were the recipients), the United States had assumed the role of expert. Talk of learning from others had disappeared.

This outcome could not have been predicted at the turn of the century or in the years that immediately followed, when many Americans were quite impressed with, or at worst uninterested in, Chinese agriculture. If either country was going to study the other, it appeared that it would be the United States that would learn from China. The USDA was interested in obtaining new plant materials from China, and a number of representatives—Fairchild, Knapp, and Meyer—went to China in search of rare specimens. Moreover, Dr. Kin's soybean mission and Professor King's popular book, *Farmers of Forty Centuries*, helped bring to the attention of the American public opportunities for improvement that Chinese examples offered to U.S. agriculture.

The notion that the United States might learn something from China did not endure for long, however, perhaps partly because of these earliest plant collection efforts, which sought exotic plant material in preference to new crops. Most damagingly, the American plant collector operated unilaterally, without pretense that his activities were part of any cooperative agreement reached between his home and the host country. Meyer went to China and unabashedly took what he wanted, raising Chinese hackles in the process and confirming Chinese mistrust of foreigners. This was not a strong base upon which the two countries could build agricultural exchanges of mutual benefit.

2

INSTRUCTION

Early Advisers and Grand Visions, 1890s–1910s

China did not stand still. During the years when the USDA was dispatching uninvited agricultural explorers to serve American interests, China on its own initiative hired American agricultural experts to serve Chinese interests. The time did not offer a propitious setting for testing American methods, however. The early American advisers were hired not by the national government but by individual provincial governors, whose own powers were limited and whose support for the Americans proved flighty. As the Qing monarchy lost its grip, then collapsed in 1911, political turmoil engulfed all levels of the government, including the hired hands from America. First in Hubei, then in Manchuria, Americans were appointed to agricultural improvement projects that foundered in the stormy transition from monarchy to republic. Finally, in the early Republican years, American experts insisted on the most ambitious project of all—a giant river conservancy. The scheme resulted from the sense of unlimited capability that Americans had gained from the engineering success of the Panama Canal—a sense that led them to believe that technology would solve the agricultural problems of China.

Zhang Zhidong was the first to employ an American adviser for agricultural improvements. Zhang was one of the best-known Westernizing reformers of the late nineteenth century, a politically savvy bureaucrat, an enthusiastic promoter of industry, an educational innovator, and a scrupulously honest person. China's humiliating defeats at the hands of the Western powers had caused some officials to call for rededication to Chinese tradition and Confucianism, while others proposed imitating the West in order to acquire the power to repel it. Zhang, however, developed a compromise position, prescribing a dualistic formula for China: Chinese learning was to be preserved as the foundation (*ti*), and Western learning was to be selected for its utility (*yong*). Theoretically, China could enjoy the best of both its own traditions and the new techniques from the West.

When Zhang was appointed governor general of Hubei and Hunan in 1889, he immediately began installing the machinery that he had ordered for an iron foundry, which became the Hanyeping Iron and Steel Works. Coal and iron mines, cotton mills, and an arsenal were soon opened as well, and all required foreign expertise. Zhang contracted with a number of European countries to send technical advisers to provide assistance. Initially, he ignored both agriculture and the United States. But in 1891, one of Zhang's British engineers at the cotton textile mill complained about the poor quality and short staple of Hubei cotton, and suggested that Zhang try importing American cottonseed for experimental planting. Zhang immediately liked the idea.[1]

Cotton improvement became another one of Zhang's crusades, and he wrote to the throne about its importance. Since the opening of China's ports to Western traders, Zhang noted, imports of cotton cloth and yarn had drained millions of taels of silver from the country. Some means had to be found to reduce the imports, and planting American cotton seemed a promising course. Zhang declared the characteristics of American cotton—large bolls, fine lint, and a color of beautiful, bright white—to be the best in the world, though his opinion was based on hearsay. He wired the Chinese minister stationed in the United States to select and send back the leading American varieties and those best suited for conditions similar to Hubei's climate. Of one hundred varieties considered, two were finally chosen, one for moist conditions, the other for drier conditions, and 3,700 pounds of seed arrived in 1892.[2]

Zhang was anxious to see improved results as soon as possible. He distributed the American seed to fifteen scattered counties and districts, asking cotton-growing households to begin experimental planting. He promised that at harvest time his Textile Bureau would send buyers to purchase the American cotton at generous prices so that the farmers need not worry about incurring financial losses. Zhang also planned to have samples of both Chinese and American plants turned in after harvest for judging, with prizes awarded to the households with the best specimens. "This seed came from tens of thousands of miles away," he emphasized, "with no expense and trouble spared in securing it"; accordingly, county and district officials were instructed to ensure that those who picked up the new cottonseeds would take care in planting and not casually abandon the experiment. By collecting the seed from the participating farmers, Zhang planned to extend the new varieties rapidly. He confidently predicted that the beauty of locally grown cotton would match that of Western cotton in a few years.[3]

The plans for contests and for the quick diffusion of American cotton proved to be premature, however. By the time the imported seeds had been distributed to households, the best weather for planting them had passed. Zhang also discovered that the farmers, unfamiliar with the new varieties, planted the seeds too close together. The result was a poor harvest. Still, he was encouraged to see that of the little cotton that was harvested, the staple was long and the color promising. Declaring that its potential had yet to be fairly tested, Zhang ordered another batch of cottonseed from America, and this time he also asked for printed instructions for planting it.[4]

The technical instructions were translated into Chinese, and a pamphlet was prepared. It opened with a few words of patriotic exhortation: the financial drain from cotton imports was even more severe than that from opium, so planting American cotton was an act to protect the country's most vital interests. Detailed instructions followed, describing soil preparation, proper planting, insect control, and appropriate fertilizers. Farmers were assured that the American cottonseed had been selected from along thirty degrees north latitude in America (southern Georgia, Mississippi, and Alabama), the same latitude as Hubei, so that the climates would closely match. But the effectiveness of the reassurances and technical instructions was limited by their form—written, unpunctuated classical Chinese, which the largely illiterate masses could not read.[5]

Another year passed, and all cotton, both Chinese and American, fared poorly in 1894. Zhang remained optimistic that American cotton could surpass local varieties. He called for continued experimental plantings,[6] but the outbreak of the Sino-Japanese War claimed his attention, and the experiment lapsed.

❖ ❖ ❖ ❖ ❖

Zhang's interest in agricultural improvement would return, however. After the war and the mortifying Treaty of Shimonoseki in 1895, he prepared a long letter to the throne. In it, Zhang proposed a sweeping reform package, including a School for Gathering Talent that would offer a program in agricultural education.[7]

Criticizing general education, Zhang appealed for more specialized training. His agricultural program provided for particular emphasis on crops, waterworks, animal husbandry, and agricultural engineering; other programs in the school would cover international affairs, industry, and commerce. Moreover, Zhang proposed hiring foreign instructors for all subjects. Notwithstanding (or perhaps because of) the experiments with American cotton, Zhang ignored America and recommended France and Germany as authorities in agriculture. In 1896, when Zhang heard that Berlin was planning to host an agricultural exposition, he hurriedly wired a Chinese consular official in Germany to ensure that all available agricultural books were purchased and mailed back to China for translation.[8]

Enthusiasm for European agriculture proved brief, however, and Zhang continued to cast about for models. The School for Gathering Talent was finally established in 1896, but was soon taken out of Zhang's hands and reorganized exclusively for training translators.[9] Zhang persisted in planning for agricultural improvements and tried to arrange for a French instructor who could teach both agriculture and sericulture.[10] Failing that, he decided in 1897 to turn once again to the United States, at the urging of Sidney Partridge, an Episcopal missionary in Wuchang. Zhang had Partridge write to the president of Cornell University for a suitable person from the agricultural school. In his letter, Partridge noted that His Excellency Zhang Zhidong wanted an American to come to China for two or three years to take charge of the construction and operation of a model farm. Zhang's idea, Partridge explained, was to fit the model with "all the latest and best agricultural appliances as are in the United States of America" and "to have this to show and explain to visiting officials—and to make it the nucleus of an agricultural school here."[11]

The invitation carried only one restriction on ideas or equipment that would be considered for the model farm: large machines could not "at present be used successfully in China." Otherwise, the candidate was to be unfettered and would enjoy generous remuneration. Partridge wrote that he did not know the precise salary that Zhang would offer, but he guessed that an annual salary of $3,000 could be secured, and more if the "right man" could not be attracted by that sum. Partridge added, "It would be a grand thing for Cornell and for our Country to have this new branch of Education Enlightenment in the hands of an *American*."[12]

Beginning what was to be a long series of associations with Chinese agricultural programs, Cornell accepted the invitation and contacted a recent graduate, Gerow D. Brill, who expressed interest in the assignment. Brill was thirty-three, unmarried, and an 1888 graduate of Cornell's College of Agriculture. Brill had done some graduate work, then returned to the family farm in Dutchess County, New York, where he had grown up. He had improved the land, lectured at farmers' institutes during the winter season, and kept in touch with his old teachers in Ithaca. His background combined both practical agricultural experience and the latest in academic training, and he was willing to go to China.[13]

Brill accepted a contract that provided for travel expenses to and from China, living quarters, and an annual salary of $3,000 for three years. To prepare, Brill visited cotton and rice plantations in South Carolina and acquainted himself with the rudiments of tea culture. He also traveled to Washington and called upon the Chinese minister, who advised him to go slowly and not become discouraged if American methods initially encountered opposition in China.[14]

Meanwhile, Partridge wrote that Brill's appointment was under criticism. Zhang was besieged with recommendations from European agents "who extolled the merits of European methods to the depreciation of American ones." Fortunately for the American cause, one of Zhang's leading secretaries was a Yale graduate (like Partridge) and had "endorsed most cordially" all that Partridge had claimed of the "superiority of our American agriculture system."[15] Brill tried to get an official appointment for his China mission from the USDA, and even the congressman from Brill's home district was enlisted in the campaign and testified to his good character. The possibility of agricultural machinery sales to China was also mentioned, and one firm, D. M. Osborne and Company of Auburn, New York, promised to donate its machinery for demonstration on the Hubei model farm. But the USDA was timid and refused to officially sanction Brill's mission.[16]

Arriving in Wuchang in the fall of 1897, Brill's first assignment from Zhang Zhidong was to carry out an agricultural survey. The area was limited to the hills in the vicinity of Daye, near Wuchang, but it provided Brill with an opportunity to become familiar with the local terrain and to make recommendations to Zhang. In his report, Brill began by praising the neatness of the terraced fields he had seen, the diligence of the farmers, and the wise use of animal fertilizers. But he then raised criticisms of some agricultural practices and offered suggestions about afforestation, plant breeding, irrigation, and other matters. He was plainspoken and direct.[17]

Brill did not automatically promote American solutions to the Chinese problems he observed; indeed, his report conspicuously lacked mention of American practices. When he advised the Chinese to invest in afforestation to help prevent floods and to provide timber for profits, he pointed to the experiences of various European countries that had regularly provided annual appropriations for forests. Lamenting the lack of attention given to fruit trees, Brill recommended that hill farmers plant Chinese grapes on lower, comparatively level or rocky land and Chinese chestnuts and walnuts on higher reaches. Chinese varieties, he emphasized, should be planted first; foreign varieties could be planted later, if desired.[18]

Almost every aspect of the region's farming scene drew a suggestion from Brill. He advised using a double team of oxen, or at least one healthy ox, to plow the soil deeply and break up the clods. Poor selection of seeds, he added, kept wheat, rape, and bean yields below their potential. The experimentation with American cotton varieties had fared poorly, Brill wrote, because the farmers had not followed proper procedures to select varieties carefully, dig drainage ditches, and apply lime to neutralize acid in the soil. Noting lush stands of wild oats that seemed to be ignored, Brill unknowingly echoed Kang Youwei's earlier proposal and suggested that they be used to raise bees, which could in turn produce profitable honey.[19]

Brill's report was a detailed agenda of practical measures that could quickly improve local agriculture. The only reaction that he received, however, was silence. Weeks passed, then months. Nothing more was heard of the report, and arrangements for securing land for the model farm repeatedly fell through. Brill did not accept the delays with equanimity. He had come to Wuchang with the understanding that he was "employed for the purpose of improving the Agriculture of this part of China" and that for this work he was to have "a large tract of land on which to grow grain, cotton, fruits, mulberries, tea, etc.; and also to stable and breed horses [and cattle]." But no land, large tract or small, was made available, and Brill grew increasingly impatient to begin his model farm.[20]

✢ ✢ ✢ ✢ ✢

Dependent on Chinese translators whom he regarded as unreliable or insincere, Brill was unaware of the preoccupations of his employer, Zhang Zhidong. Zhang had not forgotten agriculture, but he had shifted his enthusiasm away from an American model. The shift was signaled early in 1898 when Zhang issued the *Quan xue bian* (Call to learning), a collection of essays that the emperor himself made it possible to publish thousands of copies, and one source estimated that a million copies of the pamphlet were sold.[21]

In Zhang's new reform platform, agricultural education occupied an important position and reflected an amalgam of many Western sources, including Brill's agricultural survey. Zhang deplored the backwardness of Chinese agriculture; one *mou* of land (about one-sixth of an acre) in the West could support up to three persons, but if one *mou* in China supported one person it was regarded as bountiful. (Actually, Zhang's comparison was unfair to China, whose yields were not lower per unit of land. The important difference was the higher productivity in extensive American agriculture, which permitted one family to work much larger farms.) To achieve higher yields, Zhang listed two critical elements: chemistry, to properly control fertilizers and soil nourishment; and machines for pumping water, killing insects, plowing, weeding, and milling. With wind power or hydropower, Zhang wrote excitedly, new machinery could save labor and multiply yields— twin benefits that Zhang misunderstood to be synonymous.[22]

Agricultural chemistry, Zhang explained, was not something that could be readily mastered by farmers, nor could the new machines be easily operated and maintained. Agricultural schools were needed to provide the necessary training. Then, if local gentry and rich households with large landholdings tried new methods—and if the new techniques were effective—"the people will naturally follow them."[23]

Zhang singled out for particular praise the new agricultural paper, *Nong-xuebao*, as a useful source to consult for information about new Western methods. He himself ordered every district and county in his jurisdiction to subscribe, stipulating that large counties should get ten copies and smaller counties three, and that all should be distributed widely to the gentry for reading. Zhang was so impressed with *Nongxuebao* that he hired its editor, Japanese-educated Luo Zhenyu, to come to Hubei in 1898. Luo's arrival, however, meant that Zhang's interest had shifted away from Brill and American models and toward Japanese models of agricultural improvement. Chinese such as Luo and now Zhang believed that Japan had already sifted through the mass of Western knowledge and had cast out the less important information. Zhang urged China to use Japan's selections as an expeditious way to learn what aspects of Western knowledge would have practical applications in China.[24]

Brill continued to wait impatiently for land on which to start the model farm. He still had not been granted an interview with Zhang, and when Brill had difficulty securing even ordinary household items, he wondered if his simple manner failed to impress the Chinese authorities sufficiently. He asked another resident whether he should "put on more style" and was told that he should indeed be much more insistent in pressing his claims.[25]

Finally, in the spring of 1898, Zhang made preparations to put Brill to work, starting not with the model farm but with the agricultural school. Zhang announced to the throne and to the public the imminent establishment in Wuchang of a new school of agriculture. The expenses of construction, land rental, supplies, and staff salaries would be paid by the provincial government; however, a small tuition would be required of students to help pay for living expenses and stationery supplies. The tuition income was not intended to cover all such costs, for the government would supplement the fund, but payment of the fee, Zhang explained, should serve to impress upon the students the "deep significance" of their studies.[26]

Brill regarded plans for the school as useless without accompanying experimental land, for which he pressed Zhang when he finally was granted an interview in June 1898, almost a year after his arrival. Brill was especially anxious to begin work by the time his American assistant, John Washington Gilmore, arrived that summer. Gilmore, another Cornellian who had just graduated from the agricultural college, brought with him seeds, nursery stock, a large agricultural library, tools, machines, and fertilizers.[27]

✧ ✧ ✧ ✧ ✧

Meanwhile, in the capital, startling edicts were being issued from the throne. The Reforms of 1898 had begun. The Guangxu emperor, under the influence of Kang Youwei and other reformers, issued a stream of proclamations calling for fundamental changes in all realms of public and economic life. Agricultural reform was one of the subjects, and two edicts called for the establishment of an Imperial University in Beijing that would include, among many departments, a department of agriculture. For a brief moment it appeared that China was about to inaugurate a far-reaching system of agricultural education. The master plan was supplied by Kang. He asked the emperor to establish agricultural schools in every county in the country, to put fallow public lands into production, and to establish agricultural newspapers and associations. Thinking ahead to a time when China could export its agricultural surpluses, Kang even proposed that the throne establish export-promotion offices in the major ports so that foreigners could conveniently examine samples and place orders. Other countries had departments of agriculture and commerce; why, Kang asked, couldn't China?[28]

The emperor responded on August 21 with an edict that ordered agricultural schools established in all provinces, prefectures, and districts.[29] Before the edict could be implemented, however, the emperor's power was effectively ended by a coup d'état. When the Empress Dowager Cixi took control in September, the Westernizing reforms were aborted, and the period became known in retrospect as the "Hundred Days of Reform." Of the agricultural measures, virtually the only proposal to survive was the plan to establish the Imperial University, with an agriculture department.

Despite Zhang Zhidong's sympathies with much of what had been proposed during the summer, he had kept his distance from the reformers who advised the emperor; therefore, when the coup came and the reformers were suppressed, Zhang was spared. His new agricultural school, under Brill's direction, had opened during the last days of the reforms, but it was not visible or successful enough to draw conservative attack. Originally, plans had called for three departments: agriculture, forestry, and animal science. But a shortage of instructors meant that the school could open with only two departments: agriculture and sericulture. It was not only the first agricultural school in China but also the first government school to charge tuition—a radical and unwelcome departure from tradition. The only students who could afford the fees were precisely those least interested in farming. Other occupations seemed to offer a more promising future to ambitious young men. When Zhang had advertised the previous year for applicants to his military academy, he had four thousand men clamoring to enter; when he opened the agricultural college, however, only ten students enrolled in the first class (with no less than eight custodians to look after them).[30]

Brill wanted to work with students drawn from farm backgrounds, but Zhang's enrollment campaign had been explicitly directed toward the sons of officials, gentry, and merchants. Thus the first students were all city boys who had no knowledge of farming and little more of English and other subjects that Brill regarded as prerequisites. Brill wrote to Zhang, "I believe if the students of this school are to be leaders or teachers of Agriculture they should have a thorough knowledge of English, for to-day there are more Agricultural Experiment Stations in English speaking countries than in the rest of the world combined, and extending over a greater variety of climates. More agricultural books and papers are published in the English language that in all others combined." Preparatory work in physiology, zoology, chemistry, and geology was also needed, and "these we would gladly teach," Brill offered, "but to teach English and the other elementary studies is not really our proper work. . . . We came here with the understanding that we were to do agricultural work alone; as it is we are devoting most of our time to teaching elementary subjects."[31]

When the first term ended in January 1899, Brill still had no farmland to complement the school. The students had proved to be a disciplinary headache, regularly disappearing for nighttime revels in the city. (Brill requested that Zhang move the school outside of the city, where the students "would have no inducement to go out nights.") Even more distressing, Japanese classes had been added at the school, and Japanese influence seemed to be crowding out American. Brill wrote home, "Our time will be up before we are fairly started I am afraid. The Japs will work for one third what we will and at present they are very familiar with the Viceroy [Zhang]." When the second term opened in March, only seven students appeared.[32]

Brill continued to appeal for experimental land and was finally granted a 30-*mou* (5-acre) tract that had been used as the drill grounds for the local military academy. It was not, Brill felt, well suited for a farm, but he made the best of it and set assistants to work digging ditches and removing stones and bricks. "I asked if we would have the land permanently, and was told positively that we would have it as long as we wanted it," Brill wrote, but after he planted fruit trees, corn, sorghum, and five varieties of American cotton, he was told that the land had to be returned to the military academy for its parade ground. Brill was disgusted: "This method of working is absurd." After another change of plans, he complained, "They don't know what they want anyway. It's like working for a child that needs a spanking."[33]

In the summer of 1899, Brill left Wuchang and toured Japan "to see what improvements had been made there in Agriculture, as nearly all the teachers and workers were from America in the beginning." He returned with an enthusiastic report of Japan's progress. The students at the agricultural college in Sapporo knew English and had completed necessary preparatory coursework. Their college was well equipped with experimental fields close at hand, and their livestock and sericulture research had produced visible improvements. Brill used the occasion of his trip report to try to change Zhang's conception of the school farm. Zhang had asked Brill to plan a farm that would earn enough profit to run the school. Brill explained, "To run a farm for profit and to run one experimentally for improving the Agriculture of a country, and for teaching students, are two entirely different things." An experimental farm should have the freedom to try new crops; it should be given government funds, not asked to show a profit. Brill pointed out that Japan had invested heavily in the experimental fields connected with the Imperial Agricultural College, and that "as far as the Agriculture of the country is concerned they have paid for themselves many times over."[34]

Whether or not the school farm should be run for profit remained moot, however, as yet another piece of land that Brill had been promised slipped from his grasp. This time the site was to be below a city lake, where Brill had suggested that the government build a dike and reclaim land. But after Brill was promised his choice of reclaimed land and the dike was completed, squatters moved in, and Brill noted with dismay that "people are rapidly plowing it and putting down boundary stones." His entreaties to Zhang to intervene were to no avail. The broken promises drove Brill to write home, "I begin to think that the Chinese make an official study of making excuses and telling plausible lies." The Chinese authorities did not understand why Brill was so upset: "They say, why do you care, don't we pay you?"[35]

Frustrations multiplied. Brill wrote, "They expect a fellow to know everything here from the management of silk worms to raising forests. I told the Viceroy it would need about twenty men and a fully equipped University to teach on all subjects." The Chinese, Brill felt, did not appreciate the investment that would be needed: "They think all is necessary is to translate a few books and read them over then buy a few machines and have men turn the cranks."[36]

By the fall of 1899, after more than two years in Wuchang, Brill decided to give Zhang one more chance to make the improvements necessary for the work to progress. In a long report that summed up his experiences to date, Brill wrote to Zhang, "We are willing to work, and to work hard, but we want a chance to accomplish something; but so far we have not had this, and outside of school work we have accomplished very little." He made a final appeal: "Some one must have authority to settle with us definitely what lines of work we are to carry on, and then these plans must not be interfered with. At present every thing appears to end in talk."[37]

Brill later heard that Zhang had received his blunt criticisms of the work without reacting angrily. But one of Zhang's senior assistants had a "two days' talk with the Vice Roy," and the upshot was that Brill was asked if he would accept six months' notice to end his contract. Brill replied, "I would, with pleasure." He explained in a letter home, "Living in China has some advantages as well as many disadvantages, but I do not care to stay here and see no prospect for doing anything."[38]

✧ ✧ ✧ ✧ ✧

Brill and Gilmore left Wuchang early in 1900, and during the rest of the year Brill traveled through other parts of China as an agricultural explorer for the USDA, until repercussions from the Boxer Uprising forced his evacuation. In the meantime, Zhang hired Japanese agricultural experts to carry on the work of the school. The first Japanese instructors were asked, just as Brill had been, to conduct an agricultural survey and submit recommendations, and their report was strikingly similar to Brill's earlier one. Perhaps because they were less confrontational than the Americans, the Japanese stayed in Hubei for eleven years, until 1911, expanding the agricultural college to the size Zhang had originally envisioned, securing the large tract of land needed for experimentation, and adding a major sericulture research program. Japanese instructors were also used in the agricultural department at the Imperial University in Beijing.[39]

After leaving China, the two Americans worked in the Philippines for several years, organizing an agricultural school system there. Brill then returned to the United States to work for the USDA (his only publication about his China experiences was a short article on Chinese egg incubators), while Gilmore went on to a distinguished academic career at a number of American universities.[40] In the years immediately after Brill and Gilmore's 1900 departure—and after the Boxers were suppressed by a multinational expeditionary force and a heavy indemnity was levied upon China by the United States, among others—Americans were not welcomed as agricultural advisers.

In 1910, an American consular official passed on to Washington a sharply critical report of the experience of another American who had been hired by China as a college teacher in 1908 (the identity of the school and the author were kept secret). The teacher's frustrations were quite similar to those Brill had experienced a decade before. Trying to dissuade other Americans from accepting assignments in

China, the embittered teacher wrote:

> Men who have come to the work with high hopes have been disappointed.
> They have found an educational system badly organized—school
> administration often in the hands of officials indifferent or antagonistic to
> Western methods—students badly classified and not properly disciplined—
> Chinese colleagues, some fit and some not, and the unfit often advanced above
> the better trained.... The young American [who comes to China] may very
> likely have to postpone his time of marriage, and lose his chance of American
> advancement.

In an emotional tone, the teacher went on to catalog a long list of additional complaints, ranging from the professional ("a teacher of chemistry and physics may find regulations forbidding his students to use the laboratory") to the personal (some men had "broken down" under the strain). The crowning indignity was that the Chinese government replaced the Americans as soon as there were enough Western-trained Chinese staff to take their place, "even though these Chinese do less work for greater pay." Claiming to speak for other Americans hired by the Chinese, the anonymous teacher wrote, "Most Americans in the government educational service are dissatisfied."[41]

Apparently China was determined to adopt Western models without relying unduly on Westerners in the flesh. In 1903, the imperial government established a new office for China, the Ministry of Commerce, which was chartered to regard agriculture as "the foundation" of the entire economy (and which may or may not have been partly modeled after William Preston Bentley's suggestions). Three years later, a separate Central Agricultural Experiment Station was established outside the West Gate of Beijing, staffed wholly with Chinese personnel. (Later, the station was criticized by China's own agriculturalists, who complained that it was run more as a botanical garden than as an agricultural research facility.)[42]

✤ ✤ ✤ ✤

An exception to the rule was Manchuria, where the Chinese sought American advice and seemed eager to treat a visiting American well. The northeast corner of China, Manchuria was a region that China was afraid of losing and in which the government was desperate to try new agricultural programs to strengthen its hold on the territory. Especially after the Russo-Japanese War of 1904–05 called attention to the designs that Russia and Japan appeared to have on Manchuria, the Qing court was anxious to check the influence of both countries. Toward this end, Xu Shichang, a protégé of Yuan Shikai, was appointed governor general. Xu appointed Westernized men to serve under him, including Tang Shaoyi, who had studied at Columbia and New York universities in the 1870s as part of the China Educational Mission, and Chen Zhenxian, a recently returned graduate in agriculture from the University of California. The newly appointed leadership in Manchuria looked to the United States for assistance.[43]

Railroads and finances occupied much attention, as Tang negotiated with Willard Straight, the American consul general at Mukden, for help with building a new railroad and underwriting currency reforms.[44] But agriculture was not ignored, for Manchuria remained a largely unpopulated frontier, and China needed to attract farming settlers to it. Chinese officials hoped that use of American expertise would help check Russian and Japanese influence, so the Manchurian government asked the U.S. State Department to help secure the services of an agricultural expert. The State Department passed the request on to the USDA, which recommended Edward C. Parker, a young man of twenty-seven.

A graduate of the Minnesota College of Agriculture, Parker had stayed on after graduation, contributing to pioneering work at the college's experiment station which sought to discover "the best paying" systems of crop rotation. The research, which demanded that cooperating farmers keep careful accounts of all costs, gave Parker a more modest estimation of American farming than that of many of his contemporaries. He wrote, "The American is an optimist and a braggart concerning the agriculture of his native land." Although foreigners might be impressed with the apparently prosperous condition of the American farmer, Parker argued that the farmer's prosperity was "due more to the advantages he has had in unlimited soil fertility and large acreage, in the use of improved machinery and from the appreciation in land values, rather than from successful management or the application of strict business methods." American farmers, he felt, needed to keep books for their business and periodically stop to consider such things as the "relation between prices of feeds and prices of beef and pork." In short, American agriculture needed to be put "on a more business-like basis."[45]

Aside from work in the new area of farm management, Parker had developed another specialization: wheat. American wheat production was not increasing as fast as demand, and research at the Minnesota experiment station suggested that a five-year crop rotation, which included corn, oats, and fallow periods, produced better aggregate results than continuous cropping of wheat. In Parker's eyes, the American wheat farmer was not a figure to be emulated: wheat farming was carried out "in a slothful and careless manner," and when continuous cropping depleted the soil's fertility, "the common proceeding of the wheat farmer is to move westward, and begin the process of soil robbery anew." Much could be done, Parker argued, to improve American practices and raise wheat yields.[46]

Parker wanted to increase world supplies of wheat as well. He told American readers in *Century Magazine* that "vast regions of land in South America, North Africa, and Asia are awaiting the demand for 'still more wheat' which shall bring to them the steel plow and the self-binder, and cause them to yield a food product sufficient to feed a new population of untold millions." With his interest in wheat and his pertinent experience, Parker was the perfect candidate for the Manchurian reformers. At the time inquiries were being made for an American adviser, the Chinese unveiled a wide vista of opportunities in Manchuria for Americans.

A Chinese visitor in New York at the time told the Republican Club: "In the thousands of square miles of virgin soil in Manchuria, there is grand opportunity to employ your surplus capital, the ability of captains of the great farms in your Middle West and your good farming machines." [47]

Taking the "grand opportunity," Parker accepted a three-year contract to serve as an adviser to Cheng Dequan, governor of Fengtian province, and began work in August 1908. The first few months were spent familiarizing himself with the region, which he was surprised to find so richly endowed with natural resources. Manchuria, he wrote back to America, "has sufficient potential wealth within its boundaries to cause exclamations of surprise from even the inhabitant of North America accustomed to the vast rolling prairies of the Mississippi Valley and Canada and the forests of the Pacific Slope." Parker declared, "It is no exaggeration to say that an equal area of contiguous land could not be found in North America that would contain so many forms of natural wealth and in such quantity." [48]

Drawing an analogy with the United States, Parker described Manchuria as "newer, bigger, and freer" than the provinces of south China, in the same way that Montana, North Dakota, and Minnesota were different from the New England states. The native Manchus, he added, were "more vigorous of body" and "more typically an outdoor people" than their south China countrymen. Yet Manchuria remained sparsely populated. Labor shortages at planting and harvesting meant that migrant laborers from Shandong had to be brought in every year. "Colonization," Parker wrote, "is one of the large problems essential to the full development of the country." [49]

Agricultural practices in Manchuria, Parker observed, were crude and wasteful. Few livestock were kept, so the nutrients of the soil were not replenished with manure; no grass crops were grown, and the farmers knew nothing about soil tillage; and crops were sown and collected "almost unaided by the skill or mechanical genius of man." The thousands of square miles of deep-brown, loamy soil still yielded bountiful crops, but the methods used "would soon bankrupt the American farmer." Parker neglected to mention that the wastefulness he saw on the Manchurian frontier was similar to the wastefulness he had recently condemned on the American frontier. [50]

As a sparsely settled and richly endowed frontier, Manchuria was "the ideal experiment ground of all Asia for the testing of Western methods of economic progress on Eastern people." Parker wanted to see Manchuria's development hastened by "the far-sighted genius of such men as J. J. Hill and Shaughnessy, who built the steel paths of commerce into the heart of North America and waited patiently the coming of settlers and the coming of dividends." With the Manchurian region's acute labor shortages, a market for agricultural machinery— if affordable and practical—also beckoned. Parker declared, "If the use of Western agricultural machinery, mining and lumbering methods, and transportation methods fail here they will certainly fail in other Eastern regions."[51]

The choice that Manchuria faced, Parker believed, was one of determining whether Chinese or Americans would direct its development. Would Manchuria "fill up with the overflow of Chinese from the Southern provinces and gradually develop the social and economic customs of the thickly settled districts of South China or will it absorb Western ideas and have a portion of its people produce food for local consumption and for export, while another portion develop the mines, man the railways, and prepare the surplus products for exports"? The prospects for American influence appeared bright. Parker noted that the Manchurian officials appointed after the imperial reorganization of the region's government in 1907 included many who had studied in America and had a good command of English. And Parker's very presence in Fengtian illustrated the government's receptiveness to American advice. The situation, with its exciting possibilities, wrote Parker, "fires the imagination."[52]

After several months of travel and observation, Parker was ready to submit a report to the provincial government, outlining his recommendations for developing Manchurian agriculture. The advice was both practical and surprising. Parker eschewed suggestions that could not be readily implemented: "the farmer's ability to take advantage of improved methods must be taken into consideration." He also suggested that the depletion of soil fertility that he had observed was not really the most acute problem, nor was spreading the latest advances in chemistry, physics, and botany. "The chief problems of agricultural development in Manchuria at the present time are economic, social, and political problems," Parker wrote, "rather than scientific problems relative to the stimulation of greater productiveness in the soil." In Parker's opinion, what Manchurian farmers needed most was an improved transportation infrastructure that would open wider markets.[53]

Trains of heavy, two-wheeled mule carts, sometimes traveling four hundred miles, were the primary means of carrying the wheat, tobacco, hemp, and other agricultural products to market. Parker once described them for American readers as a "picturesque" sight, and was both fascinated and horrified by the carter's use of a long whip to guide the animals ("often in his maneuvering and whipping he cracks his whip about the head of a mule or pony and snaps out an eye, and hardly a mule team can be seen that has a full set of eyes"). But the inefficiency of the system was appalling. The carts cut deep ruts on the road and tipped over at the slightest provocation. The ruts became "canals and rivers" in the rainy season. "At times," wrote Parker, "traffic is absolutely stalled and business stops even in the cities, because nobody can get anywhere."[54]

Parker told the Fengtian government that, first and foremost, it should build better roads and bridges and extend rail lines from the seaboard to trading centers in the interior. Such improvements would assure "the greatest benefits to the agricultural interests of Manchuria that a wise government could bestow." An agricultural expert such as himself, if given proper facilities and support, could help introduce improved seeds and machinery and spread information about better methods of crop cultivation and livestock breeding. But transportation improvements were needed first to revolutionize "the old system of 'produce-and-consume-what-you-produce,'" a lesson that had been learned in the United States: "The agricultural problem of Manchuria is not so much the problem of making two blades of grass grow where one grew before as to change the existing economic and social conditions of farm life into an advanced condition of commercial agriculture." [55]

Opening an agricultural college in Manchuria seemed premature to Parker. He questioned the appropriateness of talk of college programs when "primary education is at present not well enough organized in Manchuria to prepare young farmers for studying the science and theory of agriculture." Moreover, if instruction in a new agricultural college were given in English, students would have to come from elsewhere in China. Parker reasoned, "On graduation many of these would return to their native homes and little would be accomplished of actual benefit to the Manchurian farmer." [56]

A more practical beginning, he advised, would be to set up demonstration farms to show local residents improved practices. The Chinese farmers were "noted for their quickness of perception and ability to learn and adopt new methods when the new method is demonstrated. There is little doubt but that labor saving machines, better methods of soil cultivation and improved varieties of fruit and grain would be adopted by the Manchurian farmer if it could be practically demonstrated to him that these methods would put money in his pocket, and that the cost of the materials was not too great for his pocket-book." Parker proposed establishing four demonstration and experiment farms, with varying specialties; he preferred starting with a modest number of farms at first and concentrating on careful supervision, rather than with a large number that would lack adequate "intelligent management." [57]

✧ ✧ ✧ ✧ ✧

Parker was told that his recommendations were "ratified" by the provincial Bureau of Agriculture, Industry, and Commerce, and he set about establishing the demonstration farms. When he wrote to Montgomery Ward and Company, in Chicago, for the mail-order price of a small threshing machine, Ward's forwarded the letter to International Harvester, which was instantly interested in Parker's project. [58]

Since its formation in 1902 as the conglomeration of five agricultural machinery companies (including Cyrus McCormick's), Harvester had aggressively doubled its initial foreign trade within four years. The fastest growth was the Russian market, which represented a third of the company's foreign sales. But on the eve of Parker's arrival in Manchuria, the prospects for developing a China market had seemed poor. In early 1909, Charles H. Haney, supervisor of foreign sales, had been asked by the company's general manager what could be done to develop sales in China, where the company had no offices or representatives and had shown virtually no sales since the promising year of 1900. Haney had replied pessimistically, "I doubt very much if we would be justified in spending very much money to investigate how to educate the populous portions of China to the use of agricultural machinery. The first thing for them to do would be to learn how to use modern plows. There is no hope of our getting into the field until they have learned to use the simple tools." [59]

Haney had regarded Manchuria as "probably the most progressive and probably the most likely to develop trade in our line than any of the other provinces of China." With an office in nearby Vladivostok, Harvester could try to promote its machines and test the China market. "If we fail to develop trade in Manchuria," Haney said, "then in my judgment it is not worth very much in other portions at this time." But despite all the talk he had heard about eventual trade possibilities, the sales record as of 1909 was dismal; only three machines, one reaper and two mowers, had been sold recently in all of Manchuria. It was precisely then, when Harvester was eyeing China, and particularly Manchuria, but feeling that sales opportunities were still small, that Parker came to the company's attention. [60]

The head of Harvester's Vladivostok office, August Heid, agreed to supply Parker with harvesting machines that would be needed for the farm's demonstration of "the American system." But Parker did not lead the company to have false hopes of success; his letters to Heid were pessimistic, and Heid, in turn, reported to his superiors that the outlook still was not bright. Heid wrote, "Considering the present lack of transportation in Manchuria there certainly could be no market, and until railways and public highways are built, we would be wasting money advertising farming machinery and making demonstrations amongst the Chinese." Harvester would proceed conservatively: "We will work this matter slowly and keep in close touch with the situation, so that if anything develops we would be ready to take advantage of it." [61]

Parker made preparations for his demonstration farm. Wheat seed was ordered from the United States; fruit trees were imported; livestock was purchased. But much of the material sat in warehouses, for Parker—like Brill, earlier, in Hubei—found that land was very difficult to secure. In Parker's case, his search for suitable land was handicapped by insufficient funds. Land was purchased or rented for two small orchards, but a year of waiting failed to yield a start on wheat farming. The seeds and machines remained in storage. [62]

Reviewing an itemized account of his expenses, Parker was appalled at the large percentage that went to his and his assistant's salary, modest though they were. A larger budget was needed so that investments in land and permanent improvements would be possible—investments that were needed if agricultural improvement was to be supported by a viable organization. Parker also requested more regular support, since funding came at irregular intervals and in unpredictable amounts. He wrote to the Manchurian government, "It is a recognized fact in business, in government and in educational affairs that continuity of policy is necessary to secure results. It is particularly true in government projects to foster industries that if ideas and plans are to be capitalized and made to return dividends in increased economic efficiency among the people, the original idea or plan of work should be closely adhered to and the plan developed from a definite budget of money."[63]

Parker's entreaties fell on deaf ears, for he lost his American-leaning patrons because of events in the capital. The death of the Empress Dowager Cixi in late 1908, and the accession to the throne of Puyi, the Xuantong emperor, in early 1909, set in motion the retirement of Yuan Shikai and the removal of his lieutenants, including Xu Shichang and the officials who had brought Parker to China.

He kept his spirits up, however, despite the frustrations and setbacks. In 1910, a group of American farmers who had emigrated to Alberta, Canada, wrote to the State Department of their interest in "going to Manchuria to investigate the possibilities of wheat growing on a large scale." Their request for information was forwarded to Parker, who seized the opportunity to set forth his still optimistic vision of opportunities for Americans in Manchuria.[64]

The Americans wanted to know whether wheat farms of two to five thousand acres would be profitable in Manchuria; Parker replied, "Under skillful management I am absolutely positive that wheat can be produced thirty percent cheaper in Manchuria than in America." He added, "This is not guesswork on my part for I know what it costs to produce wheat in the Red River country and I know what can be done in Manchuria."[65]

Calculating the cost of Chinese labor, Parker told the Americans that "the efficiency of the coolie depends to a large extent on the skill of the manager. You cannot expect him to work as fast or as intelligently as the American farm hand, but they will do a surprising amount of work if properly handled." If taught with patience and tact, Parker explained, Chinese farmhands could be taught to drive mule teams hitched to American machinery. Parker employed a Chinese teamster "who can plow a beautiful furrow and drive a disk grain drill so carefully as to put many of our American farmers to shame."[66]

Machines could be used without fear of encountering difficulties in obtaining repairs and spare parts. Local smiths and carpenters, Parker said, could duplicate all broken parts except castings. And replacement castings were close at hand in the Harvester warehouses maintained at Vladivostok and Omsk. The only remaining concern was that of securing land. Acquiring outright title would be impossible, but Parker advised the Americans to obtain a lease from the Manchurian government. With reasonable terms, the venture would not be unduly risky, "providing the American Government would take some interest in the concession and give some assurance that concessionaires would be backed up in case of radical political changes that might arise to injure the concession." With backing only for emergencies, Parker concluded, "most Americans could thereafter be relied upon to look after themselves."[67]

The precise form in which the United States was to "back up" the farmers was not detailed, but the possibility that American gunboats would be deployed to protect American wheat farmers in Manchuria never came to pass, because the Chinese government denied permission for a lease. And in the course of American inquiries, which were made with assistance from the American minister in Beijing and the consul general in Mukden, Russia learned of the affair and protested. A Russian newspaper reported that the United States had asked China to set aside in Manchuria land lots of five to fifty thousand acres for cultivation "according to the very latest American system," which was intended to "give Americans quite as firm a footing in Manchuria as Japan and Russia now possess there." The Russian report also bitterly observed that "the syndicate of the American [sic] Harvester Company, which will supply the agricultural implements for the enterprise, has as its director the American minister in Peking." The American minister promptly declared that there was "no foundation for this report," but in fact, bolstering American influence in the region through agricultural projects was a conscious strategy of the American government at the time, and when Parker's three-year contract came up for renewal in the summer of 1911, the State Department was most interested in the matter.[68]

Also interested were the directors of International Harvester, who continued to look to Parker for advice on how to develop the company's still elusive sales in Manchuria. The Vladivostok office was asked to supply machines for a number of different demonstration projects, most of which seemed questionable. In 1911, a Chinese director of a Manchurian experimental station wanted the use of large numbers of machines for an indefinite term, gratis. A Harvester executive in Chicago regarded the proposal as reasonable and as a valuable point of entry, but Heid vetoed it, based partly on Parker's counsel. Instead, Heid proposed that Harvester supply machines for a first year, after which the proposed "model farm" should be able to prove that it could be self-supporting. In the same year, A. L. H. Ledeboer (a foreigner who may have been American, European, or Russian) asked Harvester for credit for the machines he would need on a 50,000-acre concession that he expected to obtain from the Manchurian government. Ledeboer, however, knew as little about agriculture as he did about Manchurian politics, and Harvester was cool to his inquiries. After failing to convince Ledeboer of the impossibility of plowing and seeding uncultivated sod in a single season, Heid gave up talking with him and advised Ledeboer to obtain his concession for land, after which the matter of farm machinery could be addressed. Several other men with more modest plans also expressed interest in Harvester implements should their applications for concessions be approved. For all, Parker served as a one-man review board, sorting out for Harvester the feasible proposals from the foolish.[69]

✢ ✢ ✢ ✢ ✢

By the expiration of his contract, Parker had not been successful in starting the wheat demonstration projects that he had wanted to establish, whether under his own direction or that of the other Americans. But he had been persuaded to start an agricultural school despite his initial feeling that the school was premature. He was willing to renew his contract, provided that questions about his salary and authority to operate without Chinese "interference" were resolved. Parker wanted the power to set specifications for needed machines and tools and to have purchases made by public bids; he also wanted the power to "control and dismiss my assistants." He planned to have a new contract in hand before he went to the United States for a six-month leave of absence at half pay, during which time he planned to visit home and collect materials for writing the basic textbooks he hoped to use upon his return to the agricultural school in Fengtian. But on the eve of his departure, the Manchurian authorities presented him with contract papers that differed from what Parker thought had been agreed to, so he left for the United States with the terms of his new contract unsettled.[70]

The American legation in Beijing was concerned, and protested that the contract Parker had been offered "too greatly restricted his authority" and seemed to have been "purposely made unacceptable in order to get rid of Parker whose attitude offended." The State Department was asked to try "to secure for experts such freedom of action and control of subordinates as will make their work a success." International Harvester also wrote to Secretary of State Knox, "respectfully" asking that he use his good offices to retain Parker's appointment. Parker was described as "active, energetic, and efficient," and as a man who "desires to introduce modern methods and accomplish something for American trade." Internally, company officials viewed Parker's reappointment as a boon for their business. Heid wrote his superiors a company memo in which he stated that if Parker were appointed head of colonization and agricultural development in Manchuria, "the trade that the Chinese government has to give will be ours." (If the Russians had seen the internal memorandums at Harvester, their worst suspicions about American expansion into Manchurian agriculture would have appeared to be confirmed.) In response to the pressure from both the State Department and Harvester, the acting secretary of state skirted an official declaration of support for Parker's reappointment but cabled Beijing that the department "would not view with equanimity" Parker's elimination, "especially his displacement by a foreigner of any other nationality."[71]

In October 1911, shortly after Parker left Manchuria, revolts spread throughout China, toppling the monarchy; the following January, a republic was formally inaugurated with Sun Yat-sen at its head. Sun, however, soon had to step down to allow Yuan Shikai to assume the presidency, and a confusing period of political musical chairs commenced, dominated by military warlords who had private armies but lacked sufficient power to assert stable control over the entire country. The political changes that engulfed most of the nation in this period did not affect

Fengtian as much as elsewhere because Zhao Ersun, the last governor under the Qing, managed to have himself appointed the provincial head under the new republic. But Parker, busy in Washington collecting photographs and drawings at the USDA for his new textbooks, wondered how the general political upheaval might affect the plans for agricultural work in Manchuria. In January 1912, he wrote to the Bureau of Colonization in Manchuria: "Should the unsettled and indefinite conditions continue into the year 1912 it would appear to me to pre-clude the possibility of there being much development work done and therefore a real use for my services. Should I return to Manchuria under such conditions the Manchurian Government would be burdened with an unnecessary expense for my salary and I should be wasting my time and be unable to give the Government 'value received' for my salary." [72]

Conditions in China did remain unsettled, and Parker did not return. He continued work on a textbook, however, and *Field Management and Crop Rotation* was published in 1915. For his American readers, Parker included a chapter on "Lessons from Other Nations," which used his experiences in Manchuria to drive home several lessons for the United States. He pointed out that, contrary to popular impression (resulting from Frank King's recently published *Farmers of Forty Centuries*), soil-conserving "permanent agriculture" was not practiced throughout China. In Manchuria and north China, where within the memory of living farmers the crop yields had once been double or triple the current levels, the sad depletion of the soil that Parker had seen was "an object lesson worthy of consideration by the American farmer of the Middle West." [73]

After Parker's departure, the agricultural college in Manchuria struggled on, but it had only the general curriculum of a primary school and lacked courses on agriculture. The school was permanently closed in 1919, because of, in the words of a later American consul, "its isolated position, lack of pupils, and the gross mismanagement." Other Americans tried to raise capital for large-scale wheat-farming ventures in Manchuria, and International Harvester continued its market-ing efforts in the region with improving results. In 1912 and 1913, the company sold about a hundred walking plows and a few mowing machines, disk harrows, drills, and rakes. But company retrenchment caused by antitrust reorganization in the United States and the advent of the world war in 1914 cut short both its China campaign and the dream of using the open lands of Manchuria as an "ideal testing ground" for American machines. [74]

✧ ✧ ✧ ✧ ✧

When Parker left China in 1911, Americans talked of a new agricultural development project, a project of immense scale that far surpassed the preceding American attempts to launch schools and farms—namely, a scheme to tame the Huai River in eastern China. The scope of the project, requiring what was believed at the time to be at least $30 million (an unrealistically conservative figure), far exceeded any other proposal to date; still, it seemed small and perfectly manageable, given the tremendous success that Americans were enjoying in construction on the Isthmus of Panama. But unlike the earlier Americans in Hubei and Manchuria, the Americans who proposed the Huai project were essentially uninvited—and often unwelcome. The Chinese, led by the successful entrepreneur Zhang Qian, had their own, quite different ideas about the Huai, and the ostensibly shared goal of serving the Huai basin residents became obscured in the nationalistic fighting between Americans and Chinese involved in planning the project.

The Huai was a major river that lacked a natural outlet to the sea. It began near the Henan-Hubei border and ran eastward through Henan, Anhui, and into the Hongze Lake, from which it had difficulty leaving. In the early nineteenth century, its waters had passed through the lake and joined those of the Yellow River, flowing to the sea in a channel that stretched across northern Jiangsu. But in 1855, the Yellow River had changed course, moving to the north, and without its force, the outlet channel for the Huai disappeared. Not only did the Grand Canal, the man-made waterway built to link the northern and southern parts of the old empire, act as an obstacle but the new Tianjin-Pukou Railway, which also ran north-south, had a rail-bed embankment that lacked sufficient drain canals, further impeding drainage of the Huai. With scarcely any precipitation, the river flooded the region, groping for a path to the sea.[75]

The American Red Cross, which had spent hundreds of thousands of dollars on famine relief in China, was interested in a Huai conservancy project as a flood-control measure, and both Americans and Chinese saw the benefits that such a project would bring to agriculture. Paul Reinsch, the American minister to China, declared that a Huai project "would be the beginning of reclaiming the waste lands of China and utilizing the forces of nature, as represented in the rain-swollen streams, with the result that, according to the computations of competent experts, the agricultural productivity of China could be increased by nearly one hundred per cent." And an editorial in a Chinese newspaper described the conservancy of the Huai as "the turning point of the future development of Chinese agriculture."[76]

The American initiative began in early 1911, with an offer by the Red Cross to the Chinese throne to send an American engineer to study the problem of the Huai. The man selected was Charles Davis Jameson, a civil engineer whom the Red Cross regarded as the perfect expert for the job. Actually, Jameson was not a hydraulics specialist; his previous experience had been mostly on railroad and mining projects. But he had lived in China for many years, beginning in 1895. Moreover, he could point to a short stint of work on the Panama Canal, before "Panama fever" sent him back to the United States for a year of recuperation in New York and Boston hospitals. Jameson's involvement with Panama was important, for the Red Cross interest in the Huai was spearheaded by its central committee chairman, General George W. Davis, the famous engineer who had served on the Isthmanian Canal Commission and as governor of the Canal Zone in Panama.[77]

The Qing government gave its permission for the American study of the

Huai and promised to provide Jameson with assistance. The American arrived in 1911, just as the Huai was in high flood and was creating one of the worst disasters in decades. As he toured flood districts in Anhui, passing streams of traveling beggars who were on the verge of starving to death, Jameson wrote that "there was not a day that I did not pass two or three bodies of men, women and children lying on the road." Still, Jameson recommended that aid organizations require physical work for aid given and not dispense charity. While preparing his Huai study, he advised foreign relief organizations that if matters were arranged "so that every one who received relief has to work for it instead of getting it for nothing, two-thirds of the present sufferers will not suffer any longer." He explained, "There are a great many beggars and loafers. The crops are uncertain; famine relief is certain; and they are satisfied to sit down and wait for it." [78]

The advice (though implemented) was given only in passing; Jameson's main task was to find a feasible outlet for the Huai, and he was fortunate that when the Qing government was overthrown by Republican revolutionaries in the midst of his study, the new government reaffirmed its predecessor's promise to provide assistance. But the central government was busy with other business; a provincial figure, the energetic Zhang Qian, took the most interest in the project. Zhang was the promoter of a successful cotton mill in Nantong, Jiangsu, which had spawned other enterprises, including a flour mill, an ironworks, a steamship line, and a land reclamation company. Zhang established new schools, served in official appointments, dispensed charity, and made his influence felt in the region in countless projects. Controlling the Huai was a long-standing interest of his, predating Jameson's arrival.

At first, Jameson had nothing but praise for Zhang's work on the Huai problem. Eight years before, Zhang had established a surveying class at one of his schools and had hired its first forty graduates to begin a thorough survey of the region, gathering the topographical data needed for planning the Huai conservancy. Jameson described their work as "most excellent" and was flattered that they had come as a group to the rail station at Qingjiangpu to greet him: "They are the greatest monument to any one man's work that I have so far seen in China. Every one is Chinese; there is not a foreigner amongst them." The man responsible for training the men who were such a credit to their nation was Zhang Qian. Jameson had no reservations about Zhang: "There is no man who knows more about the needs of Kiangsu [Jiangsu], and what ought to be done there, than Mr. Chang Chien [Zhang Qian]." [79]

These kind words, however, were soon withdrawn. When Jameson completed his final report, he wrote to the Red Cross that Zhang had "shown himself an obstructionist and in other works a great grafter." The completion of the study had been delayed five full months which, Jameson charged, was mostly a result of the machinations of Zhang, who was supposed "to provide me with all assistance and money needed—which he did not." [80]

Despite the delays and obstacles, Jameson submitted what he regarded as a satisfactory study and was anxious to act on his own recommendations for conservancy. He proposed discharging the Huai primarily east along the old Yellow River bed, with some diversion also to the south into the Yangzi. The scheme would not only lower the flood level but would also, he said, drain one million acres of rich land that stood useless in the form of swamps or shallow lakes. He estimated the cost at 25 million *yuan* (about $15 million), and said that the project would take only six to seven years to complete. Jameson foresaw no engineering obstacles; the obstacles, in his opinion, were the Chinese officials. Writing in 1912, after his report was completed, Jameson complained that "there is practically no Government in China today." He also wrote, "Never since I have been in China has the anti-foreign feeling been so strong and vicious. This feeling is principally noticeable among the new governing classes and the foreign educated Chinese." He asked the Red Cross to use every means possible to, in his phrasing, "force" the Chinese to begin work on the project.[81]

✢ ✢ ✢ ✢ ✢

Zhang Qian was outraged by Jameson's report. Both the maps and the survey data used in it had originally been prepared by Zhang's own corps of surveyors. In a lengthy rebuttal in Chinese, Zhang accused Jameson of baldly appropriating their work without proper acknowledgment. Plainly offended that Jameson had omitted earlier Chinese research and ignored Zhang's own plans for the Huai, Zhang had portions of his own papers, along with a flattering biography, translated into English and printed as a pamphlet. Addressing American readers, his criticism of Jameson was more restrained: Mr. Jameson's investigation was most welcome, and maps and plans had been provided for his use. It was a matter of "extreme regret," however, that "Mr. Jameson's investigations, conducted under pressure of time, added to what was already known nothing in the way of theory or discovery that would serve for our guidance."[82]

Zhang was not about to step aside for this rude American. Calling for a joint Jiangsu-Anhui effort along lines he already had in mind, Zhang appealed to the central government for creation of a new agency to control the Huai. The request was approved, and Zhang was appointed director of the Central Bureau of Huai Control. Because Zhang sought to train Chinese engineers as quickly as possible for the work ahead, he planned no long-term role for any foreign advisers, and he had no use for Americans like Jameson at any time. If foreign engineers were needed, he said, he would use the Dutch.[83]

Jameson did not go away, however. After sending his report to the Red Cross, he stayed in China to lobby for an American-directed project. He had completed the preliminary work; now he asked the Red Cross to give him "charge of the actual work and carry it on to a finish." He wrote to Mabel Boardman, the powerful member of the Red Cross executive committee who directed the Washington head office, "It is a magnificent proposition, and I am in it with my whole being. Please pardon the openness with which I am writing you."[84]

Jameson sought an audience with the president of the young republic, the man who had earlier made Parker's hiring possible—namely, Yuan Shikai. The meeting went well. Yuan gave Jameson forty minutes and appeared to be quite interested in the project. The only problem was arranging financing; as Jameson soon realized, "the whole thing turns upon the possibility of getting the necessary money." Jameson reported, "It is impossible to raise any considerable amount of money from the Chinese, as they have no faith in the financial probity of any Chinese government." Thus a foreign loan would be necessary if the project was to proceed and avert dire tragedies: "Robbery—murder—riots—starvation—and cannibalism unless this conservancy work is seriously undertaken and that soon."[85]

Jameson wanted the United States government to support him officially in his efforts to have the Chinese name him over Zhang Qian as head of a Huai project, and this remarkable wish was fulfilled. Persuaded by Jameson's argument that the project would be hurt by "an immense amount of graft" if left in Zhang's hands, Boardman convinced President Taft (who was also the titular head of the Red Cross) to support Jameson's candidacy. The American minister in Beijing was authorized to raise the matter with the central Chinese government.[86]

In the meantime, however, Jameson did little to endear himself to Beijing. An interview with the minister of agriculture and forestry, a graduate of the University of California, did not go well. In a subsequent letter to the Red Cross, Jameson described the minister as "a poor example," a fool who could not understand Jameson's Huai report: "Oh! the hopelessness of the new Chinese. This is a fair example of the half-baked type." The minister had suggested that he would immediately dispatch the engineer on his staff (whose specialty, unfortunately, was electricity) to assist on the Huai project; another man, with a B.A. from the United States, was offered, but Jameson thought "the B.A. undoubtedly stands for Bally Ass."[87]

Chinese Minister for Foreign Affairs Lu Zhengxiang initially promised the American chargé d'affaires, E. T. Williams, that Jameson would be considered for the position of engineer-in-chief. But Williams panicked when he heard rumors that Zhang Qian was negotiating with a Belgian syndicate for financing. Humanitarian aims were momentarily forgotten when American interests seemed threatened. Williams vigorously protested the Belgian negotiations to the Chinese minister, "inasmuch as any such loan, if made, would in all probability require the engagement of a Belgian engineer and shut out Americans from participation in the enterprise." Williams warned, "My Government could not see without keen disappointment the surrender to engineers of another nationality of an enterprise begun under American auspices."[88]

Lu was not sympathetic to the American protest. His own wife was Belgian, and he was an old friend of Zhang Qian. Lu wrote to Williams, "Since Director-General Chang [Zhang Qian] has had plans in hand for this work for some years, naturally it should be he who, with due regard to circumstances, shall decide all questions relative to the raising of funds and the employment of men." The matter of Jameson's appointment, Lu added, should be taken up directly with Zhang. Williams wrote back that "the American government has no desire to force any man or any plan upon China"; its only interest was "in the relief of the famine and prevention of floods." But he still regarded "American friendship" as improperly reciprocated if China refused to put an American engineer in charge.[89]

The American Red Cross continued to put pressure on Washington to have Jameson appointed by the Chinese. A choice of fundamental approaches was at stake. General Davis wrote that the Chinese could either organize the project as a national one, "as is customary in rivers and harbors in the United States," or place the project in the hands of provincial authorities like Zhang, in which case the bulk of the funds would go to "graft and plunder for the benefit of those in power." If the Chinese shunned the American model, "the American Red Cross will be—indeed, has been—entirely ignored, notwithstanding its disinterested efforts and expenditures freely given for the Chinese public good."[90]

✢ ✢ ✢ ✢ ✢

American financing proved as hard to arrange as appointment of an American engineer. Worried that Belgium or another country would make an offer before American banks did, American Minister Paul Reinsch persuaded the Chinese in January 1914 to give a one-year exclusive option to the American Red Cross to secure a loan for the Huai project. A New York construction firm, J. G. White and Company, began plans to start work as soon as financing was arranged. The project seemed close to realization. The Americans even began to talk seriously of allowing Chinese to participate—but only, Reinsch explained, so that they would have a personal financial stake in the work and would control the subcontractors and workers, who "are apt, unless restrained, to cooperate against the interest of the foreign managers by way of raising the price of labor and materials." The cost of labor for moving earth was exceedingly cheap, but foreign concerns "would usually be made to pay considerably more unless they had secured beforehand a complete mastery of the situation."[91]

J. G. White wanted assurances that the United States government would lend its backing to the venture, but President Wilson was more circumspect than Taft had been. Wilson was happy to promise "good offices and diplomatic support" on behalf of an American contractor in China, but these good offices, he added, "would not go to the extent to which some governments have gone in seeking to enforce the rights of their nationals in the matter of contracts." Still, the prospects for an American project appeared promising, and in 1914, the Red Cross appointed a new engineering commission to visit China, check on Jameson's recommendations, and make plans for construction. Colonel William L. Sibert, the engineer famous for overseeing the construction on the Atlantic side of the Panama Canal, headed the commission.[92]

The Sibert report recommended an entirely new route for diverting the Huai (sending all the water to the Yangzi), estimated that the project would require $30 million and six years to complete, and suggested that the needed foreign loan could be repaid with taxes from the 7 million acres of land that would be benefited.[93] Zhang Qian, never one to relinquish his own opinions on hydraulics, criticized the commission's recommendations regarding the Huai and the Yangzi.[94] But the matter soon became moot because in August 1914, world war broke out, and arrangement of financing proved impossible.

An era had ended. After the war, talk of taming the Huai would resume, other Americans would make new studies, and Zhang Qian would continue to push his own plans (and even briefly hire his own American engineer).[95] But the later talk never came as close to realization as had the discussions in the prewar era, nor did American cockiness ever again match that of Jameson, Davis, Sibert, and other veterans of the Panama Canal project, who, emboldened by their success in Central America, had wanted to tackle another giant challenge—that of controlling the Huai and transforming the agriculture of the largest country on the globe.

The Americans who lobbied for the Huai project had the most grandiose ideas about aiding China, but the others—Brill, Parker, and the International Harvester representative—also had ambitious plans that went astray. These early Americans shared a presumption that China would welcome their sensible suggestions. How could there be any objection to the opening of new agricultural schools (staffed by Americans), to giant wheat operations (directed by Americans), or to a massive conservancy project (engineered by Americans)? The American advisers did not see that their foreign presence offended many influential Chinese, nor understand the tenuous position of their most sympathetic Chinese clients. Enlightened Qing officials were part of a government that was collapsing, largely because of the loss of public legitimacy in the face of foreign encroachment. Enlightened Republican officials were hardly better off, for they were part of a government that had difficulty establishing itself, again largely because of foreign encroachment. Ignorant of the difficulties of their Chinese hosts, the Americans tended to view China as a blank canvas, open and receptive to the improvements that they wanted to direct. Their advice to the Chinese was not bad, technically speaking, but it was offered with little understanding of the political circumstances that prevented it from being put into practice.

3

ZEAL

Joseph Bailie's Secular Crusades, 1910s

One man, more than any other, hurled himself upon China, determined to improve conditions and help rural Chinese. Joseph Bailie, a naturalized American, acted on his own, without invitation from anyone, and embarked upon a number of schemes to uplift Chinese agriculture. He was energetic and impatient, farsighted and grandiosely ambitious, a man who gloried in strenuous effort and advertised for a certain kind of Chinese follower—the fellow "who has the grit to work and isn't afraid to dirty his hands and shoes when the occasion demands it." [1]

Not incidentally, Bailie was also subject to wide swings between elation and depression, alternately embracing and reviling the Chinese people. In the abstract, he loved China, and sought repeatedly to be naturalized as a Chinese citizen; in practice, however, he regularly lost his temper with individual Chinese he encountered. Six feet tall, with a solid frame and a walking stick always in hand, Bailie was known to strike Chinese who angered him. His diary dryly registers a sample incident: "Hit a man with my stick. First time for a long time. Shall try hard not to hit another." The next month, however, he thought a Chinese acquaintance had "double-crossed" him by not supporting one of his projects. Bailie tracked him down and started beating him, before learning that there had been a misunderstanding and he had not been double-crossed after all. [2] Violent, irascible, often paranoid, Bailie nevertheless started a university department of agriculture that grew into the largest and most influential college of agriculture and forestry in China.

The route by which Bailie arrived at his decision to start a new program of agricultural education was a long, unpredictable one, marked by various careers and abandoned projects. The supreme irony is that Bailie, the "father" of modern agricultural education in China, was not qualified by any conventional standards for the role. He was no more an agricultural "expert" than anyone else who had spent a boyhood on a farm. Born in Ireland in 1860, he had left the family farm as soon as he could, migrating to the United States to study at the Union Theological

Seminary in New York City. He went to China in 1890 as a Protestant missionary but left the mission soon after.[3]

Disillusion with mission work had begun almost as soon as Bailie arrived in China. It stemmed primarily from feeling helpless when he encountered waves of famine refugees who traveled from town to town in large gangs, desperately seeking aid before succumbing to starvation. Bailie later recalled, "What a hell it was to be able only to go out in the midst of such a crowd and talk of the love of God to people desperate with hunger and cold." He tried to help the victims in the way he had been taught by the church—dispensing charity:

> In desperation I went and changed a few dollars into cents and attempted to distribute the money, but several of the crowd set upon me to get all that was in the bag. I ran, taking the coppers out in handfuls and throwing them on all sides, but before I could get half of what I had distributed in this way I was cornered, my bag wrenched from my grasp and my clothes almost torn to pieces before I could extricate myself from the hungry wolves. That was my first and last attempt to alleviate suffering in this manner.[4]

✧ ✧ ✧ ✧ ✧

·Long years of residence in China usually hardened Westerners to the most heartrending spectacles, and Bailie, too, developed an armor of protective indifference. After resigning his mission appointment, he lived a placid and unremarkable life in Chinese treaty ports for twenty years, from 1890 to 1910, trying his hand at various jobs, including a stint as an insurance salesman in Shanghai. In 1911, when American missionaries organized the University of Nanking and needed an English-speaker to teach mathematics, Bailie was hardly a well-prepared candidate, but he was available and willing, and he got the job. He arrived in Nanjing to take up his post just as the worst flooding in the modern history of the Huai River pushed tens of thousands of refugees into Nanjing, crowding the streets and the tops of the city walls. The spectacle of suffering on such a massive scale was too overwhelming to be affecting, but an encounter with a single victim changed the direction of Bailie's life:

> One night as I was in my bed in the garret of the science building, I heard a poor man crying "O.Sz, O.Sz," which means, "I am dying with hunger." Although I understood what he said and had heard many a beggar say the same before, I went to sleep, but in the morning on going out of our front gate, this man was stark dead right in my path.... I knew I had dollars in the bank and a very few of them would have saved this man's life. I went about like one crazy for a couple of days without letting anyone know what was within my soul.[5]

✧ ✧ ✧ ✧ ✧

To redeem himself, Bailie devoted himself to aid projects with the narrow intensity of a fanatic, dropping his new teaching duties (though the university indulgently continued his salary) and clearing from his life all family obligations: "My wife and I came to an agreement to divide the family possessions so that I felt that I was not wronging my family by devoting what remained of my share over and above my expenses, to helping those people who were dying with hunger." He maintained a household separate from his wife (while apparently keeping the marriage intact) the rest of his remaining ten years in China.[6]

Since he had learned that distributing charity in a crowd was a "dangerous thing," Bailie did not repeat his earlier mistake; instead, he visited several huts in the refugee quarters, distributing small sums and earning gratitude such as he "had hardly ever seen before." The visits also afforded an opportunity for Bailie to expand the social consciousness of the Chinese students whom he taught in a Sunday Bible class. He took them along on his visits to the squalid refugee camps and found that, with but one exception, the students balked at wading through the slush and mud: "Not so Mr. Tan [the son of a district magistrate]. He had on his silk top boots and followed me through the dirtiest places. Finally when we returned to the University, he came up and thanked me for letting him see what we had seen. He said he had lived in the midst of this all his life and had never conceived there was such misery around him until I, a foreigner, had come and taken him where he could see it." [7]

✢ ✢ ✢ ✢ ✢

Bailie used his students as a sounding board for a new project that he was considering—the colonization of Purple Mountain (*Zijinshan*), another destination for his Bible class outings. The "mountain" (actually a number of adjoining hills) provided an excellent view of Nanjing, the encircling Yangzi River, and the surrounding area. The hillsides were uncultivated, protectively occupied by scattered graves and treated by the local populace as a giant cemetery that was off-limits for farming. The legal status of the land was confused; individual Chinese in the area presumed that it belonged to the government, while the government presumed that it belonged to individual Chinese. However, Bailie had noticed that in some places an intrepid farmer had planted a small corner of the land. For his students, Bailie contrasted the healthy-looking families tilling the mountain with the thousands of families living in squalor down in the city. The logical conclusion was supplied by Mr. Tan as he surveyed the mountain's scenery: "Let us pray to God to give this to the poor." Bailie joined in the prayer, and wrote, "No sooner had I uttered the words than I felt my feet standing on ground that was ours." [8]

Under the title of "Bailie's Colonization Scheme," the program that Bailie launched in 1911 sought to appropriate the unused land on Purple Mountain and create farms for "colonists" drawn from the ranks of famine refugees. Bailie had decided that provision of simple relief was not only materially insufficient but morally wrong, because it undermined the refugees' work ethic: "Where they can obtain relief without working, they flock, with the inevitable result that many lose all inclination to do a hand's turn." [9] Bailie had experimented with a work-relief program that employed about 130 Nanjing refugees on road construction, paying a daily sum "so long as a man proves faithful and worthy." [10] But he had soon realized that he was continuing the common practice of putting refugee labor to work on projects that simply made the lives of Westerners in China more comfortable. The object behind his Purple Mountain colonization scheme "was not to engage a horde of laborers during famine time [for road-building], on our own compound . . . to enable Americans to reach their own doors without having to wade knee deep through mud," but rather to use relief contributions "to produce results which would also be for the poor and not for their wealthy benefactors." [11]

Another danger to be avoided, he thought, was allowing large private companies to operate the colonies. The companies in question were owned by wealthy Chinese capitalists and were a fairly recent phenomenon. They organized labor into large gangs where, in Bailie's opinion, motivation to work hard was scarce and supervision was often the responsibility of a man "who does not know a potato from a cabbage and who cannot tell whether a man does a day's work or not." Instead, Bailie championed the individual family as the basic unit of farm labor. In the early 1910s he declared (in a passage that is striking in its resemblance to official agricultural policy pronouncements of the late 1970s in the People's Republic): "When the family is on its own soil, everyone in the family is working late and early and is careful of what is grown." Bailie saw not only economic advantage but political advantage as well, for "there is the capital that develops the resources of the country—*the hard work of free men striving to make themselves independent.*" [12]

The Western press in China immediately embraced his colonization program, showering it and its originator with praise, and betraying a hint of exasperation that the Chinese had not thought to cultivate the land themselves. The *North China Daily News* commented, "But for the reverence paid to graves in China, it is well nigh impossible to understand why the Chinese have never cultivated the ground here. Never is, perhaps, too sweeping a term to use, but at any rate in the memory of man, and probably for many generations, they have not utilized this soil for agricultural purposes." Bailie claimed that he had produced crops in Ireland upon "infinitely inferior soil," and the newspaper reported that the Purple Mountain land was rich, fertile, and well suited to the crops that were being planted there. [13]

The presence of the graves, it seemed, was the only factor that could explain the abandonment of the land. The low burial mounds and circular enclosures were meant to commemorate, in Bailie's sarcastic words, "the virtue exercised by some worthies (who died somewhere between Adam and Noah) for having condescended to come to earth and live among us mortals as men." Subjecting Chinese practices to withering criticism, Bailie wrote:

> The country that attaches more importance to the graves of the dead than it does to the lives of its present inhabitants and will allow the grave of General Wong to occupy ten *mou* of good land maintained in an unkept condition while the Chen family of seven mouths have a hut on a corner of this same grave and

attempt to support themselves by digging roots of trees and the like from this
and the hundreds of graves surrounding, while they are most anxious to break
up and cultivate some of this very land—the country, I say, that does this is
committing suicide.[14]

Bailie proposed that "public cemeteries should be laid out and properly
beautified and all should be compelled to bury their dead there ... under pain of a
heavy fine if they refuse to do so."[15] When the first group of settlers began to
break the land at Purple Mountain, Bailie directed them to disinter any coffins that
were discovered and to move them to a central cemetery, where small markers
were placed so the families of the deceased would be able to find their ancestors'
new resting places. Most of the graves were so old, it turned out, that no trace of
coffin or corpse was visible. Privately, Bailie joked with a correspondent about a
famous person who slumbered in the ground of Purple Mountain: "Don't be
astonished if I send you the first joint of his little finger some day as we dig the
place over."[16]

The coffin removal was soon interrupted, however, by a visit of protesting
gentry. Bailie's account of the visit reads like a parable, with Bailie's logic triumph-
ing over native superstition: "I explained, 'These graves have no claimants; besides,
the dead that were buried here don't need this land, while these poor refugees
whom I'm trying to help are dying with hunger, and by cultivating this land I can
save their lives.' The [Chinese] spokesman turned around and addressed his colleagues saying ['The foreigner is right']. After chatting for a while with me and
some of the men, they went away."[17]

Bailie knew that fresh pieces of sod, termed "caps," were placed on graves by
family members in the spring of each year; since the graves that he had been
moving had no caps, he reasoned that no local families were personally related to
any of the dead who were being exhumed and evicted. He was not free to proceed,
however. The Central China Famine Relief Committee, a charity operated by
Western missionaries, granted $3,500 to the colony project, but on the condition
that the project would not again provoke the anger of local Chinese residents over
the "grave" question. Worse, the governor of Jiangsu issued a proclamation pro-
hibiting any Chinese from selling land to Bailie's project. In the nationalist climate
of the early Republican period, disturbing the graves was less worrisome to the
provincial government than the fact that it was a foreigner who was the instigator
of the trouble. The verdict of influential Chinese in the province was that Bailie had
no proper business in the countryside.[18]

A sympathetic Chinese friend suggested that Bailie try to earn the patronage
of high-ranking Chinese; reaching into a desk drawer, the friend pulled out a piece
of paper and quickly drew up in Chinese a short proclamation: "The Famine
Colonization Association was organized by Mr. Joseph Bailie, Instructor of Mathematics, in the University of Nanking, to enable the destitute to earn their own
living by cultivating abandoned lands. Being practical as well as unselfish, this

program has secured the hearty endorsement and support of the undersigned."
"Here," Bailie was told, "go and get somebody to sign it."

On a whim, Bailie first sent the document to Sun Yat-sen, who in 1912 was the provisional president of the new republic. Sun sent it back with his signature (Sun Wen) and stamped with the seal of the republic. With that in hand, picking up additional support was easy: Yuan Shikai, Tang Shaoyi, Huang Xing, Song Jiaoren, Cai Yuanpei, Zhang Qian, and others added their signatures, forming a "Who's Who" of early Republican China.[19]

Help also came from Westernized Chinese. K. P. Chen, a Wharton School of Finance graduate and the director of the Jiangsu Bank in Shanghai, saw the flattering article on Bailie's colony that had appeared in the *North China Daily News* and wrote Bailie an encouraging letter. When Bailie wrote back, complaining that the Chinese-language press had ignored his colony, Chen invited Bailie to Shanghai to meet personally with members of the local press. Bailie was unprepared for the reception he received. When he arrived in Shanghai and went to the appointed meeting, he was greeted by nine young, urbane men, who were American-educated, fluent in English, and extremely complimentary about his work. Bailie had trouble keeping up with them: "The head of the Associated Press for China asked me whether what I was doing resembled what Hawthorne spoke about in his book. I had to confess that I hadn't read any of Hawthorne except *The Scarlet Letter* and had forgotten whether there was any reference to a scheme for social reform laid down there. He then referred to the George Junior Republic and I was very glad that at this point the meeting was called to order."[20]

After a short presentation, Bailie opened the floor to questions and discussion. As a tactical measure, the group advised appointment of a Chinese secretary who could speak English but who could also "appear before any of the modern officials and advocate our cause if necessary, and who should at the same time be able to hold his own with the old literati." Final touches were made on the colony's "Rules and Regulations," and a volunteer took charge of polishing a Chinese translation. Bailie exulted, "I haven't felt so close in touch with the Chinese since I came to China twenty-two years ago as I did sitting at this table with these vigorous young men any one of whom, as you know, would make a name for himself in any country he chose to settle in."[21]

While Bailie's coterie worked on devising a suitable organizational structure that could deflect criticism that the project was run by foreigners, a hostile group of Chinese formed another organization to challenge Bailie's group. Both groups raced to file for incorporation and be the first to claim the Purple Mountain land, and Bailie was in trouble. He had not yet rounded up the necessary board of trustees for the project, and he faced eviction from the land the colony occupied, because foreigners had no legal right to purchase Chinese land. The challengers sought to have the law enforced and the foreigner displaced; even Bailie himself, who until then had ignored the legal problems of his project, admitted that the other group, composed entirely of Chinese, "had law on their side." On Bailie's side, however, was a more valuable asset: well-placed influence. A sympathetic official within the government provided critical assistance and held off the challengers, preventing them from filing before Bailie's group. Bailie wrote, "The [official] informed us through the Foreign office (of course *sub rosa*) that unless we hustled he would have to give a reply to this organization which kept hammering at his door day by day." Bailie "hustled" to complete the necessary paperwork, and it was his group, not the challengers, that was permitted to file claim to Purple Mountain. In a period when foreigners felt that the Chinese government was a xenophobic monolith, it was encouraging to find a split within official Chinese ranks and some firm support. Bailie wrote, "To have the Chinese so far with us as to work against their own people is proof, I think, that we have their confidence." [22]

Bailie's Colonization Association was finally incorporated with a constitution that included some legal legerdemain. To meet the letter of Chinese law, all land purchased by the association was placed in the name of five Chinese members, but they had no formal voice in shaping policies. A board of seventeen members, composed of twelve Chinese and five foreigners, preserved the fiction that foreigners had only a minor role in the organization, but the real power remained in the hands of the organization's founder, Bailie, who was entrusted with "management."

The formal purpose of the association was "to put the destitute poor on vacant land by supporting them while they break up the land and until the first crop is ripe, and to teach them improved methods of farming." Each family was to be leased sufficient land to support the family's size; in return, "rent" was to be paid to cover the government's land tax, and for schools, roads, and other local projects. In addition, the original price of the land was to be repaid in installments. If the payments were made on time and the land kept in productive cultivation, the tenant had the option of leasing additional land. But no land deeds would be given to the colonists; title would always remain with the association, to prevent land from being sold to "some wealthy land shark." Even subletting would not be permitted. If a tenant felt pressed to borrow from outside sources, the association would provide whatever loan was necessary to keep out subtenants and usurers.

The Colonization Association also sought to provide instruction in both farming and democratic management. The colony was to provide a 35-acre model farm "which will be kept as a standard both for size and efficiency for the colonists to imitate." Tenants who survived an initial probationary period and proved themselves "worthy" were to be declared "colonists" and to receive a vote in some affairs of the colony, such as determining appropriate compensation for land improvements to be paid to a member who wanted to withdraw from the project. The Colonization Association's constitution made it clear that Bailie envisaged the Nanjing colony at Purple Mountain as an inspirational model for emulation by other colonies that would spring up throughout China. [23]

✧ ✧ ✧ ✧ ✧

The work at Purple Mountain produced mixed results the first year. Although the Western press had chided the Chinese for not cultivating this "rich" land that had been allowed to stand idle, Bailie found that the fertility of the soil fell far short of what he had first estimated. Privately, he confided, "I knew when I began to break Purple Mountain that it wasn't the best land, but I never dreamed that it was so dead." Bailie reasoned, however, that there was no room for regrets, since there was no alternative at the time but to start at Purple Mountain, despite the fact that the 4,000-acre tract was too infertile and dry for most food crops; it was suitable primarily for trees.[24]

By necessity, then, Bailie had to pay attention to the problem of afforestation, and he saw that forestry work was economically as well as ecologically connected to agricultural development. He reasoned, "The first principle in Agriculture is to put as much manure into the land as possible. The straw and grain should be fed to cattle and in that way most of the ingredients would return to the land. As it is now the straw is all burned and large quantities sent into the large cities with the result that the land is being drained of its available plant-food."[25] In other words, if forests could provide more wood, straw could be spared and used for agriculture rather than for fuel. With this hope in mind, Bailie began tree plantings. A thousand saplings of various kinds arrived from the United States, along with pines from north China, and all required careful nursing: each week, every tree was carefully rubbed from top to bottom by hand to kill insects and their eggs. Most of the imported fruit trees survived at least their first year, but pear trees obtained from the vicinity perished after transplanting.

Potatoes and wheat were also planted as an experiment. The potatoes failed; the mountainside had been repeatedly stripped of its grass by local residents in search of fuel, and the soil was too depleted to support even tough tubers. However, Bailie claimed some success with the wheat. A San Francisco firm, Morse Seed, had donated a ton of seed, hoping to open the China market. Bailie planted it immediately, without testing, and declared it far superior to the local variety: "When we reaped the wheat we sold the seed . . . to the farmers around the city so that this coming spring I hope to see patches of this wheat everywhere. If it is only nearly as good as we had it, it will double or in some cases give four-fold the yield that the Chinese miserable little wheat gives."[26]

Little time was wasted in spinning off plans for related rural industries. Wheat straw, which Bailie had used at first for roof thatch, was found to be a satisfactory material for braids, and Bailie set up classes to teach the craft of braiding straw to local women and children. Once the classes were established, Bailie intended to turn supervision over to others, "as soon as the infant is able to walk." Bailie also planned to use his colonies to destroy the institution of "coolie" labor in the cities. He wrote to Western treaty-port residents, "If we could only be successful in getting families on to all the vacant lands in China, human flesh and blood would not be cheaper than horse or mule flesh and blood as it is now." His colonies would draw urban coolies back to the land, and then "we would see conveyances on Shanghai streets hauled no longer by human beings but by animals, and the ricsha coolie problem would be no longer a problem as there would be no ricsha coolie." Bailie acidly asked, "How then would we ever be able to get around in Shanghai? Carriages and autos are so dear! Well! Either walk or go home and live honest lives. Just think of asking a man in San Francisco or Chicago to haul you for an hour in a ricsha for a dime!"[27]

Despite some encouraging initial successes, the Purple Mountain Colony faced a dismal struggle with the poor soil. Bailie thought that human and animal manure could be brought up from the city to fertilize the land, but his efforts to begin construction of a road that would accommodate wagons were soon thwarted by local gentry, who regarded the foreigner's plans for a thoroughfare as a violation of Chinese sovereignty. The road work was halted, and Bailie seemed to be stuck with the inhospitable soil conditions at Purple Mountain. But the neighboring province of Anhui appeared to offer a promising alternative.

✣ ✣ ✣ ✣ ✣

Bailie had tried earlier to secure land for his colony scheme in Anhui and had been driven away by local xenophobes. In late 1912, however, Anhui officials had a change of heart and decided that Bailie's colony was the lesser of two evils—the other, more threatening one being the specter of demobilized soldiers taking over the province's hill land. In the wake of the 1911 Revolution, a number of armies had disbanded, creating thousands of ex-soldiers who had taken advantage of the absence of land registers and had moved, sometimes forcibly, onto whatever land seemed handy. Considered a dangerous "lawless element," the soldiers were not welcome, and Anhui officials decided that Bailie's colony project was a more easily controlled means of occupying vulnerable land.[28]

Arriving in Lai'an, Anhui, on January 6, 1913, Bailie learned that local dignitaries "guaranteed us that they would provide us with all the land we need free of cost"—but only on the condition that Zhang Qian personally approve the proposal. (Zhang, it will be remembered, was the powerful industrialist who took a close interest in the plans to control the Huai River.) Bailie called in the local representatives for a meeting:

> They objected to our attempt to form a branch [colony] here, saying that to do that properly a representative from Chang Chien [Zhang Qian] ought to have been sent who could come to organize. I admitted the irregularity but said that Chang Chien couldn't get a man to send. After we had mellowed them down on their subject they made objection to using Foreign money as it might lead to foreign control. I asked what foreign control the use of the money given by the Famine Relief Committee had brought with it? Then they decided they would write to Chang Chien asking was it safe to use this foreign money.[29]

✣ ✣ ✣ ✣ ✣

In the meantime, the Anhui dignitaries offered to show Bailie the tract of public mountain land that they had selected for donation to the colony. After looking over the parcel of land, Bailie tried to look at the bright side: "It is about two miles English long and a quarter wide. There are five rounded heads, four of which we went over. Number Two has about forty acres of just as good land as I have ever seen, black loam, more than a foot deep in places, and all this could be used for agriculture. The others would not do for farming, but would make excellent land for tea or fruit trees." Bailie confessed that he was disappointed in the land and did not want to "risk the future of our colonization work" by again trying to farm unsuitable land like that on Purple Mountain. But he conceived of an alternative use for the Anhui tract: "I shall try to get a hold of this place to be part of a 'Forest colony,' in which the colonists can pay off what we spend on their land by planting a certain number of trees which we will supply and afterwards pay their rent by each tending the forest he planted."

Finding suitable land for agriculture remained the most urgent problem. Bailie thought that if he could secure suitable agricultural land elsewhere in Anhui Province, he could always return later and claim the mountain tract for an experimental station and forestry colony. But he agonized over his decision, because he could see that magnificent trees on the mountain site were at that very moment being cut down; any postponement in acquiring the land would mean further forest losses. In the end, Bailie decided to press on and try to secure better farmland: "I want to make sure that we have really got a hold of the tract of good land on which we can prove our point and then nail this. What hurts me tho' is that in the meantime more of the big trees will go. But that will make us hustle to get the other land fixed upon." [30]

The search for suitable land dragged on for weeks, then months. At the same time, Bailie found that his extended absences from the University of Nanking were no longer placidly tolerated, and he was given an ultimatum: return, or lose his university salary. Bailie wrote back to the vice president of Nanking: "I'm not going to give up Colonization work unless the good Lord throws me off my legs, and I do want to stay with the University. I know the University needs something of the sort of work I'm doing to keep it in touch with facts and things and to get more closely hooked onto people; and I need the University. I can do more by reason of having Prof. put in front of my name than I could by having a Mr." The salary dispute, Bailie thought, could be easily settled: "Can't you get some men that will pay my salary for the purpose of going on with this work and have it so arranged that I can still be associated in some way with the University?" [31]

Nanking renewed Bailie's absentee appointment, and he was able to remain in Anhui, trying to organize the new colony and negotiate terms for suitable land. Twenty-seven Chinese supporters formally endorsed the Anhui colonization scheme and registered the Lai'an Branch of the Colonization Association with the local authorities. The branch members drew up a list of organizing rules and regulations, but Bailie felt that too much power would be left in the hands of the Chinese members. He held out for a revised agreement that allowed him to retain, as in Nanjing, the power of the purse: "We discussed matters from 8:00 to nearly 2:00 in the morning and managed to draw up an agreement such as will in no way take the power of spending money out of my hands. While at the same time it gives the Chinese the power to have things run in such a way as to prevent their losing face." The Chinese members had to accept the terms that Bailie imposed, for he brought authorization to spend $10,000 granted by the Central China Famine Relief Committee.[32]

The county officials of Lai'an remained friendly and as helpful as they could be: if the first tract offered was unsatisfactory, then any public land that Bailie thought would be useful was his for the asking. All Bailie had to do was go to the various districts, where the head of the local gentry would take him around and point out which land was public and available. Bailie felt confident that with a representative of the local *yamen* (government office) in his party, the on-the-spot determination of a tract's availability would be reliable: "In this way we can decide upon using public lands without making several visits and having no end of dickering with the yamen." Bailie asked that an official proclamation be issued prior to any visits in the field, "so the people of the district cannot afterwards say that we came up in some backhanded manner, and when they were asleep got hold of land belonging to some of their number."[33]

As Bailie toured the country, he soon learned that the best unoccupied land was privately owned. Although the Colonization Association had the legal option of purchasing land, Bailie and his foreign associates felt that they had to outwit both the Chinese officials and private landowners: "We (that is, the foreigners) decided sometime ago not to purchase any land for if we left that loophole nobody would ever show us any public lands." When Bailie did find attractive, relatively flat land that was public, he found that local elders had appropriated the land themselves and registered it in their own names. The county official who was assigned to help Bailie proved to be powerless in such instances, and the case was rendered even more frustrating because the elders had no intention of putting the land into production, being content to enjoy the land-tax exemption that the government granted for unused land. Bailie perceived collusion between the local elders and soldiers in the vicinity: "In order to insure the carrying out of their illegally withholding lands from our Association, [the elders] have arranged with some discharged soldiers to go down there and plant their flags all over the great region." Bailie's only hope was that the soldiers, who reportedly were antagonizing their new neighbors by extorting "protection" money, would become a problem that the provincial authorities could no longer ignore and would thus "bring matters to a head."[34]

Several more months of fruitless searching for acceptable agricultural land ended with Bailie abandoning his plan to push agriculture before forestry. In the end, he accepted the five parcels of hill land, totaling more than 10,000 *mou* (approximately 1,700 acres): "It is mountain land it is true but as the Association is getting it free we cannot grumble." Adjusting to circumstances, Bailie conceived of an important rationale for accepting the free hill land instead of purchasing better land at lower elevations: "When one considers the unlimited amount of vacant hilly land the importance of proving that it can be successfully used cannot be over-estimated."[35]

✢ ✢ ✢ ✢ ✢

Bailie had no doubts that his colonists would do well in the forest colony. He estimated that about one hundred families could be accommodated, with each family paid to take care of its "farm," planted in a stipulated number of trees. Bailie's ultimate goal was to use the successes achieved on the hills to undermine the farm tenancy system down below. In southern and east central China, the majority of farmers rented their land in a system that was beginning to be spoken of as exploitative and enslaving, and that would be the focus of increasingly heated debates in subsequent years. Bailie was an early (and, as it turned out, rare) foreign critic of the tenancy system; to him, there was no justifiable reason for the tenant farmer "to pay four-tenths of the crop for the privilege of farming." The tenancy system created a squalid picture: "The farmers live in miserable huts, with the families all in rags and poorly fed, and only once in a while one of them has one of the sons going to the neighboring village every day to read and write." Bailie pictured his forest colony as an emancipatory model that would free tenant farmers from the "slavery" of the landlord system: "If we can prove that when farmers are given fair play they can cultivate the mountain land and make a better living than those living under the [landlord] system, we will give that system a knock-out blow."[36]

For Bailie, the moment was full of possibility because the new Republican government had yet to declare what direction it was going to take. Bailie reasoned, "The theory that is backed up by some running concrete example is the one that is likely to be copied." By keeping China's Ministry of Agriculture informed of the colonies' progress, "it is just possible that if we succeed in getting the thing properly a-going, the [ministry] may adopt this method or some modification of it to relieve congestion in overcrowded places and the development of the unused lands." Echoing Bailie's own confident sense of possessing the answer to China's rural problems, a story in the *North China Daily News* lectured the government: "Of course private enterprise such as Professor Bailie's could do little more than provide an object lesson for the governing classes to follow, and it is fully realized that to confer a lasting benefit on the destitute multitudes for whom an appeal had to be made year by year, the Government would have to take the work in hand itself and do on a large scale what has been accomplished on a small scale at Nanking."[37]

The Lai'an Branch Colony was where Bailie intended to show China the model to be emulated. In June 1913, the Colony Association's legal possession of the five parcels of hill land was formalized with the receipt of land maps "that are made official not by being very exact but by being stamped by all the officials concerned." It had taken two years to secure the land, and Bailie reflected, "I have been compelled to organize in a legal fashion and have everything water-tight, which I would never have taken time to do had I not been compelled to organize for fighting purposes." The most difficult part of the undertaking was behind him; ahead lay putting the colonists on the land, and though there would be problems, "these can all be overcome by my own hard digging" (or, mixing his metaphors, "I'm where my own feet can stand on the bottom, and by hard paddling I can stem the stream"). At least, he happily noted, he would no longer be "at the mercy or the whim" of the Anhui gentry.[38]

The local gentry had been obstructionist, but the farmers seemed more welcoming. Their welcome must have been dampened to some extent, however, by Bailie's coercive style. Bailie wrote that when surveying the land, "all the countryside knew that we were coming and as the chief men of the place were in our party when I asked any one to do anything he knew we meant business." Three farmers enlisted to help begin nursery work, but it is impossible to determine whether they volunteered out of fear or, as Bailie thought, out of gratitude for his coming. Bailie claimed that "these people who live among the hills appreciate the fact that any one is coming to help in the work of forestation. They know the advantages that will accrue from it and all have but one opinion of it." Bailie recognized the critical importance of local support: "If the people didn't want the forests, there wouldn't be much use in planting."[39]

✛ ✛ ✛ ✛ ✛

Before the first seedlings were planted, however, Bailie was distracted by a new scheme that had occurred to him: contracting with the Shanghai-Nanjing Railway to have the Lai'an colony provide lumber for the ties that were used in rail beds. Bailie had secured free rail passes for his personal use, and whenever he was exhausted or depressed (which was frequently), he boarded the train and fled to Shanghai to rest. He had gotten to know a foreign superintendent of the railway, who one day complained that timber imported from Japan and Australia was prohibitively expensive. Bailie instantly thought of a number of schemes whereby he could come to the rescue. His first plan was to have the railway endow a chair at the University of Nanking, to provide for someone to attend to the problem (i.e., Bailie himself). Next, he proposed that the railway company begin experimental plantings of several timber species to determine which were best for rail ties; the results would be shared with the university. Developing Chinese wood sources seemed the best solution for all parties involved—especially, Bailie pointed out, when the cost of imported wood threatened to double or, worse, when "the governments concerned may intervene and prevent the woods that are adapted for sleepers [ties] from being exported at all." Preparations in China for such a possibility could not be started too soon, and fortunately, Bailie explained, he was just at that moment deciding which woods to plant at his Anhui colony. He had been planning to grow varieties suitable for firewood, but he was more than willing to work with the railway company to plant the woods deemed best for rail construction: "I single out sleepers because I realize the millions that will be needed here inside the next few years."

Bailie offered railway officials the opportunity to cooperate in another way, by helping them plant trees for timber on each side of the rail tracks. He wrote to them: "You have now a double strip of land 140 miles long. If that were used for the purpose of growing trees, you would have in say fifteen years all the sleepers you would need on your own line and in five or ten years more be able to send supplies to places where sleepers were needed." The proposal had much to commend it. The rail line would be enhanced by the beauty of the trees; the trees would provide seeds that could be used to start nurseries elsewhere; employment for several hundred poor families would be provided when arranging for families to plant and care for the trees; and this, in turn, would "lessen the number of marauders that would be adrift to destroy the trees."

The more Bailie expounded upon his proposal to plant along the right-of-way, the less he wanted to return to start a forest in the remote hills of Anhui. The Anhui site was far removed from a rail line, so that the timber it would eventually produce could be transported to the nearest railway stations only at enormous expense. Bailie asked the company, "Now why not grow these right beside the railway where they can be cut and thrown onto wagons at a trifling expense?" [40]

Bailie's many offers to the Shanghai-Nanjing Railway were spurned, but he returned to Anhui undaunted. The John Deere Company had donated a set of plows, an encouraging sign. Moreover, the Chinese seemed to be taking the initiative to follow in Bailie's footsteps. The Jiangsu Provincial Assembly voted $10,000 to open a new colony in Jiangsu, and Bailie was asked to assist. He was delighted, and he took pleasure in noting that the Chinese representative seemed ashamed that a foreigner had taken the lead in developing such a praiseworthy enterprise. Bailie wrote in a letter to the university president, "Well, isn't it good to be able to corner these fellows so that they have to do something to save their face?" Bailie assumed that corruption in the Chinese project would keep all but a fraction of the money from reaching the poor. Still, he was glad to see a branch colony started independent of his own resources. The spread of his model seemed imminent: "The virus has taken." [41]

✧ ✧ ✧ ✧ ✧

Progress at his own colony at Lai'an stalled, however. By late summer, no colonists had arrived, no trees had been planted. The money promised by the Famine Relief Committee had yet to show up, and Bailie found himself sinking deeper and deeper into debt while building a small house for himself and waiting for the grant. The brutal summer heat destroyed his morale, but it was the inefficiency of the local transport system that was most dispiriting. Among sundry gifts, Bailie's colony had received a thousand feet of rubber garden hose, which was in Nanjing and which would rot by the time it could be put to use at Lai'an. Bailie exchanged the hose at a Nanjing hardware company for construction supplies for his house at Lai'an, but transporting the materials proved extremely troublesome. The trains were not running because of recent bandit attacks, so everything had to go by boat, with numerous transfers to successively smaller craft, and when the boats could go no farther, wheelbarrows had to be used for the final leg of the journey.[42]

Always searching for a panacea with which to save China, Bailie let his attention drift from forests to roads. From the interior of Anhui, he wrote to the university of his newly gained insight: "A barrel of cement is worth gold here, and it is the same with everything, not to speak of the time one wastes in transferring from train to boat and from boat to wheelbarrow, and at every change and all along the line pilfering and other affairs that tend to excite sulphurous thoughts in one's mind and to bring words with more d's in them than we are supposed to indulge in." A new road, he calculated, would pay for itself in five years, simply on the basis of pack animals that would be saved. Indeed, a new road would change everything: "If a good road were made here more progress could be made in developing the place in one year than could be made in ten years with things as they are." The problem of corruption would be solved at the same time, for "the temptation to be wicked [by pilfering, etc.] would be taken away."[43]

Bailie began planning a local road project, to be started the following winter. "The present road," he wrote, "is wibble wabble among the rice fields, and is 45 *li* [15 miles] and in wet weather practically impossible." He proposed a straighter route that would cut through fields and shorten the road by 10 *li*. The owners of the fields would not present a problem, for Bailie had obtained a promise from a local official that a proclamation of eminent domain would be issued when needed. A broad avenue at least 20 feet wide, the road was to be planted with a row of trees on each side. In Bailie's mind, the most troubling problem in the whole scheme was deciding whether to plant walnut trees or willows.[44]

Bailie's mood lurched up and down, and his excitement in August about the road plans was followed by a depression in September. He abandoned the Lai'an site, leaving the actual work of breaking ground and planting the first trees for a future year. Returning to Nanjing, he found a discouraging sight at his original colony on Purple Mountain. In his absence, armies that were for and against Yuan Shikai had fought in and around Nanjing, overrunning the Purple Mountain Colony. The colonists had escaped injury—one fled to safety while warding off troops with a spray pump that resembled a gun—but a month of severe drought had passed with no one on the site to water the trees. By the time Bailie returned, hundreds of thousands of seedlings had died, including most of the pine seed that the U.S. Department of Agriculture had sent. In addition, the prospects for the few remaining trees were poor because a nearby garrison of soldiers had requisitioned all water in the vicinity for its own use. Worse, "the [military] rascals won't carry the water themselves, but compel our men to take it to them instead of watering the remaining trees."[45]

In October, another disaster struck the colony. A small fire that started in the lower reaches of the Purple Mountain tract was fanned by a strong wind and swept across the parched land. Bailie and his assistants raced to try to save the houses; they faced less danger of being burned than of being peppered by thousands of rifle cartridges that colonists had once hidden in the haystacks for unknown reasons and that now discharged under the intense heat of the fire. The commandant of the nearby garrison sent over a detachment of his men to prevent the fire from laterally crossing a ravine, but no one could prevent the flames from charging up to the top of the mountain. Two hundred thousand trees were lost.

Bailie's initial reaction to the catastrophe was mild. In the first letter he wrote after the disaster, he skipped over the incident with a philosophical shrug: "One consolation is that I couldn't help the fire."[46] But later, he must have realized that his own shortcomings as a forester were directly responsible for the latest setback. Firebreaks, a simple but effective measure to ensure against such losses from fire, had been completely overlooked during planning. It was clear to Bailie that he could no longer masquerade as an expert, and he wrote to the university urgently requesting that a "good forester" be sent out at once. Bailie pleaded, "I would almost resign my job in order to secure the salary I'm now drawing to pay for a specialist's salary."[47]

Bailie was, however, too filled with a sense of mission to be afflicted long by self-doubt. The disastrous fire at Purple Mountain did not preoccupy him, but merely deflected his energies to other projects. The dormant plan to build broad roads was now revived, only this time he planned a route between Nanjing and the Purple Mountain Colony. The practical benefits of improved transportation seemed obvious, but there was an additional, civilizing aspect to the project: "I shall try to make a few very simple W.C.'s [water closets] so that then people may not be compelled to act as the inmates of the farmyard."[48] The civil governor granted Bailie permission to begin work on the project, once Bailie and the university president had signed a declaration guaranteeing that "we laid no claim to the road after we had made it."[49]

Funding for the road was provided by a foreign charity, and in November 1913, construction commenced. Once begun, however, the project put the foreigners in the awkward position of appearing to value their road more than the homes of local residents. The district, which lay outside of Nanjing's Taiping Gate, had witnessed some of the hardest fighting in the aftermath of the 1911 Revolution; virtually all of the houses in the area had been destroyed, and it was loose brick from these razed homes that supplied Bailie's road project. Defensively, Bailie wrote to the university community: "Sympathetic reader, please do not judge me too harshly, for taking such a mean advantage of a poor family, as to purchase the brick of their home to make our road. In every case it was they who approached me. At first I protested but the answer was we are dying with hunger and suffering with cold. If you purchase the brick of our ruins, which are no use to us, we can purchase matting and put up straw huts before the severe winter comes on." Bailie hired the able-bodied as laborers and purchased grass from the others, but treated the project as a business and resisted the temptation to distribute charity: "I would have been eased in my mind if I could have given them the money and left them the brick as well, but the money I had was for road construction." Work proceeded until the road was nearly finished and the money ran out.[50]

✧ ✧ ✧ ✧ ✧

In the spring of 1914, Bailie's attention turned once again to colonization plans. In March, the "First Convention of the Nanking Branch Association of the Colonization Association of the Republic of China" was held at a Nanjing social club. The elaborate organizational structure that was voted on and approved by the branch's members created a reassuring illusion of solidity and accomplishment, which was much more pleasant to contemplate than the charred ruins up on Purple Mountain. The association enacted bylaws that provided for executive direction by an impressive number of officers: president, vice president, chief instructor, director of the agricultural station, treasurer, secretary, and an executive committee of ten. Membership in the association was open to "those (Chinese or foreigners) living in Nanking who have enthusiasm for the welfare of the poor, and who have the development of agriculture and forestry at heart."[51]

Meanwhile, the few trees on Purple Mountain that had survived the recent fire were destroyed by a new calamity, wrought by Chinese folk customs. Every spring, for the Qing Ming festival ("Sweeping of the Graves"), Chinese visited the graves of their ancestors, decorated them with small presents, and stuck willow branches in the mounds, all as part of a holiday excursion. On Qing Ming in 1914, crowds from the city came trooping out to Purple Mountain to visit the recently consolidated cemeteries, which were adjacent to the forest colony. A horrified Bailie found that "as most of them were ignorant of whether a tree was a willow or an apple tree, our poor trees began to melt away, despite the attempts to station as many as fifty workmen at different places over the planted area." Bailie realized that the visitors acted without malice: "They meant no harm, they were merely doing as they had always been doing on Tsing Ming, and when asked why they plucked out the apple trees, would answer 'just to see what it was like.'"[52]

Some of the trees that the crowds pulled up were still in satisfactory condition and could be replanted, but the overall damage was extensive. In a depressed mood, Bailie boarded the Nanjing-Shanghai Railway for a recuperative weekend in the Big City. "Somehow the Railway trip," Bailie wrote, "acted as a sedative and enabled me to think out things that I could not think out with the constant stream of trouble that the poor people had to tell me when in Nanking." With the damage wrought by the Qing Ming festival still freshly in mind and graves decorated with dead willow branches whizzing by the train's window,

Bailie was struck by an inspiring thought: turning the traditional Qing Ming holiday into an Arbor Day, "to try to change the practice of sticking branches that would wither and die into the graves, and substitute real trees."[53]

As soon as he arrived in Shanghai, Bailie wrote to Zhang Qian, then the Chinese minister of agriculture, and his proposal was well received. Zhang convinced Yuan Shikai to issue a presidential proclamation declaring Qing Ming to be Arbor Day, and a ceremony at Purple Mountain the next year commemorated the occasion as a kind of Sino-American friendship day. Zhang, representing the Chinese government, and Consul Williams, representing the American government, planted a few walnut and gingko trees and offered polite addresses. Bailie's favorite passage was in Zhang's speech, where the minister of agriculture had "likened the two Gingko trees, one on each side of the road, to the two great Republics on the two sides of the Pacific, as growing bigger and as they grew larger would also grow closer."[54]

Arranging for a proclamation and a tree-planting ceremony was, of course, the easy part, whereas getting the Chinese public to adopt Arbor Day was not a simple matter. On the day that the minister of agriculture visited Purple Mountain for the ceremony, every official in the vicinity made a conspicuous display of planting a tree himself. But these were not men who would be energetic promoters of forestry when the minister left town, and the farmers could hardly be reached by the issuance of an edict.

If adults were virtually unreachable, at least schoolchildren could be taught to celebrate Arbor Day. Bailie claimed that the Qing Ming festival which followed Yuan's proclamation of Arbor Day was a success at Purple Mountain, bringing out scores of banner-waving schoolchildren who were ready to plant trees for the holiday.[55] But sustaining their interest—and that of their teachers—was difficult. "Arbor Day for China," a pamphlet prepared for schoolteachers several years later by the Chinese Forestry Association, stressed the need to make Arbor Day educational as well as fun: "The diversion of setting out a few trees, although exciting and calling forth enthusiasm, must be regarded only as a means to the desired end rather than as the end itself. The students should be taught on Arbor Day the use and value of the tree in the life of the nation." Two suggested techniques were post–Arbor Day field trips to observe soil erosion damage and essay assignments on "the importance of forest trees." Also recommended were classroom demonstrations. For example, "A mountain slope may be pictured by a cloth upon a tilted table or inclined board; then if water is poured on the higher edge it will creep downward through the cloth and drip slowly from the lower edge as would rain falling upon the forest." This kind of display, the pamphlet claimed, "would make vivid before the students the relation of forests to streamflow and floods."[56]

The foreign press continued to provide uncritically flattering coverage of "the great success" of the Purple Mountain Colony. In 1914, Bailie lectured a reporter on the virtues of firebreaks, which he had belatedly included in the colony's future plans. Bailie admitted that mistakes had been made in the past: "We are learning from experience. Last year a fire destroyed about 200,000 young trees. Had we had the firebreaks then that we now have the loss would have been limited perhaps to one-tenth of that amount and perhaps have been averted altogether." But the press took Bailie's confession of error as the pronouncement of an authority, not of a dilettante. Analyzing Purple Mountain's "success," the *National Review* explained, "The first and most important factor has been the application of expert guidance. Professor Bailie is himself a practical and expert agriculturalist, and not merely a zealous amateur. It is owing to his expert guidance that the work has been rightly directed and has been brought to its present stage of success."[57]

÷ ÷ ÷ ÷ ÷

The abstract idea of Bailie's colony was apparently so attractive that the practical problems of implementation were completely ignored. And the more Bailie was praised and flattered, the bolder he became. In 1914, he decided to open a department of agriculture at the University of Nanking—an inspired decision if judged by the department's later successes, but an audacious decision in view of Bailie's qualifications at the time. He presumed that he had learned far more as a boy on the farm forty years earlier than adult Chinese farmers knew from a lifetime of working the land. No training in the agricultural sciences was needed, for he viewed Chinese agricultural practices as so crude that almost any Westerner had much to offer in comparison. He once confessed in a letter, "I'm not qualified to lecture on Agriculture except in a place like this where the very rudiments are a mystery."[58]

Bailie was inspired by his own growing concern that educated Chinese were pursuing professional careers in everything but agriculture or forestry, where the need was most acute. He observed, "This is the weakest point in the new China. They have plenty of engineers for railroads and mines, abundance of lawyers, a fairly good number of graduates from Textile Schools but almost no graduates in Agriculture and Forestry. The country must have [these] two branches developed and the sooner the better."[59]

Deemed unworthy of Bailie's improvement efforts were the agricultural schools that the Chinese themselves operated. At the Imperial University in Beijing, the agricultural department that had initially relied upon Japanese instructors had been reorganized in 1912 as a separate institution—the National Agricultural College (*Beijing nongye zhuanmen xuexiao*)—and was now staffed by Chinese instructors who had been trained in Japan. In the same year, the new Republican government gave agriculture a higher priority than before by reorganizing the inherited Ministry of Commerce and establishing a separate Ministry of Agriculture and Forestry. At the same time, a number of provinces began to set up their own agricultural experiment stations and agricultural-technical high schools. The high schools numbered only four or so in 1912, but by 1914 there were thirty-five, enrolling thirty-two hundred students.[60]

Foreign residents regarded the accomplishments of these new schools and stations as meager, and Bailie wanted to start his own school. He himself would lead the instructional staff, and "the whole province of Kiangsu will be our Experimental Station." Moreover, Bailie's colonization project would provide field opportunities for practical training: "In this way our students from the beginning will have the opportunity of employing their energies on practical problems. ... A good part of the first year will be spent in the field learning to use the implements used by the workmen and in learning how to handle squads of men." [61]

Bailie believed that the need for agricultural education in China arose not from insufficient knowledge of agronomy but from the elite's traditional disdain for physical labor. Bailie was concerned, first and foremost, with changing his prospective students' attitudes: "The student who will not learn the use of the pick and shovel, the plow, the seeder and mower will be treated in the Department of Agriculture just as a student who will not learn to use the knife or forceps in the Department of Medicine will be treated." Even permission to continue in the program after the first year of study would depend on the student's performance in the field. [62]

The new department was headed by Bailie, who gave himself the title of "Dean, Field Work." He laid out a detailed four-year curriculum that emphasized English and science fundamentals in the first two years and specialized agriculture courses in the last two. Third-year students would study manures and fertilizers, horticulture, plant physiology, political economy, economic entomology, and animal husbandry. Fourth-year students would take courses in irrigation and drainage, plant improvement, poultry management, farm management, rural economics, soil survey, agricultural chemistry, and fruit culture. [63]

✣ ✣ ✣ ✣ ✣

The announced curriculum was more a hope than a definite plan, for the department was desperately short of qualified instructors. Two Chinese faculty members who had been trained abroad provided instruction in chemistry and biology; an American was put in charge of teaching surveying; and the only person on the faculty of five with an agricultural degree was John Reisner, a young graduate of Cornell who did not arrive in Nanjing until after the school year had begun in the fall of 1914.

Reisner had grown up on a farm in Pennsylvania, graduated from Yale with a major in biology, and then decided to go to China as a missionary. But he felt that he was insufficiently prepared, so he enrolled at Cornell to earn bachelor's and master's degrees in agriculture. The curriculum in American agricultural schools, however, offered little that was geared toward agricultural problems abroad. Reisner wrote his thesis on "A History of Wheat in New York State." [64]

At least Reisner had attended an agricultural college and had majored in field crops and minored in plant breeding and soils. When he arrived in China in 1914, he was one of only two persons in the country who had a master's degree in agriculture or forestry (the other was a Chinese with a master's degree in forestry from Michigan State). Reisner later recalled, "Almost anything that one did in China at that time was a first."[65]

As the first person on the faculty with any training in agriculture, Reisner found that he could not spend his first year in intensive language study, as he had originally planned. The students were too restless, waiting for substantive courses. Thus Reisner's language program was cut short, and he was put to work teaching technical courses.[66] If the department had postponed its opening for a year or two and removed the pressure of student demands, Reisner would have had an opportunity to develop Chinese language skills that would have hastened the Sinicization of the curriculum, a goal all agreed was desirable. But in the press of wanting to accomplish a great deal as soon as possible, the department locked itself into using English.

Reliance on English, in turn, affected the efforts to recruit students. The department required applicants who were "thoroughly acquainted with the English language"; no exceptions were permitted.[67] At least two years of college-equivalent study were also required, restricting the pool of qualified applicants to a very elite, privileged few. The pool was narrowed even further by the unglamorous nature of the field of study—agriculture—and by Bailie's stern warning that the degree could not be used as a means to secure a government sinecure: "Men who are looking forward to making the knowledge gained at our school a means of gaining an official position or of acquiring any situation by which they can sit in an office and get other men to do the actual work, will be disappointed if they apply and are admitted."[68]

Bailie had originally announced that he intended to limit the size of the first class to twenty students, but he did not foresee that his demand for English-speaking, college-educated students devoted to the calling of agriculture would reduce the number of applicants to almost none. Instead of opening with twenty students, the department opened with only eight, two of whom did not stay through graduation. The department needed more students if it was to establish legitimacy, and Bailie did find twelve more in 1915, when he arranged to have the forestry students at the central government's College of Agriculture, in Beijing, permanently transferred to the University of Nanking. Technically, no department of forestry was then in existence at Nanking, and no course in the agriculture department's four-year curriculum touched directly on forestry. But Bailie talked persuasively of his "Forestry School" as if it, not a department of agriculture, was already in operation.

The new forestry students would arrive in the fall; in the meantime, during the summer, Bailie scrambled to make preparations to have a "Forestry School" in place when they arrived. His main hope was to secure two American foresters, and when he submitted an appeal for help to Paul Reinsch, the United States minister in China, Bailie chose an interesting tone, simultaneously boastful and self-deprecating: "Though having been trained after a fashion in Agriculture and having been brought up on a farm in Ireland, where my father taught me to do everything done on the farm, and though I have been dabbling in Forestry in China for over four years, I am not qualified to organize and conduct a Forestry School, even if I had the time, which I have not." Alluding perhaps to the forgotten firebreaks and disastrous fire, he noted the problem of "bungling that inevitably comes when an amateur attempts to carry out the work of an expert." Bailie explained, "I am in the position of one gathering the materials out of which a building is to be constructed. Can you secure for us a master-builder from your government who can make the most of them?"[69]

Bailie claimed that he was speaking not only for the University of Nanking but also for the Chinese government, which had demonstrated its earnestness about tackling afforestation by openly confessing to its own failure and deciding to send its students to an American-affiliated institution. Bailie pleaded, "Our University and the Chinese government cry out loud for help from your Government." Reinsch supported the request and passed it on to Washington. The secretary of agriculture promptly cabled back that a forestry expert would be furnished "if Chinese government so desires," provided that the salary and expenses be paid by China. Chinese earnestness did not go that far, however, and no forester was hired.[70]

When the forestry students arrived on campus, there was no one who knew both forestry and Chinese to teach them. Unlike the first agriculture class, this group of students, inherited from the Chinese government, knew little or no English. The only way to provide them with useful instruction was to have them become their own teachers. Thus they were put into English classes full-time, after which they were to translate English-language forestry textbooks into Chinese; these translations would serve as the texts for succeeding classes.[71]

Attrition soon reduced the combined number of agriculture and forestry students from eighteen to ten, but it was a start. Bailie's fertile imagination spun out dozens of ambitious new projects and plans for the department. One of his better ideas was to have a course in agriculture taught in all rural schools, with teachers trained by a short course at the university. Each school would maintain a practice field for student use, and a roving agricultural "demonstrator" would provide advice and assistance. Another idea was to finance scholarships for promising agricultural students at middle and high schools by establishing dairies at each school, to be operated by the students themselves. Bailie claimed that profits from each dairy could support fifty to a hundred students—calculations that seem more appropriate for Wisconsin than for Republican-period China.[72]

✠ ✠ ✠ ✠ ✠

Though Bailie spoke fondly of his School of Agriculture and Forestry, he clearly enjoyed starting projects more than carrying them through. He did not want to stay in Nanjing, especially when he had to work and share power with other foreigners. With classes started, Bailie had to rely heavily on the services of

Reisner, the resident agriculture expert, who was half Bailie's age. In public, the two men maintained a facade of cordial relations; in private, however, Reisner's respect for Bailie was limited, and Bailie, in turn, felt threatened. Bailie's authority was not strengthened when it became apparent that he had not investigated the availability of Chinese translations of agricultural textbooks until after the second term of instruction was under way. Knowing his own limitations, Bailie removed himself from administrative and teaching duties in his newly established departments, retaining the title of dean in name only, and boarded a ship for the United States on a fund-raising tour.

The American Forestry Association hosted Bailie's visit and lent a sympathetic ear to his appeals. An article Bailie wrote for *American Forestry* explained the extraordinary opportunity the United States had at that very moment to send American foresters to China, earning the undying gratitude of the country that "is to be the greatest nation on earth when she is developed." Bailie explained that Chinese friendship could not be taken for granted but, once earned, would be secure: "Foreigners have come and have done things in the name of helping China that make us all hang our heads. But once the Chinese trust you, there's no such a thing as trusting half way. You're a bosom friend." Bailie maintained that American prospects were excellent and that America was "on the straight road to become that bosom friend of China." All that was needed to seal the friendship was a positive response to "China's" (i.e., Bailie's) appeal for American experts. A negative response would risk an alienated China: "Are we to fight her or are we to have her as a close friend?" All seemed to hinge on the United States sending the experts.

Taking his pitch to Washington, Bailie was cordially received by the Department of Agriculture, and the Forest Service promised to provide a leave of absence for interested staff members who wished to serve in China. But authorization to pay for salaries would have to come from Congress. Sensing the political impossibility of securing congressional approval, Bailie turned to the professional community of American foresters: "I appeal to the patriotism of our countrymen to assist in one of the greatest schemes now before the human race, the afforestation of China." [73]

The campaign did not succeed, and Bailie returned to China dour and unhappy. Back at the university, he inflated small incidents into large ones—a dispute over reimbursement for a bicycle was taken all the way to the university president's office, and Bailie was offended when the university president refused to see him about the matter. Bailie became increasingly paranoid, feeling that everyone was working against him. His diary noted in early 1917: "I realized that Professor Reisner wanted to run affairs, and me. This I would not go along with." Even the university's vice president, John Williams, whom Bailie had regarded as a close friend for many years, now appeared to be bent on control, like Reisner: "Williams is preparing to take into his own hands all the items that I have been running. The manner in which Williams is now on my trail shows that he wants to suck me dry and spit [out] the shell as soon as he can. Let him."[74]

The worst insult came when Bailie was told at a university function "to take another carriage than that reserved for the University Professors." His letter of resignation and subsequent conferences with the president and others were dramatically described in his diary as a time when everyone suddenly realized the value of his services. But real events must have fallen short of the fantasy because Bailie soon left for north China, never to return to his School of Agriculture and Forestry and his colonies at Purple Mountain and Lai'an.[75]

✣ ✣ ✣ ✣ ✣

Starting a new colony in Jilin and hatching new schemes to aid China, Bailie continued to do what he had been praised for in the past. But this time, in the remote northeast corner of China, he had neither the security of an institutional affiliation nor the encouragement of an appreciative gallery of Americans and American-educated Chinese. In self-imposed exile in Jilin, Bailie nevertheless tried to start another colony while his behavior veered toward the pathological. He fought constantly with the families that he had recruited as colonists, regarding them as lazy shirkers. The colonists apparently returned Bailie's contempt, and Bailie discovered that he could not give commands and instructions as he had before: "When I reprimanded one for anything, all threw down their tools."[76]

The colony project soon fell apart. In the spring there was a mass exodus, so that only eight families remained. Bailie absolved himself of responsibility, viewing the mass departure from the camp as confirmation of his low estimation of the colonists' character. A cynical pastor had earlier predicted that "the [colonist] refugees planned to live in for the winter and to clear out in spring." In Bailie's mind, the prediction had proven true.[77]

The colony's population was dwindling to a handful. Then, in April 1919, Bailie received a letter from Henry Ford, who offered to provide a tractor in order both to "ascertain what merits the tractor together with the necessary plow implements possess" and to pave the way for tractor sales in China. Bailie excitedly replied that he would be delighted to accept the offer and predicted, "If it can run over rough swamp land and rip up the sods, I believe there will be a big sale for it." There was no question in Bailie's mind that tractors were appropriate; the problem was predicting when China's backwardness could be overcome: "It is difficult to say when China will waken up to do things as in other countries. When she does waken up, whoever is in the field with light tractors . . . will certainly make big sales." There was no need to fear competition from John Deere, Bailie explained. Their breaker couldn't break the local soil even when pulled by six oxen.[78]

Bailie treated Ford to a bit of local color in the letter. He wrote, "I'm surrounded by a lot of thieves. Everyone trying to make out of me." The roads were horrible, the clay soil so sticky that "when you get your foot into it, you can't get it out," and horses and carts became stuck whenever the roads were wet. As welcome as an American tractor would be, Bailie realized that his remote location would pose certain problems. The colony was a hundred miles from the railway terminus, and carrying fuel from the railway would be difficult and costly. Bailie hinted that Ford's assistance would be appreciated in securing equipment to produce fuel out of wood, which was in abundant supply. But then, worried that his description of the colony's remoteness would create misgivings and that Ford would take his gift elsewhere, Bailie added brightly, "I should have said in connection with our being well located here for exhibiting your tractor, that we are on the main road leading through the province, and what is done here is known all over the district." [79] But the Ford tractor was not tested in the rugged remoteness of Bailie's Jilin colony after all. Before the tractor arrived, Bailie was robbed and beaten unconscious one night by unknown assailants. Not knowing whether they were roving brigands or disgruntled colonists, he did not stay at the colony to find out: "I then and there decided I could take no more. I made up my mind to resign." The next day, with a broken rib and numerous bruises, Bailie retreated to the provincial capital with a protective escort of Chinese soldiers. He soon left for a recuperative trip to the United States and "rest away from the Chinese." [80]

✢ ✢ ✢ ✢ ✢

The physical assault that Bailie had experienced was less painful than the psychological bowl of having his efforts to start agricultural colonies be so unappreciated and end in such hostile surroundings. Bailie returned to China in 1920, but he would never work on agricultural projects again. His new crusade was to build an "Industrial University," a scheme improbably devised by C. W. Woodworth, an American entomologist. Woodworth was on the faculty of the University of California and in 1918 had spent his sabbatical teaching courses on sericulture at the University of Nanking. The experience gave Woodworth an expansive sense that he had the answer to China's problems—namely, gathering together the Chinese graduates of foreign colleges and universities and teaching them "how to apply their foreign learning to Chinese conditions." The school that Woodworth envisioned was to be no less than "the greatest educational organization in the world." [81]

Woodworth had no way of implementing his scheme and returned to his teaching duties at Berkeley, but he found the perfect person to take up the project in Bailie, with whom he talked at length in 1920, when Bailie spent six months in Berkeley recovering from his wounds. Bailie returned to Beijing the next year with a revised plan to start a "Bureau of Industry" at Beijing University, but he found that neither Beijing University nor the University of Nanking was willing to pay his salary. Obsessed with the need to hasten China's industrialization, he spent his remaining years ferrying between the United States and China, working to place Chinese students in American factory apprenticeships (including a number who were sent to Ford's giant Rouge plant in Dearborn, Michigan). Bailie never again tried to improve Chinese agriculture. He died in 1935.

Bailie's memory was honored in China during World War II, when New Zealand expatriate Rewi Alley and other Westerners started "Bailie Schools," which trained Chinese students in industrial crafts.[82] Honors were also bestowed posthumously at what had become the College of Agriculture and Forestry at the University of Nanking. "Bailie Hall" housed the college, and regular eulogies of the founder of the college praised Bailie in absentia much more fully and tenderly than when he had been resident.

Viewed dispassionately, Bailie's commitment to the cause of helping Chinese agriculture was a strange one, consuming him intensely for a short period of time, then receding as his hyperinflated expectations and he himself were battered. Bailie believed that he had the answers to the rural problems of China, but he could work with neither Chinese nor Westerners, and his colonization work ended in dismal isolation.

The problem went far deeper than weaknesses in the personality of one individual. At the heart of the situation was the fundamental tension that defined American-Chinese relations in the early twentieth century. Each side preferred to treat the other in abstract terms: to Chinese weary of foreign incursions, Americans were imperialists seeking private gain, and to Americans eager to fulfill benevolent impulses, Chinese were more acceptable as idealized images than as imperfect human beings. Thus Bailie found that his schemes for China were generally un-welcomed, and he had to constantly shift his enthusiasm to new enterprises. In the end, all he gave rural China was the unneeded nostrum of hard work, a colony scheme that never proved self-sustaining, and new departments of agriculture and forestry that he left for others to develop.

4

MISSION

Christianity and Agricultural Improvement,
1910s–1920s

Joseph Bailie was an apostate who abandoned his original mission assignment in China to pursue what he deemed to be more practical forms of service, such as improving agriculture. At the same time, however, some voices within Protestant mission councils were advocating an expanded conception of mission work—a conception that would include the agricultural work which Bailie had found only outside of the church. Indeed, by the early twentieth century, a hundred years of evangelical work in China had succeeded in converting only a handful of people in the most populous country in the world, so it is not surprising that church reformers cast about for new, more practical avenues. A call for "agricultural missions" sounded in the 1910s and 1920s, providing some missionaries with a hopeful vision: If the church could improve production on Chinese farms, China's grateful rural hinterland would open up and accept the Christian faith.

American missionaries in China had not been entirely oblivious to agricultural concerns. Many were from farm backgrounds themselves and had planted gardens at their mission stations in China, and some had introduced imported seed or plants into their neighborhoods. The informal extension work of a single missionary could lead to spectacular results; in the late nineteenth century, American fruits spread spontaneously throughout Shandong, in north China, through their introduction by John Livingston Nevius, a Presbyterian missionary stationed at Qufu. But as late as the turn of the century, American missions had no formal programs in agriculture. Gardening was viewed as a sideline unrelated to the work of spreading the Gospel, and Nevius was disturbed when he observed that some people seemed to take "more interest in the material vineyard than the spiritual." He wrote to his mother, "I am afraid I am in danger of being known among them chiefly as a successful horticulturalist!" [1]

The arrival of college-trained agriculturalists in mission positions around the world marked an important change in the missionaries' approach. In 1897, a Cornell graduate, William C. Bell, took his agricultural expertise to Africa and was credited by church historians with "getting African men to use the plow to replace the old-time hoe wielded by women." India received its first American agricultural missionary in 1902. Then, in 1907, pioneers in this new field of endeavor were sent to Brazil and Rhodesia, and China's first such missionary, George Weidman Groff, arrived the same year. The agricultural missionaries were recruited from the Student Volunteer Movement for Foreign Missions, an influential movement on American campuses in the late nineteenth and early twentieth centuries, whose slogan was "The Evangelization of the World in This Generation." A participant in the movement explained: "Just as the United States government sends out to every nook and corner of the world especially trained and qualified 'agricultural explorers,' so the churches of America and of Europe are sending forth agricultural crusaders to serve among the needy peoples of the world." [2]

✧ ✧ ✧ ✧ ✧

"Daddy" Groff, as George Weidman Groff was known to friends, originally went to China as a young man of twenty-three to teach at a missionary middle school in Guangzhou (Canton). He later established a small agricultural school at Canton Christian College and lived in China for thirty-four years. His Christian fellows accorded Groff the honor of being "first agricultural missionary" in China, although he never actually had a mission board appointment. Groff had graduated from Pennsylvania State College in 1907, with a B.S. in agriculture and a specialty in horticulture. Under the influence of John Mott and the Student Volunteer Movement, he had tried to enter foreign missionary service. But technical agricultural expertise was still unappreciated by many mission boards, and he had been turned down.

Groff managed to secure passage to China nevertheless, as an instructor hired to teach geography, mathematics, and English at the middle school attached to Canton Christian College. Technically, Groff's job included neither missionary nor agricultural work, but he did both when, upon arrival in China, he set out to provide his students with the practical knowledge "that will enable them to fight with the Christian armor their own battles for a comfortable livelihood." [3]

No agricultural courses were offered at the time, so Groff initiated a school garden program after class for those who were interested. He also began to lobby for the school to include agricultural instruction in its curriculum; it took four years, but in 1912 the middle school began formal instruction in "school gardening." Living in a semitropical region of China, Groff was fascinated by fruits and tried to introduce a number of imported varieties. One of his most successful experiments was the introduction of the Hawaiian papaya, which came to be grown widely throughout south China. He also developed a research interest in the Chinese lichee (lizhi), which would form the subject of a master's thesis when he returned to Penn State for graduate work.

Groff did not develop an interest in rice, the staple crop of the region, however. He was a horticultural scholar, not a crop specialist, and preferred to spend his time compiling a Chinese-Latin index of fruits and garden plants. Yet he captured the imagination of an American audience who pictured American agricultural expertise as helping the Chinese see the light of Christ. To Groff, and to many American readers of the articles Groff published in the 1910s, China represented an opportunity to do what had not been possible in the United States— that is, to instill a Christian direction in economic development. In the United States, Groff lamented, "The training of leaders with a knowledge of ways and means for overcoming our economic and agricultural ills has not, for the most part, been under Christian direction. The result has been that many of our leaders in these lines of effort have been dominated in their work by materialistic motives." China offered a clean slate upon which to start anew.[4]

Groff dreamed of a model farm established at every missionary post in China. At such farms, Chinese college students would test what they had learned in the classroom, and "the mass of the people could see for themselves what modern methods of cultivation and the introduction of new varieties will accomplish." If not all mission stations could afford their own farms, they could split the costs of a shared operation. "For the successful installation of such a farm," Groff advised encouragingly, "all that is necessary is a suitable piece of land, preferably close to some mission property, and a farm manager. Eight or ten thousand dollars' gold would equip the farm for successful work, and the sale of products should, in a very short time, more than cover the running expenses." The success of the farm would impart a lesson in good management: "The Chinese would watch the work of the farm with keen interest and would soon adopt its profitable features."[5]

An objection could be raised, however, that the farms were the proper responsibility of the government and not of the missions. Groff had a ready answer: "The missionary is at present in closer touch with the people and is in a better position to help and influence." The Chinese government lacked sufficient men "properly qualified to organize and carry out successfully the work of model farms and agricultural courses"; American mission boards could supply the personnel that China lacked. It was an opportunity that Groff talked of tirelessly.[6]

✥ ✥ ✥ ✥ ✥

Groff was never successful in securing funding for his ideas from American mission boards, but he did have support from friends at his alma mater, Pennsylvania State. Although Groff went to China with no official connection to the university, in 1909, Pennsylvania friends organized a "Groff Day" at the campus chapel, taking up a collection to support Groff's work in China. The collection became a regular institution, and by 1913 it was only one of a number of fund-raising activities at the Penn State campus on behalf of Daddy Groff. A committee, the Pennsylvania State College Mission to China, was organized, and a formal agreement to provide for Groff's support was negotiated with Canton Christian.

State College, Pennsylvania, became the center of review for Groff's agricultural program, and the Penn State in China supporters felt closely bound to the work taking place on the other side of the globe. Approving Groff's annual expense budget was an opportunity for the imagination to travel around the world: sitting in their library meeting room on the Pennsylvania campus, China mission committee members studied expense accounts for Groff's Guangzhou gardens (sample item: buffalo cow, $30.00) and participated imaginatively in the work.[7]

Groff was careful to explain all of his reported expenses in detail, for he wanted to "conduct this work on a business basis." His original hope was to make his gardens self-supporting, just as he intended future off-campus model farms to be. They earned little, however, and money became a dominating source of worry. Groff wrote to Penn State, "The question of the support for this work is one that concerns me not a little. I have seemed able to do so little in the way of centering any large funds for it and this is what we really need." Working on one small garden seemed frustratingly insignificant; if only more funds could be secured, "we will be able to swing larger things." Groff was looking toward "a big proposition along agricultural lines here in South China" (the details were unspecified). He was the first to register a complaint that fellow church agriculturalists would echo over and over: medical missions were well established in China and were the recipients of generous board support, but the idea of an agricultural mission was regarded as heretical by the mission establishment. Until the notion of agricultural missions received the recognition it deserved, Groff said, "we must peg away."[8]

Without backup support from a larger church board, the campus group at Penn State had only its own voluntary contributions to send to Groff. To make matters worse, Canton Christian College seized upon Penn State's support as an excuse to shed any financial responsibility for Groff: the school cut off his salary and gave notice that he was to move from the house that the college had provided. The mission college assumed that Penn State would come to Groff's rescue. When writing Pennsylvania of his financial difficulties, Groff avoided criticizing Canton Christian, for they were "carrying out a big proposition with very little funds and find it most difficult to find support for the work they have already started." Agricultural programs were simply beyond their financial capability. "This means," Groff wrote to his supporters back home, "that for a number of years at least we must carry this agricultural proposition alone." A minimal budget required at least $1,500 a year to meet Groff's living expenses in China. Groff realized that it would not be easy to raise but emphasized, "I am confident that the fight is worthwhile."[9]

Penn State in China decided to appeal to fellow agricultural colleges for assistance. Writing that "the field of work is too large for the one agricultural college in the United States to support as it should be supported," the Pennsylvania mission group asked for money "needed for equipment and land for farming and horticultural purposes at the Christian College." If many colleges were willing to combine their efforts, a "United States Agricultural College Mission to China" could be formed. "It would be advisable to place more in the field," Penn State explained, "because Mr. Groff is primarily a horticulturist, but there is room there for a dairyman, animal husbandry man, agronomist, and in fact all branches of agricultural work." [10]

Five colleges expressed mild interest, but only Kansas State organized a mission support group, sending one of its graduates, Carl Levine, an animal husbandry specialist, to Canton Christian. When the "United States Agricultural College Mission to China" failed to materialize, Penn State had to continue to shoulder complete financial responsibility for Groff. A Penn State Mission secretary wrote to Groff in late 1915, "I have been more or less discouraged from time to time in regard to the Penn State Mission to China. We worked trying to get money from the faculty and student body but have been unable to accomplish very much." While the students had given quite liberally in the chapel collections, "it is like pulling teeth to get anything out of the faculty." Discouragingly, the prospects of tapping off-campus support now seemed to be nil. No one at State College had been able "to suggest any ways or means of procedure with such men as Wanamaker, Carnegie, etc." With the world war raging, "there has been so much collecting in the past year for help in all quarters of Europe that it seems nearly out of the question to ask help from the larger capitalists of the state at this time." [11]

Without outside assistance, the Penn State Mission needed to raise more money to provide for Groff's support, and a partial solution to the problem was suggested by the mission secretary, F. N. Fagan. The chapel collections had not all been destined for China; half had gone toward the support of "a darkey worker in the South." Fagan wrote to Groff, "When I look at this work sanely and weigh it up on all sides I cannot help but feel that State College has taken on more than they can care for. I am in sympathy with the Mission work but I feel that instead of supporting two men in the Mission such as they are doing at the present time, they should support one man and support him well." Fagan felt that "it is only natural that I would say that the money should be given to the support of the Chinese work," and the others apparently agreed. Support for the "darkey worker" was dropped, and Groff's stipend doubled. [12]

Penn State remained a steadfast supporter of Groff in China. Donations varied from year to year, but a minimum floor of support was provided annually until Groff left China in 1941. As the Penn State in China program acquired a history, the appeal of supporting a campus tradition was added to the appeal of contributing to exciting work in a distant land. A fund-raising pamphlet printed in 1921 offered students the opportunity to help extend their school's influence "as far away as China." With help, "China could develop her marvelous land and labor resources to the point where she could not only provide her own but also world needs for food and raw materials." American economic self-interest was not to be ignored, either: "Unitil China produces more at home, she cannot buy more abroad." [13]

✢ ✢ ✢ ✢ ✢

Practical reasons for support were augmented by Groff's colorful tales. Resolving to serve his home campus as its on-the-scene China reporter, he wrote to Penn State in an open letter in 1924, "The very recent experience of the [Canton Christian] College with Kwangtung bandits has had widespread publicity. You have doubtless read of the episode, and your heartfelt interest in the College, in Penn State's work here, and in our own welfare have possibly aroused your thoughts to the point where you wish 'Daddy' Groff would give you some first hand 'dope' once or twice a year with regard to just what is going on over here in China." Groff indeed had a tale to tell. [14]

Canton Christian College occupied a long island in the Pearl River, opposite Guangzhou. On the ferry that connected the college to the city, six armed kidnappers, "disguised as ordinary Chinese gentlemen," commandeered a launch in midstream and headed off with thirty-six students and staff members, whom they held for ransom. When the college received the kidnappers' demand for 300 Hong Kong dollars (about $150) for each hostage, it turned for help to General Lei Fuk Lam, whom Groff described as the civil governor at the time and a longtime friend of the agricultural school (the general had his own fruit orchards and was interested in Groff's research). The following days "were exciting ones and parents and friends of the boys came in large numbers to give the college authorities advice. The great point of discussion was whether or not any ransom should be paid." The consensus was against payment. Groff reported, "It was a great inspiration to talk with outstanding Chinese gentry and hear them say that as for them they had reached the point where, even at the sacrifice of their own sons, they believed in an aggressive policy with these bandits." Groff agreed: "Herein is the only hope for a check to this awful practice so common out here. So long as ransom is freely paid, so long can we expect further kidnapping and extortion." [15]

With the General in charge, payment of the ransom proved unnecessary. By holding the heads of villages in the area personally responsible for the incident, he soon flushed out the kidnappers and secured the safe return of the hostages. Groff did not want his readers to assume that such excitement was routine—for the most part, the college campus had "the air of peace, protection, and happiness that usually characterizes the joyful college life." The college generally escaped the prevailing "whirlpool of unrest" because "after all we have come to bring peace to China and not a sword. And most of the Chinese, including the bandits themselves, realize this fact and, except when driven by an unusual opening for worldly gain, are slow to disturb us." Now that he had his readers' attention, Groff explained, "I have written a long letter regarding the bandit experience for I knew you would be interested. But events of this kind are not the usual run of life out here, at least not for us. The most interesting and inspiring part of our life and work is tied up in the details of the constructive side of our college program." [16]

The Pennsylvania campus heard a great deal about Groff's projects: the large herbarium; the farm with attached dairy (Groff claimed it was self-supporting); the Sino-American plant exchanges. But kept from public view, for obvious reasons, were Groff's constant concerns about money and housing. When Penn State supporters had been unable to raise enough funds to fully support Groff, Canton Christian had relented and had not carried out its threat to move the Groffs out of faculty housing. But the college had assigned Groff and his wife to accommodations that were shared with another couple, an arrangement that felt increasingly suffocating when Groff brought his parents and a sister to China. In 1918, Groff threatened Canton Christian with his resignation over the issue, writing, "One cannot help but feel that after almost eleven full years of service in the work, with family and parents both in China, and with growing obligations to both students and visitors, it is high time that he be establishing a home which to a degree at least he shall be able to call his own." [17] When the Groff's only child died of influenza in 1919, the campus community at State College heard rumors that "unhealthy housing conditions" had brought on the fatal illness. A total of $7,000 was raised to build a permanent home, "Penn State Lodge," on the Canton Christian College campus for Penn State's representative in China. The Groffs stayed on.

In 1921, Canton Christian College expanded and established a separate College of Agriculture with Groff as its first dean. With only four professors and eighteen students, the new "college" was quite small, and remained small, perpetually strapped for operating funds. Though it belonged to a mission institution, the agricultural school did little to join agricultural improvement and religion: students were required to take only one religion course in a four-year program. Primary emphasis was on agricultural courses and hard work in the field. The college proudly stated: "Six hours of practical work a day are required of each student in the [major] he has chosen." [18]

The agricultural school also did not require its students to attend chapel. Its system of rules and regulations, though hardly liberal, merely copied the standards common at the time on the campuses of American colleges and universities. "Mixed parties" for men and women required prior arrangement of chaperons and the permission of the dean of women. Students were expected to be in their dormitories for unannounced roll calls at 10:15 P.M., and quiet hours between 10:00 P.M. and 6:00 A.M. prohibited noise such as "loud conversation, laughter, singing, typewriting, walking about in wooden shoes." [19]

Groff was a devout man, but though his writings and speeches tirelessly called for spreading the church's influence in the countryside, in his own work he tended to keep religion in a realm apart. Despite being credited by his contemporaries as the first agricultural missionary, he never ventured off the campus to build agricultural programs for the church; he spent most of his time conducting horticultural studies on his college campus in Guangzhou.

÷ ÷ ÷ ÷ ÷

Farther north, John Reisner, Bailie's young successor who had arrived in Nanjing in 1914, was the second agricultural missionary in China. He too spent his time on a campus, not in rural mission posts. Like Groff, Reisner maintained a vigorous campaign to draw more church support for agricultural improvement work, and in the late 1910s and early 1920s the missionary movement increasingly addressed agricultural questions. Numerous speeches and articles and conferences seemed to herald a new era that would merge agricultural improvement and spiritual awakening.

As early as 1918, Reisner declared an early victory in the drive to secure church support. He observed, "The body of missionaries is becoming more awake to a sense of possibilities of agricultural activities, if not to a full sense of realization of the intimate relationship between the future of the Christian church and Chinese agriculture." The encouraging proof that he had found was the inclusion of a paper on the "Relation of Education in Agriculture to the Christian Movement in China" at a recent meeting of the China Christian Educational Association in Shanghai. And he had heard that a paper on "The Place of Practical Agricultural Education in our Middle and Lower Schools" was scheduled for presentation at another church conference. These were reassuring "evidences of interest." [20]

At Reisner's own school, the University of Nanking, the College of Agriculture had become the largest college on campus, and the importance of agriculture was underscored when the students held an intramural debate in 1919 on the resolution, " Resolved that the improvement of agriculture is more important for China than the development of new industries." A team from the College of Agriculture faced opponents from the College of Liberal Arts, but to make the confrontation less partisan, the liberal arts majors took the affirmative, and the agriculture students the negative.

The affirmative side and the cause of agriculture triumphed that afternoon. Agriculture, the winning team argued, was the very foundation of industry; moreover, China was "better adapted" to agriculture than industry. Aside from mentioning the plain economic reason that "our people need more food and clothing," the debaters included a moralistic rationale in their brief. Like the Physiocrats of eighteenth-century France and the Jeffersonians of the United States, the Chinese students argued that farmers are morally superior to urban residents, who are subject to the corrupting influence of the city. They claimed, "Rural people are usually more healthy, more moral, and stronger in personality, which makes the people believe that the farm is the seed bed of true citizens." [21]

The University of Nanking stood ready and willing to help Chinese agriculture but found itself in an awkward position. On the one hand, it tried at every opportunity to generate greater interest in agricultural affairs among members of the missionary community, but on the other hand, it would not abide by any other church institution developing its own college of agriculture. Its administrators felt that funds were too scarce to be spread over more than one program—its own. When Reisner received a friendly request for guidance in the establishment of a new department of agriculture at another mission college in China, he wrote disapprovingly in reply: "Don't ask me to develop plans for another college of agriculture or department of agriculture of college grade in connection with the present Christian educational system, until we have developed in China at least one college that is adequately staffed, equipped and financed, *of which as yet there are none*. We are doing our best here at Nanking to deserve the confidence of the Christian movement in China so that they will take us and make us what we ought to be, but our needs are many." Reisner closed his letter by asking that his missionary colleague shelve his proposed plans.[22]

Contention over limited funds transformed church support for agriculture into a political matter within mission councils. Nanking took its case for sole proprietorship of church-sponsored agricultural work to the newly formed Association of Christian Colleges and Universities in China. The five-year plan of Nanking's College of Agriculture called for increasing its staff from the current thirteen persons (five foreign, eight Chinese) to twenty-seven (sixteen foreign, eleven Chinese); the annual budget was to go from $22,000 to $127,000. But the proposed increase was actually modest, the school explained, if measured by American standards. The Massachusetts Agricultural College, not even one of the largest institutions in the United States, had an annual income of more than $600,000, and its staff numbered more than a hundred. The Association of Christian Colleges and Universities was persuaded by Nanking's argument that the College of Agriculture's ambitious plans were "not excessive."[23]

Once it had agreed that Nanking's plans were reasonable, the association was led to affirm a sequence of corollaries: since "any school representing the Christian Church should have the highest possible standards" and maintaining a "high-grade" school was so costly, and "considering the limited funds available for Christian education work in this country, as well as the difficulty of securing large numbers of experts willing to serve on a missionary basis," only one agricultural school in China, it seemed, could be supported under mission auspices.[24]

Nanking seemed to be the only choice. Its "successful work hitherto has secured a remarkable degree of recognition." It had "the additional advantage of central location, being within easy reach of the wealthy cities and farming districts of the lower Yangtze region, and accessible by an easy journey of only a little over a day from such northern centers as Peking and Tientsin." And it was "near and in close touch with one of the most, perhaps the most influential and enterprising industrial communities in China"—namely, Shanghai. Groff's limited program in the south, at Canton Christian College, could not match such competition; over Canton Christian's strenuous objection, the association recommended against support of an agricultural school in Canton. Thus the other Christian colleges and universities that had not yet developed agricultural or forestry courses were told that students interested in agriculture were to be sent to Nanking.[25]

✦ ✦ ✦ ✦ ✦

While Reisner and the University of Nanking pushed hard for church support of their agriculture program, the world mission movement also began to give formal recognition to the importance of agriculture in its work. In 1919, the International Association of Agricultural Missions was established, and representatives from China were prominent. A related World Agriculture Society, dominated by mission groups, sprang up as well, with the purpose of furthering "a better understanding of world problems in agriculture and country life." The recent world war had shown that "to feed the World adequately, without waste, with just remuneration to the producer and without extortion from the consumer, agriculture should be planned on World lines."[26]

In an early issue of the World Agriculture Society's magazine, Reisner published an article reviewing the agricultural missionary work in China and similar efforts in other countries. With the appearance of Sam Higginbottom's *The Gospel and the Plow*, which told of the author's agricultural mission work in India, and with the news of a large church investment in a model farm in Chile, Reisner noted that "there has been a marked increase in interest in the whole problem of agricultural missionary work." Although "still being spoken in somewhat of a whisper," agriculture appeared to be "the outstanding new development in foreign missionary work in the next ten years." Reisner predicted: "It is going to have at least as important, if not a greater place, in the missionary program for the future as medical missions have had in the past."[27]

Kenyon Butterfield, president of the Massachusetts Agricultural College, the American Country Life Association, and the new World Agriculture Society, helped to draw American attention away from European agriculture and toward Asia. Lecturing and writing extensively about his six-month study of "the Far East" as a member of a foreign missions conference, Butterfield in 1922 told the society of the importance of China "in the problem of agriculture viewed as a world question" and of the weighty significance of the region's population: "Half of the world's population lives in the Far East. Four-fifths of these eight hundred million human beings live on the land and secure their living directly from the land." He concluded, "Nowhere else in the world does the population press so hard upon the soil for sheer subsistence, nowhere is the margin between life and death by starvation so narrow."[28]

Chapters of the World Agriculture Society were formed in China by the handful of agricultural missionaries in Nanjing, Guangzhou, and Beijing. But their mandate to promote "better understanding" of world agriculture was rather vague. Butterfield, however, offered what he called "a few concrete suggestions" during his China visit. First, Butterfield advised, practical projects needed to be launched for "rural community development"; he liked best the slogan originally adopted by an Irish society: "Better Farming, Better Business, Better Living." Second, "representatives of all important agencies, government and private" should be brought together to work out a program for agricultural development. Butterfield called this "An All-China Agricultural Program." And each branch society was to "inform its members and the general public regarding all enterprises which look towards the development of the rural community." These proposals, the *World Agriculture* editors explained, were "applicable not only to China but also to other places to which the World Agriculture movement has been, or may be, extended." [29]

In practice, these tasks were quite daunting. The China chapters occupied themselves with more modest activities. Typical was a report from the Nanjing chapter: "We are hoping that at each meeting some member may present a paper on some phase of agriculture which may be published in the Chinese papers and, in some instances, which may be suitable for publication in *World Agriculture*." [30]

In the United States, where chapters were established at a number of American agricultural colleges, the World Agriculture movement might not have been noticed off campus, but it did briefly spark the interest of a few American students in agricultural problems abroad. At Cornell, the "International Agricultural Society" had a membership of thirty a year after its founding in 1922, and its members gave talks on social and agricultural conditions in different countries: China, India, England, and Russia. The chapter's secretary reported that the "memorable event of the year" was the program of international music and "stunts" that it had prepared for a campus "Student-Get-Together-Social," including presentation of a pageant called the "International Spirit of Agriculture." Livingston Farrand, the president of the university, spoke at the occasion and declared that "folks were folks the world over." [31]

Within China missionary circles, however, resistance to agricultural work remained. Opposition was based partly on the conviction that the Chinese were master farmers—Franklin King's book, *Farmers of Forty Centuries*, was read by church leaders and exerted a tremendous influence on their thinking (see chap. 1). When William Overholt, a young graduate of Iowa State College who had volunteered for mission service in 1920, asked his mission supervisor in Fujian about starting an agricultural program, he was told, "We can't teach the Chinese anything about agriculture." Overholt disagreed: he felt that King's book, while accurately describing Chinese fertilizer practices, ignored other aspects of soil management in which Chinese techniques were deficient. It vexed Overholt to see sweet potatoes, for example, planted in rows up and down unterraced hills, where the soil was washed away in one or two summers. King's book, he later reflected, "did a great disservice to Chinese agriculture. It took a long time for the church to see the place of agriculture in the program of the church." [32]

Church resistance also stemmed from theological objections to secular pursuits. John Reisner did his best to wear down such objections with a new exegesis:

Christ said He came, not that men might have life, but that they might have more abundant life. Is He referring only to spiritual things, or does the term life have a more comprehensive designation, and include the elements (in addition to spiritual) that enter into the normal daily life that we live here on earth, producing necessities for ourselves and others, combating the stern realities of economic pressure, and otherwise trying to maintain ourselves as a unit of society, and possibly leaving the world a little better place for those who come after us?

Like Groff, Reisner was pleased that the church had supported medicine and education in its mission work in the past, but he was frustrated that "the idea of utilizing agriculture in any of its varied aspects seems not to have taken much root in the minds of mission administrators or missionaries." Fortunately, he claimed, this was passing, and the possibilities of agriculture in mission work were "being realized from the missionary on the field to the Board secretary at home."[33]

✢ ✢ ✢ ✢ ✢

A Methodist conference in central China led the way in calling for new agricultural programs. To prepare their future ministers for country churches, the Methodists took what Reisner described as "what may seem to some to be a very radical step": they resolved to ask that their divinity schools offer "such courses as deal with agricultural production, rural economics, and rural sociology." The Methodist reformers declared that "the vital relationship between these courses and practical evangelism" was to be "kept constantly before the minds of the students."[34]

The Methodists also planned to establish primary schools and "preaching halls" in small towns to provide services "specially adapted to rural and agricultural communities." Lectures ("illustrated if possible") on topics of interest to farmers and demonstrations of improved methods, seeds, and machinery seemed appropriate: "By helping to improve the grains, fruits and vegetables, the cotton or silk, we shall win the confidence of the people and again save by serving." The Methodist planners added, "No other agency contemplates this form of service." The church could only benefit, for "all this reacts on spiritual issues."[35]

Similar talk filled the air in the early 1920s, as other mission gatherings made plans for converting the long-ignored rural folk of China. At its 1922 meeting, the prestigious National Christian Conference recognized the important facts of demography: "It is commonly said that three-fourths of the people of China are directly dependent upon agriculture for a living. . . . It is in itself a convincing argument for the importance of agriculture and village life in the program of the Church, if that program is the Christianizing of China." Landlords were singled out for particular attention: "It is the duty of the Christian Church to bring home to the landowners of China their duty toward their tenants and their responsibility for the introduction of better methods of agriculture, for the promotion of education, and for the improvement of village life."[36]

Titled, with martial flair, *The Christian Occupation of China*, the 1922 report of mission activities in China gave prominent attention to agricultural missions, whose possibilities in China were "unlimited." The arithmetic held the same fascination for American missionaries as it did for American businessmen who dreamily pondered the immensity of the "China market." *The Christian Occupation* calculated that since 85 percent of China's population was rural (10 percent more than the estimate of the National Christian Conference), "this means that 350,000,000 people or more are in real need of a new rural outlook and of scientific knowledge of better methods of agriculture." The potential was vast: "In the light of these conditions the Christian Church faces one of its greatest opportunities."[37]

The mission movement unabashedly saw itself as a competitor with the Chinese government. The agenda for church agricultural work was as secular as an extension agent's: promoting improved seed, animals, tillage and fertilization methods, farm management, roads, and control of insects and plant diseases. The Chinese government, the mission survey noted, had begun a few agricultural schools, but the emphasis was "too materialistic, having as it does, in too many cases, the sole aim of bettering the economic condition of the farmer, without much attention being given to moral and social problems of rural life upon which the uplift of any community or nation depends, as much as upon better crops." Moreover, the Christian mission community was confident that it could draw trained agricultural specialists from American colleges, while the Chinese government had to contend with the problem of "non-availability of trained experiment station workers and competent teachers of agricultural subjects."[38]

The church demonstrated its ability to usurp the role of the Chinese government as the leading force in agricultural improvement when Reverend A. Torrey, stationed in Shandong, staged in 1923 what the Western press called "China's First Agricultural Institute." With the help of the staff at the University of Nanking, Torrey secured the grounds of a Buddhist temple in the county seat of Linyi and set up a tent for farm exhibits, lectures, and a plowing exhibition. He obtained the permission of the local authorities by inviting them to be members of the organizing committee. The local magistrate, school principal, and chairman and vice chairman of the chamber of commerce were recruited as sponsors. Schoolteachers acted as stagehands, and their stage manager was the head of the local prison.

For three days the tent drew an audience estimated at four to five hundred people. Lectures were given in the mornings, and plays were performed in the afternoons. On the side of the stage, an American plow was a star attraction: "When the foreign plow drawn by two ordinary Chinese animals easily broke a deep furrow through the hard sun-baked soil of a much trodden threshing floor, excitement ran high." The agricultural fair was declared a rousing success by Western reporters, but a parenthetic statement revealed how unsettled the Chinese countryside was in the 1920s: the Americans needed an armed escort to accompany them to and from the nearest rail station, twenty-five miles away.[39]

✣ ✣ ✣ ✣ ✣

The agriculturalists were given an opportunity to address the full mission community in China in 1924, when the *Chinese Recorder* devoted an entire issue to "The Church in China and Its Rural Task." The opening editorial discussed the need to reach the "three hundred million" rural residents so as to lead them "from darkness into light," and two photographs of Chinese agricultural students illustrated the promise of using agricultural instruction. In one, two college students were bent over pear-tree grafts, while the caption declared, "Joy and pride in work and practical accomplishment in other than literary pursuits is a lesson more Christian schools should be teaching to more boys." In the other—a group photo of a class in the field, farm tools in hand—the caption explained that these are "some of the Huping College garden boys ready for action." Readers who were church contributors were assured that "all Mission financial help to these boys must be 'worked out.' The work plan has toned up the spirit of the whole school." [40]

The *Chinese Recorder* featured the two agricultural spokesmen who had been sounding the call for more than a decade—Reisner and Groff. Their message was familiar: a church confined to China's cities was destined to remain unsuccessful. Reisner singled out the inappropriateness of traditional church training for rural work: "After a hundred and more years of missionary work, we find only one theological seminary with a specially trained teacher devoting his time to the special problems of the rural church." The church, Reisner said, needed to encourage divinity students to see that there could be "a great future right here on earth, in China, as well as in the life to come." But the "exegeses" and "learned introductions" then emphasized in seminaries were "foreign to the rugged and simple needs of rugged and simple minded rural China." [41]

Groff asked his readers to notice the danger of China's rural residents "turning to the city as a place of refuge" from poverty and banditry. In Groff's view, this represented a threat to "the life of the nation. . . . If the cities try to assimilate them as they are now doing, these very cities will become the Sodom and Gomorrah of China." The church had to do what it could to ensure that the farmers would "stay where they are." To serve China's rural areas, the church needed missionaries sympathetic to the needs of the countryside. Groff pointedly asked how many of his missionary readers had "ever ridden upon the back of a water buffalo or yellow cow, or have served as a laborer in a field of ripened grain or any agricultural crop?" [42]

Groff and Reisner separately tried to answer the objections to agricultural programs that had been raised by parts of the missionary community. Groff combated the idea, which seemed to "permeate the minds of Christian teachers, students, laymen and preachers throughout China," that the countryside was "not a becoming place for our best educated Christian men and women." Groff wrote, "This mistaken idea must certainly be corrected before any progress in a constructive program for the redemption of the country, and the nation, can be effected." [43]

Others seemed to think that "if the rural chruch should consciously launch out in the role of good Samaritan," it would lose its "spiritual meaning and message." This, Reisner emphasized, would not be so. But the very nomenclature of "agricultural missionaries," he claimed, created the mistaken impression that the work did not have "spiritual sanction." Reisner proposed that "the name rural workers or rural missionaries would more nearly indicate their missionary interests." He asked his readers, "If schools have been necessary to train men, if hospitals have been necessary to heal broken bodies, why not rural services to help in the every day things of every day rural life?"[44]

Two conferences on agriculture and mission work, in 1924 and 1926, represented the apogee of talk about the subject. Both were held at the University of Nanking; both drew American and Chinese church representatives from around the country.[45] But despite the workshops on "Realignment of Christian Forces in China" and "Ruralizing the Christian Rural Program," the campaign to use agricultural improvement in mission work had failed in the field. The rhetoric would continue into the 1930s, but without the intensity of the two previous decades. The fundamental problem, which was never resolved, was finding—and keeping—American mission representatives who had both the technical expertise and the spiritual commitment that agricultural mission work required.

Groff and Reisner discovered that few American missionaries followed their call to improve Chinese agriculture. By the early 1920s, after a decade of strenuous appeals for agricultural missionaries to China, a mission census found only fifteen who had had college training in agriculture. The count a few years later was hardly larger. Even after 1928, when the International Missionary Council gave its considerable support to a worldwide effort in rural mission work, the number of participating agricultural missionaries remained minuscule. In 1931, of twenty-nine thousand Protestant missionaries distributed about the globe, only one hundred were said to be directly engaged in agricultural work.[46]

The two pioneers in China were most exceptional: both Groff and Reisner had college degrees in agriculture and were deeply religious. Each was based on a college campus which, though not ideal, was an entire world distant from the hardships and isolation of a mission post out in the field. Among the American college students who signed pledge cards in the Student Volunteer Movement committing themselves to foreign mission service, the combination of technical expertise and willingness to live in uncertain circumstances in China proved to be a rarity. The difficulty in recruiting agricultural missionaries for China bears a striking resemblance to the problems that the U.S. government's Peace Corps experienced many years later in recruiting technical specialists for overseas service. In both cases, volunteers tended to be generalists who were imbued with a high degree of idealism but who lacked the desired technical expertise. Individuals with technical qualifications did not volunteer, or if they did volunteer, were difficult to keep. The experiences of two missionaries in particular, Walter Lowdermilk and J. Lossing

Buck, reveal the challenge the church faced in recruitment and retention of its precious crew of agricultural specialists.

÷ ÷ ÷ ÷ ÷

The University of Nanking discovered that recruiting Walter Clay Lowdermilk for service in China was a tricky business. Lowdermilk had been born in 1888 in Liberty, North Carolina, reared on farms in Oklahoma and Arizona, awarded a Rhodes scholarship that led to forestry studies at Oxford, and was a rising star in the United States Forest Service when he wrote to a mission board in 1922 of his interest in China. Characteristically, his opening line emphasized secular rather than spiritual interests: "May I ask you to outline for me the possibilities in the extension of forestry and reforestation work in China, working out from a Presbyterian Mission University as a base?" [47]

Lowdermilk did not explain the real source of his interest in China: his girlfriend. Inez Marks, an old acquaintance, had just returned from five years of missionary work in Sichuan, China; the two had become reacquainted in Pasadena at the 1922 Rose Bowl game, and within forty-eight hours Walter had proposed. "She accepted me," he later recalled, "but immediately said, 'I hope we can go back to China together for China needs you more than does our Forest Service. Others will take your place here, but in China there is no one to do the big job required on famine prevention but you.'" [48]

At the time, Lowdermilk was "very dubious about going to China"—it would mean jeopardizing his career in the Forest Service. But his fiancée talked him into sending a letter of inquiry to the Presbyterian mission board. The letter was passed on to Reisner at the University of Nanking, who was delighted that a qualified forester was knocking at the door. At the time, Reisner had only two foresters on the faculty—Chinese who had been trained at Yale and Harvard. Reisner wanted "two or three strong American foresters," and wrote that he would be glad to hear further of Lowdermilk's interest. "I know of no line of work," Reisner told him, "in which there are greater opportunities for real Christian service than in the development of forestation in China at the present time." [49]

Lowdermilk did not inquire into the opportunities for "Christian service," but he did have a number of questions about mundane matters: teaching load, time permitted for fieldwork, living accommodations, Nanjing's climate, and contract conditions. The foreign language was also a concern: "Is the instruction to be given in the Chinese language entirely?" [50] Reisner's reply was reassuring. English was used for all of the college's courses, and gaining a command of Chinese would not be difficult: "One can begin to make his wants known fairly intelligibly after a month or two in the Language School which is connected with the University." [51]

Reisner also assured Lowdermilk that life in Nanjing imposed no special hardships: "Living conditions in Nanking are very good indeed. We live in foreign, or semi-foreign houses in the very highest and nicest part of the city." No health problems deserved worry, for Reisner had found that "one can be just as well in

Nanking as they can be in the United States. Of course there are certain precautions to be taken." As for the climate, Nanjing offered admittedly damp and cold winters but the compensation of lovely springs. The city also offered a school for American children and the companionship of a foreign community of about four hundred people.[52]

The most intimidating part of Reisner's description consisted of the details of the appointment to the university faculty. The term of appointment was that of other missionaries—namely, for life; lest that appear too long, Reisner explained that he would consider candidates who would serve for a shorter term, but at least ten or fifteen years. The first five or six years were usually needed simply "for one to get his bearings and acquire a working knowledge of the language and the larger problems which he wishes to tackle." Reisner's experience had been that "conditions are such that a longer time is required for one to get hold of his job in China than in America, and I should say Europe as well." The starting salary was $1,300 per year, which Reisner hastened to explain had more purchasing power in China than in the United States.[53]

Reisner's letter campaign appears to have worked, for Lowdermilk and Marks submitted formal applications for mission appointments to the University of Nanking. But just as Reisner was preparing for their arrival, complications arose. The first set of problems was presented by Miss Marks, who wrote from California asking for a southerly transpacific route, stopping in Honolulu, and for a center cabin to avoid seasickness. Her main request, however, was for the university to provide the couple with a house of their own in Nanjing: "Mr. Lowdermilk and I were friends more than ten years ago, and during all those years, we have only been together six days." When they had been engaged, Marks had promised Lowdermilk that they would have their own bungalow, and she had made plans to bring everything they would need, from kitchen utensils to a piano.[54]

Marks couched her request for the house in terms of what would be best for "Mr. Lowdermilk's work and happiness in China." Though veiled in polite phrasing, she threatened to delay their sailing for Nanjing. If they had to board in another household in Nanjing for their first year, as Reisner had told them, then Marks wondered aloud whether "it would be better under the circumstances to delay sailing for awhile, rather than have Mr. Lowdermilk not be able to have the home he has been longing for all these years, and risk circumstances which might make Mr. Lowdermilk wish that he might have accepted the urgent offers of the government here, where a beautiful home is assured us."[55]

Had serving the spread of Christianity been Lowdermilk and Marks's primary motivation in volunteering for mission work, Reisner would have been able to prod his balking prospects with a few words about higher causes and duty. But he understood that that would not work in this case. Spiritual considerations were conspicuously absent in the arrangement, so Reisner restricted himself to saying only once, in reply, that "sometimes we have to put personal preferences second in a work such as is going on in Nanking and other missionary centers in China." Most of his response to Marks was practical: don't delay sailing, for Lowdermilk would miss the beginning of language school; don't worry about the house, for it was being built and would be completed soon. The Reisners offered to have the new couple live with them until it was finished.[56]

This mollified Marks, but Lowdermilk, writing separately from Montana, had presented Reisner with another set of concerns. Now, as his departure approached, Lowdermilk wanted to make sure that he would not be saddled with the responsibilities of an instructor—he wanted to spend his time on "regional study and extension." He wrote to Reisner, "You will understand I am sure when I say that I do my best and original work under this condition: where I have a field of activity in which I am left to my own initiative with guidance only as to general policies." In Montana he had a "pretty free hand," and he expected the same in China.[57]

A gingerly tone was adopted in Reisner's response. "You would not have a great deal of instructing to do," Reisner suggested, "but I think it would be wise for you to count on doing some teaching in order to get in closer touch with students." The students would be the ones who, after graduation, would administer the major forestry projects in China, and "a close relationship with them while they are under-graduates in the College" would create useful contacts for Lowdermilk's future work. But Reisner, recognizing what most appealed to Lowdermilk, emphasized the exciting potential of being a forestry pioneer: "Scientific forestry is a virgin field in China from almost every standpoint, and you will be one of the first foreigners in China who will have been in a position or had a mind to make a serious study of forestry conditions and the problems which must be solved in order to better them." There would be no problem, Reisner wrote, in being given enough responsibility: "There is so much to be done in China and all of which is so necessary that I am quite sure that you will get into that particular line of work which will bring out the best that is in you."[58]

Before Reisner's letter had an opportunity to make its way from Nanjing to Missoula, Lowdermilk had fired off a testy letter to Reisner full of new questions about his going to China. The opportunity of serving the Chinese and the cause of forestry in general was appealing, as was the "possible international reputation" that Lowdermilk, without false modesty, planned to secure "if I make good." But he wanted to know more about "what is to be done for me and my family." The mission board's care for its charges had not impressed Lowdermilk: "You say that you will take good care of us. If you mean good care such as Miss Marks received formerly I do not consider it good enough for her, nor such as I propose that she have." Her care, Lowdermilk wrote, came "first of all—to put it rather bluntly—regardless of what becomes of the Chinese." Money was also a big worry. Lowdermilk declared that he did not "come under the category of a recruit in missionary work," and the financial sacrifice that he was being asked to make seemed un-reasonable. If he stayed in the United States, he would earn three or four times as much as in China.[59]

This time, Lowdermilk went too far; Reisner could make no more accommo-dations. In his reply, Reisner repeated the financial terms of the appointment, with an assurance that it would be "not only sufficient to live on most comfortably but will be sufficient, unless your tastes are extravagant, to save some money." Reisner was rankled that Lowdermilk did not regard himself as a missionary recruit. This notion was mistaken: "We are all doing missionary work and its Christian sig-nificance depends entirely upon our motive and purpose in doing it." Noting that Lowdermilk had not mentioned anything about Christian service in listing his reasons for coming to China, Reisner warned Lowdermilk that unless he felt the "real missionary possibilities and implications" of his work, "my very frank opinion would be to consider carefully before accepting the work at Nanking."[60]

Reisner added that "there has been no question at all in my mind of your missionary motive" and that he looked forward to the contributions that Lowder-milk and his fiancée would make to "our missionary and University community, perhaps I should say in our University missionary community, for it is all one and the same thing."[61] But Reisner was wrong; it was not all one and the same thing. The Lowdermilk case revealed how the church had to compromise its standards when searching for its ideal: the missionary-agriculturalist who combined religious fervor with technical expertise. In the end, Lowdermilk and Marks were married and came to Nanjing as originally planned, equipped for a long stay (and even for tennis and golf). But Lowdermilk was interested in forestry and soil conservation, not in spreading the Gospel. He spent most of his time on land surveys and taught infrequently, which was exactly what he had originally planned to do. He even secured the international reputation for which he had hoped. Although he and his wife lived in China for only five years, from 1922 to 1927, he made important discoveries of soil erosion in north China. He went on to high posts in the U.S. Forest Service and to appointments as consultant to Mexico, Algeria, Morocco, Tunisia, Yugoslavia, Japan, and the United Nations. China had given him inter-national visibility, yet he had used his missionary appointment to pursue strictly lay interests. The vexatious recruitment of specialists like Lowdermilk may have advanced agriculture and forestry in China, but it did not contribute to the spread of Christianity.

✣ ✣ ✣ ✣ ✣

John Lossing Buck, unlike Lowdermilk, began with the perfect combination of technical expertise and missionary commitment. Still, retaining such a person and his ideals in the field proved to be extremely difficult. Buck had been born in 1890 and reared on a farm near Poughkeepsie, New York. Maintaining his family-nurtured religious interests while at the state agricultural college at Cornell in the early 1910s, he participated in a Bible study group that met weekly. Its leader was John Reisner, then a graduate student who was soon to leave for Nanking with his master's degree. After Buck graduated in 1914, he spent a frustrating year employed at a New York reformatory farm, charged with using farm work and fresh air to transform juvenile delinquents into responsible young men. He then pledged service in the Student Volunteer Movement to do mission work abroad. He declined an invitation to go to India, waiting instead for the opportunity to go to China. In 1915 he got what he wanted: assignment as an agricultural missionary to a tiny rural station at Nansuzhou, Anhui.[62]

When Buck arrived in China in 1916, he had a B.S. in agriculture and a strong desire to serve the church. He wrote home, "The great pressing need of China is Christianity and education. I am mighty glad I have come, the field is unlimited."[63] After a few unsuccessful weeks of language study at the University of Nanking, Buck gave up and headed for his post at Nansuzhou. On his way, he stopped for a while at a resort where the foreign missionary community spent its summers. There he met Pearl Sydenstricker, the daughter of longtime China missionaries. Her parents did not consider Buck's assignment of teaching farmers to be true missionary work, and they regarded Buck, with his agricultural degree, as a bumpkin unsuitable for their daughter. Despite her parents' disapproval, Sydenstricker and Buck quickly became engaged and were married the next year.[64]

Their first home, Nansuzhou, was anything but romantic. Located on the dry, desolate north China plain, a market town distinguished only by its immense city wall and protective moats, Nansuzhou was surrounded by countryside that was some of the most impoverished in China. The new Mrs. Buck described her first impression: "Outside the walls and beyond the moat the countryside stretched as flat as any desert, earth and houses were all dust color, even the people, for the fine sandy soil was dusted into their hair and skin by the incessant winds."[65] Her husband was undaunted. Here was an excellent opportunity to improve Chinese agriculture, which would enable Christian farmers to better support the church financially and non-Christians to accept the teachings of Christianity. For Buck, agriculture was to be used as "a practical way of teaching Christianity and as a means of making friends."[66]

Buck's work got off to a slow start. It took two years of language study (still unsuccessful) and bicycle excursions into the neighboring countryside before he was ready to form definite plans about where to begin his agricultural work. He decided to establish a test farm for experiments, a demonstration farm for a model, and a school program for farm boys. Young students, he felt, would more readily accept new ideas "as compared with the ignorant farmer, who can be best reached through farm demonstration work." Buck planned to show his students that "farming is a very well worth while occupation, and that there is more to it than mere drudgery." The school that he had in mind would be "based largely on the principles in vogue at Hampton Institute" (a Virginia vocational school for blacks staffed by whites only—its founder, General Samuel C. Armstrong, believed that "negroes needed white leadership in education").[67]

Buck wanted to buy a single large tract of land for his various projects, as in the United States, but this proved impossible in Anhui, "owing to the fact that land is owned in such small portions and to the feeling amongst Chinese against selling land unless absolutely necessary." For the moment, Buck settled for the lease of a few acres to begin experimental comparisons between the yields of Chinese and American wheat varieties. He found, however, that it was difficult to grow the American wheat "without some of it being stolen for seed by the natives." The thefts made yield comparisons inconclusive; however, if not prompted by curiosity, the thefts provided an informal testimonial to the apparent superiority of the new American varieties.[68]

With a group of two dozen high-school boys, Buck began an informal general-agriculture class that met for three hours a week, with an additional three hours of work in the individual garden plots that Buck marked out for each student. Buck was pleased with his pupils: "In a land where manual labor is considered such a disgrace it did one's heart good to see the boys go out there and work with enthusiasm." But he observed that local farmers seemed to be quite conservative and untouched by new ideas, even though Nansuzhou was located on the Tianjin-Pukou rail line. "The people," he wrote, "are very backward in starting or accepting anything new."[69]

Buck had to learn, however, that some of his new ideas would not work. Among his early mistakes was an attempt to promote an improved American plow with an iron beam, which proved too heavy for the local farmers to carry on their shoulders from home to often distant fields. He also encouraged farmers to grow grass as a forage hay, until one farmer pointed out that Chinese millet provided a source of forage and was an edible grain at the same time. And early in his apprenticeship at Nansuzhou, Buck was unaware of the "right to glean," a customary privilege of anyone in the Chinese countryside. Anxious to plow under wheat stubble to add organic matter to the soil, Buck one day waved off gleaners who were waiting at the edge of his experimental field for their opportunity to comb the field. It was a mistake. A colleague informed Buck that his action had earned him the less-than-endearing nickname of "foreign dog."[70]

Despite these initial problems, Buck believed that since he was a farm boy, he naturally knew how to talk with and engage Chinese farmers. Later, he reminisced about his technique in China:

> The important thing is when you go out and see the farmer plowing or hoeing, the thing is to talk with him about what he is doing. If the soil is dry and a little hard to hoe, when you first greet him you say, "It's pretty hard, isn't it, hoeing today? We haven't had any rain for some time." In that way he knows that you understand his situation. Then you have an entree immediately. I used to go out

and if a farmer was plowing ... I would say, "Let me try plowing." The farmers would laugh at first—it sure is funny, this foreigner here trying to plow—but it worked.[71]

The image that Buck's description evokes is that of two men, one American and one Chinese, separated by different nationalities but readily finding their shared rootedness to the soil.

One wonders whether Buck actually had such satisfying encounters, however. His Chinese-language skill remained so poor that he was dependent upon his wife to act as a translator, and even if his own foreign presence did not create a commotion, hers certainly did. Consider the very different image, based on a contemporary letter, of Lossing and Pearl Buck when they decided to visit a mission station sixty miles away. It was not an inconspicuous entourage—Buck, a tall American perched on a bicycle, accompanied by his wife, carried in a curtained sedan chair that was shouldered by four "coolies." Pearl wrote to her mother-in-law that all along the way they encountered people "who had never seen a white woman and were wildly curious about me. In one place they tried to take the top off the chair to see me better." With "literally hundreds of people" packed against her chair, she and her husband must have presented an interesting sight.[72]

Buck was probably most effective not when he went out to farmers but when farmers came to see him. The accomplishment in which he took the most pride was organizing a 1919 course in agriculture for adult farmers; with a dramatic flourish, Buck announced Nansuzhou's first agricultural class "in over four thousand years." The class, which consisted of twelve clearly well-educated landlords, was actually taught by Buck's Chinese assistant, who was one of the first graduates of the College of Agriculture at the University of Nanking, and it met for one hour a day for two months during the winter. Buck's greatest frustration was the lack of books in Chinese on general agriculture.[73]

Working with these landlords gave Buck an opportunity to try to combine church and agricultural interests. Although he viewed agricultural improvement as a means by which interest in and economic support for the church would be strengthened, in practice he unconsciously reversed matters and used the church to help further the cause of improved agriculture. A member of the local church, a large absentee landowner known to Buck as Mr. Hwang, was "one of the many who are loafing and have no interest in life." But Buck counseled Mr. Hwang to change his indolent ways, and soon Hwang had removed tenants from some of his land and was farming it himself (a development that Buck cheered). Hwang had even become interested in buying a foreign harrow, if only one could be found.[74]

Yet even when he felt he was making some progress, such as with Hwang, Buck found maddening frustrations in his work, and these became harder to bear as his initial enthusiasm for fieldwork wore off. Hwang's interest in an American tool that Buck had no way of obtaining for him underscored the limits imposed by

Nansuzhou's remoteness. The Shanghai agents for agricultural implement companies were unwilling to loan Buck's mission station any tools for demonstration. Buck lamented, "Unless the companies themselves will loan samples for demonstration work as an advertisement for possible future sales, it will be necessary to purchase them outright and this cannot be done with present funds." Buck knew that mechanized irrigation would help local farmers contend with a drought that had persisted for three years, but again, lack of funds placed the simple pumps out of reach.[75]

Similar instances when he could not provide simple assistance, Buck complained, "can be multiplied by the dozen," and he had little hope of enlarged resources. The Chinese government offered no prospect of funding agricultural improvement work until its worth had been demonstrated, and this, Buck felt, was "doubly so in a locality of such 'good for nothing' officials as we have here." Buck appealed directly to American mission supporters for financial assistance. Anticipating a common question, he asked rhetorically, "Why don't we secure funds for [the agricultural mission work] by growing crops and produce for sale and in this way be a little easier on the pocketbooks of others?" His answer was that it was "pretty hard to earn money to run a department financially and at the same time accomplish much in the way of education among the farmers." He explained to his American readers that "it is undoubtedly a great deal easier for many at home to earn this money and in much larger amounts than it is for us out here in a strange land."[76]

The requested funds never came, and problems seemed to outweigh successes. For most of 1919, no Chinese agriculturalist could be found to serve as an assistant; this was a crippling problem. Agricultural work was also limited, Buck complained, by the aggravations attendant upon the building of their home: "Building in China is an entirely different proposition than it is in America owing to the fact that there are no reliable Chinese contractors and to the fact that most of them have to be told how to do a great deal of their work." And the foreign community in Nansuzhou, never large to begin with, dwindled to one other couple, making the post even lonelier than it had been.[77]

The wider political environment also became increasingly difficult to ignore. When Buck's landlord-students formed their own agricultural society, local military officials stepped in and appropriated it for their own purposes. The officials assumed the society's offices of president and vice president and ensured that the organization would accomplish little. Moreover, the militarization of the Anhui countryside was hard to overlook when local warlords battled in and around the town. As Pearl Buck wrote to her in-laws, "This week we had a real battle. Once Lossing ran outside and a bullet just missed his head, so after that we all stayed indoors and away from windows."[78]

Under such conditions, little headway in agricultural work seemed possible; moreover, Lossing Buck's interest in the religious side to his mission assignment had faded considerably since he had arrived in China four years before. Then, in 1920, when his mission work was most in need of a boost, he was told that funding for his agricultural mission would be discontinued. The news provided an occasion to escape the frustrations of the field, for John Reisner invited Buck to join the faculty at the University of Nanking. The Bucks were delighted to move.

The Nansuzhou years were important to Pearl Buck, who later used her experiences there to write *The Good Earth* and thus begin a popular literary career. But for Lossing Buck, Nansuzhou ended his career as a missionary in the field. When he moved to Nanjing, he became a desk-bound academic. Pioneer agricultural missionaries such as Reisner and Groff could call for volunteers like Lowdermilk or Buck to join them, but Lowdermilk was based on a campus, as Reisner and Groff were, and Buck moved from the field to the campus at the first opportunity. As long as the voices that called for an agricultural mission movement in China came from the campus rather than from the field, the movement's limited influence on the Chinese countryside was inevitable. The isolation imposed by the university's walls exacerbated the cultural separateness that kept American missionaries apart from the China that surrounded them.

5

COMPETITION

King Cotton and Collegiate Rivalry, 1920s

An American visitor touring China in 1925 tried to convince a group of Chinese students that American farmers were in desperate economic straits. The speaker told of a Wisconsin farm family whom he knew personally. The family had been so devastated by the recent drop in wheat prices that its seven grown children had been forced to leave the farm and go to the city to seek a living. But after listening to the story, the Chinese asked a few questions and learned that

> this family has a large home, grain silos, barns, over 10,000 *mou* of land, many cattle and horses, plus two cars, two pianos, electric lights, telephone, running water.... Can you imagine how this kind of farm family, with the loss of one or two years' income, becomes "very pitiful"? If you compare this with the living standards of our country's farmers, what a difference there is![1]

The difference between the two countries suggested to some Chinese that America should be used as a model. "China Should Adopt the American Policy of Promoting Agriculture," proposed the title of a Chinese magazine editorial that appeared in 1911. It noted that Japan offered an undeniable success story, but that the experience of an island country could not guide a country as large as China. The United States, however, was comparable in size and had achieved "surprising" success in its agricultural development, based upon scientific advances, motorized transport, ingenious agricultural machines, government support of agricultural specialists, and a protective trade policy. Like other articles that were to appear with increasing frequency in the Chinese press, this editorial reflected China's search abroad for solutions to its agricultural problems.[2]

The Chinese were impressed by America's own boasts. Peng Jiayuan, a Chinese analyst of American agriculture, translated for his readers in China a long section taken from the 1921 USDA Annual Report:

> America produces 70% of the world's corn, 60% of the world's cotton, 50% of the world's tobacco leaf . . . 20% of the world's wheat, 13% of the world's

barley.... Average figures show that each American farmer can produce 12 tons of agricultural products. The average of the farmers in other countries is only 1.4 tons per person.

Peng explained that the bounty of American agriculture stemmed from one thing, and one thing only: "Science." [3]

✧ ✧ ✧ ✧ ✧

Early in the twentieth century, Chinese students began to earn degrees at American agricultural colleges, expecting to learn practical knowledge that they could apply to problems in the Chinese countryside. Young Hu Shih was typical of many of his fellow Chinese students. He enrolled in 1910 at the New York State College of Agriculture at Cornell University, choosing agriculture, he later recalled, based "on the belief then current in China that a Chinese student must learn some useful art." (An additional motive, he said, was to save money to send home: the College of Agriculture charged no tuition.) Like most of the other Chinese students who enrolled at agricultural schools in the United States, Hu Shih had no prior experience working in fields. [4]

The curriculum of the American agricultural college, Hu discovered, was not designed to serve Chinese agriculture. At Cornell, one seminar in particular infuriated him—pomology. The course was supposed to survey fruit growing, but in the state of New York this meant "more strictly the science of apple growing." In their laboratory sessions, students were required to identify dozens of varieties of apples, which the American students already seemed to know. Hu and his Chinese compatriots cut up the fruit, struggled to distinguish "signs of identification," and searched for the proper scientific names in the pomological manuals, while the American students were able to leave the lab early, with their uncut, properly identified apples tucked in their pockets. [5]

Before examinations, Hu could memorize enough material to do well, but he doubted the utility of knowing the names of the four-hundred-odd varieties of apples then known, most of which were not to be found in China. After three semesters of frustration, he decided that the study of agriculture was "sheer waste" and transferred to the College of Arts and Sciences, where he indulged his personal interest in philosophy, a pursuit that later earned him much fame.

Other Chinese students felt similar frustrations at American agricultural schools, but most completed their degrees nevertheless. Their numbers were not large—perhaps as few as forty students were enrolled at agricultural colleges in the United States at any given time during the 1910s and 1920s—but they did bring back to China a critical and sophisticated perspective on the question that D. Hoe Lee, studying at Ohio State University, succinctly posed in 1918: "What can China learn from American agriculture?" [6]

Lee answered the question by emphasizing the things that China should not learn. "While power machinery," he noted as an example, "is a dominant factor in making American agriculture profitable, its hasty introduction on Chinese farms will not only bring about unnecessary bankruptcy, but will beyond doubt [raise] undesirable disturbances among farm [workers] resulting from the rejection of their services." He suggested that "in order to acquire some knowledge directly applicable on Chinese farms with as little variation as possible, the student ought to go to an institution in such a locality as bears a close comparison in natural surroundings to the place where his future work is intended." [7]

Few of the Chinese students who earned an agricultural degree in the United States stayed in agriculture upon their return to China. Lee wrote, "It may be said with no hesitation that a great part of the total energy spent by former students of American agriculture has become wasted, viewing that only a small percentage of the returned agriculturalists are working along agricultural lines." Chinese journals often echoed the same note of disappointment, though one experienced rural worker, Zhang Fuliang, took a more sympathetic stance and spoke up in defense of the returned graduate who ended up in the city: "Unless he is a saint or a fanatic, the temptations of living away from the farm are too great for him to resist." Some Chinese writers blamed the students themselves for lacking a farm background and a strong commitment to agriculture. An editorial in a Chinese farm journal claimed that Chinese students who left for American agricultural schools had never been to the Chinese countryside and "wouldn't even be able to tell wheat from beans." And like Lee, other Chinese writers emphasized the inappropriateness of the foreign curriculum for help in addressing agricultural problems in China. Deng Zhiyi, author of a 1923 essay entitled "A Comparison of Chinese and American Agriculture," questioned whether China had anything to learn from the United States. Deng pointed out that China was much more "efficient" than America, raising food for twenty times as many people on a given unit of land. [8]

✤ ✤ ✤ ✤ ✤

With the utility of their foreign educations frequently challenged and with few opportunities to pursue a career in agriculture upon their return, the Chinese students with agricultural degrees from American schools faced bleak professional prospects. They had to wait for the development of a stronger institutional apparatus dedicated to agricultural education and research. One institution in particular, the College of Agriculture and Forestry at the University of Nanking, funded and administered by Americans, took the lead and did the most to call Chinese attention both to the importance of agriculture and to the role that American expertise could play in developing China's agricultural resources. When John Reisner took over as dean after Joseph Bailie left the fledgling college (see chap. 3), he aggressively expanded the activities of the school, campaigned to increase public concern about the state of Chinese agriculture, and then channeled that concern toward benefiting his institution and increasing its ability to offer assistance. Almost every aspect of agriculture and forestry needed improvement, and Reisner tried to address every problem that appeared. Continuing in the tradition of Bailie, Reisner was fond of exhorting everyone to greater efforts for the cause. His terse slogan was "Interest! Enthusiasm! Work!"[9]

As he had seen Cornell's agriculture faculty do in Ithaca, Reisner tried to make the college at Nanking a center of service to the farmers of the area. He published a pamphlet entitled "What the College of Agriculture and Forestry Can Do for You!" in which he explained in English the multifarious services offered by the college. Vegetable and flower seeds, shade and forest trees, improved corn and other field seeds, spray pumps, planters, and plows were available at the college "at very reasonable prices." Pecans and black walnuts were free to whomever wanted to plant them. A plant identification program offered to send to the United States any specimens that the staff members themselves could not identify. Various college publications were distributed and questions about any aspect of agriculture were answered as fully as the staff was able: "We are not specialists in everything and some questions may have to go unanswered. Your letters, however, will be answered."[10]

These vigorous efforts to develop extension services, even before the college had much to offer, were characteristically American. But Reisner was not an uncritical proponent of applying American methods to Chinese agriculture. For example, he did not encourage the introduction of American farm machinery where agricultural conditions were fundamentally different. "In the United States," he pointed out, "production is measured per capita while in China high production per unit of land must be the goal." Labor-saving machinery from America was simply inappropriate for the crowded Chinese landscape.[11]

Reisner viewed chemical fertilizers with equal skepticism, even though there was considerable talk in China at the time that such chemicals were essential to the improvement of Chinese agriculture. Ideally, they could be important, Reisner granted, but practically speaking, their advantages over night soil had not been demonstrated. Night soil would prove to be "the keenest of competitors when commercial fertilizers enter the field." The supply of human waste was constant, its price cheap, and its acceptance by Chinese farmers long established.[12]

To demonstrate the impracticality of substituting commercial chemical fertilizers for night soil, Reisner offered some persuasive arithmetic. First, he estimated the total annual production of night soil. Assuming annual human feces production of "1,073 pounds per capita" (an interesting figure, from an unspecified source), Reisner calculated annual production in China of about 428 billion pounds, estimating that two-thirds of this was saved and used as fertilizer. The amount of nitrogen, phosphoric acid, and potash that it provided, if purchased commercially as chemical fertilizer, would cost $500 million. Reisner asked how an individual farmer could be expected to pay for commercial fertilizer and give up the use of night soil, which provided the same results at a fraction of the cost.[13]

The one role that Reisner did see for chemical fertilizers was as a supplement to balance the high nitrogen content of night soil. But he ruled out promotion of American imports and instead called for the development of Chinese sources of phosphate and potash. He also advised China to protect its own interests and prohibit the export of bones, which were an important source of phosphates but sold in large quantities and at low prices to the fertilizer industry in Japan.[14]

✥ ✥ ✥ ✥ ✥

Instead of imposing American chemical fertilizers upon a country that could not afford them, Reisner sought to expand agricultural production in China by scientific improvement of the country's own products and crops. His early emphasis on indigenous products led Reisner to try to improve sericulture, a field for which Cornell had not provided training. But Reisner was willing to learn, and with financial assistance from the Silk Association of America, among others, he launched a sericulture research project that tinkered with an eclectic range of methods from China, France, Japan, and the United States.

Disease afflicted an astounding percentage of Chinese silkworms—the college found that 61 percent of 12,000 moths it examined were diseased. An inexpensive, easy means of identifying diseased eggs needed to be devised so that problems could be caught early. In France, Louis Pasteur had devised a method of placing each silk moth in a paper bag to lay its eggs. The moth was then removed, crushed, and examined under a microscope. If any signs of disease were visible, the eggs in the bag were discarded. This was an effective system, but cumbersome if tens of thousands of moths needed testing. The Japanese used a simpler method whereby a large number of moths laid their eggs on one large piece of cardboard, rather than in paper bags, but it was difficult to keep the eggs from each moth separate.[15]

Nanking tried to combine the best features of the Japanese and European systems by using a large sheet of cardboard for the egg-laying process and keeping the moth eggs separated in tall cardboard cylinders, which were cheap and reusable. The researchers immodestly hailed their discovery as one that would perhaps "be one of the greatest contributions yet made" in sericulture improvement.[16]

Next, as an experiment to see if the incidence of disease could be controlled by low temperatures, the researchers placed silkworm eggs in a cold storage plant in Nanjing for the winter. When the eggs were brought out in the spring and warmed up, the resulting crop of silkworms was found to have a much lower than average incidence of disease. The project staff also worked on an improved way of hatching the eggs. With the traditional method, the eggs were wrapped in cotton and then worn next to a person's body for five or six days, until the young worms appeared. This was a technique that a college publicity release said "might seem humorous to the mind of the layman," but it did not provide the silkworm with a constant temperature and adequate ventilation (nor the wearer with much comfort). By converting an American poultry-egg incubator into a silkworm incubator, the research team found a solution to the problem of temperature control.[17]

The college also inaugurated a three-month short course in sericulture for any interested persons, but the courses and innovations failed to have much effect, even in Nanjing. Five years after the excited announcement of new sericulture discoveries, the *Chinese Economic Bulletin* reported that "most of the local farmers in Nanking still cling to time-honored methods." Eight different diseases had been identified as afflicting the local silkworms, and most could be prevented by giving greater care to proper feeding. But, the *Bulletin* said, "Nanking silk farmers, being ignorant of these causes, call all diseases 'plague,' which they think is beyond their power to check or prevent." [18]

Moreover, even those farmers who received specialized training at the College of Agriculture had difficulty applying their newly obtained knowledge when the silk economy was depressed and their personal financial means were limited. The American-inspired incubator was still unaffordable for most. Graduates of the "new school" of sericulture were observed to be careful about lighting and ventilation, but temperature and humidity control continued to elude even the most conscientious of them, because the needed equipment was too expensive to be found anywhere but in the showcase rooms on campus.[19]

✣ ✣ ✣ ✣ ✣

To Reisner, the American efforts to improve Chinese sericulture represented the success of Yankee ingenuity applied to an unfamiliar problem. Still, sericulture remained too foreign to sustain the interest of American agriculturalists. Cotton fell within more familiar territory, and the largest effort in plant improvement work at the college was directed at applying American expertise to improving Chinese cotton. Significantly, the high priority attached to cotton improvement was not the result of Chinese analysis of China's top agricultural needs but was instigated by Walter T. Swingle, a visitor from the U.S. Department of Agriculture. Swingle was head of the USDA's Office of Crop Physiology and was interested in Asia, like David Fairchild, his USDA colleague who had earlier dispatched agricultural explorers to the region (see chap. 1). When Swingle visited China in 1918, he casually observed diverse mixtures of cotton varieties. He decided on the spot that China needed to develop pure cotton varieties and that the United States could help. When he returned to Washington, he persuaded the USDA's principal cotton authority, O. F. Cook, to do a more thorough study. John B. Griffing, a cotton specialist who was then working on pure seed production in Arizona, was recruited to serve as assistant.[20]

Swingle's passing interest in Chinese cotton soon led to a massive testing and improvement program that was based at the University of Nanking. Other Chinese institutions copied Nanking, and researchers in China soon had little attention to spare for any other crop. The program started modestly however.

Before visiting China, Cook sent seed packets for planting in a variety of locations as a test. Unfortunately, the Chinese were not made partners in the project. Cook sent the seeds to the American commercial attaché, Julean Arnold. Arnold entrusted John Reisner with the task of distribution, and Reisner, in turn, relied on intramural missionary contacts to carry out the test plantings. At the time, using Reisner and the University of Nanking must have seemed a natural way of avoiding the vexations of working with Chinese officials and poorly educated Chinese specialists. But it was, in fact, a case of unilateral operation. China was to be the laboratory, but no Chinese were called upon to participate in the experiment.

Funding came from the "Chinese Cotton Millowners' Association," which, despite its title, was composed of foreign enterprises—mostly British—that had a natural interest in improving the quality of local cotton. In the spring of 1919, Reisner wrote to more than two dozen missionary friends at stations scattered in six provinces in eastern and northern China. He explained, "The purpose of the experiment which we shall carry on is to find the one particular variety of foreign cotton which does best under the climatic and soil conditions under which it is planted. After this has been determined, *all other* varieties will be discarded." It was assumed that foreign varieties were superior to Chinese; the only question was which one was best suited to Chinese conditions.[21]

Reisner assured his friends that "the extension of cotton culture in China in the next ten years will be one of the most important agricultural developments, and foreign cotton will play a big part in it." With the promise of participating in an important project, and with Reisner's personal appeal for a favor, all the needed "cooperators" were secured. The USDA seed packets contained eight varieties that included a wide range of characteristics, and the test plantings that summer revealed several varieties that showed much more promise than the others. No attempt was made to quantitatively measure differences, but the gross results seemed quite clear. Trice, an early maturing, short-staple variety, did the best of all; two others, Acala and Lone Star, both with large bolls, also did well in areas where the cotton achieved maturation. Many stations reported that "the experiment was drowned out" or that "drought at the time of planting gave poor stand."[22]

At the end of the summer of 1919, Cook and Griffing arrived from America for a tour of the cotton districts, and at that point a member of China's Ministry of Agriculture and Commerce was invited to join the group in its survey of eight provinces. During their visit, the Americans repeated one message again and again: the importance of developing pure seed. After assessing the situation in person, however, they no longer automatically prescribed American varieties of cotton. First, they cautioned that expectations should be restrained: "It must not be understood that pure seed from the United States will give uniform plants in China, that produce pure seed. This is because of the variation that is induced by change in climatic conditions." If constant selection was necessary in the United

States to keep out variations in a given type, even where cotton was planted year after year under similar soil and climatic conditions, then "how much greater care in selection is necessary when the factor of acclimatization is introduced." Moreover, the American experts decided to take a second look at Chinese varieties. If a pure variety of Chinese cotton could be developed, considerable improvement over existing yields seemed likely. The problem, they believed, was that there probably was not a single stand of "pure" Chinese cotton in the entire country.[23]

✧ ✧ ✧ ✧ ✧

In 1920, the University of Nanking decided to launch a formal cotton improvement program, which was aimed at acclimatizing an American type of cotton and creating an improved strain from native varieties. O. F. Cook had returned to Washington, and the university hired John Griffing to direct the new project, with the Cotton Millowners agreeing to provide funds for three years. The cotton work gave the College of Agriculture a definite direction, outside funds, and much publicity, although no one paused to ask whether cotton was the crop that deserved to be the object of the first concerted plant-improvement project in China. Griffing was well trained, with a B.A. from Drake, a B.S. from Kansas Agricultural College, and an M.A. from Columbia. But his specialty was cotton and he looked at nothing else; the broader agenda of China's agricultural needs did not concern him.

Griffing started his tenure in China sharply focused on what agriculturalists refer to as "cultural practices"—that is, the methods that foster plant growth. His early advice was technical, but sensible and sensitive to the varying character of the Chinese landscape. For Chinese who asked what type of land was best for cotton, he analyzed the different characteristics of Chinese soils in terms familiar to a Chinese farmer, although the touchstone was his experience with cotton growing in the United States. The best climate, he thought, was found in north China, where conditions most nearly resembled those of the southern United States: "Hot summers with abundant sunshine, dry air, and sufficient summer rainfall to maintain continuous growth give an ideal condition for the growth of the cotton plant." Only the lack of sufficient rainfall in north China presented a "limiting factor."[24]

Although anxious to initiate cotton research, Griffing did not want to spend time conducting tests at Chinese experiment stations. He wrote, "Practically nothing could be gained by adding one more [experiment station] to the list of stations already in China comparing varieties, cultural methods, etc." Griffing had been most unimpressed by the experiment stations that he had visited in China; the testing of varieties, "in spite of the attractive show and museum effect that it gives to station work," seemed wasteful and irrelevant: "The majority of the experiment stations . . . have been devoting their attention to elaborate tests of varieties or to various cultural methods, the spacing of rows of plants, and in general, what seemed to be an attempt to rediscover common facts already known to experienced cottongrowers. With nearly all variety tests the fact of cross pollination was disregarded and the seed replanted year after year, so that in most instances no actual varieties were really being compared, but only degenerating mixtures." Fortunately, Griffing said, the incompetence of the stations had prevented them from introducing their seed to farmers, so no great damage had been done.[25]

Griffing felt that superior American varieties were already in hand and that the primary task yet to be undertaken was creating, "in the shortest possible time," a commercial supply of the improved seed and a suitable organizational plan to introduce the seed to Chinese farmers. He decided to start by promoting two varieties that had done well in the test plantings. Trice offered an early maturation date; in north China it would beat the frost, and in central China its earliness would help prevent destruction from insects and diseases. The other variety, Acala, required ten days to two weeks longer to mature, but it had a finer lint and longer staple.

Neither Trice nor Acala had yet been introduced to China. Other American varieties of cotton had been imported for a number of years, but in no instance had their original quality and character been maintained. Griffing observed, "The general experience was apparent success at first, followed by degeneration, even to the grade of Chinese cotton, in a very short time." Specimens of degenerate American cotton could be found in nearly every field of Chinese cotton "save where an enterprising farmer hoes out such plants in disgust at their appearance."[26]

To avoid repeating past failures, acclimatization was necessary before the new American varieties could be distributed. "There is nothing magic or unpreventable about the deterioration of cotton varieties," explained Lawrence Balls, a cotton expert whom Griffing quoted in a pamphlet for Chinese readers. "Every case known can be explained in terms of crossing, seed mixture, and natural selection." Many farmers, Griffing warned, disregard the principles of heredity and find that in a few years a new seed variety turns inferior, or has "run out." Thinking that the problem is due to unfavorable soil or climate conditions, the farmer tries to recapture earlier results by bringing in new seed from a better environment. And because the fundamental problem is ignored, consistent results remain elusive.[27]

Griffing tried to explain the necessary scientific principles to his lay audience of American missionaries and Chinese farmers. One reason that cotton varieties deteriorated so quickly was that they had been "artifically raised to a high standard of perfection and utility by mass selection." When the artificially ideal conditions were removed, the variety tended to break up into differing forms and drift back into an inferior state. Another factor was "the effect of a radical change of environment such as moving from one country to another." In such circumstances, nature stimulated wider variations of the plant and more pronounced reversion to earlier types: "A stock of seed, though pure when imported and even though grown under conditions of isolation, will in the course of a few years become a mixture of types corresponding to a group of different varieties, which interbreed through cross fertilization of the flowers by insects, thus hastening the process of deterioration."[28]

Cotton fields in China displayed the results of unchecked deterioration of American varieties. Each field resembled no particular variety, yet showed the characteristics of many. Griffing observed, "Predominating in fields from older seed is a little bushy, wiry type of plant with small, rather fuzzy leaves, and a profusion of undersized bolls which when open show very short and weak lint. This is the typical degenerate specimen, often mistaken for a superior plant on account of the number of bolls, a fact still more unfortunate when we consider the reproduction of degenerate seed."[29]

To prevent deterioration when moving a plant to a new country, Griffing explained, the first task is to establish uniformity and "fix the type," by eliminating plants that are "off type" or "rogues." As soon as young plants are sufficiently developed to reveal visible differences, they are ready for "roguing." Griffing described the process:

> As one proceeds down a row it soon becomes evident that all the plants bear slight differences toward each other and here and there will be one that is radically different from the rest. Such a plant may attract the eye from some little distance because it is tall and spindling while its neighbors are stocky and compact; or it may be that its leaves are all deeply lobed, crinkly, and small, while the adjacent plants though similar in structure have broad smooth leaves. It is the plant which bears a marked difference to the majority which is the rogue and should be pulled.[30]

No fixed percentage of plants were to be destroyed. At the university, no less than about a third of the new cotton plants were rogued to purify the type, with no concern for the high cost. Individual farmers could not afford such losses, however, and for them Griffing recommended the destruction of "only plants that were distinctly bad," or about 5 to 8 percent of the plants. But he told the Chinese: "The more severe the roguing in the first years, the more quickly will the type be fixed."[31]

Griffing believed that few farmers would be experts in roguing. Aside from the necessary knowledge of botany and heredity, the work required patience. The master, he said, "must not only have a scholarly mind but he must be both willing and able to indulge in the physical hardship of spending the hottest days of the summer in walking up and down the rows of the field pulling undesirable plants." It was also something of an art: "The roguing of cotton like the welding of iron or swimming is an art in which success cannot be attained by the reading of books but only by persistent application to the practice." Rather than entrust the task to amateurs, Griffing felt that it was best to centralize the work and keep roguing in the hands of experts. The American practice seemed best, devoting "a certain area to seed farms where scientific roguing is practised, and then to plant the rogued

seed in all of the surrounding farms so that the rogued stock will not be con-
taminated and so that it may be multiplied for wider distribution."[32]

The college at Nanking established the first seed farm and launched what was
the most extensive plant-selection program ever attempted in China. The two
American species, Trice and Acala, were planted on widely distant seed farms
to prevent crossing. During the summer of the first year, about 30 percent of
the plants were pulled up and thrown away. Then seven thousand of the most
promising plants were picked, tagged, and taken to the laboratory for study. Ten
lint samples of each plant were measured and a hundred seeds of each were
weighed, a formidable task of detail work that was possible, Griffing noted, only
because of "the large number of interested students available for technical measure-
ment work and the low priced labor for simpler operations." Three hundred of the
best seeds of this select lot were grown the next year in progeny rows, supplying
the seed for distribution the next year. By 1922, within three years of the beginning of the project, the process of acclimatizing the two American varieties was
declared accomplished.[33]

✢ ✢ ✢ ✢ ✢

The successful introduction of American cotton varieties depended on more
than careful laboratory work, however, and formidable problems that lay beyond
the pleasant confines of the university campus became an increasing concern as the
project proceeded. John Reisner worried that impure cotton varieties, both native
and American, were spreading rapidly over broader areas of China. He maintained,
"It is a fact beyond refutation, that of seed grown in China and distributed last
spring not over an infinitesimal share of it was pure. The more the cotton growing
area is extended and cotton seed indiscriminately distributed, the greater will the
problems of improvement become." One Chinese agricultural-improvement
agency had recently distributed more than sixty varieties of cotton, an example of
what Reisner called "mistaken enthusiasm." There were no safeguards to prevent
native seed produced in insect-infested regions from being extended to new
regions, nor were there any controls on imported American seed to prevent the
introduction of new cotton insects and diseases to China. An unregulated chaos
prevailed.[34]

Reisner pointed to lessons that the United States had learned when plant
insects and diseases from foreign countries had caused severe cotton losses. Large
sums of money and strict controls had been needed to limit damage and prevent
the introduction of new pests. The U.S. government had instituted plant quaran-
tines, destroyed infested cotton acreage, banned cotton planting in infested areas,
monitored freight shipments of cottonseed, and inspected and fumigated all imported cotton. Reisner did not suggest that all such measures should or could be
practicably adopted in China, but he pushed for immediate action on controlling
foreign cottonseed imports. If imports were limited to one or two ports of entry,
he argued, then fumigation could be systematically carried out and the danger of

introducing pests and diseases reduced. But import controls were far beyond what a university could institute and administer itself.[35]

The American example was also held up by Griffing, who recounted the story of acclimatizing foreign cotton in Arizona. Twenty years before, superior varieties of Egyptian cotton had been introduced but had met with early failure. Yet the new cotton, Arizona Pima, had gone on to become "in many respects the best cotton to be found in the world" and commanded a better price in world cotton markets than the best grades from Egypt. The successful adaptation of the imported variety had depended on firm governmental controls. To prevent hybridization, no other type of cotton was permitted in the district where Pima was grown. Only pure seed of the Pima strain could be planted there, and a central seed farm, with specialists trained for roguing, provided a supply of seeds, thus ensuring that no seed more than two years removed from rogued plants was ever planted.[36]

Without similar policies in China, the effectiveness of Nanking's cotton improvement work would be quite limited. The most vexing problem was "the common policy of indiscriminate and widespread distribution of American varieties of varying character and a great deal of impure and degenerate seed." When the university was ready to distribute pure, acclimatized varieties, the "mongrel plants" would cross with the improved varieties, destroying their uniformity and quality. This was particularly aggravating because there was no botanical danger of the improved American cotton crossing with native Chinese varieties. Pure American seed could be easily maintained in a community even though native Chinese varieties were present, but only if there were no other American varieties in the vicinity.[37]

The prospects for successful maintenance of a pure American cotton seemed dim, but encouraging results had been achieved in the isolation of promising native Chinese varieties. The Nanking cotton project bragged about its own foresight: "Hitherto practically no interest had been taken in Chinese cotton by any experiment station, as attention was attracted to the apparently more spectacular possibilities of the foreign varieties." Actually, Nanking had also been bedazzled at the outset by the apparent superiority of American cotton. But Griffing and his assistants had seen that American cotton would not be appropriate for all areas in China. Since the American cotton matured three to four weeks later than the Chinese varieties, and the growing season near the coast was shorter than in the interior, a large proportion of the bolls never opened on American cotton in the coastal districts. Moreover, planting American cotton prevented the planting of a second crop of beans or a small grain, and one crop of American cotton could not earn the income of two traditional crops. Thus Nanking had decided to search for promising native varieties as well.[38]

To find a better variety of Chinese cotton, students combed hundreds of fields in various provinces in search of superior individual specimens, and selected more than a thousand plants that stood out from their neighbors. After laboratory study, the most promising three hundred were grown and multiplied for further testing. After three years and some forty thousand selections, progeny rows that required incredible attention were grown. Griffing reported: "The self pollination of all blossoms of the most likely plants has involved the making, the placing on the square, and the removing from the withered blossom, of several hundred thousand paper bags." The best cotton, a strain the students named "Million Dollar," was originally discovered near Wusong, Jiangsu, and produced lint that was pronounced by a Shanghai cotton broker to be "equal in value to standard American cotton." [39]

✧ ✧ ✧ ✧ ✧

By 1922, the preliminary results of the selection work on American and Chinese varieties showed dramatic gains in yield over common varieties. Exact comparisons were difficult because the improved seed was too precious to be planted in the usual generous fashion and thinned later; each seed had to be carefully spaced at the desired distance at which the plants were to grow. Even so, Trice on one plot produced almost double the lint of a common Chinese variety. The college was ready to send the seeds out to the farmers.

Initially, the seed supply was so limited that only a small number of willing farmers exhausted it. But Griffing saw that large-scale extension would not be easy for a number of reasons—some peculiar to China, others not. Griffing was quite sympathetic to Chinese farmers who resisted the introduction of the new cotton varieties. "In the first place," he explained, "practically all farmers depend absolutely for their living on a comparatively small area of land and the margin of subsistence is so small that no risks may be taken. Any new crop, even though it seems to give promise of greater returns, is tried with reluctance and then only on a very small area, for the farmer feels that only the crops that he has grown all his life and are true and tried may be counted dependable." [40]

The predatory social conditions of rural China at the time also interfered with extension work. In one area, farmers who had been quite impressed with the size of the bolls of American cotton nevertheless refused to plant it because "others would steal it." Theft was so prevalent that even ordinary Chinese cotton was stolen from fields at night unless picked prematurely by the owner. For other crops, an American tried to persuade farmers in one village to replace the traditional sickle with a cradle, an improved American-style hand tool for harvesting, and demonstrated the new tool's usefulness in a field demonstration. It cut eleven times faster than a sickle, and the villagers, duly impressed, agreed to consider its adoption. But two weeks later the villagers announced that they had decided as a group not to use the new cradle, reasoning that its adoption would mean that thieves working at night would be able to take advantage of the new tool's speed and would steal eleven times as much as before. Better that no one had the tool. [41]

In most areas, Chinese farmers viewed extension agents as representatives of a corrupt officialdom, and damaging stories circulated about extortion and trickery.

Griffing wrote, "When the plan of giving out tickets good for a small quantity of cotton seed was tried, the farmers about Hochow all shied at them, inasmuch as a previous distribution of mysterious tickets had turned out to be a forerunner of a special tax collection." At Wujiang, many farmers were afraid to accept pure seed samples because local officials had made a "free" distribution of mulberry trees in the interests of "agricultural improvement," and had later returned to collect for them at treble their original value.[42]

Before he had begun to actively extend the new cotton, Griffing had been quite harsh in his criticism of Chinese conservatism and resistance to change. He had written: "There is the problem of the farmer himself. Although in every country the farmer represents the most conservation [sic] element, here his habits are fixed by centuries of custom. He obeys the mandates of the rural deities rather than the printed advice of experiment station experts which he cannot read." Even when presented with a superior product, the Chinese farmer rejected it simply because it was "different." For example, Chinese farmers commonly rejected American cotton because its bolls pointed in the "wrong" direction, sticking up instead of down. Griffing was critical of such apparent irrationality: "In this [the Chinese farmer] overlooks the fact that the downward droop of the Chinese boll necessitates picking the crop every three or four days to save it from falling to the ground while the American type is considered stormproof and can have its pickings a month apart."[43]

Not long after he had lectured on the stubborn conservatism of Chinese farmers, however, Griffing gained more experience by talking with farmers out in the field and adopted a more sympathetic attitude. In his eyes, Chinese farmers were still conservative, a "characteristic of the farmer group throughout the world." But the factors that strengthened their conservative nature were beyond the responsibility of the individual: "illiteracy, age old customs, farm practices ingrained with superstitions, and the indifference of city landlords who control the cropping policy of their tenants and resent any change in the fixed habits of rent collection." The example that Griffing had used earlier to point out how the superiority of American cotton was insufficiently appreciated by the hidebound Chinese he now saw in a new light: since the bolls on American cotton turned up instead of down, they were more vulnerable to the fungus diseases that afflicted cotton in the humid cotton-growing districts. The attachment of Chinese farmers to familiar native-cotton varieties was not as irrational as Griffing had first thought.[44]

Still, Griffing regarded China as similar to "that part of the United States where the farmers are the most conservative and illiterate; viz., in the cotton belt of the South." He decided to use the extension techniques pioneered by Seaman Knapp, which had "revolutionized" agriculture in the American South in recent years—demonstration farms, boys' clubs, and exhibits. In China, Griffing planted improved cotton along well-traveled highways as a kind of advertisement for the project. In the fall, the college organized country fairs with displays of improved crops and new tools, accompanied by entertainment to draw in the curious. Huge posters extolled the benefits of planting the improved cotton varieties, and pictorial symbols of crops and coins made the message clear to those who could not read: one *mou* of rice earned only a few coins (captioned $6.20), while one *mou* of acclimatized American cotton earned a treasure of coins ($12.70) that filled up the poster.[45]

An audience hungry for live entertainment was willing to overlook heavy-handed didacticism and welcome the play that was staged at each fair. Written and acted by students of the college, the melodrama narrated the story of a cotton farmer who, discouraged with his harvests, resorted to "superstitious idol worship." But when a Christian pastor introduced the farmer to an extension agent from Nanking, the farmer was able to purchase better seed and was shown improved ways to plant and cultivate his cotton crop. The profits from the resulting harvest meant new clothes for his family and school for his sons. A conservative neighbor, who had scoffed at the new seeds and new methods, was left sinking into heavy debt.[46]

The college's traveling show piqued interest in the new cotton varieties, but it was left to rural mission stations to distribute the seed and provide instruction and advice to the farmers. Provincial and county governments were bypassed in the project because Griffing lacked personal contacts, language skills, and respect for extension work that the Chinese offices had accomplished to date. The mission stations offered a convenient network of rural "offices" that were already in place in the field and staffed by highly educated people. Since their personnel were often foreign and were "working for community improvement," Griffing felt that the missionaries were "especially appreciative of the value of crop improvement." Where government extension workers would encounter popular hostility in the field, missionaries would enjoy popular trust, Griffing believed, because the Chinese farmers had "learned in times of famine or sickness that the mission works for their good and without mercenary motives."[47]

✥ ✥ ✥ ✥ ✥

Although Griffing was confident that American varieties of cotton could help China dramatically increase production, he was careful not to claim that American machinery should be imported as well. A number of limitations restricted the suitability of foreign implements for cotton production in China—a lack of working capital, a general "lack of adaptation" to China's type of "fields, animals, and workmen," the mechanical complexity of the machines "with parts easily lost or broken if the operation is not understood," and difficulty in securing repairs and parts.[48]

Only a small number of tools and machines seemed appropriate and affordable for Chinese farmers. One was an old-fashioned American plow that had been invented in the early nineteenth century: its chilled metal point could be inexpensively replaced when dulled. Other foreigners had tried to promote more modern steel-pointed plows, which Griffing discovered had "nearly everywhere been thrown into the scrap heap because of the inability of country blacksmiths to sharpen and temper a steel share." The college imported ninety chilled-point plows, demonstrated their usefulness in the field, and sold them at cost to whomever was interested.[49]

No phrase had yet been coined to describe what the project was groping toward, but Griffing and Reisner were clearly concerned with finding "appropriate technology" for the impoverished and labor-intensive agricultural economy of China. Another tool that the college promoted was a newly designed cultivator, which could be made with local materials for a very modest sum and could "quickly pay for itself in the labor saved by cutting down the hoeing operations." Work on improving traditional Chinese irrigation pumps was also begun, and the one form of modern American machinery that seemed to have an important role to play in China, the cotton gin, was adapted to the different seeds and lint of native Chinese cotton. In a market town in Anhui, a demonstration gin was installed in a rented storefront strategically located at a busy corner. Farmers occupied themselves with exhibits in one room while their cotton was ginned in the other. The increased efficiency of the imported machinery enabled the service to charge less than native gins yet still pay its own way.[50]

The real showpiece was a power gin that was built at the central seed farm in Nanjing; it handled all of the area's cotton with ease. Using blueprints and iron parts supplied by the Continental Gin Company of America, Chinese craftsmen built a giant press to form the ginned cotton into compact bales that reduced losses in transport. Griffing declared, "It should be the duty of every seed farm to demonstrate not only efficient ginning but compact pressing and efficient marketing of the product in high class condition."[51]

Like Joseph Bailie before him, John Griffing wanted to incorporate the large areas of fallow land in the Nanjing area into his improvement project. Griffing thought that the "wild land" that grew nothing but grass was idle partly because of the difficulties in breaking up sod, and partly "because many areas once cultivated reverted to natural conditions when practically depopulated during the Tai Ping rebellion and have not yet been settled to the point of intensive cultivation." A team was sent from the college to Purple Mountain, where Bailie's Nanjing colony had quietly vanished into the grass, and plowed a tract for a demonstration plot of the improved cotton. Oblivious to the legal and political difficulties of appropriating idle land, Griffing excitedly wrote of the Purple Mountain field, "The establishing of this precedent has opened up a considerable field of opportunity in the expansion of the cotton growing area."[52]

The real importance of the plowing was not the psychological "precedent" but the technological advance it represented, for Griffing actually underestimated the importance of his own American plow. Until the introduction of this new implement, the Chinese had to break sod with a hand tool because native plows were too dull and fragile for the task. The traditional method of breaking the land was slow, expensive, and inefficient, since large clumps of sod were left and a newly created field could not produce much until the sod was broken down further, which usually took a year or two. The American plow turned an uneconomical, cumbersome task into an affordable, reasonable one, and several "gentry" farmers immediately began to shift from intensive to extensive agriculture, opening up new land and planting it with the improved cotton. Griffing praised the example of one man who had planted 150 *mou* (25 acres) of poor-quality upland fields and had earned over 1,561 *yuan* (about $800) from cotton. The success was attributed to his close attention to costs: "He is a careful student of both Chinese and modern methods of farming and is able to work out a semi-extensive system of operation that combines the economics of both." [53]

Griffing liked the Chinese farmer-entrepreneur who farmed and managed his own land, but he was unimpressed by nonfarming opportunists who tried to produce cotton as a form of agribusiness. The success of the individual farmer-entrepreneur demonstrated the possibilities of the new cotton varieties, techniques, and tools, but this system of farming, Griffing warned, "may not be easily duplicated by those who are less skilled in the art of farm management because of no practical experience." Land companies, formed by several men with land and capital, hired graduates of Chinese agricultural schools to serve as managers of ambitious cotton-growing ventures: "The number of such undertakings that has come to the writer's notice is astounding, but not a single instance has yet been discovered where the operation has proven profitable." Most quickly fell into bankruptcy or were abandoned. The reasons, Griffing felt, stemmed from the nature of the graduates, who had never worked on a farm until they arrived at the agricultural college. Then, the agricultural school provided "much theory but little practice," and attention was devoted to "that which is foreign and expensive or impractical rather than that which is a skilful selection and adaptation of those modern tools, methods, and ideas from foreign countries which tend to affect efficiency and economy under Chinese conditions." The policy of the college at Nanking was to discourage attempts to apply machinery designed for extensive agriculture in the United States to the intensive conditions of the lower Yangzi River valley in China. Griffing had little patience for "the use of tractors where plowing costs under local conditions would mount up to more than six times the cost of the same operations with the presumably old fashioned buffalo." [54]

The cotton improvement project at Nanking directed its educational efforts toward two separate audiences, the specialists and the general farming public. For the college's own students and graduates of other agricultural schools, translations of technical articles from the United States were distributed; for the farmer who could read only a little, simple vernacular was used in short instructional pamphlets that were passed out by the thousands. Griffing also started a one-year short course for young local farmers and overcame "a few handicaps such as no dormitories, no funds for budget, no teachers, no Chinese literature, etc., etc." By converting an old silkworm shed into a dormitory, by budgeting no more than the tuition collected, and by enlisting his colleagues to donate their time to provide instruction, Griffing was able to get his program under way with forty-six farmers enrolled. These short-course students were Griffing's favorites: "These boys appeal to me as being a step toward real 'dirt' Agriculture as they have manifested a far greater interest in the actual work than our more philosophically inclined senior Agriculturalists, who for example struck on the proposition of spending a Summer on our school farm a year or two ago." [55]

Griffing felt that while his college was endeavoring to provide practical suggestions, other colleges and experimental stations were overly concerned with theory and experimental research. He wrote of his Chinese colleagues at other institutions:

> Education in cotton which consists of memorizing descriptions of foreign varieties, mathematical systems of breeding, and foreign systems of culture, which make up most of the existing literature on the subject, are not only confusing but harmful to the average station operator. What is needed is more education in the practical phases of growing, harvesting, and ginning cotton, and the methods of keeping seed fields pure; a promotion of seed farm development instead of detailed experimentation; and an aggressive campaign of extension based upon demonstration farms, boys' clubs in country schools, small ginning and buying units, etc.

In other words, programs were needed that were identical to his own plans for the College of Agriculture at the University of Nanking.

✣ ✣ ✣ ✣ ✣

Griffing, Reisner, and the others at the college tended to view themselves as lonely voices of reason crying out in the wilderness, but another agricultural college, also influenced by American models, attempted to carry out improvement projects that were similar to those of the University of Nanking. By coincidence, it was also located in Nanjing, just a few blocks from the University of Nanking's campus, and was also influenced by American models and experiences. But the College of Agriculture at National Southeastern University was founded and run not by Americans but by American-educated Chinese. Notwithstanding their shared educational background, the University of Nanking rarely condescended to notice Southeastern; for the most part, it was ignored.

Despite the lack of encouragement from the University of Nanking, Southeastern's struggle to apply American methods to Chinese agricultural improvement was energetic, and for one brief moment, it seemed to rival Nanking's program. Ultimately, Southeastern was overshadowed by the greater power and resources upon which Nanking was able to draw; still, it represented the most successful attempt by Chinese to develop their own institution of agricultural education. Southeastern University began as a government-funded teachers' college, established in 1915 by Guo Bingwen (P. W. Kuo), a graduate of Wooster and Columbia. By 1921, its faculty had grown to sixty-five members, most of whom had been trained at American universities, and the school was distinguished as the first college in China to introduce coeducation. Guo decided to expand the college into a university, turning departments such as the small agriculture department into colleges. John Davis, the American consul in Nanjing, took a measure of proprietary pride in the school's expansion. He wrote to Washington, "It is especially gratifying to know that not only has the first modern university in Nanking been established by American missions [the University of Nanking], but that the second institution of this grade is being brought into existence through the ability and energy of an American educated citizen." Even though the new Southeastern University was to be directed by an all-Chinese board of trustees, Davis saw it as an American product.[56]

In 1921, when the University of Nanking was in the second year of its cotton improvement project, the College of Agriculture at Southeastern formally opened its doors. It began with a respectable base of human and material resources. The faculty consisted of seventeen professors, divided among seven departments: biology, agronomy, horticulture, animal husbandry, sericulture, plant pathology, and entomology. Aside from three sericulture experts who had been trained in France, almost all of the college staff had studied in the United States, mostly at Cornell and Illinois, but also at a number of other agricultural schools, such as Kansas State and Iowa. Three professors held doctorates. The dean, Zou Bingwen (P. W. Tsou), only had a B.A., but he earned his position by dint of administrative and political skills that his more bookish colleagues lacked. Like Reisner, the dean down the street, Zou was a product of Cornell.[57]

The research and extension programs established at Southeastern grew quickly. The college had one central experiment station and fifteen substations where sericulture and cotton improvement received considerable attention, though without the cooperation of Nanking. Faculty members pursued other research projects as well, including the study of botany, farm machinery, soybeans, sugar beets, hogs, and the tricky science of coaxing more eggs out of laying hens.[58]

Southeastern took its mission of serving the nation more seriously than Nanking did. Despite their advanced training abroad, Southeastern's staff members were instructed not to use foreign books or materials. Since agricultural books from abroad lacked practical value for China, the administration held that "all teachers in the college, no matter what they teach or how heavy their courseload, must work on carrying out one or several kinds of agricultural research." A college memo also directed attention to the issue of language: "If scientific research, no matter how deep or shallow, relies upon foreign languages for help, then science will never be able to be born in China. So our college advocates that all classes be taught with Chinese lectures prepared by each faculty member, and foreign language materials are to be used only for reference purposes." [59]

The agriculture school at Southeastern set high standards for itself and warned its faculty and staff that the responsibility "to assist the country, the province, and the society" could not be shirked. Consequently, work rules were imposed that left no room for the relaxed coming and going that other academics enjoyed: "All faculty and staff are to work a minimum of eight hours each day. Normally, personnel are to report to the readiness room at 8 A.M. and leave at 12 noon; report again at 1 P.M. or 1:30, and leave at 5:00 or 5:30." The agriculture faculty did not have the leisurely calendar that the university faculty did: "Our college of agriculture works around the year without vacation. The vacations set for the University are inappropriate for use in our School. Our faculty and staff are to rest by rotation." [60]

Southeastern sponsored farm surveys, extension lectures, and distribution of agricultural leaflets and improved seeds "to render the greatest possible service to the nation by administering to the needs of the farmers who make up the bulk of the population." The school's agricultural survey of Jiangsu Province was the first of its kind in the country (a fact that rival Nanking would later ignore), and its lecture parties regularly toured rural districts. For special occasions, farmers were invited to the central experiment station for farm machinery demonstrations. An American tractor loaned by Dodge and Seymour Company for a three-day demonstration drew the largest crowds to the station.[61]

÷ ÷ ÷ ÷ ÷

The cotton improvement program at Southeastern did not have an American cotton expert in residence, as the one at Nanking did, but it developed along parallel, if separate, lines. The goals of the two schools were identical: acclimatizing American cotton, improving native varieties, controlling cotton insects, and developing improved implements for cotton culture. Like Nanking, Southeastern quickly succeeded in selecting improved varieties, and it launched seed farms in several provinces to provide large quantities of improved seed for extension. The school also blanketed the countryside with fifty thousand pamphlets on cotton improvement.[62]

Although Southeastern never made public comparisons, in one respect its cotton improvement program was more successful than Nanking's. John Griffing at Nanking often spoke of the usefulness of the American model of "boys' clubs" in cotton promotion work, but it was Southeastern in 1922 that was the first to succeed in organizing them. The Young People's Cotton Improvement Clubs were open to farming males between the ages of ten and twenty; each member tilled half a *mou* of cotton on his family land and engaged in friendly competition with the other club members. Points were assigned in a number of categories: highest yield, best display samples, best report and tables and, not ignoring economics, best net profits. In the first year, prizes were awarded in silver currency, but popular though it must have been, the extravagance was impossible to sustain. The next year the prizes were school supplies and farm tools.[63]

When the clubs were started, Southeastern's original plan was to provide biweekly "tea chats" where refreshments would draw the members and cotton production problems would be discussed. Ideally, the chats could prove to be useful. One participant testified that he learned something about each of many topics, from weeding techniques to world cotton-market trends.[64] But Southeastern soon learned that its original plans to hold frequent get-togethers would have to be modified; locations were too remote, and professional staff members were too few.[65]

Transferring knowledge from the campus to young farmers in outlying districts proved to be no easier for Southeastern than it was for Nanking. Southeastern's first extension agent, Zhu Chunyuan, discovered that rural residents were alarmed when he toured fields: "What is he up to? Is it the first step in expropriation of our lands?" Eventually Zhu learned that an extension agent should "link up with local notables," because villagers were "fearful and submissive to them" and would do as they were told.[66]

Zhu's efforts to encourage cotton-growing clubs in Jiangpu, Jiangsu, met with varying success, depending upon the social background of the young participants. At Yongning, club members had not had any formal schooling and had been kept at home to help their families with farm work. Their farming knowledge was considerable, as was their "tolerance for work," and Zhu praised their cotton-raising results as excellent. Zhu used vernacular speech when explaining techniques to this group, but they did not always retain as much information as he had hoped: "At the time of explanation they understand, but after a while, it is often forgotten." Zhu attributed the problem to the fact that the club members "did not use their brain enough in the past and their memory capacity hasn't been expanded." To counteract this, Zhu provided his instructions when everybody was actually working in the fields, so that the information might register more easily.[67]

Much less successful was the club at Dougangji, where members were drawn from an upper elementary school. Although they were older than their counterparts in other clubs, their comparative maturity proved to be of little value. Since they were the sons of merchant or absentee-landlord families, they had no personal experience with farming and assimilated Zhu's instructions only with difficulty. A cotton field was provided for the club's use, and each member was assigned a portion for which he was personally responsible. But Zhu reported that "although at first the students were very interested, subsequently they dreaded the labor, their fields went untended, and the results were terrible." The group that possessed the best combination of farming experience and education was at Huolongji, where elementary-school students had good memory retention as well as experience working on farms. They were Zhu's favorites but were located too far from his home office for him to visit them very often.[68]

Southeastern's cotton improvement work, like Nanking's, faced tremendous obstacles that could not be removed by the efforts of an extension agent out in the field. Zhu Chunyuan was no less aware than was Griffing or Reisner of the problem of degenerate varieties of American cotton crossbreeding with the pure improved varieties his college was trying to promote, yet Zhu himself could do little to curb the widespread planting of degenerate strains. Zhu also realized the importance of raising the market's purchase price for improved American cotton: "The peasant's aim is profits. If one *mou* of cotton earns more than one *mou* of beans, then beans will be set aside and cotton will be planted. If the price of American cotton is higher than Chinese cotton, then it must lead to American cotton being planted." But Zhu was frustrated by cotton brokers who did not yet appreciate the improved quality of pure American cotton and who valued both it and degenerate American varieties well below Chinese cotton.[69]

Most extension workers in China steered clear of political controversy, but Zhu blamed part of the problems he encountered in cotton extension work on the land tenure system. In many cotton-growing districts, a share-rent system predominated, in which the landlord and tenant split a field's produce. "The harm to society is enormous," declared Zhu, "because the tenants are unwilling to expend more labor and put out money to buy fertilizer to increase production so long as the landlord will be the beneficiary." Improving cotton simply meant "twice the work for half the benefit." Tenancy stood in the way of improving not only cotton but other crops as well. Zhu hoped that "society" would recognize the problem, enlist the power of the government, and "completely change the rent system."[70]

✢ ✢ ✢ ✢ ✢

Zhu's call for a revolution on the land was ignored, but his cotton program brought attention and funds to Southeastern, just as cotton improvement did at Nanking, and in 1922 the Cotton Millowners' Association designated Southeastern as the base of the association's cotton improvement project. The attention given to sericulture at Southeastern also attracted outside support, and $18,000 was donated by the International Committee for the Improvement of Sericulture in China for a modern silkworm hatchery, which was equipped with special underground stoves and numerous measuring instruments to maintain the desired temperature and humidity.[71] The American consul, John Davis, described Southeastern's choice of activities as an "imitation" of Nanking, but a different argument could be made.[72] Both Southeastern and Nanking shared a need to find funds to build up their programs, and both welcomed any support that outside commercial interests were willing to provide. It happened that organized interests in the cotton and sericulture industries in China were generous in providing funds to both agricultural colleges; not coincidentally, cotton and sericulture received most of the attention of researchers at the two schools. The outside funding did not purchase favoritism toward a particular company, but the industry associations did effectively set the research and extension agendas at both schools.

Unfortunately, research on rice improvement languished. Southeastern, for example, included rice as one of many "projects," but few funds and little attention was given to it. Although an improved rice variety was identified, there was only enough seed to distribute to twelve farmers one year and ten the next. The staff knew that seed farms were desperately needed, but available money went into research on cotton, not rice. It was cotton that the visitor from the USDA, Walter Swingle, had said needed improvement, and it was cotton that had a strong commercial constituency to encourage university research. Because the colleges did not set their priorities independently of outside influences, rice improvement was ignored, and would remain so until after World War II.

Southeastern and Nanking never had the financial means with which to impose their own priorities on their activities. Internal funds were limited, especially for Southeastern, and the competition for external funds was fierce. The schools were forced to spend a large portion of their time marketing themselves, by telling the world of their splendid accomplishments.[73] Dean Zou at Southeastern was skilled in the statistics game that the colleges constantly played. He provided the public with an impressive number to illustrate the success of every aspect of Southeastern's work: Eighty-eight courses were offered by the college of agriculture. The college owned 3,322 *mou* for experimental work. Seventeen thousand people had seen Southeastern's cotton exhibits. If farmers in Jiangsu Province used Southeastern's improved cottonseed, production would increase by 2.4 million piculs, and no less than 36 million *yuan* in increased annual income would result.

Southeastern, getting a later start in the race, was more aggressive than Nanking in soliciting funds, and in the early 1920s a string of contributions from a number of sources, both Chinese and foreign, appeared to give it an edge over Nanking. A Cornell graduate, H. Y. Moh, who owned a large cotton mill in Zhengzhou, donated money for a "Farm Mechanics Hall"; another mill owner funded research on cotton insects. International Harvester donated a few machines for school use; the Tung Tai Reclamation Company (a prime example of the new company that Nanking's John Griffing detested) gave the school money for cotton improvement; and the Wheat Millowners' Association provided some funds for wheat experiments. The provincial government provided money to open an entomology bureau, and two Americans were hired as staff entomologists.[74]

In 1922, when Jiangsu Province designated Southeastern's College of Agriculture as its "central agency for the control and promotion of agriculture" and promised the college an annual appropriation of 50,000 *yuan* (about $25,000), the school seemed to have a bright future. John Davis was pleased with the university's prospects in general and reported to his superiors at the State Department that "the institution is ... in effect a laboratory experiment in determining the ultimate value to the Chinese people of the education of Chinese young men in American institutions." [75] In 1923, Southeastern's College of Agriculture had three times as many professors and three times as large a budget as Nanking's, but Zou Bingwen was dismayed that his school and Nanking continued to work separately, wasting efforts and precious funds on redundant projects like cotton improvement. Even though Southeastern was the larger of the two, Zou was willing to merge his school into a new institution that he proposed: a separate agricultural university, formed by the consolidation of Southeastern, Nanking, and smaller schools in the province. The university would bring under one umbrella training, research, and extension, providing the centralized direction that, in America, each state's land-grant agricultural school seemed to provide so effectively. [76]

✧ ✧ ✧ ✧ ✧

Although Southeastern had the most to lose, it was willing to join a collective effort; Nanking, however, was not. It had applied for, and later that year received, a long-term grant that brought its annual income up to a level that far exceeded Southeastern's. Nanking's grant not only undermined the possibility of a merger but dealt a crippling blow to Southeastern's financial future. The reasons for the grant being awarded to Nanking rather than to Southeastern reveal much about how allocation of international funds and channels of personalistic networks worked against the interests of native Chinese institutions.

The multiyear grant, of $675,000, was awarded to Nanking in late 1923 by the American Committee of the China Famine Fund. The committee had been appointed by President Woodrow Wilson to raise money to aid victims of Huai River floods in 1921 and 1922 (no Huai River conservancy project had been implemented since the discussion and debate of a decade earlier; see chap. 2). After disbursing money for relief, it had found that it had a surplus of $1 million. Nanking was given two-thirds of the total, and the smaller agricultural college at Yenching received the remainder. The American Committee had decided that, rather than keeping the funds for future disaster relief, it was better to apply them "to the prevention of future famines." [77]

The committee agreed with the University of Nanking's argument that the "cornerstone" of a famine prevention program was "the improvement of Chinese agriculture and the conditions under which the farming population lives." [78] And if agricultural improvement projects were to be viewed as contributions toward famine prevention, Southeastern had as legitimate a claim to funds as did Nanking and Yenching. However, it did lack several advantages enjoyed by the other two schools. Both recipients of the funds were missionary institutions and were well-known to the Protestant denominations that contributed toward their support. The China Famine Fund was a nondenominational charity, but it relied on American churches to help raise money and naturally viewed the Christian educational work in China with approval. Furthermore, the top administrators at Nanking and Yenching were Americans who could present their appeals for funds in correct

English and with chummy familiarity. Reisner had even traveled to New York and had personally presented his appeal at the annual meeting of the International Association of Agricultural Missions.[79] Southeastern had no American administrators to press for the interests of the institution. Cornell-educated Zou Bingwen did the best he could, but his written English was stiff and the fact that he was Chinese, not American, imposed a subjective distance between the American Committee and Southeastern's case.

Undoubtedly the most important factor in Nanking's obtaining the lion's share of the famine funds was its ability to present a thoughtful, comprehensive, and persuasive plan of what it proposed to do with the money. The substance of the plan was less exceptional than was the form of a "famine prevention program," the newly created package in which the specific programs were placed. The opening assumption was that "the problem of famine prevention is both immense and complex," thus involving more than giant conservancy engineering projects alone. Even if floods could be substantially averted and the damage from droughts minimized by better water control, plant varieties needed to be improved, insects and diseases needed to be controlled, and credit facilities needed to be made available if the farmer was to be raised beyond the vulnerable margin of subsistence.[80]

Nanking's plan called for strengthened instruction at the college and a required project for all seniors which appealed to American interest in practical education. Each student would be required to develop a detailed working plan for the reforestation of a large unforested area. The task demanded that the student "survey, map, divide the tract into the several planting sites, determine the suitable tree species for each site, locate the nursery and plan its operation, prescribe the planting practice to be followed, and draw up a plan of management for the reforested area." To keep the project from lapsing into an exercise in armchair planning, the student would also be required to conduct actual nursery and field-planting work, "to acquaint him with the processes needful to the reforestation of wide areas."[81]

Farm-crop improvement was also an important part of the program. The college emphasized the American roots of its own earlier efforts, and it hailed the achievements in the development of drought-resistant varieties that had "transformed the agriculture of the semiarid sections of the United States." Those successes, the college claimed, gave "a suggestion of the great field of opportunity in the famine areas of China." The college's cotton improvement work, which had consumed the bulk of its attention thus far, did not readily fit into a program of famine prevention, so it was not mentioned. Instead, wheat improvement work was described as if it, not cotton, had been the mainstay of plant breeding experiments.[82]

Plans for agricultural extension were placed into commercial jargon: extension was the "sales end" of agriculture and involved "creating a demand and developing a market" for improvements. Chinese farmers were presented as a harder "market" to crack than their counterparts elsewhere. The college's plan explained, "Agricultural improvement—on the Chinese farm—must come largely from without. The farmer will not seek it." The most persuasive means of extension was providing concrete, visible improvements; a small amount of improved seed that could be given to a farmer for trial was "worth any amount of talking." Aside from developing new seed varieties and seed farms to produce the necessary supplies, the college planned to introduce new tools, promote the digging of irrigation wells, and demonstrate cooperative credit, savings, and marketing methods.[83]

"Famine prevention" was a term elastic enough to encompass anything, including Nanking's plans for internal curricular reform. University graduates had not proven to be the dedicated agricultural professionals for whom their teachers had hoped, so the college decided to add a new program that was expressly for rural schoolteachers. "The first and fundamental step in rural progress," the college asserted, "is to produce a class of teachers that come from rural stock, are adapted to rural work, and are of such a type that they will enter into village improvement as a life work notwithstanding its discouragements, handicaps, low salary, etc." A special normal school was planned to provide training in "rural leadership." Admission would be limited to those who came from a "rural environment" and "in whom the aversion of the traditional scholar to practical activities is not liable to prove a handicap." Bright students were desired, whose educational careers had been "retarded rather by circumstances than by intellectual qualifications." Yet they could not be too bright or they would use the program as a stepping-stone to other careers: "Consideration will also be given to taking only those whose circumstances and relationships are such that they cannot aspire to further education but hope rather to go into the work permanently."[84]

To enable its staff members to remain abreast of developments in their various fields, a fund was designated for developing the college's library collection. China, it was pointed out, lacked "the personal connections possible in countries like the United States, with its large technical personnel, its scientific societies, and its conventions." The only way staff in China could keep in touch with American advances in agriculture and forestry was through published literature. But the college did not regard the United States as the sole source of agricultural wisdom; it looked to Chinese sources as well. The college explained,

> It is not generally known that China possesses a fairly rich literature pertaining to agriculture; in horticulture, sericulture, irrigation, land tenure, botany, zoology, entomology, farm crops, forestry, animal husbandry, fish culture, etc. Much of this old literature is as useful in many ways for China as the more modern books, and the possession of the knowledge which it contains will be not only valuable but should be considered an absolute necessity in any serious study of any phase of Chinese Agriculture.[85]

Nanking offered a recently compiled list of famines in Chinese history as suggestive evidence of the usefulness of Chinese source materials. Some 1,068 famines were recorded between 1644 and 1911; the pattern was "an annual average of four in the last 267 years." A more detailed study, the administration felt, would reveal historical factors that would be useful when working on current famine relief and prevention. The problem was cataloging and indexing the Chinese literature. With the cooperation of the USDA, the college had already borrowed the services of a staff member, Katherine Wead, to provide guidance in establishing bibliographic control of the materials, and part of the famine-prevention funds were earmarked for extending the work. It was a cross-national mix of components: American money and library-science techniques applied to organizing the historical Chinese agriculture literature.[86]

The famine funds given to Nanking were so generous that it was as if the dean's most outlandish wishes had come true. In 1918–19, the College of Agriculture and Forestry had a budget of $17,700; five years later, with the new annual appropriations from the famine fund, it was $175,000. Student enrollment jumped as well, and by the late 1920s, the college had close to two hundred undergraduate and graduate students. The American Committee may not have realized that its decision to award Nanking most of its surplus funds meant that the college would expand far beyond the scale of any other school of agriculture in China.

Southeastern's program had lost the opportunity to secure a steady source of funds, and in the next year, 1924, it would lose the opportunity to participate in one of the first formal American programs to improve world agriculture. Southeastern's eclipse by Nanking meant an end to China's best bid for developing an excellent agricultural college that was not dependent upon missionary support. Southeastern lost not because it was undeserving but because its leaders lacked the personal American connections that enabled Nanking to secure the surplus famine funds and then—the crowning honor—a cooperative program with one of America's leading agricultural colleges, complete with funding provided by a new American foundation.

6

TIMIDITY

The International Education Board and Cornell,
1920s

Few professors of philosophy have been given $27 million to establish and direct their own philanthropy, but in the early 1920s, John D. Rockefeller, Jr., gave Professor Wickliffe Rose of Peabody College, Nashville, Tennessee, that sum to realize Rose's idea of a foundation devoted to "the promotion and advancement of education throughout the world." Rose had come to the attention of the Rockefellers during earlier administrative service. When he was asked to head the Rockefeller Foundation's General Education Board, which was charged with promoting education within the United States, Rose accepted on condition that another board be established with funds available for use outside the United States. With Rose as its president, the International Education Board (IEB) was formally established in 1923.[1]

A friend described Rose as "possessed by the faith of Aristotle that the salvation of mankind lay in the extension of knowledge." But when given millions to spend as he and his board wished, Rose suddenly realized that "extension of knowledge" embraced a hopelessly broad range of activities. Thus he settled on the promotion of the natural sciences and agriculture as "the fields in which lay the greatest promise of human service." Rose chose agriculture because "the development of farming and of men on the farm" was "the basis of democratic civilization." The recent world war had called attention to the precarious sufficiency of world food supplies and distribution. Moreover, success in the United States with farm demonstrations, cooperatives, boys' and girls' clubs, and traveling fellowships seemed to demonstrate that rural life and agricultural production were amenable to improvement.[2]

After designating the general focus of attention, Rose was willing to entertain applications for grants from any institution anywhere. He set few specific guidelines. Permanent institutions were preferred, for "the education of a people can be accomplished only by permanent agencies rooted in the soil." And "nongovernmental" institutions were to be favored over official ones, because they had "greater freedom for initiative and for experiment" and could thus "serve to stimulate and guide governmental effort." The IEB, which regarded itself as a "bird of passage," had no wish to establish and maintain its own institutions; instead, it sought to help institutions that "may be depended on to derive their support from the people they serve." [3]

Rose visited several agricultural colleges in the United States to evaluate programs and collect ideas. The notion of an international role for American agricultural schools was a novel one—indeed, when Rose wrote to Cornell in late 1923 of his interest in visiting and discussing "a scheme in agriculture on an international scale," both the president of the university and the dean of the agricultural college were mystified. After the visit, Dean Albert Mann wrote to Rose: "We all felt greatly stimulated by your outlook." [4]

The IEB's fraternal relationship with Cornell was tightened when Mann took a leave of absence to serve as the director of the IEB's agriculture program in Europe. No definite program plans were formed, but both the IEB and Cornell were concerned with how to strengthen agricultural education abroad. Into this window of opportunity walked Nanking's John Reisner, a Cornellian who asked for help in building a stronger agricultural college in China. Reisner was the right person in the right place with the right proposal.

Perhaps Reisner heard of Rose's interest in working with Cornell and calculated that the moment was ripe for a proposal from Nanking. But it is more likely that his propitious timing was mere coincidence. Excited by the news of receiving the China Famine Funds, Reisner had made plans early in 1924 to expand programs at Nanking, and had naturally turned to his alma mater for assistance. He wrote to Cornell, "We are looking for a plant breeder—a man who is interested in the practical applications of the principles of plant breeding and in getting practical results as quickly as possible, rather than one who is interested in the subject from a purely scientific rather than an applied scientific standpoint." An attractive feature of the position was the availability of large numbers of "inexpensive" assistants, so that a single plant breeder would be able "to make his time go a very long way." [5]

No one at Cornell was willing to trade Ithaca for Nanjing on a permanent basis, but several members of the plant breeding department expressed an interest in spending a sabbatical at the University of Nanking. Harry Love, a specialist in small grains and statistics, presented a counterproposal to Reisner: Love would spend a portion of the next year in China, and his colleague, Clyde Myers, would go the next. But this two-year plan seemed too short, so it was decided to try to arrange a cooperative program between Cornell and Nanking of five to ten years, "until such time as local workers are fully prepared to go ahead independently." The new plan meant that scheduled sabbaticals would be insufficient to cover the salaries of the visiting American participants. After conferring with Cornell, Reisner decided to attempt to secure financial assistance from the IEB. [6]

Reisner was by then an experienced hand at writing attractive grant proposals, and the one he submitted to the International Education Board was elegant. The financial assistance he sought was not simply for the University of Nanking but also for review of experimental work and plant breeding projects at "nearby Chinese institutions." The money, he promised, would have a profound impact on Chinese institutions at the grass-roots level. He explained, "Experiment stations in China at the present time are really making almost no contribution to agricultural advancement. They tend more or less to museum interests, and while in many places they have the fields all cut up into small plots and have very detailed experiments worked out, they, in effect, are valueless because of the many factors of error which they fail to take into consideration." Reisner proposed to hold conferences with experiment-station workers and persuade them to work on more practical projects. To have a lasting impact, the project intended to train a staff of Chinese workers "to conduct the work after we shall cease to have direct supervision." [7]

The proposed Cornell-Nanking project, Reisner pointed out, was based on a strong existing program; would last long enough to do some good but would not drag on indefinitely; would build foreign technical competence; would be staffed by familiar faces from among the Cornell faculty; and would not cost much money. Albert Mann, former dean and now an IEB director, forwarded the grant application to the IEB's executive committee. It was one of the first proposals to be considered and was approved by the committee in December 1924, "with a view to improving agriculture in China."

✢ ✢ ✢ ✢ ✢

The IEB still did not have a clear geographical focus for its agricultural work. Initially, the board appeared to favor Europe, and Wickliffe Rose personally toured nineteen countries in western and eastern Europe to canvas funding possibilities. The Cornell-Nanking project, however, called attention to other opportunities, so before committing the IEB to a course of funding primarily European projects, Rose decided to commission two systematic surveys, one of Latin America, the other of Asia. Thus in 1925 he hired H. L. Russell, the dean of the agricultural college at the University of Wisconsin, to undertake the tour of the "Far East": Japan, China, Siam, the Philippines, Java, Australia, and New Zealand. [8]

Russell was charged with surveying the physical facilities of campuses and evaluating equipment needs for the agricultural and natural sciences. The IEB was cautious about what it would consider donating; Russell was instructed to "consider improving equipment if such aid would have a stimulative rather than a replacement effect [and would] make for a more rapid advance of science and a quicker diffusion of scientific knowledge in the countries concerned." Equipment was to be supplied only for outstanding faculty members, whom Russell was to identify, not for the general use of the Chinese school. [9]

The International Education Board also wanted Russell to interview university and government authorities in Asia about prospective candidates for advanced training abroad. The contemplated fellowships would be for one year of study in the United States and would be restricted to applicants younger than thirty-five; moreover, candidates would have to promise to "remain in service in their own country" after the award. Providing fellowships and equipment grants seemed the best means of supplementing existing programs and avoiding the high costs of starting new programs from scratch. It also met the board's own criteria of being short-term in nature and of keeping the board free of permanent commitments.[10]

Russell sailed for Asia a stranger to the region, but he had an observant eye and a good sense of humor, treating the trip as an adventure as well as serious service. He visited schools, conducted interviews, and dealt bravely with the gustatory perils of being the only English-speaking person on dining cars. When he arrived in China, one of his first visits was to the central government's Bureau of Agriculture and Forestry in Beijing. On paper, the bureau was in charge of an agricultural experiment station, three forestry stations, and four colonization projects, but when Russell visited the central offices, he found a most unimpressive sight. There was no minister of agriculture because the incumbent had "fled the capital" a few weeks previous, a victim of the political shifts that chronically rocked Beijing in the early Republican period. No summary of the bureau's work was available in English, so Russell had to rely upon "collateral sources" (i.e., gossip) to form an impression. He decided that "the work of this department is merely perfunctory and the frequent changes of administration make it quite impossible for constructive permanent policies to be carried out."[11]

At his next stop, outside of Beijing, Russell visited the National Agricultural Experiment Station, which had about 180 acres and claimed a staff of forty. The fields, however, seemed to be used primarily as a botanical garden and zoo; research was clearly at a low ebb. At an agronomy exhibit building on the grounds, Russell found interesting displays of hemp, cotton, tobacco, and medicinal plants, but "these are prepared primarily for general exhibition rather than for scientific use." In search of some sign of scientific work in progress, Russell asked to see the chemical laboratory. He was not impressed with what he found: "A few chemicals are on the shelves, and a small amount of simple apparatus; the laboratories were locked, and from the accumulation of dust, it was obvious that no scientific work was then in progress." Here, too, political upheaval was evident. "I have been told by those who are familiar with the history of the institution," Russell wrote, "that in earlier years considerable scientific investigation was carried on, but that unfortunately in this institution as in so many others in the government organization, the continual political changes have resulted in this institution being made a football of politics. As at present constituted, the institution has no scientific value."[12]

The more Russell saw of the dismal state of government agricultural agencies in China, the less optimistic he became that IEB money would make an appreciable difference. Fellowships for outstanding researchers seemed inappropriate when

Russell discovered that members of the faculty at the National College of Agriculture were receiving only 10 percent of their stipulated (and already modest) salaries. Most professors had to moonlight at other jobs to survive; such conditions, Russell observed dryly, were "probably not conducive to high grade research work." And Rose's dream of having the IEB purchase equipment seemed misguided when Russell discovered that the instruments already on site were underutilized. At the National College, he toured the biology and chemistry laboratories and reported: "Most of the apparatus had apparently been purchased at the time the institution was organized; a number of elaborate models were evidently intended for show purposes and not for class use. A great deal of apparatus [was] purchased without reference to its practical utilization with classes."[13]

✢ ✢ ✢ ✢ ✢

Russell's arrival in Nanjing was eagerly awaited both by administrators at the agricultural college at the University of Nanking, who hoped to secure funds beyond those allocated for the Cornell-Nanking program, and by those at Southeastern, who had been pushed from the funding trough by their growing neighbor. Shortly after the IEB had announced the Cornell-Nanking project in late 1924, Southeastern had put together its own request for an almost identical program, which proposed bringing to China another Cornell expert to work in the college's horticulture department. The Southeastern administration reasoned that if Nanking could receive Cornell's help, surely it could, too. Guo Tanxian, the associate dean at the college, wrote to the IEB of Southeastern's plans to invite its own Cornell expert and explained, "As our institution is in such a very serious condition that we cannot afford to invite him we therefore make this request to you." Rose wrote back that the board "considered it inadvisable to enter into any other arrangements affecting China until a representative of the Board shall have had an opportunity to study the situation on the ground." Russell finally visited Nanjing in 1925 and gave Southeastern an opportunity to show the IEB that it was just as deserving of support as the University of Nanking.[14]

Zou Bingwen, Southeastern's Cornell-educated dean, opened his formal written appeal to Russell by emphasizing the global importance of Chinese agriculture: "I am given to understand that the International Board of Education is taking steps to devise and finance a large constructive plan for the promotion of World Agriculture." No such program could ignore China, the country with "one-tenth of the land surface of the globe and one-fourth of its total population," and Zou praised Russell's very presence in China as an indication that its importance had been recognized.

Zou recommended two general courses of action for improving Chinese agriculture: "training additional agricultural experts," and "accelerating a few lines of urgent activities already undertaken by established institutions." Both courses were in keeping with IEB priorities, and Zou's supporting analysis was cogent. He told Russell, "Although native graduates of Agricultural Colleges from Japan, Europe and America total some few hundreds, the majority of them have had only a general training, sufficient to qualify them to teach perhaps, but inadequate for the persecution [sic] of research and the solution of technical problems." By Zou's count, China had only two or three people in each agricultural discipline who were truly qualified to contribute to the "modernization" of Chinese agriculture. "Such a staff is hardly sufficient to man a first rate American agricultural college. How can it be sufficient," he asked, "to leaven and quicken the forty-century old agriculture of this vast country?"

Zou argued that a short period of support from America would put "scientific agriculture" in China on a firm basis. He explained, "I have had five years of experience in seeking [Chinese] governmental help for agricultural development. I am convinced that the slow response is solely due to our inability to demonstrate results on account of the time element." China also had "a further handicap of an unstable government," but if the current political difficulties could be weathered, agricultural development would progress rapidly: "The beginning in modern agriculture has been made through native initiative, and if foreign help could safeguard it through a period of acute crisis, native support will become a certainty when the value of agricultural work becomes known."

Southeastern's own growth was a demonstration of the inherent strength of native institutions. In 1913, when the first course in agriculture was offered, the school only had 2 professors, 27 students, and 40 *mou* of experimental land; in 1925, the college had 26 professors, 52 assistants, an enrollment of 180 students drawn from every province in China, and 3,330 *mou* of land. Knowing that American foundations preferred to grant money to institutions that had already demonstrated excellence by drawing financial support from other sources, Zou listed a long list of previous donors to his college, ranging from the nearby provincial government to the distant International Harvester Company. Unfortunately, financial support from several principal contributors had recently been curtailed. "We believe," Zou told Russell, "no financial support can be given to the College more opportunely than at this time."

Zou made two specific requests. He asked for support for a trained American entomologist to work for five years with the college and with the provincial bureau of entomology. Southeastern would pay travel and living expenses; all that was asked of the IEB was the money to cover an adequate salary. Second, he requested money to help erect a new building to house the college. The school found itself without one central building, Zou explained, because "from the beginning the College expended its appropriations in securing first class men, in purchasing equipment, and in prosecuting research, instead of using funds for the erection of an imposing building of brick and mortar." Settling for a "poorly constructed building," the college suffered a devastating fire in 1923, which destroyed all of its equipment, books, and research data. Since then, the different departments of the college had been housed in widely scattered buildings. The IEB was asked to contribute half of the sum needed to build a "semi-fireproof" building to house the college; the balance would be raised from Chinese sources.[15]

Russell did not have the power to formally approve or disapprove such requests, but his recommendations to the IEB's directors would carry considerable weight. In private reports sent back to IEB offices in the United States, Russell praised Southeastern as an institution that "is so far ahead in its agricultural work of any of the other *Chinese* institutions examined that it is in a class by itself." But Russell nevertheless attributed this achievement to the "stimulus" of the neighboring agricultural college at the University of Nanking, and being the best of Chinese agricultural colleges was not sufficient to earn his support in the competition for IEB funds.[16]

✣ ✣ ✣ ✣ ✣

The principal problem that bothered Russell was the politics that disrupted the work of Chinese schools, and Southeastern was unable to hide the fact that during 1925 its work had suffered embarrassing interruptions in the months preceding Russell's arrival. The campus had boiled with protests early in the year when its famous president, Guo Bingwen, was dismissed from his post by the Ministry of Education. The university's charter supposedly insulated the school from politics and stipulated that Southeastern's board of trustees was to have sole authority to make changes in the administration. But the charter had proved meaningless because the school's funds came from the local military governor; when Guo's military patron was displaced by rivals, the school lost its primary source of income and, soon after that, its president. Southeastern's students were not happy about Guo's irregular departure and the appointment of his unpopular replacement, Hu Dengfu.[17]

Campus demonstrations over sundry issues, large and small, were not uncommon in China in the 1920s, and the students at Southeastern did not hesitate to express in public their unhappiness about Guo's dismissal. A crowd of several hundred angry students marched to the president's office, where they found Hu and his brother, who was a member of the faculty. An American consul reported what then happened:

> Recognizing the temper of the crowd the Hu brothers locked the door of the room in which they were. However, the upper half of the door being glass it was quickly broken in, and the unfortunate pair were subjected to a volley of ink wells and such articles as were handy. They were then subjected to the indignity of being spat upon by hundreds of students until they became nauseating objects to look upon and as a crowning indignity were taken out and photographed in their unfortunate condition so as to perpetuate their humiliation.
>
> In order to prevent future claims of bodily injury, which was not inflicted, the students had their victims given a careful examination by a competent

physician. They then wrote out a letter of resignation addressed to the Ministry of Education for Hu Dengfu's signature, and upon his stating he had no seal with which to sign it, they compelled him to affix his thumb-print. Finally a carriage was called and the Hu brothers were placed in it and sent away.[18]

Russell heard the story, and though he might have been entertained by the embellishments added in its retelling among Americans in Nanjing, the tale had serious implications for Southeastern's bid for IEB funding. Russell learned that after Hu's ignominious "resignation" and subsequent transfer to a girls' school in Beijing, Southeastern's troubles had continued. He discovered that "at the present time the salaries are from six to seven months in arrears, and only about 60 to 70 per cent of the normal income of the university has been paid during the present fiscal year." The financial distress and continuing political turmoil had led a number of faculty members to resign and go elsewhere. Russell praised Zou for "masterful leadership" in such a time of crisis, but no single person could overcome the negative impression created by the institution's political and financial difficulties.[19]

Southeastern's requests did not fare well in the end. In the evaluations that he sent back to IEB offices, Russell was emphatically unsupportive of the request for help in constructing a building for the college: "Work has got to be placed on a very much more secure foundation than it is at the present time before a Board would be justified in spending very much in the way of capital improvement of these institutions that are now having a struggle even to keep their doors open." Southeastern's case had not been helped when Russell noticed an item in a newspaper reporting that another Chinese university, Beiyang, had been forced to close until further notice. Russell wrote, "As this university recently celebrated its thirtieth anniversary and has held a prominent place in Chinese education work, it shows the difficulty that even the longer established institutions have in maintaining themselves under these conditions."

Southeastern's request for money to hire a Cornell entomologist was also turned down. In Russell's opinion, the control of pests fell under the jurisdiction of pest control organizations rather than research institutions, and thus was an undertaking that "normally should be covered by the government itself." Even if the IEB were to help support a department of research in entomology, "from past experience with these problems I know too well the pressure that always comes from field outbreaks to absorb the time of scientific men in carrying out ordinary methods of control." Since the provincial government had not demonstrated its interest and ability to fund a pest control program, Russell thought that support for Southeastern's plan would be "injudicious."[20]

The only area in which Russell was willing to give even qualified support to Southeastern was that of fellowships. The college requested traveling professorships for two of its faculty members, one of whom Russell described as "not one of those highly brilliant men from whom extraordinary results are likely to be obtained, but he is an earnest and conscientious worker." Russell thought that if this man, whose specialty was plant breeding, had the opportunity to see plant breeding operations at U.S. experiment stations, it would "enthuse him with new life." But Russell did not support Southeastern's request for funding five fellowships for instructors who had recently graduated from Southeastern and wanted to study abroad. Despite the kind words that he had for the college's accomplishments, Russell recommended little concrete support for Southeastern.[21]

÷ ÷ ÷ ÷ ÷

The University of Nanking, in contrast, made a tremendous impression upon Russell: "This institution is the outstanding place that we have yet found in China so far as the possibilities of research in the fields of the fundamental sciences, agriculture and forestry are concerned." He praised John Reisner as a strong executive whose past accomplishments showed that "it is safe to bank on him for a wise and economical use of funds that may be placed in his hands for development." Russell was also impressed by the trust that had been placed in Reisner and his programs by the China Famine Fund and the other recent donors to the college at Nanking.[22]

At the time of Russell's visit, the IEB had already pledged $7,600 to help support the Cornell-Nanking plant improvement program, which had just begun. But that sum was a trifle compared with the $50,000 Nanking now requested of the IEB. Russell reviewed Nanking's requests carefully and ruled out funding fellowships for training recent graduates abroad: "After having studied this proposition in the various institutions which we have visited in China, I am strongly of the opinion that it is unwise to send over to America immature students to complete the later years of the regular college course or the beginning of their graduate work." Such students usually ended up spending a long period of residence in America. According to Russell, the extended stays had resulted "in most instances in the Chinese student being swept away from his home moorings so that he was quite out of touch with conditions in his own country upon his return." Russell believed that the university should continue to operate as it had in the past, dissuading its young graduates from going to the United States until after they had acquired considerable work experience in China following graduation. Thus, he felt that the IEB should "concern itself with the outstanding man, rather than immature men who might develop later."[23]

Russell endorsed most of the other items that Nanking requested; even after trimming, he still recommended that the IEB grant the college more than $32,000 during the next three years, which would more than quadruple the level of support that had already been promised. But by providing a dismal picture of Westernized agricultural students, Russell inadvertently undermined the prospects of the IEB increasing its expenditures in China, whether to Nanking or to any other institution. Reporting on the experiences of Chinese students who had been sent to the United States with Boxer Indemnity funds, Russell wrote, "They came back quite Americanized, at least so imbued with the American point of view that they were

often unable to adapt themselves readily again to the Chinese point of view."
Moreover, once they had returned with "an American training that doesn't fit
Chinese conditions," they had had little opportunity to find practical work in
agriculture: "The Chinese farm is, generally speaking, only a few acres; no labor
saving machinery is used. There is no demand for these men from the land, and
there is no especial desire on their part to go to the land. Not even the graduates of
the agricultural colleges here go into the applied field; practically all of them seek
to become teachers or to occupy a government position."

Explaining why so many American-trained agricultural specialists were to be
found in government positions was difficult until Russell learned more about
government life in China: "With us in America the official class do not receive
anything like as large an income as men in business or the more lucrative professions. In China an official receives a higher salary than is secured by most of the
other groups. Moreover in a great many positions the opportunity for 'squeeze'
makes it still more profitable to enter this field." On his tour, a group of Wisconsin-
trained Chinese met Russell and presented a small gift; Russell used the occasion to
inquire into their present occupations. Of the two who had majored in agriculture,
one was now in the Ministry of Education, and the other was a provincial commissioner of industry. Concluded Russell, "One is quite as likely to find a man
trained as a chemist in the Ministry of Communications as engaged in chemical
industry or research."

The executive board of the IEB could only be dismayed to learn from Russell
that in China there were no research positions available to students who had
returned from graduate training in the United States. Russell reported: "In fact
there is no research atmosphere in any of the Chinese institutions that we have yet
seen. Research cannot thrive on a dung hill or a pile of brick bats; nor even within
the four bare walls of a so-called college." When salaries of university professors in
China were months in arrears, the professors could "hardly be expected to throw
themselves soul and body into research." Indeed, Russell wondered "how some of
them have hung on as long as they have."

Russell collected applications from Chinese professors and students for fellowships abroad, in anticipation of the International Education Board's inauguration, as planned, of a program of training fellowships. But he soon felt swamped
and pessimistic about the prospects of accomplishing anything with such a
program. His last report to the IEB ended on a decidedly negative note: "I am
having all kinds of applications from men here who want to get away, go anywhere for further study, or get out of China for the present, but when you check
up on their probable productive scientific future, it gives you too low a batting
average." As long as China presented a face of political disorganization, potential
foundation donors from the United States would be scared off: "Until China,
somehow or other, is able to stabilize herself, so that 75 to 90 percent of the taxes
raised does not go to maintain a military machine that is dragging the country to

ruin, it is not much use to offer opportunities for research training to men who have to face this condition on their return."[24]

China should put its own house in order, Russell recommended, before the IEB invested heavily in its future. He was not hopeful. China would probably "muddle through," but "no one here on the ground is optimistic enough to be able to tell me when this is going to happen."[25] Disturbing signs of radical agitation further darkened the picture in Russell's mind: "There is very positive evidence (I have had opportunity to see the confidential files of an American consul in one of the leading cities) to show that the Bolshevists are spending no inconsiderable sums of money for propaganda to inflame the Chinese against the introduction of foreign ideas." The recent organization of Sun Yat-sen University in Moscow and the scholarships provided to several hundred Chinese students to study revolutionary doctrines were "an index of the length to which the Russian party is now going to ally the Chinese in their world movement against 'Imperialism,' and 'Capitalism.'" Student organizations on Chinese college campuses seemed to be caught up in this Bolshevik movement as well. Although Russell dismissed part of the Chinese student movement as "the froth and exuberance of very immature youth," he did grant "a growing nationalism that is striving to express itself in terms of 'China for the Chinese.'"[26]

✧ ✧ ✧ ✧ ✧

If Russell had been reporting on "Bolshevik" influence on China in a later period, he might have suggested funding a massive program to try to win for America the hearts and minds of Chinese students. But in late 1925, Russell was extremely cautious and recommended, in essence, that the IEB stay out of China until China's future seemed less subject to upheaval and Soviet manipulation. The "uncertainty" created by the nationalist movement led him "to hesitate in the development of any very large plans for the future."[27]

The IEB had no idea that Russell would return with a recommendation to stay out of China. The very month that Russell was preparing his trip report, but before it had been mailed, Wickliffe Rose spoke excitedly of developing a center of agricultural science that would soon be able to "run under Chinese steam." Albert Mann, who was also unaware of the imminent arrival of Russell's negative report, leaned toward support of Chinese schools like Southeastern over foreign schools like Nanking. "Other things being equal," he said, "preference would be given to public and governmental institutions, rather than those supported by missionary agencies."[28]

At that moment, however, Russell was in Shanghai preparing to submit the report that would scuttle Southeastern's hope of receiving IEB funds. Russell wrote to Rose in New York, "I heard this last week that for the month of December the Southeastern staff only got five percent of their regular allowance. They are certainly in desperate straits, and are to be admired for the loyalty with which the agricultural crowd is holding on." But Southeastern's neediness made it an unattractive candidate for support. Russell was not unaware of the paradox: "This is of course the time they need help the most of any, but on the other hand, until things become more stabilized it would look to me as a useless procedure to spend any material amounts for the work which they ask." [29]

Russell recommended increased support for the University of Nanking, but his report of his trip to China was dominated by so much negative commentary about the general conditions in the country that Wickliffe Rose lost interest in developing new programs there. The Cornell-Nanking program had started and would continue, but the IEB would make no new commitments. Rose axed almost all of Russell's recommendations for expanding support to Nanking. He explained his new outlook: "China is a backward country. Conditions in science and in agriculture are primitive. Under such conditions the Board cannot undertake the burden of developing either science or agriculture in any country." Although a limited role of providing some assistance to existing institutions would be possible, Russell's report on Chinese nationalism was disturbing, and it caused Rose to rule out any support for schools like Nanking, which had too close an association with Western interests: "Nanking is at present a Missionary institution, that is, a foreign institution planted on Chinese soil. The plan of the Board would be to cooperate with institutions rooted in the soil of the countries they are attempting to serve." [30]

Despite Rose's abstract interest in developing native institutions, the particular conditions reported in the case of China made him skittish; consequently, Chinese institutions like Southeastern received no IEB money. In effect, China was dismissed as a hopeless case. Although Rose wrote in 1926 that the Cornell-Nanking project would be observed closely and that experience gained there would guide any further China programs, a critical moment in the board's history had passed, excluding most of China. By 1928, the International Education Board had spent virtually all of its funds, and Rose retired. The Cornell-Nanking project turned out to be the only Asian project in the board's short history, and it was started before Rose and the board were familiar with actual conditions in China and the region. South America and other parts of the undeveloped world fared no better. Instead, the IEB developed a policy of "helping the already strong" and spent its millions in Europe and the United States. In the end, this "international" foundation gave its largest grants to American projects at Harvard, the California Institute of Technology, and the University of Chicago. [31]

✢ ✢ ✢ ✢ ✢

The Cornell-Nanking program, designated by Rose as a trial, barely had time to begin before the IEB virtually liquidated itself by committing its funds to large projects elsewhere. In one respect, Rose's concern about growing Chinese nationalism was borne out, when the Cornell-Nanking program was interrupted in 1927 by antiforeign violence that shut down the University of Nanking. Harry Love had been the first participant in the program and had spent most of 1925 at Nanking;

Frank Meyer in Shanxi (1908). Courtesy of USDA and Isabel Shipley Cunningham.

Joseph Bailie. Courtesy of American
Forestry Association.

Groundbreaking at Purple Mountain (Bailie in slouch hat). Courtesy of Yale
Divinity School Library.

John Reisner, dean, College of Agriculture and Forestry, University of Nanking. Courtesy of Yale Divinity School Library.

Bailie Hall for Agriculture and Forestry, University of Nanking. Courtesy of the Rockefeller Archive Center.

Lossing and Pearl Buck on their wedding day, 30 May 1917. Courtesy of Paul Buck and the Pearl S. Buck Birthplace Foundation.

Picking cotton on experimental plot, near Nanjing. Courtesy of the Rockefeller Archive Center.

Shen Zonghan at Cornell
(1924). Courtesy of Linking
Publishing Company, Taiwan.

Prizewinners at an agricultural exhibit. Courtesy of the Rockefeller Archive
Center.

Selskar Gunn, vice
president, Rockefeller
Foundation. Courtesy
of the Rockefeller
Archive Center.

Insecticide experiment, National Agricultural Research Bureau. Courtesy of
the Rockefeller Archive Center.

Soldiers on Purple Mountain assisting in pest control campaign of NARB (1935). Courtesy of the Rockefeller Archive Center.

Experimental plots on University of Nanking farm. Purple Mountain in background. Courtesy of the Rockefeller Archive Center.

Officers of the Nanking Branch of the Colonization Association. Courtesy of
Yale Divinity School Library.

Clyde Myers had gone in 1926. But in early 1927, just as R. G. Wiggans, the third participant in the Cornell-Nanking program, was about to arrive, Nationalist troops under Chiang Kai-shek reached central China, clearing rival warlord armies from their path. When Chiang's troops reached Nanjing, they celebrated their achievement by terrorizing the foreign community. The University of Nanking, as the leading missionary institution, was a prime target.

At first, American professors in the agricultural school were complacent when large numbers of soldiers entered the city and combed the neighborhoods where the foreign residents lived; their Chinese students heard the soldiers say that they "were only after the British and Japanese." But then shocking news swept the community: John Williams, the vice president of the university (and the man with whom Joseph Bailie had worked closely ten years earlier) was shot dead by soldiers on the campus when he refused to give them his watch. Complacency turned to panic as the Americans at the University of Nanking realized that they were not immune to the violence that was sweeping the city. The foreign staff of the agricultural college took refuge in the attic and closets of Bailie Hall. R. H. Porter, a member of the plant pathology department, later wrote to his friends at Cornell of the ordeal that ensued when a group of soldiers stormed the building where the foreigners were hiding:

> They called for us to come out, we heard them draw the bolts of their guns and we knew they would shoot into the doors so we decided the best thing to do was to come out. Accordingly every one came out and there before us were about 8 men, or rather boys about 17 to 18 years of age, armed with rifles, bayonets and knives. They began a systematic search of every one, taking anything of value, jewelry, money or clothing. Unfortunately, most of the people had been robbed in their homes so that the soldiers were not pleased with their booty. Accordingly they became desperate and two or three stepped back, drew the bolts in their guns and threatened to shoot us if we did not give them money. I remember distinctly that the worst one of the lot stood directly in front of me with his bayonet within a few inches of my heart region and I expected any minute either to be run through or shot.

Fortunately, a young Chinese officer appeared, took control of the "ruffians," and used good English to calm the terrified Americans. Porter wrote, "He talked with us for some time, explaining the ideals of the nationalist party and their three principles of government and emphasized the prize of liberty. By the time he got on that subject the atmosphere in the room became charged with a bit of the humor of the situation for we had just experienced the direct opposite of what he was teaching." Porter described the soldiers who had tried to shake him down as "the most reckless, high handed, insolent, ignorant youths I have ever seen." [32]

Having witnessed mob violence and feeling that Chiang's officers hardly had control of their own men, the Americans at Nanking evacuated the city, fled to Shanghai, and boarded ships for Japan and other destinations in the Pacific. In the midst of the commotion, Wiggans, the representative from Cornell scheduled to spend 1927 in China, arrived in Shanghai, turned around, and returned to Ithaca. The next year, political conditions in China were still regarded as unsettled, so Cornell decided not to send anyone; only in 1929 did Love return and the program resume. Wiggans finally got his chance to see Nanjing when he was the 1930 Cornell representative, and Myers returned to Nanjing in 1931 as the last participant in the program.[33]

In total, Cornell had a representative in residence in China for five years, between 1925 and 1931. If the International Education Board had been interested in evaluating the progress of the program, it would have been quite pleased. The Cornell professors held to their institution's promise to emphasize the training of Chinese experts. Gains were made in plant breeding work, and the Americans were quite unassuming. They simply wanted to provide China with the most improved crops possible, while causing the least possible disruption of traditional practices.

✢ ✢ ✢ ✢ ✢

Love and his colleagues decided at the outset to concentrate on selecting the most promising existing varieties rather than on hybridization work; selection was seen as "the cheapest and quickest way" to raise yields. The plant breeder picked a number of different plants from a range of fields and planted them in controlled field tests to observe which were the best. The Cornellians demonstrated the use of "head rows," in which the seeds from each head were planted in separate rows that preserved identical conditions but allowed for comparisons. Other standardized experimental procedures were followed, with explanatory Chinese-language brochures prepared for the staff and students.[34]

The Cornell representatives apparently thought that John Griffing's work on cotton improvement was unscientific, and Griffing was quietly deprived of university resources to continue his work (see chap. 5). The Cornellians, free of the financial pressure to serve the local cotton-mill interests, shifted Nanking's emphasis away from cotton and toward food grains. Love dabbled in rice improvement, but his unfamiliarity with the crop hampered progress. He tried planting rice seed, directly, without using the labor-intensive process of transplanting rice shoots into a prepared field bed. His claim to have obtained yields that were equal to those of transplanted rice proved difficult to verify when tried again; moreover, Nanking did not own much irrigated land upon which to proceed with experimental work on paddy rice. But important progress was made on the improvement of dryland crops such as wheat, sorghum, soybeans, and millet.[35]

The most spectacular results were obtained in the area of wheat improvement. From selections that led to the planting of more than ten thousand head rows, one variety, named "Nanking No. 2905," stood out from all the rest. Love had happened upon the variety by chance in 1925. Touring the countryside for head selections, he noticed that one field seemed to have outstanding characteristics that deserved immediate inclusion in the selections. He talked with the field's owner, explained the university's experimental program, and offered to purchase a number of plants for testing. The owner readily agreed, but while Love and his assistants were busily gathering up what they thought was a rare find, a farmer who had been quietly observing the scene spoke up: "You think this is good? You should see the wheat across the way." Love was directed to a field a short distance away, where he found the best wheat he had seen, which subsequently became "Nanking No. 2905." [36]

The best selections were planted at a number of mission stations, and "2905" was found to yield about 30 percent more than the wheat varieties then commonly used in China. A new soybean variety that was isolated during experimental work promised yield increases of 80 and 90 percent above usual levels. As further selection produced superior varieties of a number of crops, the staff began preparing to distribute the new varieties to the public.

Extension to the countryside would be the hardest part, for "it was much easier to produce an improved variety than it was to introduce it to the growers and have it produced successfully." When discussing extension problems, Love and Reisner, like Griffing earlier, took pains not to appear condescending to Chinese farmers. They declared, "The Chinese farmer is no more conservative by nature than was the farmer of the United States [at the turn of the century]." Chinese lack of willingness to adopt new varieties merely reflected economics; their landholdings were generally too small to permit experimentation, whereas the American farmer "could usually spare a strip of land for some experiment without seriously affecting his income." The Cornell visitors recognized the difference in circumstances.[37]

As long as enough Chinese farmers were willing to try the limited supplies of improved seeds that Nanking could produce, no one examined the wisdom of distributing the seeds to whomever would accept them; the college was simply grateful that all of its seed supplies were distributed. But late in the program, Myers realized that the policy of distributing a small supply of seed through the college and through widely scattered mission stations diluted the potential impact of the crop improvement work. He proposed that a small area be selected as the target of improved seed distribution: "If results were satisfactory, the plan would be to move out in a more-or-less general circle surrounding the area where the seed was first distributed, and continue on in this way until an entire area, or at least the majority of the farmers of the area, were growing the new variety." Unfortunately, the idea came too late to be implemented as part of the program, and the practice of unsystematically distributing improved seed over a wide area continued.[38]

✣ ✣ ✣ ✣ ✣

The Cornell participants emphasized that an important part of the plant improvement program was the training of Chinese counterparts to carry on after the Americans' departure. Thus the visitors used a portion of their time in China presenting formal lectures, leading field trips, and holding summer institutes. "By the end of the formal cooperation between Cornell and Nanking," Love and Reisner wrote, "it was estimated that over 125 men, who had little or no previous experience, had been trained to where they were independently able to conduct crop improvement experiments." Later, the official history proudly claimed, "To a large extent, the Cornell team members had worked themselves out of the job. They left the program in efficient hands." Yet it is doubtful that more than a handful of the Chinese scientists and assistants had both adequate background and adequate exposure to the single American plant breeder who was in residence at any given time, and hence unlikely that many of them learned as much as the Cornellians claimed.[39]

The American participants also tried to heal the rift between Nanking and Southeastern. The feud was no secret: Clyde Myers learned about it the first day he arrived in China, when he was literally rushed off the pier in Shanghai by John Reisner, with Southeastern's Zou Bingwen in close pursuit. Myers was mildly amused by the melodrama into which he had walked. He held no prejudices against Southeastern and was initially quite eager to help that school as well as Nanking. When Zou was finally able to contact him, Myers cheerfully accepted an invitation to visit Southeastern's experimental wheat farm, examine procedures, which they translated into English for him, and make suggestions for improvement. Here was work similar to Nanking's and equally in need of expert guidance; Myers was happy to be of service. Nanking's refusal to cooperate with Southeastern seemed silly, and Myers thought that he could iron out the problems by arranging for both sides to meet in person.[40]

The peace council did not go well. Reisner had nothing positive to say about his Chinese colleagues from across town and took pleasure in noting Southeastern's most recent setback: a key member of their faculty had left, placing their college "in a very embarrassing position." In Reisner's view, Zou Bingwen was acting irresponsibly by "going ahead and planning for another experiment station.... His big difficulty is, in my judgment, always wanting to overreach his resources both in men and money." Reisner claimed at the meeting that "we went just as far as we possibly could" with the Southeastern representatives, and he left the matter of cooperation unresolved until Southeastern had submitted its specific proposals for cooperation.[41]

When Southeastern presented its suggestions in writing, including a request to work with Myers, Reisner would have none of it. Myers was the property of Nanking and not to be shared. Myers himself was disappointed that his efforts to reconcile Nanking and Southeastern ended so unsuccessfully. He attributed the problem to mutual jealousy between the two institutions: Southeastern staff felt that they were "as good as anybody," while "a lot of people at Nanking feel that they (Nanking U) are better than anybody else—a little bit of the Harvard attitude." The conflict between Reisner and Zou was intensified by their personal similarities. Myers wrote, "The two Deans are very much alike in some respects in that they are both aggressive and hustlers and genuinely and sincerely interested in the future welfare of their own institutions."[42]

If official cooperation seemed unlikely, unofficial cooperation remained a possibility, and Myers encouraged informal contact between members of the faculty. In the summer institute that he gave at Nanking, he was happy to see a number of people from Southeastern who were sitting in without registering. "I guess that they felt they might lose face if they registered," Myers speculated. The Southeastern auditors were in fact in a difficult position, since they had been encouraged to attend the Nanking institute by one Southeastern supervisor but forbidden by another.[43]

By inclination, the Cornell participants were more than willing to work with whomever was interested in improving China's plant breeding efforts, but they were unable to free themselves of the restraints imposed by their hosts at Nanking. Institutional self-aggrandizement (*danwei zhuyi*) was a phenomenon among Chinese institutions then as well as now, and was frequently criticized by Americans who lived in China during the Republican period. The problem afflicted not only institutions operated by the Chinese government but also the Americans' own college, Nanking.

The interuniversity cooperation between Cornell and Nanking rested upon ad hoc financial arrangements, and the program fell victim to money problems. After the International Education Board grant was spent, no new source of funding was found to carry on the work. The United States government was preoccupied with the Great Depression; assisting agriculture in China seemed a noble but very distant concern. In China, notoriously little of the national budget was available for nonmilitary spending, and absolutely no money was considered for a foreign. missionary-sponsored school. Only if Southeastern had been included in the program might the national government have assumed the responsibility of continued funding. When the Cornell-Nanking program ended in 1931, Myers spoke for others as well as himself when he wrote, "There was some feeling of disappointment to have the formal cooperation discontinued at the close of the 1931 season, with only five years of actual, formal cooperation, when from five to ten years were originally contemplated and planned for." He mentioned that unspecified "changed conditions" necessitated early termination but affirmed his belief that "the work has been placed on a permanent basis and that it will come to its full development in due season."[44]

Full development, however, depended on more successful programs for extending improved seeds into the countryside. The Cornell-Nanking participants were scientific experts who knew little about the social, economic, and political problems that weighed upon the Chinese farmers whom they wanted to help. The scientists did not know the language, their visits to China were relatively short, and they were busy with campus-related responsibilities. Despite their awareness of the importance of extension, the American visitors remained personally unfamiliar with conditions beyond the University of Nanking. They achieved beguiling success—selecting improved crop varieties and training dozens of Chinese "experts"—but it came without real acquaintance with the obstacles that lay in wait for the reformer who ventured away from the campus.

7

MYOPIA

Lossing Buck and Agricultural Economics,
1920s—1930s

When Lossing Buck, the young agricultural missionary, moved in 1920 from his rural mission station in Anhui to the campus of the University of Nanking, he embarked upon a new career as an academic authority in agricultural economics, a career in which he became an almost instant authority. Yet the more recognition he attained as an agricultural economist, the more estranged he became from the conditions in the rural economy that he purported to know. By the time he became an expert adviser to the governments of both China and the United States, he had long been out of touch with actual conditions in the countryside. He held the ear of many Americans and Chinese only because no one else in China had marked out so powerful an academic fiefdom so early as he.

When John Reisner considered Buck for appointment as the College of Agriculture's sole professor of "agricultural economics and farm management," Buck was thirty years old, with a B.A. and a number of years of agronomic experience in the field, but he had absolutely no experience or training related to economics. Buck was an agronomist, not an economist. Nevertheless, Reisner thought him perfectly suitable—he was a fellow Cornell graduate and Christian, his living stipend would continue to be paid by his mission board if he moved to the University of Nanking, and he clearly wanted very much to leave Anhui. There were too few Americans on the scene for Reisner to be overly choosy about academic qualifications. He appointed Buck as the new professor with the assumption that Buck could train himself.

Not only did Buck start as the head of a new department, he also began academic life as the head of the entire College of Agriculture and Forestry. It happened that Reisner was eligible for a two-year leave of absence in the United States just as Buck arrived, and Reisner appointed Buck acting dean of the college for the interim.[1]

The academic community of the university lived on missionary stipends, which were far less than the incomes enjoyed by other Americans living in Nanjing at the time, such as the expatriate staff of Standard Oil Company or the

United States consulate. An American member of the Nanking faculty later recalled a split among Americans between "the missionary group and the commercial group." The main difference was in the number of servants: families in the
commercial group would have at least one Chinese servant per American, while
missionaries generally had only one servant for every two Americans. Still, it was
granted, missionaries lived quite comfortably. Said one, "In China we all live like
lords and kings on fifty-five dollars a month."[2] The Bucks were installed in a
commodious brick mansion, staffed with a crew of servants that rivaled the ratio
enjoyed by American businessmen: cook, housewoman, nursemaid for their new-
born daughter, and a gateman-gardener. Their entertaining was constant, with
guests for lunches, teas, and dinners. A relative later recalled that whenever
Lossing met "a man who might help him in some way," Pearl would invite him to
dinner at the family's home. The Bucks's busy pace of life in Nanjing was as
dramatic a change as could be imagined from the lonely life of just a few months
before, when they had been posted in Anhui (see chap. 4).[3]

✢ ✢ ✢ ✢ ✢

Meanwhile, Lossing Buck began teaching courses that no one else in China
had taught (and that he himself had never taken): agricultural economics, farm
management, rural sociology, and farm engineering. His only guides were the
American textbooks that the college library had on hand, the most important of
which was George F. Warren's classic, *Farm Management* (1913). Farm management was emerging as a subject distinct from agricultural or rural economics and
was devoted wholly to the internal operations of an individual farm. Warren
explained: "How shall I grow corn is agronomy. How shall I grow an animal is
animal husbandry. But shall I grow animals or corn, or both, or neither, is farm
management."[4]

Warren was interested in learning "why certain farms pay better than others."
His method of surveying large numbers of farms—successful and unsuccessful
alike—had helped push agricultural economics away from the case-study method
of looking at a handful of farms individually and toward studying hundreds or
thousands of cases by collecting and analyzing large amounts of statistical data.
Warren was a nationally recognized authority in the United States, and he happened
also to be at Cornell. Buck had never taken one of his courses, but with the Cornell
bond, Warren's text became a natural choice as a guide to farm management.[5]

Farm Management treated the farmer as a businessman (as Edward Parker and
his Minnesota colleagues had; see chap. 2). Such a farmer needed to be not so
much a savvy trader as an executive organizer who could ensure that men, horses,
and machinery were kept fully employed at all times. "The idle horse in the barn,"
Warren wrote, "is a more frequent source of loss than is the bad bargain in buying
a horse." To calculate the success of a farming operation, the farmer was to subtract
from the year's receipts the actual business expenses and the hypothetical interest
that his capital would have earned if invested elsewhere; the resulting sum pro-

vided the value of the farmer's exertions for the year, or his "labor income." Warren held no sentimental attachments to farming: "If a farmer's labor income does not equal hired-man's wages, he would be as well off if he sold his farm, placed his money at interest, and hired out."[6]

Unlike most of his economist colleagues, Warren thought that profits should be measured per farmer, not per acre. America, he felt, was premature in turning toward intensive agriculture to maximize per-acre profits when an abundance of untilled but serviceable land stood ignored. To illustrate the point, Warren's text used China as a negative example. John Washington Gilmore, once Gerow Brill's young assistant in Hubei and by then president of the College of Hawaii, had told Warren that 70 percent of the Chinese population were farmers, yet productivity was so low that the country needed more people farming, not fewer, because land still went untilled for want of farmers to put it into production. Warren explained to his readers that in China "one family raises little more than it uses, hence a very large part of the population are farmers." Measured in terms of profits per acre, Warren noted, Chinese farming would appear to be "ideal," but "the small profit per man does not allow a high development of civilization, either on the farm or in the city." The first step in progress, Warren advised a country such as China, was "for each farmer to use machinery and animal power so that he can work more land. This would allow a larger proportion of the population to do other things."[7]

In the United States, many articles in the farm press had recently promoted small farms, with titles such as "Three Acres and Liberty," "Ten Acres Enough," and "Five Acres Too Much." But based on his own surveys of Tompkins and Livingston counties in New York, Warren argued that operators of large farms enjoyed significantly higher incomes than those of small farms. Simple economies of scale meant that a family could expand an 80-acre farm to 160 acres at only modest additional expense, thus doubling its net income. Warren wrote, "It therefore becomes a task for a genius on the 80-acre farm to compete with a very ordinary mortal on the larger area."[8]

Warren advised farmers who could not afford to purchase a large farm to rent whatever additional land they needed: better to take advantage of economies of scale on a large operation, even if rented, than stick to a small holding, albeit wholly owned. In *Farm Management*, Warren noted that 9 percent of American farmers were part-time tenants in addition to farming their own land, while 35 percent were full-time tenants. Puzzled that other writers persistently ignored the "opportunities" that tenancy provided to the ambitious farmer, Warren described America's three million tenants and part-tenants as upwardly mobile entrepreneurs pursuing a wise course of tilling as much land as they could.[9]

✧ ✧ ✧ ✧ ✧

Warren regarded 300 acres as an ideal size for a family farm, but such an idea did not suit existing circumstances in China. In 1920, when Buck tried using *Farm Management* in the classroom at the University of Nanking, he soon saw that his

Chinese students had difficulty with the material. Everything about the book seemed alien to Chinese agriçulture, from its overarching theme of promoting large-scale operations to its frequent discussion of livestock management to illustrate important points. Its main redeeming feature, Buck felt, was its revelation of Warren's farm survey methodology, which the author had used in New York to gather his supporting material and which might also be used in China to gather material more appropriate for the Nanking classroom.[10]

Securing the permission of Nanking's president and registrar, Buck offered college credit to any student who conducted farm management surveys of at least a hundred farms when home in the countryside during summer vacation. Several students accepted the offer in 1922, and the data brought back to campus by one of them, Tao Yanqiao, was used immediately in Buck's first scholarly publication, "An Economic and Social Survey of 102 Farms Near Wuhu, China." Full of Warren's jargon, as well as Buck's own prescriptions for rural improvement, the article attempted to analyze Chinese rural economy in American terms.

A sample profile of one Chinese family that had been surveyed was full of rich and interesting detail. Aside from information about crops, property assets, expenses, and income, the survey examined the family's economic history. The "operator" had begun farming in his twenties under his father, had inherited a small parcel and rented more, and at the age of fifty had purchased his own farm, where his two sons and a daughter-in-law, all in their twenties, helped him. Under "General Information," the family was described as "cleaner than the average for the region."[11]

Like Warren, however, Buck was more interested in statistical patterns than in individual cases, and he needed an analytical framework to order the data. The cornerstone of Warren's surveys, the concept of "labor income," was not easily transferred to China. Warren assumed that the New York farmer, with a low "labor income," could easily liquidate his farm, hire out as a spare hand, and do better. Although both the capital and labor markets in the Chinese countryside were much different and hardly as rich in opportunity, Buck ignored this and announced that his calculations of "labor income" revealed that the owners in the Chinese survey lost money in their operations—news that might have surprised the owners themselves.[12]

Buck also ignored problems with his own sample. His student had secured data from about half of the families in three villages near Wuhu, Anhui, taking care, Buck said, "to visit small farms as well as large ones." For some questions, such as comparing the relative efficiency of small farms to large, this was acceptable, but for other questions, such as the extent of tenancy, it was not. The student chose families to interview on the basis of family connections. If the student was from a relatively affluent family, as was usually the case, the family's circle of acquaintances could scarcely have been assumed to reflect the class structure of the village in neat microcosm. Yet Buck overlooked the problem of bias and announced nicely precise numbers—55 percent owners, 32 percent part-owners, and 13 percent tenants. Over time, he would cite these figures again and again, allowing them to take on a life of their own.[13]

Part-owners, not full owners, Buck found, earned the highest "labor income," for they worked the largest farms. Just as Warren had found in the United States, human and animal labor, tools, and equipment were used much more efficiently on bigger farms than on small. But while Warren had always argued that no group of farmers was more capable or worked harder than another, Buck disagreed, claiming to see a relation "between the character of the farmer and his labor income." "Bad character," defined by drinking and gambling, was found among 72 percent of the Wuhu landowners, which "may explain to some extent the low labor income of the owners." "Good character" was found in 61 percent of the tenants and 85 percent of the part-owners, the latter group being filled with what Buck described as "the hard working, wide awake man trying to live the best kind of life he knew."[14]

Buck concluded, "It is quite a fallacious idea that one must improve the farmer's economic condition before his social and spiritual potentialities can be developed. A large income will not help the family of a farmer who drinks and gambles, for he will only waste his profits in further profligacy." Agricultural improvement work, Buck emphasized, should thus address "all phases of rural life," not simply material production. Only then could the farmer spend an increased income wisely.[15]

Pleased with the outcome of his study of Wuhu farm management, Buck touted the usefulness of similar rural surveys for the rest of China. Toward that end, he designed a survey blank that he claimed a single student could easily fill out to describe conditions in a village, several villages, or even entire counties. For a model, Buck had his Wuhu article translated into Chinese and distributed three thousand copies around the country. He also obtained funds from the college to hire two full-time Chinese assistants to collate the farm management data that other students brought back from their summer vacations. A permanent academic industry began, devoted to rural surveys under his direction.[16]

✧ ✧ ✧ ✧ ✧

Using the information gathered from his students' surveys, Buck formulated prescriptions for China's social problems. "Idleness" was the first problem needing attention in China, he told readers of The *Chinese Recorder* in 1923. Listing the average number of months, ranging from one and a half to six, that farmers were "almost totally" or "partly" idle each year in eight communities surveyed, Buck explained, "Not only does idleness diminish the income but it is also the chief cause of gambling and often leads to quarrelling and sometimes immorality." The alternative he recommended was church-organized recreation. The salutary effect of a recent experiment was instructive: a former student, presently superintendent of the college's experimental farm, had organized the farm's workmen into a drama troupe for the lunar New Year holidays, keeping the men so "occupied and amused," Buck reported, that it was possible "to control their gambling instinct." [17]

In Buck's opinion, the popularly perceived problem of farm tenancy was exaggerated. "There is a general opinion that the landlord is getting the best of the tenant," Buck noted, but reported that his research showed that such instances were the exception, not the rule. Providing anecdotal examples from Anhui, where landlords were frequently cheated out of their lawful share of the crop, and from Jiangsu, where a school that rented out land had tenants who banded together and refused to pay rent beyond a certain point, Buck asked, "What can the landlord do under such circumstances?" [18]

Because tenancy was generally "a stepping stone to owning a farm," it was an institution that was "anything but a serious evil." The most serious problem, Buck thought, was caused by tenants who changed farms frequently or paid share rents (a set percentage of their crops). Such rents discouraged maintenance of the soil's fertility and production of a high yield, since the share tenant felt that "with any additional effort half the crop goes to the landlord." Buck advised the church to help, both by "promoting an attitude of fairness" between tenant and landlord and by convincing the tenant farmer that he was his "brother's keeper" for future generations and had a duty to maintain the land.[19]

Although Chinese activists talked increasingly of class tensions in the countryside, Buck preferred to cite the lack of rural financial services. He strongly criticized the absence of banking facilities in the countryside, noting that a farmer with a small surplus had no safe place to deposit it. Some buried their money in the ground; others wasted it on frivolities or gambling, reasoning, "Why not have the pleasure of spending it, for to-morrow it may be stolen?" Especially galling to Buck in his new role as an economist were cases such as one in Nansuzhou, Anhui, where a farmer gave his savings to a wealthy member of the gentry for safekeeping, not earning a penny of interest.[20]

Farmers needed access to credit at reasonable rates of interest, eliminating usurers, whom Buck saw charge as much as 300 percent interest. Market services also stood in need of improvement, though Buck was careful not to blame merchants alone for existing problems. True, some commission agents cheated farmers when measuring crops for purchase, but that abuse was matched by farmers who soaked their grain or cotton in water to try to obtain a higher price for it. What was needed, Buck thought, was not a fundamental change in the economy or society but the addition of new services. Thus he proposed that Chinese farmers be helped to help themselves, by forming cooperatives.[21]

Cooperatives were not unknown in the United States, but Buck was most familiar with European models, which he heard about while serving with Englishman J. B. Tayler on a committee for the International Famine Relief Commission. Buck also had read Myron T. Herrick's *Rural Credits* (1914), a survey of the dozens of varying cooperative ventures tried in nineteenth-century Europe. One group in Germany, which adopted what was called the Raiffeisen system, stood out from the rest for its apparent success in combining financial solidity with a Christian spirit. Started in the 1860s by Frederick William Henry Raiffeisen, the cooperatives attracted both wealthy and poor members and had multiplied quite dramatically in Germany. Buck was also impressed that the Raiffeisen principles had already proven to be transportable; in India, similar cooperatives appeared to Buck to have "not only alleviated the indebtedness of their members but have also done much to build up the character of the members." "Truly," Buck wrote in 1923, "the co-operation movement is one that should not be left untried in China." [22]

✛ ✛ ✛ ✛ ✛

Buck was asked by the International Famine Relief Commission to look into the possibilities of establishing a cooperative in Nanjing, and he turned the matter over to an assistant, Paul C. Hsu, who was granted a budget of 1,000 *yuan* (about $500) by the commission to help start the project. The Fengrun Rural Credit Cooperative, the first rural cooperative in China inspired by a Western model, opened under Hsu's direction in November 1923. Theoretically, credit coopera-tives offered their members loans that were drawn from the pooling of members' investments, but the Fengrun Cooperative was rather unusual, in that its sixteen fortunate members could borrow from a treasury fattened by the Relief Commission grant.[23]

Adapting to local needs, the Fengrun Cooperative also provided a service to its members that the proponents of cooperatives in Europe and the United States could not have foreseen: ensuring access to a steady supply of night soil. The Fengrun farmers, all of whom were commercial vegetable growers, needed large quantities of human waste, which could be secured only by "renting" collection rights at a privy in the city. Unfortunately, the collection fee was too high (and the quantity of waste too large) for any one farmer to contemplate rental of a privy on his own. But with the appearance of the cooperative, the farmers had a formal organization to help them share costs and benefits. The rental of a privy in the city was easily arranged, with members rotating the privilege of waste collection every two days.[24]

The Department of Agricultural Economics at Nanking organized other co-operatives with its Famine Relief Commission grant, which stipulated establish-ment of ten credit cooperatives. An additional grant to the department, from the China Famine Fund Committee, allowed for the creation of experimental coopera-tives dedicated to providing many different kinds of services. To establish a new organization in a selected village, Hsu sought out one or two local residents who could be persuaded to serve as organizers, leaving the task of recruitment to them. Once enough people were willing to invest a token share and participate in the cooperative, an organizational meeting of the charter members was held to elect unpaid officers for two boards: an executive committee to manage the coopera-tive, and a "Council of Supervision" to serve as watchdog over the executive committee.[25]

After the management was in place, the early credit cooperatives issued low-interest loans to their members, an ever-popular program. But the organizers from Nanking saw that borrowers tended to take the money and run. After the avail-able money was distributed, members did not seem interested in coming to meet-ings; thus the prospects seemed dim for an animated, self-directed organization that could survive the departure of outside organizers. To encourage cooperative members to participate beyond the initial stage of loan distribution, Nanking funded other cooperative schemes that, like Fengrun's privy rental, extended the range of services and tried to engage members in sustained participation. One cooperative used a loan to fund irrigation improvements in the area; another started mulberry plantings for silkworm feedings.[26]

The agricultural economics department saw its cooperatives not only as instruments for economic improvement but also as tutorial institutions in political democracy. Reflecting the preoccupations of his senior American colleague, Hsu wrote of the educational benefits that the cooperative brought to its members: "In the general meeting the members learn how to vote, to conduct a meeting, to discuss problems, functions fundamentally important in rural self-government." Information about how a democracy functions could be explained in schools or public lectures, but the farmers would never listen, Hsu said, whereas as members of the cooperative, "they have to learn it." The Nanking staff hoped that the entire country would soon benefit from these cooperatives, which provided the farmer's "first steps in the great lesson of self-government, the lesson which, if he learns it rightly, will make China a true republic."[27]

More immediately, the cooperatives brought "moral" improvement to their communities, Hsu claimed. If the organizations took care to ensure that "only honest men with good character" were admitted as members, "this will encourage men to be honest and will create an atmosphere in the rural community recogniz-ing that it is worth while to be a good man not only for reputation and honor but also for material advantages." Hsu heard reports that within only a few years of its establishment, a credit cooperative in Jiangning, Jiangsu, had worked wonders. Its members were no longer to be found in tea shops or gambling houses and now took an active interest in public affairs. And nonmembers, Hsu was also pleased to hear, were no longer disrespectful (aside from "those who have been refused admission").[28]

✧ ✧ ✧ ✧ ✧

With Hsu in charge of organizing new rural cooperatives and with other Chinese staff in charge of overseeing the collection of farm management surveys, the University of Nanking's Department of Agricultural Economics and Farm Management was active in experiments and research that no other institution in

China could match. By 1924, only four years after starting the department, Buck could point with pride to an impressive record of outside fund-raising and supervised research activity, although his own lack of an advanced degree continued to nettle him. Eligible for a sabbatical in the United States for the 1924–25 academic year, he returned to Cornell with his wife and daughter. There Lossing worked on an M.S. in agricultural economics; Pearl, an M.A. in English.[29]

The year was a financially difficult one for the couple. To make ends meet, Pearl tried writing articles for money, successfully publishing a piece in a popular magazine and winning a $250 prize in an essay contest at the university. In the meantime, Lossing focused his attention on his graduate courses, among which was a seminar taught by George Warren, the man whose book had been so influential in guiding Buck's survey work in China. Warren taught his graduate students the principles of farm management, as well as the Warren philosophy of life and love. (On selecting a wife, he advised: "Don't have too many girl friends because then you can't decide which one. You better not go too much on looks. Pick somebody that will make a good mother, somebody with broad hips.") The Bucks returned to Nanjing in 1925 with their degrees; with a second daughter, whom they had adopted; and with new ideas in economics and rural sociology that Lossing wanted to try in China.[30]

Writing more formally and academically than before he had received his master's degree, Buck told the missionary establishment in China that churches should be run like businesses. Church organizations were "dependent upon certain well known business principles which operate in all successful secular organizations." Thus if Chinese churches in the countryside were to be economically self-supporting, they would have to study nonspiritual matters such as the wealth of their members and the geographic area of membership necessary to ensure sufficient funds. Listing a sample budget for a rural Chinese church that paid its own pastor, Buck produced calculations that showed almost five hundred members would be necessary for support—too large a number of Christians to be found in a small community. Simple economics, Buck said, revealed the need to abandon unsupportably large budgets. Better to start small, with an unpaid pastor and donated buildings. Farm management showed that churches needed to keep to an optimum size, just as "the farms that are neither too small nor too large give the greatest profits."[31]

Aside from economics, Buck wrote that mastery of other social sciences was also essential for organizing work in the countryside, even for church work: "No matter how saintly a religious leader may feel himself or his fellows to be, or may desire himself or his fellows to be, he cannot escape the fact that as long as spirits are clad in human flesh, people behave according to the laws of psychology and sociology." The success of government programs in rural America showed the wisdom of "a few simple principles" and, Buck reasoned, "what has proved constructive and useful among other human beings may prove helpful here as well."[32]

The first such guideline, the "self-help principle," recognized the importance of having farmers take an active role in helping themselves and not becoming dependent on outside organizers. Buck was impressed by the story of a home bureau agent in the United States who had done most of the planning for a monthly public program. The agent "wondered why it was that the members of the bureau were not more interested in the work and why they did not turn out in larger numbers for the meetings." As an experiment, the agent left the responsibility for future programs entirely in the hands of the members, and the result, Buck heard, was that although the meetings "may not have seemed to the agent so good and helpful as were the programs arranged by herself, still the members turned out in much greater numbers than formerly and showed a far greater interest." [33]

The experience of organizing cooperatives in the Chinese countryside confirmed another principle that Buck drew from American programs: the importance of developing the rural organization "around a keenly felt need, or interest," so that the farmers would willingly support the program by themselves. In the United States, farm bureaus and county extension agents were not imposed from above but were an outgrowth of farmers wanting to improve their methods, so they formed a suitable organization and hired an expert. "As a result," Buck noted, "we have many strong farm bureaus which could never have been formed except by this method of beginning from the bottom—from the farmers themselves." [34]

The Christian church in China had ignored these principles and tried to impose an alien organization upon an unwilling countryside. Buck agreed with the pastor who had told him, "One could talk himself 'blue in the face' about the Church not being foreign, but so long as he was paid by an outside organization the people could not be made to believe that there was no ulterior motive behind it all." In the United States, Buck added, organizations such as the YMCA, YWCA, the Boy Scouts, and the Camp Fire Girls had found that small rural communities had regarded them as "alien" to the community. If such was the case within one country, "one can understand the more readily how the Christian Church in China is thought of as 'foreign.'" [35]

To reduce its onus of foreignness, Buck advised the church to provide the rural community with practical services, such as introducing improved seeds (as he had tried to do, a decade earlier, in Anhui), promoting the formation of cooperatives, and showing farmers how to keep accounts. Buck suggested "flower clubs" for girls and women, to promote "beautification of the home," since "a careful study would undoubtedly reveal a very close relationship between beauty and true religion." And even so prosaic a subject as road building was commended to the church's attention. "Church members can do a real Christian act," Buck explained, "by putting enough earth in the middle of the road so that water will run off the road rather than into it." [36]

Buck was not interested in personally returning to village organizational work, however; he liked his new role as professor of agricultural economics and spent most of his time sifting through his students' farm management surveys. Between 1921 and 1925, the work had continued even during his absence, and surveys from seventeen localities were turned in, each involving more than a hundred families and dozens of survey schedules. The data were voluminous, and though Buck picked up Warren's analytical framework with renewed enthusiasm, it took him several years of sustained attention to impose order on the material and fashion out of it a book-length manuscript. And in the midst of this work, in early 1927, revolution intruded.

÷ ÷ ÷ ÷ ÷

Buck had not paid much attention to the upheaval in the countryside that accompanied the Nationalist-Communist alliance in the mid-1920s and their Northern Expedition. The arrival in Nanjing of xenophobic troops and revolutionary slogans caught Buck as much by surprise as it did his colleagues in the plant breeding department. On the day that John Williams, the vice president, was killed (see chap. 6), the Bucks' Chinese tailor ran to their house and yelled an early alarm: "Get out quickly! They're shooting white people!" After hiding for thirteen hours at the home of a Chinese servant, the Bucks moved to Bailie Hall on the campus. There the Chinese Red Cross organized an evacuation to the Yangzi River, where two American destroyers were anchored, laying down a barrage of gunfire over the city to signal their presence. In the commotion, many valuables were left behind, including a manuscript that Pearl left on her desk. But Lossing had scooped up his farm survey manuscript at the first alarm and never let it go.[37]

The evacuation of foreigners interrupted not only the Cornell-Nanking plant breeding program but also the work of Lossing Buck's agricultural economics department. The Bucks went briefly to Shanghai, then moved to Unzen, Japan, a small hot-springs resort near Nagasaki. They had nothing but the clothes they were wearing—and the farm survey manuscript, on which Lossing immediately resumed work. The graphs and charts he was assembling lent a reassuring order to that topsy-turvy world where Americans such as the Bucks, who thought they had gone to China to help the Chinese, found themselves reviled as imperialists and forced to flee for their lives. Work on the farm survey was a solace; as Pearl wrote to the Reisners, "Lossing keeps regular hours, and we don't speak to him between eight and twelve and one and five."[38]

Trying to make sense of the social fury in Nanjing from which they had fled, both Bucks ascribed the problem to the pernicious presence of the Communists. Pearl explained in a letter to friends, "It seems that the Southern soldiers urged on the mobs of poor and idle people of the city, and told them to come in and take all the foreigners had, since now everything was to be in common, and there was to be no more private property. We recognized this as the red teachings of Russia, and that the Communists were in control of Nanking, and not the Conservative Nationalists as we had hoped." Because of the popular attraction of communism, Lossing saw a grave future for China. From Unzen, he wrote to a Chinese colleague on April 16, "The communist doctrine appeals to those who are near the starvation line and China has a great many such people as you all too well know. The doctrine has taken such a hold that eradication now is going to be very difficult before a great deal of damage has been done to society." [39]

Chiang Kai-shek was directing the "eradication" for which Buck hoped, even as Buck was speculating about it. The bloody purge of Communists, thousands of whom were executed in Shanghai alone, permitted Chiang's government to consolidate its control and invite foreigners to return. In September 1927, Lossing returned to Nanjing, but it was another year before the American expatriate husbands felt that conditions were safe enough for their wives and children to return.

Buck had no firsthand knowledge about what had happened in the countryside, where tens of thousands of farmers had rapidly organized farmers' unions, but reports about the phenomenon issued by the Nationalist government revealed a countryside that was far from content. The unions had demanded a 25 percent reduction in rent, abolition of rent in years of poor harvest, distribution of government land to the public, imposition of a ceiling of 20 percent annual interest on loans, and the right to participate more directly in local government. [40]

In the immediate wake of the farmers' union movement, Buck wrote that conflicts of "a very serious nature" seemed to arise when farmland in China was owned by someone other than the farmer himself. But his sympathy for some of the farmers' demands did not extend to their unions. From what he had read and heard, Buck concluded that the organizations were undemocratic and directed "from the top down," that their executive members were mostly "non-farmers," and that the unions had enlisted members by spreading "propaganda" in posters, slogans, resolutions, speeches, and publications. Buck was disturbed to learn that their posters and slogans had "vividly conveyed the idea of oppression of the farmer by other classes such as the landlords, gentry, money lenders, officials, the people's army, militarists and imperialism (foreign)." [41]

Before the Nationalists forcibly closed down the unions, some groups had achieved positive results, a fact which Buck later conceded when he returned to Nanjing. The unions had rendered considerable aid to the revolutionary armies on their advance northward and had curbed abuses in rent and tax collection and in usury. The lesson to be learned, Buck said, was that "economic and social conditions in rural districts are such that unless an enlightened government emerges soon there is almost certain to be sporadic if not more general uprisings of farmers against the conditions they now have to endure." The comparative ease with which the farmers' unions had formed showed "how quickly the spark may be fanned into a flame." The only reason most farmers endured present conditions was because they believed that the status quo was determined by fate and could not be changed. Such passiveness "cannot and will not always remain so," Buck warned. "A good government fostering the welfare of the farmer is the most desirable outcome. Failing that a real revolution initiated by the farmers themselves is not improbable."[42]

✜ ✜ ✜ ✜ ✜

To help both the farmers and the government avert future upheaval, Buck set himself the task of stripping from the farm tenancy issue all emotional clutter and analyzing the problem with the dispassionate eye of an economist. He put aside his farm management survey for the moment and published in 1927 a short essay on tenancy in China, which sought "to ascertain facts and to offer briefly suggested solutions."[43]

The extent of tenancy in the country, Buck said, was "a subject of frequent misstatement because data from exhaustive studies of the topic do not exist." But after noting the wide variations in the known distribution of tenancy and assembling all available information, Buck estimated that approximately 50 percent of China's farmers were owner-cultivators, 25 percent part-tenants, and 25 percent full-tenants. Since Buck believed that part-tenants were at least as well-off as owner-cultivators, these estimates seemed to him to show that tenancy was not nearly as severe a problem as many were claiming. To put China's tenancy in comparative perspective, Buck pointed out that in the United States a higher percentage of the farming population was full-tenants (38 percent) than in China (23 percent), while England had a much higher percentage (89 percent) than both combined. Such comparisons convinced Buck that the extent of farm tenancy in China "compares very favorably with that of other countries."[44]

Buck was sure that in China the problem lay not in the institution of tenancy itself but in certain abuses associated with it. Where landlords were absentee and uninterested in directing the management of the farm, intermediaries were hired to collect rents, and it was they, Buck said, who were responsible for the worst abuses, cheating tenants and landlords alike. Buck also disapproved of the practice of landlords requiring personal services from their tenants, such as at weddings and funerals. "It is a system evil in its effect," he wrote, "because it is indefinite in requirement, and may work real loss to the tenant in keeping him away from his work, and worse than that, perhaps, is that it makes deeper the feeling of inferiority that the tenant has, and definitely classes him as the landlord's servant."[45]

Aside from recommendations to break up large landholdings, however, Buck felt that the legal structure of tenancy should be left alone. The most important service that the government could provide was to encourage landlords, in the few places where needed, to charge what Buck termed "fair rent," based on a complex formula that sought to apportion income to landlords and tenants according to their respective investments. But according to Buck's calculations, landlords in most parts of China received a far smaller return on their capital by investing in land and renting than they would have by lending money at prevailing interest rates. Thus Buck stuck by the conclusion he had drawn several years before, when analyzing survey data from Wuhu: Chinese landlords were not obtaining "exorbitant" profits from the land.[46]

By the next year, 1928, the political situation in the capital had stabilized and the tide of rural unrest appeared to have receded. When Pearl Buck and the two children finally moved back to Nanjing in the fall, the city had returned to the quiet of the past. Lossing reported to friends in the United States, "We go about freely on the streets with only rarely (once) insults in the nature of remarks such as was made to Mrs. Buck when taking Janice to the Chinese kindergarten. Low class people in a hut full of looted foreign furniture yelled out one day as she passed 'Kill the foreigner.' Such remarks even at their worst must be taken with a grain of salt because ignorant people often pass on what they have heard soldiers and others say without real thought on their own part." But he was determined to stay in China, despite "uncertainties as to the future," because "the opportunities for service are so many and the desire for the presence of the foreigner is so evident on the part of not a few."[47]

Buck remained concerned, however, about the reappearance of unrest in the countryside in late 1928, in the wake of poor harvests and the demobilization of thousands of Northern Expedition troops. Buck noticed that "banditry has developed in East Central China, where before it was practically unknown." He wrote to Harry Love at Cornell, "The bandit conditions are really very, very serious and are hampering all kinds of improvement work in the country." Not only were bandits a menace but so were the secret societies that the farmers joined to protect themselves. Buck told readers of *The China Weekly Review* that six villages near Zhenjiang, Jiangsu, had been burned to the ground and an estimated two hundred people killed in the course of a feud between two self-protection societies, the Big Swords and the Little Swords, who ended up fighting each other instead of bandits, their common enemy.[48]

Most disturbing to Buck was the Nationalist government's apparent inability to provide law and order in the vicinity of Nanjing, the national capital—and hence the government's rural backyard. Newspapers reported that only 20 miles away, some eight thousand farmers had submitted to the extortion of outlaw gangs and agreed to regularly pay "protection" money, while other nearby villages reported recent kidnappings for ransom. Buck personally saw how terrified nearby villagers were when he accompanied a Chinese staff member on a visit to the little market town of Yanziji, near Nanjing.[49]

The two men from the university had gone to the town to talk with local farmers about forming a credit cooperative. Using the patrons of a small teahouse as a captive audience, they began their standard presentation. They were interrupted, however, by a local resident who launched a speech of his own, explaining that the last thing the village needed at the moment was financial assistance—any grant given to help start a cooperative would only serve to attract more thugs to the area. The man told Buck that bandits had already driven local wealthy families into the city and "those who are as poor as we have neither means to move to other places, nor work at home, but close the door at night and hurry away to hide with their children wet and cold, in the bushes and streams of the mountainsides, in spite of the mosquitoes and snakes." He pleaded, "If you could think out some means of ridding us of the 'Bandits' instead of introducing to us the cooperative Societies, we would be everlastingly grateful to you and we would never cease in appreciating your help." [50]

Clearly, the Nationalist government was failing to perform properly. Buck wrote privately of his concern: "It does take time for a new Government to get organized and to have things in smooth running order. Some of the bigger things in organization have perhaps been already partly accomplished, but one questions the ability of a Government which is unable to control things to a better extent in the country districts." Buck noted approvingly that a new normal school that had been established near Nanjing had taken the initiative to help villagers purchase fifty rifles for their own protection. "While such local group self protection is not the most ideal one in any nation," he wrote, "still in the present circumstances in this country, until the government is able to perform all its functions, it may be that this is the only possible solution to a problem which may assume really alarming proportions." [51]

✣ ✣ ✣ ✣ ✣

Buck's expressions of concern with current events in the countryside soon faded, however, as his attention returned to his manuscript, "Chinese Farm Economy." The book, started long before the dramatic events of 1926–1928 and the appearance of radical farmers' unions, assumed that the rural landscape in China looked very much like the politically quiescent one then to be found in the United States. Buck was explicitly testing how suitable Warren's principles of farm management were for China. Adhering to the distinction that Warren had drawn between "farm management" and "rural economy," Buck collected data that were confined to farm operations and farm family life. The "external relations" connecting the farmer to other parts of the economy and to the state were omitted. Another important aim of his study was to discuss the rural economy objectively, providing quantitative support for all statements. Buck wanted very much to earn the applause of the academic community in the United States and adopted a cool, detached tone that presented numbers, not emotions. As a result, when he reimmersed himself in his survey data and accompanying manuscript, he no longer saw revolutionary tinder in the countryside.

When J. B. Condliffe, research secretary of the Honolulu-based Institute of Pacific Relations, passed through Nanjing, Buck showed him his manuscript, and Condliffe immediately offered to arrange for its publication. In 1930, *Chinese Farm Economy* was published simultaneously in China and the United States, marking the first such Western study of rural China and establishing Lossing Buck as the preeminent authority on China's rural economy. It was also an enormously influential book in the Chinese academic community, serving as the standard text in the training of Chinese agricultural economists in the prewar years. Its influence fulfilled Buck's hope at the time of publication—namely, that the book would inform not only Westerners about China but also Chinese about their own country and the American survey method. "China has been a country without reliable statistics," Buck observed, "and it is to her advantage to obtain them, not only from the point of view of taking her place in world statistics, but also for the important reason of self-knowledge before there can be self-improvement." [52]

Despite its title, *Chinese Farm Economy* started and ended with American concepts of farm management. Readers had to wade through considerable jargon (e.g., "Man labor efficiency, then, as measured by the number of crop hectares per man-equivalent and by the man-work units per man-equivalent . . . ") and dozens of tables on every conceivable aspect of farm operations. They also had to accept Buck's claims that his data were statistically reliable. Buck used survey data from seventeen localities, concentrated in either north China or east central China. He did not insist that the seventeen represented the entire country, but he did maintain that they represented the areas in their vicinity. Yet in many villages only a tiny sample of the population had been surveyed, and that on a wholly unsystematic basis, in that Buck's students selected households by simply interviewing relatives and friends. Buck was aware of the problem and defensive, arguing that critics were "unfamiliar with the survey method." [53]

The numbers generally were not as important as the analytical framework that Buck employed, however. Chinese farms were closely scrutinized to measure their microeconomic efficiency, and in the course of explaining his data, Buck often recommended changes for the consideration of both Chinese farmers and the government. For example, the physical layout of the Chinese farm did not please Buck. China's "open field system of unfenced scattered plots of land farmed by one family corresponds very closely to the former strip system" of England and other European countries. The survey data showed an alarmingly high average number of family plots and long distances separating them. Fertilizer had to be carried to the fields, and harvested crops carried off, all by means of a bamboo carrying pole that rested on the farmer's shoulders. This cumbersome method of transportation suggested to Buck that "were the land all in one piece and the farmstead located either in the center or in some other position as convenient in relation to the whole, such transportation costs would be diminished." Consolidation of land would bring other benefits as well. Control of irrigation and drainage water would be facilitated, as would pest control. The number of boundary lines could be reduced, along with boundary disputes. And formation of a single large parcel would make protection of property easier. However, in the same breath that Buck recommended reducing the number of boundary lines, he also proposed reinforcing the remaining lines with fences, hedges, or ditches, "to obtain privacy and prevent trespassing, thieving, and gleaning."[54]

The heart of *Chinese Farm Economy* was "The Best Size of Farm Business," an analysis of the relation of farm size to profits and efficiency. In his earlier study of the Wuhu data, Buck had tried to force the Chinese data into the Warren mold of "labor income," but he had subsequently realized that this was "difficult to measure" in China. For *Chinese Farm Economy* he provided readers with no less than eight different measures of farm profits, "labor income" being only one, and no matter which one was used, the data made clear that "profits increase with the size of the farm business."[55]

This was not surprising news, but the data on crop yields were unexpected. Buck noted that "there is an impression among many people that the smaller a farm is the greater is the yield, on the basis that a small farm makes possible better care of crops." Yet his survey data showed that yields did not vary by size of farm: large farms, though operated by only a small family, produced yields the equal of smaller farms. This discovery seemed to remove the only possible argument in favor of small farms. The question, then, was this: If large farms were the most profitable and efficient, why didn't Chinese farmers move toward acquiring larger holdings? Buck's answer was: "The over-supply of farmers." The Chinese government could try to move farmers in densely settled areas to colonization schemes or to industries in cities, Buck granted, but the prospects of relocating enough people to relieve the existing pressure on the land appeared minimal. To Buck, population control appeared to be the only permanent solution.[56]

Hidden between the voluminous charts in Buck's book was good advice about farm practices. Recognizing that labor was rural China's largest resource, Buck declared, "Progress in Chinese agriculture does not depend solely, as so many think, upon the introduction of the expensive farm machinery of the West. Farm machinery can only be profitably used to the extent to which it saves labor that might otherwise be productively employed or to the extent it performs work that hand labor cannot do or cannot do as well or cannot complete quickly enough to enable farm operations to be done at the most suitable time for maximum production." Calculating the costs of buying and operating an American tractor in China, Buck showed that plowing costs per unit of land would be much higher if tractors replaced the water buffalo. Such higher costs meant that the tractor would have to be enormously more productive than the buffalo or ox if it were to compete successfully with them.[57]

Buck pushed instead for improvements in farm operations by increasing the number of farm stock, planning crops to spread peak labor demands more evenly over the year, and encouraging a more varied diet. According to his survey of farm nutrition, Chinese farmers relied too heavily upon cereal grains and too little upon vegetables for their own food. Buck had been surprised to discover that few

Chinese farmers maintained a family garden. His informants claimed that gardens took too much time, but Buck was skeptical: "This is not a reason, because it is evident from the limited amount of work done and from the labor distribution that there is plenty of time at the farmer's disposal to grow vegetables for home use. A plausible and actual reason for the absence of home grown vegetables is the plea of ignorance of vegetable-growing methods." Buck suggested that extension workers be sent out to show "the importance of the home garden to the farm business and to health" and to teach farmers how to grow vegetables.[58]

Buck also had opinions about how farmers should spend their time and money at home. Household budgets were scrutinized for wasteful expenditures, such as contributions to Buddhist or Taoist priests, whom Buck held in contempt for their exploitation of "the farmer's fears of the unknown." Yet contributions to Christian churches were criticized only for being too low. Buck also condemned "expenditures upon gambling, drinking, and opium smoking," as he had in the Wuhu survey, but now he tried to talk in purely economic terms. The same amount of money "if spent upon education or more wholesome forms of diversion or savings would do much to raise the standard of living."[59]

He also inquired into matters of what he called "sex-immorality," even though its relation to farm management was unclear. His surveyors asked villagers about concubines, prostitutes, and whether "sex-immorality" was "increasing, decreasing, or stationary." The responses were not included in the book.[60]

Buck openly criticized the rural Chinese home as too spartan, for which he blamed Chinese farm women: "The Chinese farmer's home is largely a place for shelter only and often is even inadequate for this. There is little about it to create the finer feelings usually associated with a home, and this will undoubtedly always remain true until farm women have at least a primary school education."[61]

Aside from such stray comments, Buck stuck closely to an analysis of farm operations. He drew a sympathetic description of the lot of the Chinese farmer as one of enduring a low standard of living imposed by too many people eking out subsistence on too little land. But *Chinese Farm Economy* had a grave weakness: it did not satisfactorily address existing Chinese concerns about the rural economy. The foreignness of its emphasis on farm efficiency, which accounted for its fresh insights, also accounted for its limited scope and awkward handling of the two most talked-about issues of the day in China: the seemingly explosive problem of tenancy and the questionable ability of the Nationalist government to help the rural areas.

Buck said that when designing his survey blanks, he had not paid special attention to the issue of tenancy. Consequently, his data on the subject were not as rich in detail as they could have been, and the haphazard method of selecting informants further reduced the usefulness of the data. Still, Buck sounded the same themes that he had introduced in the Wuhu survey, stressing the reasonableness of prevailing rents and proposing the calculation of a scientifically verifiable "fair rent." In some places, rents were too high, in others, too low, but in all cases, Buck implied, an agricultural economist could calculate the rent that would be acceptable to both landlords and tenants.[62]

Who was supposed to ensure that rents were properly adjusted? Buck did not say, nor did he discuss the difficulties of implementing other recommendations that he felt were more important—namely, consolidating parcels, controlling population growth, and improving rural diets. All would require the guiding hand of a strong and popular government, which the Nationalist government did not seem to be. In his private correspondence, Buck was as skeptical as everyone else, but in his book he chose not to discuss how his recommendations should or could be realized.

Buck was not reticent to dispense advice to the Chinese, but the nitty-gritty details did not interest him nearly as much as the intellectual quest he had set for himself, which consisted of demonstrating the universality of social science "truths" discovered in the United States. A major influence on Buck was *Rural Social Problems*, a sociology textbook written by Charles Josiah Galpin, the head of the USDA's Division of Farm Population and Rural Life. It contained a chapter entitled "Why Farmers Think as They Do," which Buck said "helps one to understand farmers' psychology, which is much the same the world over." The book also discussed American farm tenancy in the most benign terms, and Buck enthusiastically recommended it and similar American texts to "rural leaders" in China.[63]

The farm surveys conducted in China under his direction, Buck said, showed that "the principles of farm management were exactly the same in China as Warren found [in the United States]." Not all Chinese economists agreed with Buck's judgment, however. One unidentified Chinese scholar, who apparently had a Ph.D. in agricultural economics and rural sociology from Cornell, argued that Chinese farmers did not view their farms as a business, so it was not necessary for them to master business methods. This view was criticized by another Chinese agricultural economist, Alfred Chiu, who had been trained at Harvard. Chiu was extremely critical of Buck's sampling methods, but he defended the idea that farm management principles should be taught in China, even if Chinese farmers "may not [regard] their farms as a business." Chiu wrote in his dissertation, "It is exactly our duty as agricultural economists to teach our ignorant but educatable farmers sound business (scientific) principles in the management of their farms, for otherwise what is the use for us to study agricultural economy?"[64]

✥ ✥ ✥ ✥ ✥

Even before Buck's *Chinese Farm Economy* appeared in print, Buck had started a new, still larger survey project in China, applying a new organizational theme, "land utilization," which had become fashionable among American agricultural economists during the 1920s. Responding to increasing concern in the United States that expansion of agricultural land encroached upon forests, pastures, and other lands, economists began to talk of the need for comprehensive government planning for the "optimum use of land." An influential economist, David Weeks, of the University of California, wrote of the need to consider information about a number of topics: "soil physics, soil chemistry, moisture supply, temperature, light, topography, location, markets, character of population, price conditions, comparative advantage, friction of economic adjustment, and financial conditions." The task called for massive surveys and for joining the talents of soil specialists, economic geographers, land economists, foresters, ecologists, and farm organization experts.[65]

Land uses were mapped in agricultural atlases, and around 1925 Oliver E. Baker, an economist at the USDA who was then assembling a world agricultural atlas, became particularly interested in land utilization in China. Baker had never been to China, but his study of available statistics about agriculture and population there had led him to see a striking similarity between China's population growth in the eighteenth century and U.S. population growth in the twentieth. Baker told a conference of the Institute of Pacific Relations, held in Honolulu in 1927, that the current agricultural situation in China presented "a picture of conditions that may exist in our country two or three centuries hence."[66]

It was not a hopeful picture. Using Chinese government statistics released in 1922 by the Ministry of Agriculture and Commerce, Baker had calculated that China had only one-ninth as much cultivated land per capita as did the United States. But after analyzing soils, rainfall, and temperatures, he also had come across an unexpected statistic: China cultivated a lower percentage (26 percent) of its potentially cultivable land than did the United States (39 percent). Baker was surprised:

> One would expect that in China almost every hillside would be terraced to its top, all land it was possible to irrigate would be irrigated, all land it was possible to drain would be drained, and that long since settlers would have pressed out upon the subhumid prairies of Manchuria and the semiarid plains of Inner Mongolia, instead of having just started to do so, almost timidly, during the past quarter-century. Why do large tracts of tillable land lie untouched, as I am told, in the neighborhood of many cities, sometimes even within the city walls, as at Nanking?[67]

Once again, Americans were puzzling over the mystery of untilled land in China. Baker's answer to his own question was that the Chinese lacked both the necessary machinery and its requisite, power. By Baker's estimate, China had no less than 500 million acres of uncultivated tillable land—over twice as much as was under cultivation. With machines, Baker believed, much of the unused land, especially in China's northwest provinces, could be profitably used in wheat production. Whether tractors or horses would be the cheapest source of power could be determined by trial. Moreover, Baker assured his listeners that his proposal would not displace farmers and increase unemployment, since the lands to be opened up were unsettled at the time.[68]

Baker explained that he spoke only as a private individual; he did not want to leave the impression that his ideas and proposal were officially connected with the USDA. But Lossing Buck later heard secondhand that "the USDA" was planning to study "land utilization in China" without sending personnel from Washington. Buck thought that the topic should be studied on location in China, with himself as project director. As *Chinese Farm Economy* neared completion, he wrote up grant proposals for his own land utilization study, and in 1928 he was given the necessary funds from the Social Science Research Council and the Institute of Pacific Relations. Buck planned nothing less than surveying every aspect of land use for the entire country of China.[69]

To begin this task, Buck returned to the United States for four months to talk with specialists and learn more about "land utilization," about which he actually knew little. He returned to China early in 1929 and began setting up a new research apparatus, employing dozens of senior staff and, at one point, one hundred clerks to tabulate collected survey data. He also began recruiting American experts to serve as visiting advisers. He hoped to secure the services of George Warren, and when Warren could not come, Buck hired Warren's son Stanley, who had just completed his Ph.D. in agricultural economics in his father's department at Cornell. Other assistance came from David Weeks and Charles Shaw from the University of California, Leonard Maynard from Cornell, Warren Thompson from the Scripps Foundation, Pearl Buck's brother, Edgar Sydenstricker, from the Milbank Memorial Fund, and a number of other visiting consultants—nineteen in all.[70]

The Americans designed survey schedules, directed Chinese assistants, and sampled the life of the expatriate in China. Stanley Warren, looking back on the experience later in his life, described his stay in China as a curious mixture of luxury and poverty: "You would live on higher standards in some respects than you would at home but not as high in others. I had a bicycle and every noon when I came home, if it was muddy, a servant would wash it while I was eating lunch, a service I'm not accustomed to at home, but being able to drive a dirty automobile might be looked upon as a higher standard than driving a clean bicycle."[71]

✥ ✥ ✥ ✥ ✥

With the new grant for a land utilization study and the bustle of foreign specialists coming and going, the Department of Agricultural Economics at Nanking did not escape the notice of the Nationalist government, which began to call upon the department for special research projects. In 1931, T. V. Soong asked Buck to help the government survey the disaster relief needs of districts hit by severe Yangzi River flooding. (Charles Lindbergh, who happened to be in China at the time, was also enlisted to fly aerial reconnaissance.) The next year, Soong again asked Buck to investigate damage claims in the wake of the "Shanghai Incident," when Japanese troops attacked the city. The local farmers had filed what seemed to the Chinese government to be inflated claims of losses for which they sought compensation; Buck was hired to determine which districts had actually been severely damaged in the fighting.[72]

Buck viewed these assignments as a milestone, marking government acceptance of his work and trust in his lack of bias. When he became a consultant, however, he traded away the neutrality that had kept him distant from both the Nationalists and the Communists. In late 1930, he wrote to friends in the United States that "things in Nanking are in a more settled condition than any time since the formation of the Nanking Government." Reporting on the Generalissimo's recent victories in fighting the forces of Feng Yuxiang and Yan Xishan, Buck revealed his new appreciation for Chiang Kai-shek: "General Chiang is a man of great courage, and at a critical moment when his men were retreating and urging him to order the whole army to retreat, refused to do so, and ordered his men into battle in the face of very great difficulties. It is said that he told his men that they could shoot him or do as they wished, that he was going out to fight the enemy. In this way he instilled some courage into his own officers, and turned the tide of victory toward the side of the Nanking Government."[73]

While praising the "quality of courage" that had given Chiang "a place of prominence among the Chinese people," Buck criticized the infestation of bandits and Communists, who were "difficult to distinguish" and seemed to be found "almost everywhere." The land utilization surveyors were finding "Communist propaganda" throughout the countryside, and Buck used a report from one of his assistants to point out the insidious workings of the Reds: At a rural middle school, students had been taught "Communistic ideas," and after graduation those students had become teachers at other rural schools, "carrying on propaganda in their school districts." Later, when the remnants of the Chinese Communist party were driven out of their mountainous sanctuaries in the southeast, Buck formally took sides in the civil war, accepting the Nationalist government's request to deploy his department in rural surveys that would help guide "reconstruction" in the contested areas and redirect farmer support away from the Communists and toward the Nationalist government.[74]

Buck enjoyed his role as a sought-after expert, and took time from his land utilization survey to prescribe the use of more experts to cure China's agricultural ills. In listing 108 recommendations for agricultural improvements that China should consider (e.g., plant windbreaks, conduct a soil survey, breed new crop varieties), he said that a few measures required the farmers themselves to change existing practices, and a few others required the cooperation of different government agencies. But most relied upon "technically trained persons."[75]

The United States, Buck said, provided China with an agricultural extension system suitable for emulation. Through experience, the United States had learned the best and cheapest ways of convincing farmers to adopt improved methods—the result, he said, "of the discovery of certain fundamental principles in extension work just as 'principles' have been discovered in the various sciences." The universality of some of the extension principles was not immediately evident, however. Placing agricultural advice in farm newspapers had been found to be the least expensive method of agricultural extension in the United States, and Buck urged Chinese extension agencies to take advantage of the same low-cost method, even though in China it would not be as successful. But another principle did seem readily transferable: extension work should stimulate farmers to undertake improvements themselves. Expanding the points upon which he had lectured the missionary community years before, Buck told the Chinese in 1931 that "farmers, like other people, prefer to manage their own affairs." Just as "the Chinese people do not want another nation to come into China and run the Chinese government for them," so Chinese farmers did not want "city people or any organization to come into their village to carry out reforms for them." [76]

Buck noted that the value of agricultural economics, his own field, was often overlooked, because "the subject is more abstract than those in other types of agricultural improvement." But it had much to contribute, Buck said, and he pointed to farmers in Wujiang, Anhui, who had found that when they began to grow American cotton, local cotton growers paid no more for the improved product. However, Nanking's Department of Agricultural Economics had organized a marketing cooperative that arranged for direct sales to large cotton mills near Shanghai, which paid a higher price for the cotton, a fact that soon convinced local merchants to follow suit. This required only a little staff time and showed "how often agricultural economic improvement can be carried on with little initial expense, the chief expenditure being the use of brains." [77]

❖ ❖ ❖ ❖ ❖

As the outspoken head of the department, the author of *Chinese Farm Economy*, and the director of a new survey of land utilization, Lossing Buck was well known in China. But the Buck name became famous in the United States as well in 1931, when Pearl Buck published *The Good Earth*, which was to become one of the most popular best-sellers in the history of American fiction. Shortly after Pearl received the Pulitzer Prize in 1932, the Bucks decided to spend a year in the United States. Lossing left the work on the land utilization survey to his assistants and returned to Ithaca to complete coursework for his Ph.D. in agricultural economics. Traditionally, a dissertation precedes a book, but Buck already had the book in hand and submitted *Chinese Farm Economy* as his thesis.

The two Bucks had contrasting personalities: he was serious and untalkative, she gregarious and voluble. Without the fame that was suddenly thrust upon Pearl, the differences might have been complementary, not divisive, but their marriage foundered when Pearl became a public figure in the United States and drifted from a husband whom she regarded as cold and emotionless. On their return trip to China in 1933, Pearl broke the news that she wanted a divorce; Lossing did not contest it.

Once back in Nanjing, he returned to his university position as the leading authority in Chinese agricultural economics. A "Dr." was now in his title and he was no longer confined, as he had suddenly been after the publication of *The Good Earth*, to the obscure shadows of being "the husband of ...." His professional ego received a new boost in 1934, when he was asked by Treasury Secretary Henry Morgenthau to come to Washington to meet with President Roosevelt and cabinet members about currency issues related to China. Buck went to the United States intending to stay one month, but his services were in demand and the one month lengthened into five. He returned to China with a continuing appointment as "U.S. treasury representative to China." [78]

Final work began on the land utilization project. Data were assembled from 168 places in 22 provinces, surveying almost 17,000 farms—more than five times as many as had been covered in the earlier *Chinese Farm Economy*. With additional population and food consumption data and countywide evaluations of land use patterns, the information tumbled into three hefty volumes: a 500-page summary of results and two companion volumes, an atlas and a compendium of statistics, which were huge folios the size of a small desk. *Land Utilization in China* was published in 1937. It was the culmination of almost ten years of labor and the work for which Lossing Buck would be best known. [79]

In it, Buck dropped the modest disclaimers he had used in *Chinese Farm Economy*; this time, he asserted that his data spoke for all of China. But despite the bulkiness of the volumes, *Land Utilization* had too little material to substantiate its claims. When he had started the study in 1928, Buck had been faced with the important decision of whether "to carry out the field work, province by province, or to carry it out in different parts of China at the same time." Proceeding by individual provinces would have meant better results but would have been slow, so Buck chose to survey all of China simultaneously. Once he began the surveys, however, he discovered that as big as his staff was, it was far too small for the massive task that he was attempting. His surveyors were stretched too thin, and as a result, many provinces were represented by farm surveys gathered from only a handful of places. Fujian was covered by surveys of only five places; Guangxi, by two; Liaoning, by one. [80]

Stung by earlier criticisms of the class-biased and haphazard sampling of the survey data used in *Chinese Farm Economy*, Buck had attempted to do better in the land utilization surveys. His assistants in the field were instructed to survey all the families in a given village, not just those they happened to know. If that proved impossible, especially in a larger village, they were to select one particular street or neighborhood and survey each household in consecutive order, without choosing to interview one particular family rather than another. But because of Buck's decision not to proceed by provinces, supervision of his surveyors in the field was impossible, and by his own admission his instructions were not adequately followed "in many localities." [81]

One of the principal aims of the study was to provide information that could serve as "a basis of national agricultural policies," and to that end Buck proposed that Chinese planners mentally divide Chinese agriculture into eight agricultural regions, with labels such as "Double Cropping Rice" and "Yangtze Rice-Wheat," which would succinctly describe the predominant use of agricultural land in each area. Unlike provincial boundaries, which in Buck's words "divide like from like," the agricultural regions would encompass homogeneous physical and economic conditions, permitting better government planning. For example, the neighboring provinces of Jiangsu and Anhui straddled the Wheat Region in their northern districts and the Rice Region in their southern. The northern halves of both provinces could be served by a single experiment station specializing in wheat, while the southern halves could share a station specializing in rice. But because of the artificial provincial boundaries, Buck explained, Jiangsu and Anhui maintained redundant sets of experiment stations that did not cooperate with each other.[82]

Evaluating the total amount of cultivated and potentially cultivable land, Buck fired criticism at Oliver Baker, the economist who had never visited China but had claimed that large fertile areas in China awaited settlement. "People who have never been in the Northwest," Buck wrote, "imagine great areas only awaiting settlement, while people who have been there and have seen with a discerning eye, fully realize the very limited area available for cultivation." Baker's uninformed estimate of arable land in China was not only wrong, but also "unfortunate," Buck said, for it had fed false hopes about agricultural potential in the region. He explained, "Farmers have settled most of this country centuries ago and have already brought under cultivation not only the good land but a great deal of sub-marginal land, such, for instance, as the mountain sides which might better be in pasture or in forest." The phenomenon in China was compared to that found on the dry marginal lands east of the Rocky Mountains in the United States, "where four successive generations have moved on to the land and then moved away again because the years of good crops were not frequent enough to maintain even a meager standard of living."[83]

Buck's observations of agriculture in Northwest China were acute, but they were gained from personal travel, not from a massive land utilization survey. The quantitative data that he had collected about soils and climate and land uses and crops and farm businesses were, in most instances, answers in search of questions. *Chinese Farm Economy* had excluded some of the most pressing social and political questions that troubled the Chinese countryside, but *Land Utilization* was even more divorced from matters of Chinese concern. In 1937 the Chinese countryside still had not recovered from the devastating impact of the world depression, and the Chinese Communist party, which had recovered from earlier setbacks, was raising fundamental questions about agricultural policies in China. But these matters did not interest Buck, who declared on the very first page of *Land Utilization* that he would not discuss "the so-called agrarian situation which may be thought of in terms of the political, economic and social relationships between farmers and other classes of society." [84]

When Buck wrote in *Land Utilization* that China was a "keen competitor" in world markets because of the low "costs per unit of food," his readers received no hint that the Chinese press had spoken of little but rural crisis (and of the problem of grain imports, not exports) for the previous ten years. Unable to read Chinese publications and bound by the narrow lens of "land utilization," Buck looked only at efficiency of land use. Moreover, rural crisis or not, China by his definition was a very efficient utilizer of its land, in that its reliance on grain production rather than meat and dairy products meant that less land was needed to support a given population. [85]

The size of that population remained a source of deep concern to Buck, but he criticized little else about the "agrarian situation." The specific recommendations for agricultural improvement that issued from *Land Utilization* were generally concerned with increasing yields and production. Eliminating the risk of crop failure from drought or flood would do more to increase production, Buck said, than any other measure. Big projects were needed: conservancy, reclamation, soil, forestry. Buck also recommended that graves be removed from fields, a move which he calculated would increase China's total crop area by 1 percent—land sufficient to support more than four hundred thousand farm families. Consolidation of scattered parcels would increase available land, he claimed, by another 10 percent. In sum, Buck estimated that the rationalization of agricultural land use and the employment of the most modern methods of intensive cultivation could increase China's total agricultural production by 25 percent. [86]

In a brief nod to critics of farm tenancy, Buck recommended that "the State should encourage a diffusion of ownership in those parts of the country where the prevailing form of tenancy meets neither the cultivators' nor the State's needs and where a large proportion of the tenants desire to become owners." But tenancy in China, he added (as he always did), was no greater than in many other countries. Buck explained that talk of collectivizing agriculture in China was too untested to earn his support; China should maintain the existing system of "individual farm family units." Revolution and land reform would not do much to improve the situation, he wrote: "The problem of land distribution is not one of equal division of land among all the people, for then no family would have enough land upon which to earn a living, but rather one of the development of farms of an economic size for each farm family, so that each may have a satisfactory standard of living." [87]

In the end, Buck suggested narrowly technocratic solutions to China's agricultural policies. By bringing together various "technical professions" represented by the soils expert, the geographer, the agronomist, and the forester, all under an able director ("preferably an agricultural economist"), wise decisions could be made about land use. Such was the vision of land utilization advocates who had spoken out in the United States ten years earlier, but in a very different social and political context.[88]

✣ ✣ ✣ ✣ ✣

Twenty years after he had first come to China, working first as a missionary and extension agent out in the field and later as an agricultural economist based at a university, Buck still believed that China's rural problems could be reduced to the simple matter of matching production with population by increasing the one and reducing the other. Social tensions did not enter his field of view, except briefly in 1927 and 1928, when he glimpsed the radical impulses that surfaced in the countryside during the Northern Expedition. But Buck soon lost sight of rural dissatisfaction as he returned to establishing his academic reputation and directing his farm surveys, which were not designed to detect rural problems, and so did not. Indeed, his most ambitious and famous work, the land utilization study, was the one least in touch with existing social realities. When the war with Japan began in July 1937, soon forcing the University of Nanking to evacuate, Buck had a view of the Chinese rural economy that was based more on American teachings than on Chinese realities.

In siding with Chiang Kai-shek and an explicitly nonradical approach to improving Chinese agriculture, Buck cannot be faulted for failing to see that the Communists would eventually triumph. In the 1930s—and even the 1940s—the events that would determine the conclusion of the civil war in 1949 were, of course, neither visible nor predictable. But Buck was blind to rural problems that were being discussed in his own time. And this blindness sometimes seemed to be almost willful, in that he ignored problems simply because they did not fit into the models of ideal farm management or land utilization that he had brought with him from the United States. One did not have to be clairvoyant to see that issues of land distribution would play an important part in future events in China; farm tenancy was a topic of constant comment, even in the cities, during the late 1920s and throughout the 1930s. Even if Buck was correct that tenancy rates were no worse in China than elsewhere, the political fact was that such pedantic comparisons did not reduce the volatility of the issue in the countryside. Social tensions simply would not go away.

Many of Buck's recommendations—for improved extension, large conservancy works, and population control—were eventually implemented by the Chinese government, but only after the Communists, whom he detested, had taken power. Buck had placed his hopes on the Nationalist government, whose troubles in the Chinese countryside were of such a different and more serious nature than those of the federal government in rural America that Buck never saw them, despite his accumulation of "data" from thousands of Chinese farms. A similar inability to see political reality, and how it limited technical agricultural improvements, afflicted the premier Chinese student of American agriculture.

8

DEFEAT

The Failure of the Star Pupil, 1930s

China's preeminent agronomist, Shen Zonghan, whose career was remarkable, was trained in the United States. Born into humble family circumstances, Shen managed by dint of diligent study to win a series of scholarships that led him from Chinese schools to American colleges in Georgia and New York. He returned to China to take the lead in agricultural education, plant breeding research, and organization of new administrative structures to support agriculture. His accomplishments were sizable, and he himself saw his life story as an exemplary tale that could provide inspiration to younger generations.[1] Yet his many successes in the laboratory and experimental field failed to have much impact by the time the peacetime era ended in 1937. Like the American research scientists who trained him, Shen believed that agricultural development was primarily a technical problem of increasing crop yields. This narrowly technical approach was spectacularly successful in the laboratory, but it failed utterly in the countryside when unaccompanied by fundamental social and political changes. Foreign experts such as John Griffing had found it impossible to introduce their improved plants and techniques, and so too did American-trained Chinese experts.

Born in 1895, Shen grew up near Yuyao, Zhejiang, in a small, single-surname village of about two hundred families. His father was a member of the rural gentry who had an examination degree and much prestige but owned little property. As a young boy, Shen was taught the classics in a small academy run by a relative, but he also did farm chores at home, learning everything from applying manure as fertilizer to harvesting crops. At the age of fifteen, he did well on an entrance examination and won a scholarship to a primary school in the county seat, temporarily leaving the farm. Upon graduation he decided to study agriculture. Against the advice of his teachers and schoolmates, who thought a career in agriculture was inappropriate for a bright scholar, and in defiance of his father, who wanted his son to start teaching and contributing income to the family, Shen borrowed money to enroll in 1913 at the provincial agricultural high school in Hangzhou.[2]

Two years in Hangzhou gave Shen both his first exposure to foreign agricultural ideas and the desire to study abroad. At first his dream was to go to Japan. The school was directed by Chinese graduates of Japanese agricultural schools, who had their students study Japanese. English was also taught, but by a Chinese instructor who had studied English in Japan and who brought back incorrect pronunciation that he passed on to the students. Shen intended to join a group of his classmates bound for Japan in 1914, but he could not borrow enough money and had to stay behind. In a newspaper, he saw a notice that the Ministry of Education was offering scholarships for study in the United States. At the time, Shen knew virtually nothing about American agricultural schools, remembering only that he had seen a letter at a friend's house the year before written by Hu Shih, a student of agriculture at Cornell. (Hu was the discouraged student of apples mentioned in chap. 5; later, Shen would claim that Hu's "vivid" report on Cornell had inspired his dream of studying there, although Hu's account was probably not very laudatory.) Shen realized that he would be able to continue his education only if he won a scholarship such as that offered for study in the United States. But graduation from Beijing's Qinghua University was required of candidates for the fellowships, so Shen resolved first to get to Beijing to study at the National Agricultural College, as a preliminary step to transferring to Qinghua.[3]

Shen could continue his studies only by borrowing heavily from relatives and friends, winning a tuition scholarship from the school, and again defying his father. The courses in basic sciences and agriculture in Beijing turned out to be more advanced that those in the high school, but Shen had no trouble earning top standing in his class. Outside of his regular classes at the college, Shen spent almost all of his time studying English on his own—reading grammars, memorizing vocabulary cards, and declaiming speeches to imaginary audiences while pacing the athletic field. He also converted to Christianity and often visited the home of a Chinese YMCA staff member who had many books on religion and English literature. His ability to read English progressed rapidly, but conversational English remained a problem even with the most diligent self-study. To win the scholarship to the United States, he had to transfer to Qinghua, and despite excellent marks in his coursework, Qinghua's oral entrance examination in English kept him from passing. Deeply disappointed, Shen graduated in 1918 from the National Agricultural College with no prospect of being able to go to the United States.[4]

✦ ✦ ✦ ✦ ✦

With his agricultural studies at an end, Shen faced the difficult task of finding employment that would utilize his expertise. With an introduction provided by an American missionary he had known in Yuyao, Shen wrote John Reisner in Nanjing to ask about work. Reisner wrote back offering the possibility of a modest position paying 14 *yuan* a month (about $6.00). Final approval would depend on a personal interview. Shen excitedly took a train to Nanjing, but when he arrived, Reisner was preoccupied with preparations for a lecture and postponed the interview. When

finally available to meet with Shen, Reisner was evasive and then explained that
the position was no longer available—he had given the job to a Nanking alumnus.
Shen had no leads to other possible jobs in agriculture.[5]

Without other prospects, Shen accepted a position as a private tutor in
Beijing, preparing a young man for a high-school entrance examination. The job
meant abandoning agriculture and teaching general subjects: English, mathematics,
science, geography, and history. But Shen had learned self-discipline during his
attempt to prepare for entrance into Qinghua, and he set himself a rigid schedule
of self-study in addition to his tutoring responsibilities. His day started at
6:00 A.M. with a half hour of Bible reading and prayer, followed by an hour of
reading English aloud, then additional English study sessions throughout the day.
Two hours were devoted to reading an English newspaper, and another hour to
writing English compositions. Shen also kept up agricultural studies on his own,
reading Eduard Strasburger's *Textbook of Botany*, John Henry Comstock's *Insect Life*,
and several Japanese books on entomology, soils, and botany. Not surprisingly, he
found inspiration in the autobiographies of fellow autodidacts, such as Benjamin
Franklin, Abraham Lincoln, and Booker T. Washington.[6]

Shen hoped to secure a position related to agricultural teaching or research in
Nanjing, the center of professional activity, but after two years of tutoring, his first
offer of an agricultural job was at a small cotton research station in western Hunan,
which was so remote and unprotected from wayward soldiers that no other
agricultural graduate had been willing to go there. But the position offered a return
to agriculture, so Shen took the job. When he arrived, he found soldiers everywhere and conditions just as unsettled as he had been warned they would be. He
rented land, planted American cotton, and befriended nearby warlord Feng Yuxiang, who took a liking to the fellow Christian. But in 1920 fighting forced Feng
to withdraw his troops from the area, and the cotton experiment lost its military
protector. Fortunately for Shen, his wish to work in Nanjing was realized when
he was offered a job teaching English at the First Provincial Agricultural High
School.[7]

For someone who had taught himself English, Shen's command of the language was quite good. In fact, he won a national English essay contest sponsored
by *Millard's Review*, an English-language weekly published in Shanghai. Topping
sixty-one entries, many of which were submitted by more privileged students at
American-run missionary schools, Shen's essay on the assigned topic of "How Can
America Best Help China?" described the United States as a special friend and
protector of China. Shen suggested that Americans needed to be better informed
about China: "If possible, the Americans should teach Chinese history and
geography as required courses in their universities and high schools so that the
Americans in a general way have an intimate knowledge of things Chinese and
their friendship to us may be built on a firmer foundation."[8]

Shen also recommended that America's "great and famous" men visit China in order to point out China's shortcomings and suggest means of improvement. "Chinese social evils," he wrote, "such as gambling, immorality, drinking, public corruption, become more serious every day. Chinese in general have no idea of improvement." Shen also called for American investments, which, unlike Japan's, were free of imperialistic ambitions: "The United States of America in investing money in foreign countries has no other ambition further than to expect only a financial return." In the interests of serving world peace, Shen argued, "Americans should help China as much as they can politically, socially, intellectually, financially, commercially, and industrially." [9]

When Shen took up his new teaching position in Nanjing, he discovered that his students did not accord him much respect. They ranked their instructors in a hierarchy: at the top were teachers who had been trained at American agricultural schools; below them were those who had been trained at Japanese schools; and at the bottom were teachers like Shen, who had graduated from Chinese institutions. The students also wielded considerable power; they successfully forced a string of principals to resign, and in one of the political struggles that brought down a principal, Shen lost his job. The experience rekindled his dream of studying in the United States, partly to increase the respect he would receive, and partly to obtain more knowledge about cotton culture, which he had enjoyed discussing with John Griffing while in Nanjing. His last chance for a scholarship had fallen through when he had done poorly in a fellowship competition sponsored by Nanyang Brothers Tobacco Company, which was sending Chinese students to the United States to study tobacco growing in the expectation that they would then promote the cultivation of American tobacco in China. (In retrospect, this was one of the more controversial contributions that American agriculture offered to China in this period.) If Shen was ever to study in the United States, he would have to pay for it himself. [10]

Shen took a position at an agricultural high school in Wuhu, Anhui, added a weekend job at a local agricultural station, and bided his time, saving money by extraordinary economy. Out of his monthly income of 130 *yuan*, he sent 20 to his family in Zhejiang, used 20 for his own subsistence, and managed to save most of the rest. Within two years, he had saved 1,000 *yuan* ($500); by borrowing another 1,400 *yuan* ($700), he bought his boat passage, purchased a few sets of clothes, and had $800 in U.S. currency on hand. His plan was to study cotton for one year at the Georgia State College of Agriculture, from which it seemed that all Chinese experts on cotton had graduated, and then work for six months gaining field experience. His father was furious that his son was abandoning gainful employment for more studies, with no apparent regard for the family's financial difficulties. Going to America when both his father and mother were alive and desired that he stay nearby showed, his father said, that Shen was most unfilial. Only with the intervention of an older brother did Shen receive grudging permission from his father to go. [11]

✢ ✢ ✢ ✢ ✢

Sailing from Shanghai in August 1923, Shen met a friendly American couple, the Candlers, who were from Atlanta and who solicitously reviewed his travel plans. When Shen took the Southern Pacific across the country to Georgia, Candler was waiting at the Atlanta train station with a car to whisk him to a suite in a large hotel. The next morning, when Shen checked out and tried to pay for his room, he found that Candler had already paid. Shen was appreciative, but completely un-aware of how untypical was this first American that he had chanced to meet: Candler was Asa Griggs Candler, Jr., the man who had helped his father build Coca-Cola into an empire and who was one of the wealthiest men in the South.[12]

When Shen arrived at the College of Agriculture in Athens, he intended to enroll as a graduate student, but the registrar's office would not accept his Chinese degree. Finally admitted as a probationary student, Shen soon impressed his professors with his knowledge and experience. Most of the textbooks were ones he had read on his own before he had come to the United States. Academic standards were not as high as he had expected, and he found little challenge in the classroom, earning A's easily. In fieldwork, his earlier cotton-growing experience in Hunan was clearly evident. It also distinguished him from the Chinese students who had come to Georgia before him, virtually all of whom had come from urban backgrounds, had no farm experience, and had chosen agricultural study as a means to an office career. One of the Georgia professors told Shen, "I've taught many Chinese students, but none of them knew how to grow Chinese cotton. You're the first Chinese student I've had who actually has had experience growing cotton in China."[13]

It happened that there were no other Chinese students on campus at the time. For companionship, Shen befriended a young American who was living in the same boardinghouse; the two took after-dinner walks together, and Shen practiced his English. The town also had a Chinese laundryman who treated Shen with affection, helping to dispel Shen's loneliness with Chinese tea, newspapers, and invitations to large Chinese feasts prepared on Shen's behalf on Saturday nights. The two men did not speak Chinese dialects that were mutually intelligible, how-ever, so they had to converse in English, the only spoken language they had in common.[14]

Early in the fall term, Shen received an invitation to spend a weekend in Atlanta as the houseguest of the Candlers. Shen did not know their identity until it was explained to him by his landlady, who was amazed that her boarder was on personal terms with the richest man in the state. Shen was less excitable and took it all calmly. The tour of the Candler estate led him past hundred-acre gardens, greenhouses, a zoo, a swimming pool, an athletic field, stables, and art treasures. A huge dinner was given in Shen's honor (where he struggled to eat fried chicken with a knife and fork until one of the Candler daughters whispered that it was all right to eat it with one's fingers). Ballroom dancing followed. The next day, Candler gave Shen a tour of the university and hospital that the family had donated to the city. At the end of the visit, Candler offered to help Shen in any way Shen named. Shen declined the offer, but asked the question that had been nagging him during his visit: "Why have you been so nice to me?"[15]

Candler's answer was an interesting specimen of national stereotyping. On the basis of his recent visits to both China and Japan, Candler explained, he had discerned significant differences in the character of the people. Take the rickshaw pullers as an example, he suggested: "In Tokyo, every time we took a rickshaw, we had to give a tip in addition to the fare, and even then be asked to pay more, which was quite aggravating. But in Beijing, when we paid the fare for a rickshaw, the coolie would simply say 'Thank you' and refuse our attempts to add a tip." From this comparison, Candler went on, he had found the Japanese people to be "corrupt," whereas the Chinese were "most likable." Candler had invited Shen to be his guest in order to show his "high regard for the Chinese people."[16]

✧ ✧ ✧ ✧ ✧

Shen did not ask for special help and, it soon turned out, did not need any. He earned his master's degree within a year of arriving at the Georgia college, specializing in cotton and wheat studies. On the basis of his outstanding academic record and the recommendations of his Georgia professors, Shen was able to win a partial scholarship from the Qinghua Boxer Fund to extend his studies in the United States and pursue a doctorate. He chose the famous plant-breeding program at Cornell and moved to Ithaca in 1924.[17]

In contrast to his experience in Georgia, he now found that he had to apply himself to the coursework, a demanding curriculum that included genetics, advanced genetics, crop breeding, biometry, farm crops, soils, advanced soils, soil bacteriology, advanced plant physiology, and cytology. Shen also attended weekly seminars in four different departments—plant breeding, agronomy, plant physiology, and cytology—where he enjoyed observing the intellectual combat of professors and students, who gathered together to discuss and critique recent research. Shen plunged into his studies with a single-mindedness that left virtually no time for anything else; he worked from seven o'clock in the morning until eleven at night, seven days a week.[18]

The fellowship that supported his studies provided only half the living stipend that the other Chinese fellows in America received, so Shen could maintain just a minimal level of subsistence. He had no money for new clothes and shoes to replace the worn outfits he had brought from China, and to economize on food costs, he stopped eating at the cafeteria and cooked his meals on the Bunsen burners in the lab.[19]

His diligent study, his willingness to work hard in the experimental fields ("You're not like all the rest," he was often complimented), and his precarious financial position made Shen the ideal candidate for a special research fellowship offered by the International Education Board (see chap. 6). It was a singular honor, for he was the only Chinese recipient in the fellowship program. More important, it meant he would not have to worry about having enough money to complete his doctorate.[20]

As an IEB fellow, Shen returned to China in early 1926 to assist in the Cornell-Nanking plant breeding program. It had been three years since he had left China, traveling third class. How different his return was, traveling first class, courtesy of the IEB, with enough money to present his father with a gift of several hundred dollars for his seventieth birthday. The prodigal son had finally made good, and the old man was happy. Shen's return to Nanjing was particularly rich in irony. On his last visit, eight years before, Shen had been an unemployable nobody, easily pushed aside by Reisner to make room for a Nanking graduate. Now he was the most honored Chinese agricultural student to have studied in America, and Reisner and his arch-rival at Southeastern, Zou Bingwen, each tried to woo Shen into making a commitment to come to his respective institution after Shen completed his degree at Cornell. When Reisner saw Shen, he asked, "Haven't we met somewhere before?" Shen, enjoying the moment but not wanting to embarrass Reisner, pretended that he was not clear whether or not they had ever met.[21]

Initially, Shen postponed making a decision between Nanking and Southeastern; he was busy teaching a course at Nanking and assisting the Cornell representative in residence at the time, Clyde Myers. Harry Love, then in Ithaca, proposed to Reisner that the University of Nanking abandon its claim to Shen and allow him to go to Southeastern after graduation. Certainly he could make important contributions to the work at Southeastern, Love pointed out. In return for "releasing" Shen, Nanking could obtain the services of another person. It would be a nice gesture of goodwill, and Shen could remain in close contact with his friends and colleagues at Nanking, making possible the coordination of plant improvement work between the two institutions. But Reisner was not receptive to the idea of sharing this prize find. He wrote back that the best results for plant improvement work would come about "by the [Nanking] College of Agriculture and Forestry strengthening its own work at every turn."[22]

In the end, Shen announced that he would return to the University of Nanking after graduation. He felt that, as a government institution, Southeastern was too vulnerable to political changes and sudden departures of presidents and deans; plant breeding research required a stable environment over a number of years, a condition that Southeastern seemed unable to guarantee. The University of Nanking, as a missionary school, offered a setting better sheltered against political winds, and it also had the larger budget.[23]

At the end of 1926, Shen returned to Ithaca to write his doctoral dissertation. When the International Education Board asked him how much money he would like for a monthly stipend, he replied that $80 would be sufficient to supplement the $40 he received monthly from the Qinghua fund. The other IEB fellows must have regarded him as an insufferable prig, for they had insisted that they needed at least $200 a month. Then Shen came along, proposing to live on little more than half of that and telling the IEB that he was happy to forgo a large stipend so that a large number of students could be assisted.[24]

✢ ✢ ✢ ✢ ✢

Shen's graduate career at Cornell ended with a number of new honors, but his dissertation on winter wheat crosses had to be completed quickly during the summer of 1927, for the evacuation of foreigners from Nanjing meant that the University of Nanking desperately needed Shen to begin teaching in the fall semester. With his Ph.D. completed (after only three years' combined residence at Georgia and Cornell), Shen rushed back to China to serve as head of the Crop Improvement Project at Nanking. He also taught genetics and plant breeding, and showed the distinctive marks of his foreign education. Shen stressed fundamental principles, not rote memorization of numbers and names. He insisted that text material be integrated with field experiences, leading students into a rice field himself to demonstrate transplanting. His students, who were from urban back-grounds, flinched at putting their feet into the muck and water of the flooded rice field, so Shen had to coax the timid. His classes came to be quite popular; at times they included more than half of the two-hundred-odd students of the College of Agriculture and Forestry.[25]

Shen soon found that in some respects his education at Cornell had not prepared him for his situation in China. Plant breeding was by its very nature quite specialized. Some of the most important crops in China—rice, sorghum, millet, and sugar beets—were grown but rarely in the United States and hence had been little studied. Accordingly, the only English-language textbooks on plant breeding that Shen could give his students for reference lacked detailed examples appropriate to China. Shen also discovered that Cornell had neglected to teach him about "blank testing," which he found useful in his classes. The test called for students to plant three hundred rows of one variety of wheat, then carefully measure the heads of each and note the varying weights from row to row. The data gathered gave his students an appreciation of the relationship between soil fertility and yields. At the agricultural college in Ithaca, the lesson was too elementary for the students, who came from farm backgrounds, so blank testing was never mentioned. But Shen found it an excellent exercise for helping rusticate his urban students in Nanjing.[26]

Shen spent only about a third of his time teaching; the rest was devoted to his own plant breeding work on wheat, rice, and sorghum. The work was done well, and one wheat variety tested under his direction displayed a pleasing combi-nation of earlier maturation and significantly higher yields than common varieties. Offered opportunities to leave the university for positions in provincial adminis-tration, Shen chose to remain on campus, partly because he unabashedly liked academia, and partly because of his belief that the way to improve Chinese agriculture was to increase agricultural production, and the easiest way to begin that was to use improved varieties. "When the farmer plants an improved variety," he wrote, "he obtains an increase in yield without additional capital, fertilizer, or labor inputs. In economic terms, that is pure gain." [27]

٭ ٭ ٭ ٭ ٭

The idea of "pure gain" from improved varieties, free of any accompanying drawbacks, was obviously appealing, but Shen saw that his plant breeding research at the University of Nanking was far too small in scale to serve as a national program. A private university could train specialists, but only the inauguration of government programs, as in the United States, would assure plant breeding research on a scale appropriate for the nation. In 1928, at a national conference of the Ministry of Agriculture and Mines, Shen proposed that the new Chiang Kai-shek government establish a national agricultural experiment station to serve as the hub of a research network, conducting research and coordinating the work of provincial and county stations. The proposal was well received at the conference and was sent on with a recommendation for implementation. But once it entered the Nanjing bureaucracy, it disappeared.[28]

In the meantime, Shen encouraged interprovincial cooperation in agricultural programs until a truly national program of agricultural improvement could be started. The provincial governments of both Jiangsu and Zhejiang were interested in agriculture, and Shen was instrumental in arranging for the two provinces to jointly hire his former Cornell teacher, Harry Love, as an adviser. Love was given a three-year contract and returned to China in 1931.[29]

The presence of an American adviser was adroitly used by Shen to prod the national government into action: Shen argued that the valuable services of the foreign expert would best be utilized if Love worked not for two provinces but for a national agricultural research bureau, such as the one Shen had already proposed. A reshuffling of cabinet ministers in 1931 brought to power people sympathetic to Shen's idea, and a fourteen-member planning committee was finally appointed. Aside from Shen and other leading Chinese agriculturalists, the committee included three Americans from Cornell: Love, Buck, and Myers.[30]

The committee presented concrete recommendations for establishing a National Agricultural Research Bureau (NARB), but implementation proceeded haltingly. The initial director appointed four American-educated Chinese specialists to head programs, but he and his appointees soon resigned or were dismissed when another cabinet shuffle brought new superiors to power. The next director, Tan Xihong—whom Shen regarded as an incompetent political appointee—hired his own friends, who, like Tan, had been educated in France. Two more years passed, while the NARB, without land, existed only on paper.[31]

In 1933, another governmental reorganization provided an opportunity for Shen and his friends to lobby for changes at the NARB. Tan was fired, and the new man who was brought in, Qian Tianhe, appointed Love as chief technician. Since so little had been done in the two years that the NARB had officially existed, the new administration started with virtually a free hand. The first pressing matter was to find an appropriate site for the NARB's experimental fields and offices. The planning committee had originally recommended that both the NARB and its offices be located at Xiaolingwei, a few kilometers outside of Nanjing in Jiangning County, where a large tract of 2,700 *mou* (450 acres) was available. Love now suggested that the fields be placed in Jiangning County but that the NARB offices be built within Nanjing's city gates, for the convenience of visitors and the staff who lived in the city. But the Chinese saw the drawbacks of Love's proposal; it made little sense to keep the NARB's scientists so far from experimental fieldwork simply for the sake of "convenience." Love's proposal was rejected, and fields, offices, homes, and dormitories were planned for the rural site at Xiaolingwei.[32]

Construction of the first NARB buildings had barely begun when, in 1934, Love's three-year contract expired and he returned to the United States. Shen was chosen as the succeeding chief technician, but the University of Nanking was unwilling to let him go. In the end, Shen agreed to continue to teach at the university, but he moved his family to the new site at Xiaolingwei to show the university administration that he was serious about serving the NARB and that they should not delay in hiring a replacement for him. Shen's wife was an agriculturalist who had been appointed to the NARB before Shen, and he hesitated before accepting his new post, worried that a husband-wife appointment at the same institution would encourage whispers of impropriety and nepotism. When the Shens and their two children moved to Xiaolingwei, they were the first family there, and the only available housing was a small, dark temple.[33]

✢ ✢ ✢ ✢ ✢

Six years after Shen had made a detailed proposal for its establishment, the NARB was finally functioning. In preparation for planting, fields were leveled, irrigation and drainage ditches dug, and impressive administration buildings and dormitories, standing above the Nanjing-Hangzhou highway, were completed in October 1934. More impressive still was the long list of research activities in which the NARB staff claimed to be involved. A number of years before, Shen had advised his home province, Zhejiang, to begin its agricultural improvement work by concentrating on just a few important projects that could produce visible results, and to avoid diffusing attention on an overly comprehensive agenda. The temptation was, of course, to take on everything at once, as the earlier generation of experimental stations in China had tried to do. Shen had noted that in attempting a little of everything, the stations had failed to do any one thing well. Now, at the NARB, Shen did not follow his own counsel; the NARB, too, appeared to tackle everything at once.[34]

For an organization with a staff of only fifteen specialists, the NARB had an elaborate structure of divisions, departments, and research programs. Its Division of Crop Production included departments of agronomy, forestry, plant pathology, and entomology; the Division of Animal Production was subdivided into animal husbandry and veterinary science; and the Division of Agricultural Economics had separate departments of crop reporting, farm management, and rural industries. The studies for wheat improvement, from regional testing to hybridization, were so numerous that the list of their titles alone took up several pages in official reports; rice, cotton, and potato improvement programs also spawned long lists of ostensibly separate studies underway at the NARB. Each department boasted of its busy research activity, creating an impression that the NARB was twenty times as large as it actually was.[35]

One of the most interesting projects that the NARB started was its Department of Rural Industries, headed by John Bernard Tayler, the only foreigner on the permanent staff. The department recognized "the importance of supplementing agriculture with industry," an important need in a country such as China, "where the under-employment in the villages due to the density of the population and to the part-time nature of agriculture is estimated as equal to the whole-time unemployment of fifty to sixty million people." The department itself did not intend to create and manage rural industries, but it did plan to collect data about raw materials, power supplies, agricultural production, and markets, in order to advise others about recommended new industries for particular areas. Although the need to integrate agriculture and industry, which the department noted was then "widely felt in the Western world today," would be incorporated into national development policy only many years later, the NARB was at least aware of its importance.[36]

Beginning in 1935, the NARB annually invited a foreign agricultural authority to spend a number of months in residence, offering seminars for the staff and outside visitors. John Wishart, of Cambridge, England, was the first such visitor, and H. K. Hayes, a famed plant breeder from the University of Minnesota (and future developer of hybrid corn), spent ten months in China in 1936 lecturing at the NARB and accompanying Shen on visits to wheat-growing stations in North China. Shen thought the foreign experts contributed a great deal to the NARB, but he had to counter the criticism that their services were too costly. The NARB, Shen pointed out, did not use foreign experts without taking pains to be "extremely economizing." Indeed, it paid only for their travel and living expenses; their home institutions paid their salaries. Nevertheless, Shen and the Chinese authorities at the bureau did feel that foreigners should be given accommodations that were even more spacious and comfortable than the new houses built for the top staff. When Hayes arrived with his wife, a new three-story, four-bedroom home was waiting.[37]

÷ ÷ ÷ ÷ ÷

The national government was unwilling to substantially increase the level of its initial funding for the NARB, but it was willing to fund new organizations. Because of China's huge wheat and rice imports, the government created a new National Rice and Wheat Improvement Institute in 1935. The institute was located on the same campus as the NARB, and although it may have looked like a new, separate entity to outside observers, such as the government officials who sponsored it, Shen confessed in his memoirs that it was in fact indistinguishable from the NARB. The institute and the NARB shared the same administration, and Shen himself was put in charge of the new institute's wheat division, while retaining his old NARB position. Since the government was willing to spend much more if there were two institutions at Xiaolingwei instead of one, the staff members were happy to play along in the masquerade. The next year, still another new organization, a wheat inspection office, was established to guard against adulteration of wheat sent to market, and Shen accepted another concurrent office. Shen and his colleagues did not mind the multiple appointments, even though there was no additional salary, because they saw that the proliferation of institutions brought increased government funding for agriculture.[38]

By 1936, the Xiaolingwei campus, with its two "separate" institutes, had a total annual budget of 1 million *yuan* (about $360,000). The staff mushroomed, and one large new building was completed after another, providing expanded offices, laboratories, refrigeration rooms, greenhouses, and a gas plant. Shen was not only delighted to work amid well-equipped facilities but also liked the professional atmosphere that was so rarely seen at other institutions. The staff was required to work eight-hour days with strict hours—8:00 A.M. to 12 noon and 2:00 to 6:00 P.M.—without exception, "punching in" with their chops (personal seals) in a roll book that the director personally scrutinized.[39]

With an enlarged staff, well-equipped campus, and serious-minded administration, the NARB was an exciting place to work in 1935, 1936, and 1937. Later, looking wistfully back on these years, Shen called them a "Golden Age" for the advance of scientific agriculture in China. These years were also a golden age for Shen personally. A man who never aggressively pursued financial gain for himself, Shen nevertheless enjoyed the distance he had come since his days as a penniless student. The Shens moved to a new, eight-room house built especially for them on the NARB campus; modeled after those at the University of Nanking, it had a refrigerator, running water, and Western bathroom fixtures. The Shens were served not only by the modern conveniences but also by the traditional amenities: three servants. Shen Zonghan took particular pride in two things—his well-stocked personal library and his own Ford automobile, which took the family on picnics.[40]

✢ ✢ ✢ ✢ ✢

Shen was "doing well by doing good." Moreover, his professional success in China and the promising expansion of the NARB and related agricultural institutes during the 1930s appeared to confirm the hope that Americans had placed in him and in his American-trained colleagues. China seemed on the verge of accomplishing something important, using American ideas but its own people. This moment of promise in Chinese agriculture attracted the attention of a potentially generous patron, the Rockefeller Foundation.

The Rockefeller Foundation had a long-standing interest in China, dating back almost as far as its 1913 charter, in which it pledged to promote "the well-being of mankind throughout the world." Its first president, John D. Rockefeller, Jr., the only son of the Standard Oil tycoon, was a Sinophile and collector of delicate chinoiserie. Under his guidance, the new foundation sent several commissions to survey the needs of China. In 1914 the foundation had created the China Medical Board, which channeled a colossal sum—more than $30 million—into the Peking Union Medical College and related programs during the next twenty years.[41] However, the only agricultural program in which the Rockefellers were involved was the Cornell-Nanking project, which was funded not by the Rockefeller Foundation but by the International Education Board, the separate, administratively distant, and short-lived "cousin" of the main foundation (see chap. 6). Despite the tremendous investment that the Rockefeller Foundation had made to advance medicine in China, until the early 1930s it had ignored agriculture. In 1931, however, one of the foundation's vice presidents became excited about the potential of directing agricultural change in China, and thus decided to redress this oversight.

Selskar Gunn was the vice president primarily responsible for European programs, but on a return trip from Paris to New York during the summer of 1931, Gunn passed through China and spent almost two months surveying the scene and interviewing academics, officials, doctors, and businessmen. At the urging of a friend, he talked with rural sociologists at several universities and visited James Yen's "rural reconstruction" center at Dingxian, Hebei, where literacy education, health improvement, and "self-government" were offered to local farmers.[42] Gunn found it difficult to organize his impressions. He wrote shortly afterward, "China lives and moves, let us hope, forward. It is a mighty puzzle. No living being can pretend to find its solution."[43]

Gunn found numerous signs of instability. "The Nanking government," he reported, "really has control over a small part of the country. An authority attached to the Ministry of Finance stated that the Government actually only received revenue from three of the twenty odd provinces." Of the revenues that were collected, 90 percent were used for military purposes, he was told by T. V. Soong, the minister of finance. Gunn was not impressed with the Chinese government he encountered in Nanjing: "I had the feeling it was more like a group of youngsters running a high school society rather than the affairs of a country of 450,000,000 people."[44]

Gunn also found that "the Chinese have become touchy on the subject of inferiority." He wrote, "The danger of wholesale importation of Western doctrines is decried in an ever increasing volume. The demand is now to 'Chinafy' Western knowledge." He was not sympathetic to Chinese nationalism ("they have exalted ideas of what they could do if given the opportunity"), but he was intrigued by the state of flux that seemed to prevail in China. Gunn declared: "China has become

plastic after centuries of rigid conventionalism." Perhaps the Rockefeller Foundation could help shape the new China.[45]

When Gunn returned to New York, his appeal that China receive fresh
attention from the foundation was supported by its president, Max Mason. In
1932, Gunn was sent back to China for an extended stay, in order to prepare a
detailed list of recommendations for foundation action. The resulting report, presented to the foundation trustees in 1934, recommended support for rural improvement instead of continued funding of the elitist Peking Union Medical College.
Gunn reported that in China, "all over the country one hears of plans for national
or provincial reconstruction and with particular reference to the rural problems.
This is natural as it is estimated that over 85 percent of the population is rural."
Gunn recommended that the Chinese concern with the countryside receive the
foundation's full support. "I urgently insist," he told the foundation, "that a considerable part of any future aid which we may give be devoted toward activities
the benefits of which will be felt by the rural population." [46]

Gunn had developed more sensitivity to Chinese concerns about nationalism
and Westernization since his first brief visit to China three years before, and his
specific recommendations in 1934 reflected a new interest in developing indigenous institutions. Sending Chinese students abroad for Western training now
seemed unwise to Gunn. The majority of returned students had "lost a good deal
of their Chinese point of view and background and have picked up something of
Western life but insufficient to make them really Western in their outlook." The
result was that "many are disgruntled and become the leaders of radical movements." A better course was strengthening Chinese institutions, which also permitted more benefits for the money invested. Gunn calculated, "At the present rate
of exchange, two or three [graduates at Chinese institutions] could be paid an
adequate stipend and a thousand U.S. dollars could be given for equipment for a
cost equal to that of one foreign fellowship." [47]

In his report, Gunn also frowned on sending foreign experts on short assignments to China. He had seen dozens of foreign advisers in China, guiding the
Nanking government in financial and economic policy, rural credits, cooperatives,
public health, sericulture, land tenure, and many other programs. "It may be rather
hazardous to prophesy now what will be the outcome of all their efforts," Gunn
wrote, but "indications are none too brilliant." The usual criticisms that Gunn had
heard were that the experts stayed too short a time and that their recommendations
were "generally along the lines of what has been done in the *particular* country
from which they come." Gunn suggested that experts stay in China for three to
five years, so that they could actively participate in the implementation of their
recommendations. The College of Agriculture at the University of Nanking was
lauded for its wise use of foreign experts, and it led the list of institutions that
Gunn recommended for immediate Rockefeller funding of major rural projects.[48]

✧ ✧ ✧ ✧ ✧

The total annual cost of a new, rural-centered "China Program" for the foundation would be about $300,000, Gunn estimated. But the Rockefeller trustees were reluctant to begin a new venture when the foundation was undertaking a thorough self-appraisal of all of its programs. Gunn's recommendations were referred to the foundation's ad hoc Committee for Appraisal and Plan, which had been formed to consider the best uses of the foundation's money as if it were starting "with a clean slate." The committee's critical evaluation of previous Rockefeller funding, both in the United States and abroad, paralleled Gunn's evaluation of previous Rockefeller spending in China: too much had been spent on medicine and public health, to the exclusion of other fields. The committee asked, "Is physical health the outstanding need of the world today? Do we best serve the welfare of mankind by devoting a substantial percentage of our contributions to disease?" [49]

Previous foundation emphasis on research now also seemed unwise. Instead of paying for the acquisition of more knowledge that would go unutilized, the committee suggested that it might be preferable to support "the better dissemination and the more thorough application of existing knowledge." Gunn's China Program was immediately appealing because it was practical and full of references to agricultural extension and mass educational programs. The committee was searching for countries where "a plastic condition" offered "opportunities for service" not found elsewhere. It wanted to avoid countries that were either too underdeveloped or too developed: "There are countries or areas that are either so backward in development that there is too litttle soil for seed, or relatively so advanced in development that the Foundation could make only a limited contribution." China seemed a perfect candidate for experimentation; combining great need with "wide open opportunity," it was a temptingly "vast laboratory in the social sciences." [50]

The review committee remained cautious in making new funding commitments, however. Gunn had not mentioned how long he thought a China program would be needed, and an open-ended commitment seemed dangerous ("if we embark, we embark for the duration"). The committee was also concerned that China had already claimed its fair share of Rockefeller funds, since the support of the Peking Union Medical College already had drawn the largest total sum in any country outside the United States. Other areas of the globe, such as Central and South America and India, had received virtually nothing. [51]

In December 1934, the foundation's executive board, heeding both Gunn's appeal for a new China program and the review committee's warning not to make an open-ended commitment, authorized $1 million to be spent in China over three years along the lines suggested by Gunn. It was not a large sum, but it conformed with the foundation's interest in getting the most dramatic benefits from the least expenditure of funds. The trustees believed that "the resources of the foundation are significantly large if they are applied over a narrow front, but they become ineffectual and unimportant if they are widely scattered." A short-term commitment also permitted the foundation to retain its natural advantage over governmental institutions—namely, the freedom "to change its strategy at any moment."[52]

Foundation headquarters reserved the right to grant final approval for the specific projects, but Gunn was sent back to China in early 1935 to head a new Rockefeller Foundation office in Shanghai, where he could refine his recommendations and supervise administration. The moment he returned, however, he found that he was besieged by Chinese institutions who sought foundation grants. He wrote to Mason, the foundation president, "I am taking especial pains to spread around the news that the Foundation's new program is a very modest one and that the funds available are small. This is not easy to do, as the name 'Rockefeller' still inspires hopes of large appropriations."[53]

The College of Agriculture at the University of Nanking, headed now by Chinese administrators, was especially forceful in pressing its requests on Gunn. However, he refused to be stampeded and took a dim view of their use of the sentimental argument that the school had been "established largely by Americans with American money." That fact, Gunn felt, was irrelevant. The important question was whether Nanking—or agricultural colleges at any other mission college, such as the admittedly "pitiful case" of Groff's college at Canton Christian, recently renamed Lingnan University (see chap. 4)—could survive financially in the future. All had experienced deep cuts in funding from home mission boards squeezed by the Depression. Gunn reported to New York, "Mission colleges have either got to produce some new money or get out of the game." Sentimentality could not be permitted: "We will be completely sunk if we allow our sympathies with some of these foreign institutions to go to the extent of appropriating sums of money which will not in all probability give us the best return in terms of our main objective."[54]

Gunn was much more interested in helping Chinese institutions that were independent of other foreign funding, and these included both Southeastern—recently renamed National Central University—and the National Agricultural Research Bureau. Southeastern/National Central could not shake its checkered political history, but the NARB, being so new, was unburdened with a troubled past. Indeed, the NARB seemed a perfect candidate to support: it was a Chinese-staffed institution, invulnerable to the nationalistic criticism that had tarred with the taint of imperialism those agricultural colleges, like Nanking, that were filled with foreigners. Moreover, the NARB was bypassing the brewing land-reform controversy by offering a distinctly nonrevolutionary answer to China's rural problems: technically achieved improvements in crop yields.

With three outstanding agricultural institutions in Nanjing, Gunn was aggravated to see that the University of Nanking's College of Agriculture was unwilling to work with the other two. "I have a strong impression," he reported, "that some of the Nanking University crowd who apparently are not very keen toward cooperating with the Government would like to see us finance their institution so that they could go ahead without any particular relationship to the National Central University Agricultural College or to the National Agricultural Research Bureau." Gunn decided that the best thing the Rockefeller Foundation could do in Nanjing was to force the three institutions to work together.[55]

÷ ÷ ÷ ÷ ÷

In 1935, the first year of its new China Program, the Rockefeller Foundation treated the three Nanjing institutions generously: the NARB received $34,400; National Central, $34,600; and Nanking, which had the best programs in the country, was given $5,500 and a large sum, 72,000 *yuan* (about US $30,000), in local currency, despite Gunn's reluctance to help a mission school. Large grants were also given to James Yen's "rural reconstruction" project at Dingxian, Hebei, and to rural programs at Nankai and Yenching universities. The more a Chinese institution seemed to be independent and self-contained, the more eagerly the foundation offered grants. Yen's program of education and health projects was attractive, among other reasons, because it seemed to be supported solely by the local population, which offered to the Rockefeller Foundation the promise that its programs could be "adopted elsewhere without the use of funds other than those normally available."[56]

The foundation grants to the NARB and the two Nanjing agricultural colleges came only after "prolonged discussions" with all three institutions about their willingness to work more closely with each other. Gunn was pleased that he had convinced them of "the importance of team play" in agricultural training and research, but the agreements Gunn reached with them did not provide for their working cooperatively, only for their staying out of each other's domain. The NARB was given responsibility for insect control; National Central, animal husbandry and veterinary medicine; and Nanking, agricultural economics.[57]

Most of the time, Gunn was a shrewd observer who had little patience for the inflated claims of accomplishment that issued regularly from all Chinese offices in the Nationalist period. "The National Government," Gunn reported to New York, "for political reasons finds it necessary to carry on activities in many places and over wide areas." Gunn called this a "quantitative" approach to rural reconstruction, launching efforts in many directions "with generally inferior results." The Rockefeller Foundation's China Program, he hoped, would show the government the importance of a "qualitative" approach. Gunn was not naive and hardly believed that all components of his China Program were doing well. National Central had few accomplishments to show for its grant to develop animal husbandry programs, and the school came to lead Gunn's list of disappointments. By 1937, Gunn would candidly report to New York that at National Central, "the results obtained through our aid have been only mediocre."[58]

The NARB, however, enjoyed immunity from Gunn's critical scrutiny. With the pride of American agricultural colleges, Shen Zonghan, as a leading figure, the NARB had special appeal, and its reports were granted more than the usual credibility. Shen wrote to Gunn of the sprayers and dusters built in the NARB's new machine shop, the new insecticides developed in the laboratory, and the extension of insect control "on a national basis," all made possible by the "far sighted promotion" of the Rockefeller Foundation. Gunn, ignoring the fact that such "reports" contained no hint of any problems and were intended more to ensure grant renewal than to describe actual experiences, approvingly passed them on to New York.[59]

The foundation trustees in New York were duly impressed. The NARB was praised for its good staff, its dozen major departments, and the long list of publications to its credit though it had existed only a few years. After one year of Rockefeller Foundation support, the insect control program appeared to be doing quite well: photographs sent from Nanjing showed an entomology laboratory, a field being sprayed with an oil emulsion to control cotton aphids, and most impressive of all, uniformed Chinese soldiers ("under direction of the Bureau's entomologists") working peacefully in a campaign to control the pine caterpillar. The Rockefeller Foundation renewed its grant to the NARB for a second year.[60]

In 1937, more good news came in, with a report from Shen telling of "very successful results." Newly established training programs and printed pamphlets took insect control research at the NARB out to the farmers; extension work, in fact, was declared to be "relatively easy to do" since farmers themselves had increasingly realized the value of insect control. And Shen reported that the NARB's new sprayers and dusters had been "distributed over almost all the country." Another NARB official claimed that over $5 million in crop losses had been averted by the work accomplished to date. The trustees in New York were pleased, noting that the China programs "were essentially of Chinese conception" and that the foundation's contribution was simply to assist "Chinese institutions and workers who are spending their lives in search of adequate answers to the many complex problems which exist. Credit for the resulting accomplishment belongs to the Chinese." The NARB insect control program received funding for a third year.[61]

✧ ✧ ✧ ✧ ✧

In early 1937, Gunn declared the Rockefeller Foundation's support of the NARB to be one of the "most gratifying" activities in the China program, still believing the sunny picture that Shen drew for him. But Gunn and Shen were deceiving both themselves and the Rockefeller Foundation. An insect control program was indeed critically important to Chinese agriculture—one conservative estimate put pest and disease losses at 10 to 20 percent of China's crops—and the insecticides that the NARB worked on were, technically speaking, satisfactory.[62] But the program itself was an utter failure. The problem was the same one that held back the effectiveness of the NARB in particular and of American-inspired technical improvements in general: unsuccessful extension of the new knowledge and techniques to the farmers. The talk of an insect control program that was "popularized on a national scale" was premature. The program not only failed in its home province, Jiangsu, but also in its home county, Jiangning.

This lack of success was especially remarkable because Jiangning offered the most favorable conditions for agricultural extension in the entire country. Not only was it militarily secure and its administration free from the external disruptions posed by the Chinese Communists or the Japanese elsewhere but, by virtue of its location, it was host to the nation's capital of Nanjing and received extraordinary development aid from both the national and provincial governments. Designated a privileged "Self-government Experimental County" in 1933, Jiangning was placed under the control of the Central Political Academy. More than any other county given "experimental" status, Jiangning was intended by the Nationalists to be the showcase of rural reconstruction for the entire nation. Its special status also brought tax remittances and subsidies.[63]

Yet even in the most ideal environment in Republican China, insect control was unsuccessful. First, Jiangning's most serious pest problem, locusts, originated elsewhere, in the bogs and swamps around Hongze Lake and the Huai Basin. Without provincial cooperation and regional programs to address the locust problem, a single county, no matter how favored with special designations and funds, remained vulnerable to devastating locust attacks, against which local remedial measures could do little. Jiangning farmers did the best they could to destroy the pests as soon as they alighted in their fields, bagging them or trying innovative forms of combat (once, a battalion of 5,000 ducks was deployed, when it was discovered that they could gobble more than half their weight in locusts each day). When desperate, the farmers resorted to burning their crops.[64]

Unfortunately, the county leadership of Jiangning did not lend much assistance to the NARB and other agencies interested in tackling the problem of insect control. A chronic problem was the indifference of government personnel to rural problems. Before Jiangning received its special designation, one insect control worker complained, "According to our experiences in the past, we feel that the most difficult thing about locust control is not the locusts themselves but the human problem. The officials in each locality generally do not understand the locust control program nor do they work hard on it." The locust control workers, he said, could not be successful without support ("You can't clap with just one hand"), and they did not receive it from their lay colleagues in the government. Even after Jiangning became an "experimental" county, the problem persisted.[65]

Despite the constant talk of "rural reconstruction," the new Jiangning administration was almost as indifferent to the countryside as the old had been, and it spent its money in exactly the same ways as its neighbors—on police, roads, education, and administrative expenses. The Jiangning "experiment" was innovative in one respect: it was the most top-heavy, expensive county administration in the province, perhaps in the country. Its farmers had little reason to rejoice about the county's special status; the annual budgeted amount for administrative expenditures outran the amount earmarked for agricultural improvement by a ratio of eleven to one. The funding for the Nationalists' internal party business alone was almost four times more than the government agricultural budget. When the new county administration rejected the offices it had inherited and built a palatial office building instead, a magazine editorial politely asked whether such expenditures, used for the material comfort of government officials in the midst of a countryside suffering from economic depression and bankruptcy, might not "give rise to an unfavorable impression" among the county's residents.[66]

The NARB could not escape the stigma of association with a government that on all levels—national, provincial, county, and local—seemed callously unconcerned with the needs of farmers. When the insect control workers ventured out of the laboratory and into the field, their new sprayers and insecticides in hand, farmers were unimpressed. Experience had taught them that the arrival of government representatives was usually a harbinger of trouble, and even the best-intentioned insect control workers were unable to dispel the farmers' distrust. In an article titled "Look, What Can Be Done?" (*Nikan zenme ban?*), a Nanking graduate described how the farmers' instinctive misgivings were justified. The writer had been assigned to a pest-control work team that had gone from village to village introducing new control measures, and each village that the team visited insisted on sending guards to accompany them to the next stop. He had been mystified as to why these temporary guards always seemed so eager to volunteer for duty, until he discovered what had been happening. Upon arrival at each destination, the "volunteers" deposited the agriculturalists into the good hands of the villagers and then went off on their own, brandishing the weapons they had obtained for their temporary assignment and robbing whomever they encountered. Strictly speaking, these brigands were neighboring villagers, not government employees, but the victimized farmers could scarcely ignore the fact that the pest control team had brought the problem along with them.[67]

Even when a pest control team was able to enter a village without provoking a hostile reaction, it faced entrenched educational problems that could not be changed by the short visit of a few college-educated agriculturalists. The very best insecticides and sprayers, however perfectly they worked in tests on the NARB campus, had to be accepted by farmers whose formal educational background was minimal and whose understanding of science was often scanty. Farmers viewed the crop pests or blight as a sign of displeasure from Heaven; agriculturalists complained that villagers lit incense and prayed for relief instead of taking action to help contain the problem. In some places, locusts were viewed as a kind of angel, and any farmers who wanted to implement control measures were prohibited from doing so by their more religious neighbors.[68]

The superstitions about pests could only be circumvented, it seemed, by playing upon other superstitions. A pest control worker in Jiangning stuck a large wooden sign into the fields of all farmers who had not implemented field cleaning measures required for controlling rice-stem borers. The signs' characters announced, "This Field's Rice Stalks Must Be Removed Within Three Days," and they were fairly effective in prodding landowners to clean their fields. The deadline on the sign was not as important as the physical presence of the sign itself, which was considered an extremely inauspicious omen. To get the sign removed, the farmers were willing to comply with the pest control regulations.[69]

The farmers' low educational level also hampered effective use of the insecticides and applicators that the NARB staff tried to distribute. One extension worker, Chuan Shengfa, who tried insecticide extension work among vegetable growers in Jiangning, reported to his professional colleagues that farmers were "extremely stupid." Chuan complained, "You explain carefully to them how to prevent and control pests, but they are unable to ever remember." The insecticide base that Chuan tried to introduce had to be diluted with five measures of boiling water, followed by twenty measures of cold. But when on their own, Chuan reported, farmers never added boiling water, only warm (undoubtedly less a problem of poor memory, as Chuan believed, than one of high fuel costs and simple economics). Moreover, the farmers often tried to stretch the insecticide base by diluting it with far more than the recommended amount of water, leading to poor results and later complaints that the insecticide they had used was worthless.[70]

✛ ✛ ✛ ✛ ✛

The primary control campaign that the NARB attempted to launch in Jiangning was directed at the rice-stem borer, a pest with a voracious appetite that annually destroyed a considerable portion of the county's rice crop. The bureau printed and distributed leaflets that explained how borer eggs lay dormant in the rice stalks that were customarily left on the fields during winter; destruction of the stalks, the leaflets pointed out, would lead to destruction of the pest. The bureau held promotional meetings in every district in the county and set deadlines for having fields cleared. Farmers could remove the stalks by burning them or by pulling them up and making compost piles sealed with river mud, but whatever method was used, no stalks could be left uncovered on the ground.[71]

"Destroying rice-stem borers is the responsibility of every farmer," residents were told in the campaign's leaflet. "If everyone does not participate, if some do but some do not, then the pests in the fields of those who did not comply will spread to the others." The program attempted simultaneously to coerce and persuade all of the county's farmers into meeting the stipulated deadlines. Farmers who did not comply were to be subject to arrest; those who did were eligible for commendation. The thirty-five most diligent farmers in the county were to be awarded a certificate of merit, and the very best among them were to receive an inscribed plaque to be presented personally by the head of Jiangning County.[72]

Despite all the publicity and arrangements, the campaign flopped. To avoid embarrassment for the NARB in its quest for additional funds from America, Shen never sent Gunn and the Rockefeller Foundation the NARB's report of how poorly its campaign fared. The NARB estimated that in only one district out of seven was a majority of rice stalks properly destroyed; no estimates were ventured for two districts; and in one, a mere 1.40% of the rice stalks was reported to have been removed. Since nothing less than complete compliance in all the districts was necessary to have any effect, the NARB campaign was a total failure.[73]

The NARB then attempted to mobilize farmers for rice-stem borer control in a neighboring county—an attempt that ended the same way. Yet it should not have been a surprise that the farmers remained uninterested and would not clear their fields. Mobilization of the countryside could not be accomplished by assigning a handful of experts to launch a population of several hundred thousand on a novel enterprise. In one case, four staff members—three of whom were apt to spend their time in the county seat rather than in the field—were assigned to a county with a population of more than four hundred. The agricultural experts working for the Nationalist government tried to organize the masses in the countryside, but they did not have the organizational structure, let alone the simple credibility, to make their efforts successful.[74]

The abysmal failure of its pest control campaigns led the NARB staff to debate internally different strategies for the future. One senior staff member, Wu Fuzhen, argued that the use of force was the only way to secure compliance. Furious that farmers had tried to cheat inspectors by piling conspicuous stacks of rice stalks along the side of roads while leaving stalks on their fields, Wu called for stricter inspections and a novel measure: closing all teahouses and wine shops during future campaigns. Wu believed that the farmers were indolent and uncooperative with the NARB during the winter months because of their patronage of the shops. Conceding that the closure of all drinking establishments would be controversial, he argued that the action would "create the appropriately tense atmosphere of an emergency situation" and would also disrupt the spread of news in the countryside, thus reducing "obstructionism" caused by gossip and rumors.[75]

Others agreed that administrative muscle needed to be applied, but NARB staff member Lü Jinluo proposed a more innovative approach. "The period of implementation should be shortened," Lü said, "and everyone—from the county head down, including bureau chiefs, department chiefs, district heads, elementary school teachers, and the entire county's police force—all should be mobilized to create together a very pressing atmosphere." Lü felt that if all levels of government displayed official commitment, any farmer who did not comply could justifiably be dealt with severely. In the face of dramatic government mobilization, "the farmers will not dare to sit around staring at each other and will implement the measures on time." Experience had taught Lü that insect control would never be successful if it relied solely on "technical personnel," such as those dispatched by the NARB, as a substitute for active involvement by the entire government establishment.[76]

✥ ✥ ✥ ✥ ✥

The NARB had no opportunity, however, to retry an insect control campaign, either in the "model" county of Jiangning or elsewhere in eastern China, because the outbreak of war with Japan in July 1937 brought its agricultural improvement programs to a halt. Many staff left for west China, and in August, Shen Zonghan put his family on a Yangzi riverboat bound for safety in the interior. Shen and other staff members who remained behind in Nanjing had to abandon their research and work on emergency food plans. By October, the deterioration in the military situation forced further evacuations, and Shen prepared to leave, reluctantly closing a happy period in his life. Touring the empty NARB campus one last time, Shen recalled how the fallow land purchased just four years before had been transformed into neatly arranged experimental fields for rice, wheat, cotton, and other crops, with six laboratory and administrative buildings built and equipped with the best research equipment in the country. In Shen's mind, the NARB had also become the national model for conducting agricultural research and encouraging work for the public good rather than for individual aggrandizement. Now the campus, once home for more than a hundred staff members, stood empty. Shen said good-bye to his books, gave the keys to his Ford to a friend who was staying behind, and took his two pieces of luggage down to the tumultuous scene at the river wharf, to fight through the crowds for his reserved place aboard a steamer headed up the Yangzi.[77]

Rockefeller representative Selskar Gunn, who was in Shanghai, was forced to flee even more hurriedly; he and his wife had to leave behind all their personal possessions to obtain passage on a steamer sailing for Java. The dream of having the Chinese themselves continue the foundation's China Program was ruined by the war. Gunn wrote to the New York office, "I have never felt so futile in my whole life." As the postevacuation situation stabilized and the Nanjing universities, the NARB, and other beneficiaries of the foundation's grants set up wartime operations in west China, the foundation continued to extend emergency grants for a few more years. But the Rockefeller Foundation did not like renewing grants for emergency purposes and terminated its ties as soon as it could without appearing to be callous toward victims of war.[78]

When Shen and Gunn had to abandon their work in 1937, a larger experiment, the peacetime application of American methods to Chinese agricultural problems, was brought to a close. Nationalist officials and sympathizers would later assert, over and over, that the development efforts of their "Nanking decade" would have succeeded had they not been interrupted prematurely by the war. But the agricultural programs of the government showpiece, the NARB, designed by Shen and funded by the Rockefeller Foundation, were not on the verge of success when cut short in 1937. The foundation's financial support was due to expire that year and was to be wholly assumed by the Chinese; the intrusion of the war actually extended Rockefeller funding beyond its scheduled termination. If the

Japanese had not invaded and forced the evacuation of the NARB, it is questionable that it would have accomplished much on its own.

✢ ✢ ✢ ✢ ✢

Shen was both well and poorly served by his earlier experience in the United States. Trained to be a research scientist, he could draw upon his graduate education and research experience in America to help guide rapid development of plant breeding programs on the NARB campus. But Shen was poorly equipped to handle the world of human affairs that lay beyond his orderly experimental fields. As the insect control program showed, it was easier to deal with locusts themselves than with farmers, who for a variety of reasons did not want to cooperate with the experts. For both the Chinese and the Americans who were interested in improving Chinese agriculture, it was comparatively easy to train a Shen Zonghan in the United States and send him back to China to organize a model research laboratory. Building organized structures that would extend improvements from the experimental field or laboratory to the populace at large was a far less simple task.

Shen's colleague, Lü Jinluo, envisaged a government that was mobilized from top to bottom for agricultural improvement campaigns, but it was an idea that sprang from Chinese conditions, not American experiences. Shen himself overcame the limitations of his originally narrow, technical approach to agricultural improvement and developed an interest in land reforms and farmer cooperatives. But the change in his thinking came only after he was driven from his protected sanctuary in Nanjing and had worked as an agricultural planner for the Nationalist government during the difficult years of the war against Japan and of the civil war between the Nationalists and the Communists.

Gunn did not survive the war, but future events in China would not have surprised him. Early in 1937, before the Japanese invasion, he prepared a candid assessment of the Nationalists' weaknesses. Chiang Kai-shek's New Life Movement seemed to Gunn to be "tending towards a Fascistic state with the accompanying regimentation of the population and a good deal of lip service for National Reconstruction." Democratic measures had been discussed but had yet to be implemented. Gunn wondered, "Perhaps China is not ripe for such form of government." [79]

Rural China, Gunn realized, remained poorly understood by most foreigners: "Western people in China are almost exclusively in contact with 'Western' Chinese. They may live in China years without realizing that despite the display of Nanking and the large cities where the 'Western' Chinese are to be found, there exist the 'Chinese' Chinese who make up the backbone, power, and authority of the large part of China, including the entire rural regions where 85 percent of the people live." To Gunn, the Westernized Chinese stood for technical progress but were stymied by the conservative "landlord, gentry, and usurer group," who did not want to increase the purchasing power of the farmers. "A debt-free rural population," Gunn wrote, "would be to them a great disaster." But maintenance of the status quo "plays into the hands of the Communists." [80]

When Gunn concurred in 1937 with those who had warned Chiang that "it will be necessary to outdo the Communists and 'go them one better,'" his attitude signaled an important change in the history of American technical assistance abroad. Before that time, Americans had gone to China to try to improve Chinese agriculture for a number of reasons, combining noble impulses with the mundane. Most shared a belief that even if the content of the agricultural expertise they brought from home did not apply to conditions in China, an undefined American style of work was superior to all others and would find ready acceptance. Still, the pride taken in American ways fell far short of constituting a coherent ideology, and when Americans first confronted Communists in China in the 1920s, their inclination was not to fight for hearts and minds but simply to leave. By the eve of the Second World War, the essentially private initiative behind the early American programs to aid Chinese agriculture was about to disappear. Agricultural improvement programs for the developing countries of the postwar period would become, first and foremost, a government instrument in an ideological battle, and the early American experiences in China would be visible only through the intervening haze of the Cold War.

EPILOGUE

The end of the Japanese occupation in 1945 gave the Chiang Kai-shek government another opportunity to implement the agricultural improvement programs it had touted for so long. The war years had forced the Nationalists out of the cities and out off complacency and had impressed upon them the urgent necessity of rural improvement. The rapid growth of the Chinese Communist party in the countryside could no longer be ignored.

Chiang turned to the United States in October 1945 and formally requested help. Harry Truman answered by appointing eight American agricultural specialists (including Lossing Buck) to join with Chinese colleagues (including Shen Zonghan and Zou Bingwen) in forming a "China–United States Agricultural Mission" to survey conditions in China and offer recommendations. The resulting report recommended that almost everything be improved: plant and animal stocks, fertilizers, farm credit, land surveys, land tax enforcement, river conservancy, flood control, population control, and agricultural instruction, research, and extension. Shen later observed, "As Communism was capitalizing on the poverty and miseries of the Chinese peasantry, it was felt that the most effective way to steal the Communist thunder would be to solve the agrarian problem through peaceful reforms carried out with the technical and financial assistance of China's wartime ally and traditional friend, the United States." To direct "peaceful reforms," in 1948 the two nations formed a new bilateral organization, the Sino-American Joint Commision on Rural Reconstruction (JCRR), and Congress authorized nearly $40 million for Chinese "rural reconstruction." But by that time the Chinese partner in the arrangement was about to lose to its Communist rivals.[1]

The "loss of China" and the evacuation of the Nationalist government to Taiwan in 1949 gave additional impetus to the U.S. government to fight communism with technical agricultural assistance. If it was too late to "steal the Communist thunder" on the Chinese mainland, it was not too late to try elsewhere. Under the direction of the JCRR, rural Taiwan became one large demonstration project to test new approaches to agricultural development. The Chiang government successfully

213

carried out in Taiwan land reforms that it had regarded as abhorrent when it held power on the mainland. Long gone was its simple belief of the 1930s that an agronomic research agency like the NARB could solve the rural problems of China.

One aspect of earlier naïveté persisted, however, causing much mischief elsewhere in Asia: the assumption that improved seed varieties offered farmers higher yields without higher input costs or social dislocation. It was this belief that inspired the Cornell-Nanking Plant Improvement Program of the 1920s and that later led to the pursuit of an Asian "Green Revolution," which began at the International Rice Research Institute (IRRI) in the Philippines in the 1960s. The similarity in approach was not coincidental. When Cornell's ties to mainland China were severed in 1949, the university began a cooperative program with the University of the Philippines College of Agriculture at Los Banos, which in turn served as the base upon which IRRI was built. The Rockefeller Foundation contributed funding and provided additional continuity.[2] The IRRI staff viewed the development of high-yielding varieties as a purely technical problem and did not anticipate the extension problems encountered in the 1960s and 1970s, when "miracle" rice moved from the laboratory to farmers' fields in South and Southeast Asia. The slighting of the importance of nontechnical aspects—social, cultural, economic, and political—repeated the mistake that Americans had made in China fifty years before.

After the Americans left the Chinese mainland in 1949 (and soon fought Chinese troops in the Korean war), the Soviet Union became China's leading agricultural model. With the Sino-Soviet split in 1960, the Chinese changed paths again and took a more independent course, which they followed until the late 1970s. But during the thirty years between 1949 and 1979, when China and the United States had little direct contact, American-trained Chinese on the mainland continued to apply portions of their expertise in forming agricultural education, research, and extension programs of their own design. The two colleges of agriculture in Nanjing were consolidated into one and relocated in the rural area outside the city, rectifying old problems of redundancy, competition, and isolation from rural conditions. Agricultural research was expanded nationally, and the farming population was finally given the extension services it had always been denied. In 1970, even Shen Zonghan, in exile in Taiwan and a strong critic of the "ruthless" Communists, credited the socialist government on the mainland with implementing virtually all of the recommendations that the China–United States Agricultural Mission had made in 1947. The one exception was the early recommendation that the Chinese government "guard against a rapid increase in the growth of population."[3]

In the late 1970s, when contact and trade between China and the United States increased dramatically, both nations appeared eager to resume the earlier pattern of applying American expertise to Chinese agricultural problems. American agricultural colleges rushed forward to sign protocols of cooperation with

Chinese counterparts, and Cornell was among the first to do so. Chinese trade organizations invited American farm-machinery companies to bid on projects. When Deere and Company asked a state farm in Heilongjiang what accessories it wanted on the five tractors it was purchasing, the Chinese reply was "All." Perhaps the arrival of the giant machines, complete with tape decks in their air-conditioned cabs, only marked the logical culmination of events that had started when Edward Parker had been invited to plan wheat farms for Manchuria seventy years before.[4]

Today, both Americans and Chinese continue to share a strong faith in the simple "technical fix" for complicated problems—a faith that belies the experiences of the past and that is particularly egregious because it is blind to China's own recent history. Since the founding of the People's Republic of China, the Chinese have more than doubled annual agricultural production, a technical marvel resulting from improved seed varieties, fertilizers, and water and pest control. But these improvements could not have been extended into the countryside without accompanying political, economic, and social changes that reduced the farmers' distrust of extension agents, increased literacy, mobilized large numbers of people for major earthworks and infrastructural improvement, and channeled large sums of state money into agricultural extension and research.

The postrevolutionary government in China departed furthest from the Americans' earlier suggestions when it did not hesitate to radically change the social organization of agricultural production. In the 1950s, first with a land reform, then with the formation of cooperatives and collectives, the Chinese government dismantled the inherited system of land tenure and replaced it with an entirely new system of collectivized production which contributed to China's dramatic gains in the agricultural sector.

In the late 1970s and early 1980s, when farmer morale had dropped and the collective system no longer seemed capable of producing additional spurts in production, the government dismantled its previous system and installed a decollectivized one that returned responsibility to the family and to individuals. Agricultural production jumped spectacularly, leading some Americans today, perhaps, to believe that the pre–World War II advice given to China—by Joseph Bailie, Lossing Buck, and many of the figures in this book—has been vindicated at last. According to this view, the importance that Chinese planners have recently attached to family and individual initiative is an echo of what Americans in China emphasized fifty years ago.

The problem with this prideful conclusion is that it ignores the fact that production also jumped impressively when the Chinese adopted the socialist measures that collectivized agriculture—the very approach that was anathema to early twentieth-century American advisers in China. A more valid conclusion might simply be that the postrevolutionary experience in China demonstrates the critical importance of social organization in the battle to raise agricultural production, and that this holds true whether the reforms of a particular moment are collectivist or decollectivist. In both the 1950s and the 1980s, the Chinese government applied a strong hand in directing the organization of agriculture. When Americans were in China, no Chinese government was strong enough to gain and secure national rule, let alone play a dominant role in the improvement of agriculture.

In the earlier period, when American influence in Chinese agriculture was applied, agricultural improvement was too often regarded merely as a technical challenge for the agronomist in the laboratory. Americans at the time were captivated by a vision in which China would be guided through a technological revolution in agriculture without undergoing broader change. But a supportive infrastructure was needed for the extension of technical improvements outside of the laboratory and beyond the experimental field. The Americans failed to realize that changes in the wider polity, society, and economy were necessary. Social change was needed to make a technological transformation possible.

ABBREVIATIONS

CU	Cornell University
IEB	International Education Board
IHA	International Harvester Archives
IRRI	International Rice Research Institute
JCRR	Sino-American Joint Commission on Rural Reconstruction
NA	National Archives (U.S.), Record Group 59
Nanking	University of Nanking
NARB	National Agricultural Research Bureau (Republic of China)
PSU	Pennsylvania State University Libraries
RF	Rockefeller Foundation
RFA	Rockefeller Foundation Archives
SZH	*Shen Zonghan zishu* [The autobiography of Shen Zonghan]
USDA	United States Department of Agriculture
YUDS	Yale University Divinity School, Day Missions Library
ZW	*Zhang Wenxianggong quanji* [The complete works of Zhang Zhidong]

NOTES

INTRODUCTION

1. Everett E. Edwards, comp., *Washington, Jefferson, Lincoln, and Agriculture* (Washington, D.C.: United States Department of Agriculture, 1937), 5–6; Garry Wills, *Cincinnatus: George Washington and the Enlightenment* (Garden City, N.Y.: Doubleday, 1984), 232–235.

2. Frederic Wakeman, Jr., *The Fall of Imperial China* (New York: The Free Press, 1975), 100–101; Harold L. Kahn, *Monarchy in the Emperor's Eyes: Image and Reality in the Ch'ien-lung Reign* (Cambridge, Mass.: Harvard University Press, 1971), 123–124.

3. Kahn, *Monarchy*, 11; Edwards, *Washington*, 6.

4. Edwards, *Washington*, 31.

5. Edwards, *Washington*, 14–15; Thomas Jefferson, *The Papers of Thomas Jefferson*, ed. Julian P. Boyd (Princeton, N.J.: Princeton University Press, 1950–1982), 11 : 339.

6. Benjamin Franklin, *The Papers of Benjamin Franklin*, ed. William B. Willcox (New Haven, Conn.: Yale University Press, 1959–1984), 16 : 201, 18 : 188–189; David Fairchild, *The World Was My Garden: Travels of a Plant Explorer* (New York: Charles Scribner's Sons, 1945), 286.

7. John T. Schlebecker, *Whereby We Thrive: A History of American Farming, 1607–1972* (Ames: Iowa State University Press, 1975), 102–104, 109.

8. John W. Oliver, *History of American Technology* (New York: Ronald Press Company, 1956), 225–227, 253–256.

9. *Report of the Commissioner of Agriculture, 1862, 1863, 1864* (Washington, D.C.: Government Printing Office, 1863–1865), 1862 : 11; Oliver, *History*, 224–225, 234.

10. Oliver, *History*, 232.

11. Vernon Carstensen, "An Overview of American Agricultural History," in *Farmers, Bureaucrats, and Middlemen: Historical Perspectives on American Agriculture*, ed. Trudy Huskamp Peterson (Washington, D.C.: Howard University Press, 1980), 15.

12. Ibid.; "Agriculture at Yale College," *Scientific American*, new series, vol. 2, no. 7 (11 February 1860): 100.

13. Feng Guifen, *Jiaobin lu kangyi* [Protest from the Jiaobin Studio] (Taibei: Wenhai, 1971, reproduction of 1898 ed.), 92–93, 199.

14. Quoted in Ho Ping-ti, *Studies on the Population of China, 1368–1953* (Cambridge, Mass.: Harvard University Press, 1959), 239.

15. *Report of the Commissioner of Patents, 1837* (Washington, D.C.: Government Printing Office, 1838), 5.

16. *Report of the Commissioner of Agriculture, 1862* : 16; *1864* : 11.

17. Ibid., 1862 : 12; Oliver, *History*, 235.

18. Schlebecker, *Whereby We Thrive*, 188–205; Oliver, *History*, 372–373.

19. *Agriculture of the United States in 1860* [Eighth Census] (Washington, D.C.: Government Printing Office, 1864), v.

20. Charles Denby, *China and Her People* (Boston: L. C. Page and Company, 1905), ix–xvi; Michael H. Hunt, *Frontier Defense and the Open Door: Manchuria in Chinese-American Relations, 1895–1911* (New Haven, Conn.: Yale University Press, 1973), 23.

21. Charles Denby, "Agriculture in China," *Forum* 32 (November 1901): 328; [Denby], "Among the Plants: In Garden, Field and Forest," *Current Literature* 27 (March 1900): 258.

22. Denby, *China*, 119, 121.

23. Francesca Bray, "The Chinese Contribution to Europe's Agricultural Revolution: A Technology Transformed," in *Explorations in the History of Science and Technology in China*, ed. Li Guohao et al. (Shanghai: Shanghai Chinese Classics Publishing House, 1982), 597–637; Mark Elvin, *The Pattern of the Chinese Past* (Stanford, Calif.: Stanford University Press, 1973), 113–130; Ho, *Studies*, 169–195; and Dwight H. Perkins, *Agricultural Development in China, 1368–1968* (Chicago: Aldine, 1969), 10–11.

24. Elvin, *Pattern*, 114–117, 308–309; Su Yunfeng, *Zhongguo xiandaihua de quyu yanjiu: Hubeisheng* [A regional study of Chinese modernization: Hubei Province] (Taibei: Academia Sinica, 1981), 415.

25. Liu Boji, *Meiguo huaqiao shi* [The history of overseas Chinese in America] (Taibei: Xingzhengyuan qiaowu weiyuanhui, 1976), 374–378.

26. Thomas E. La Fargue, *China's First Hundred* (Pullman: State College of Washington, 1942), 36–66.

27. Robert S. Schwantes, *Japanese and Americans: A Century of Cultural Relations* (New York: Council on Foreign Relations, 1955), 48–49, 53–55; John A. Harrison, "The Capron Mission and the Colonization of Hokkaido, 1868–1875," *Agricultural History* 25 (May 1951): 135–142; Martin Bronfenbrenner, *Academic Encounter: The American University in Japan and Korea* (New York: Free Press, 1961), 13–15.

28. Hsiao Kung-chuan, *A Modern China and a New World: K'ang Yu-wei, Reformer and Utopian, 1858–1927* (Seattle: University of Washington Press, 1975), 324–328.

29. Jian Bozan, et al., ed., *Wuxu bianfa* [The Reforms of 1898] (Shanghai: Shanghai renmin chubanshe, 1961), 2 : 143–144.

30. James Bryce, *The American Commonwealth* (New York: Macmillan, 1889), 2 : 696.

CHAPTER 1: CURIOSITY

1. Frederick Jackson Turner, *The Early Writings of Frederick Jackson Turner*, comp. Everett E. Edwards (Madison: University of Wisconsin Press, 1938), 185–229.

2. Walter LaFeber, *The New Empire: An Interpretation of American Expansion, 1860–1898* (Ithaca, N.Y.: Cornell University Press, 1963), 416–417.

3. LaFeber, *The New Empire*, 72–95; Thomas J. McCormick, *China Market: America's Quest for Informal Empire, 1893–1901* (Chicago: Quadrangle, 1967), 105–125.

4. [Denby], "Among the Plants," 259.

5. Denby, "Agriculture," 331.

6. William Martin, "Agricultural Implements in China," U.S. House of Representatives, *Consular Reports* 62 (June 1900): 202.

7. Ibid.

8. Rounsevelle Wildman, "Chinese Agriculture and American Machinery," U.S. House of Representatives, *Consular Reports* 66 (May 1901): 121.

9. Ibid., 122.

10. George Anderson, "Agricultural Implements in China," U.S. Department of Commerce and Labor, Bureau of Statistics, *Monthly Consular Reports*, no. 291 (December 1904): 52–53.

11. Henry B. Miller, "American Fruit in China," U.S. House of Representatives, *Consular Reports* 65 (January 1901): 40–41.

12. W. P. Bentley, *Guojia zhuanshe nongbu yi* [A suggestion for a national department of agriculture] (Shanghai: Commercial Press, 1903). Individual quotations that follow are not cited individually.

13. Wayne D. Rasmussen and Gladys L. Baker, *The Department of Agriculture* (New York: Praeger, 1972), 11–13.

14. David Fairchild, *The World Was My Garden*, 18, 28.

15. Ibid., 28–31.

16. Marjory Stoneman Douglas, "The Most Unforgettable Character I've Met," *Reader's Digest* 53 (November 1948): 67–71; Fairchild, *The World Was My Garden*, 30–36.

17. Fairchild, *The World Was My Garden*, 106–107.

18. Ibid., 117.

19. Ibid., 119.

20. Ibid., 153–155.

21. Ibid., 156–157.

22. Ibid., 205.

23. Ibid., 219; David Fairchild, *Letters on Agriculture in the West Indies, Spain, and the Orient*, USDA, Bureau of Plant Industry Bulletin no. 27 (1902): 24.

24. Fairchild, *Letters on Agriculture*, 25.

25. Ibid., 26.

26. Ibid., 25.

27. Joseph C. Bailey, *Seaman A. Knapp: Schoolmaster of American Agriculture* (New York: Columbia University Press, 1945), 133.

28. Ibid., 134.

29. Seaman A. Knapp, *Recent Foreign Explorations, As Bearing on the Agricultural Development of the Southern States*, USDA, Bureau of Plant Industry Bulletin no. 35 (1903): 37.

30. Ibid., 37–38.

31. Fairchild, *The World Was My Garden*, 297, 321.

32. Ibid., 315.

33. Ibid., 118; facsimile of Meyer's official authorization, in Isabel Shipley Cunningham, *Frank N. Meyer: Plant Hunter in Asia* (Ames: Iowa State University Press, 1984), 26.

34. Frank N. Meyer, "China a Fruitful Field for Plant Exploration," *Yearbook of the United States Department of Agriculture—1915* (Washington, D.C.: Government Printing Office, 1916), 205–206.

35. Cunningham, *Frank N. Meyer*, 31–33; Frank N. Meyer, "Economic Botanical Explorations in China," *Transactions of the Massachusetts Horticultural Society*, part 1 (1916): 126.

36. Meyer, "Economic Botanical Explorations," 126; Cunningham, *Frank N. Meyer*, 33–35.

37. Cunningham, *Frank N. Meyer*, 37.

38. David Fairchild, "A New Exploration of the World," *Youth's Companion* 83 (6 May 1909): 219–220; "The People Who Stand for Plus," *Outing* 53 (October 1908): 69–76.

39. Cunningham, *Frank N. Meyer*, 40, 45.

40. Ibid., 42–43, 72–73.

41. Meyer, "China a Fruitful Field," 209.

42. Cunningham, *Frank N. Meyer*, 80–84, 206, 227.

43. David Fairchild, "An Agricultural Explorer in China," *Asia* 21 (January 1921): 8.

44. Ibid., 8–9; Cunningham, *Frank N. Meyer*, 173.

45. "Plants from China," *Wallace's Farmer* 41 (11 February 1916): 235.

46. Cunningham, *Frank N. Meyer*, 75–76.

47. Meyer, "Economic Botanical Explorations," 126.

48. "The People Who Stand for Plus," 72; Cunningham, *Frank N. Meyer*, 69, 190.

49. Cunningham, *Frank N. Meyer*, 184–185; Reginald Farrer, "Mr. Reginald Farrer's Explorations in China," *Gardener's Chronicle*, series 3, 58 (1915): 1.

50. Cunningham, *Frank N. Meyer*, 192–193.

51. Ibid., 193.

52. Ibid., 170, 193–194, 224.

53. Ibid., 206–208, 225–226.

54. Ibid., 243–248.

55. Fairchild, *The World Was My Garden*, 455; Stephanne B. Sutton, *In China's Border Provinces: The Turbulent Career of Joseph Rock, Botanist-Explorer* (New York: Hastings House, 1974), 9–19; Cunningham, ·*Frank N. Meyer*, 267.

56. David Fairchild, "Two Unknown Modern Languages," *The Outlook* 93 (4 September 1909): 43–44.

57. "Woman Off to China as Government Agent to Study Soy Bean," *New York Times*, 10 June 1917, section VI, 9.

58. Ibid.

59. Ibid.

60. Ibid.

61. National Archives, Record Group 59 (hereafter abbreviated NA), 893.61321/6a, 893.61321/7; E. J. Kahn, Jr., *The Staffs of Life* (Boston: Little, Brown, 1985), 275–278.

62. F. H. King, *Farmers of Forty Centuries* (Madison, Wis.: Democrat Printing Company, 1911), 2, 176.

63. Ibid., 1, 196–198.

64. Ibid., 10–11.

65. Ibid., 90–93, 188–189.

66. Ibid., 2, 120–121, 245.

67. Ibid., 274.

68. Ibid., 4–5.

69. Ibid., iii–iv.

70. R. P. Crawford, "World Crops for America," *Scientific American* 126 (April 1922): 226.

71. Ibid.

72. Cunningham, *Frank N. Meyer*, 261, 263.

73. J. Lossing Buck, "Contributions to Western Agriculture," in *There Is Another China: Essays and Articles for Chang Poling* (New York: King's Crown Press, 1948), 112; Cunningham, *Frank N. Meyer*, 260–267; David Fairchild and Walter T. Swingle, "China's Contributions to the World's Food," *World Agriculture* 2 (Spring and Summer, 1921): 102–103; W. H. Donald, "China as a Most Promising Field for Plant Exploration," *Far Eastern Review* 12 (July 1915): 45.

74. Buck, "Contributions," 113; Swingle to Williams, 19 December 1924, Yale University Divinity School Library (hereafter abbreviated YUDS), 226/3829.

75. Fairchild, "An Agricultural Explorer in China," 7; Reisner to Ravenal, 12 June 1925, NA 893.6106.

CHAPTER 2: INSTRUCTION

1. Su Yunfeng, "Waiguo zhuanjia xuezhe zai Hubei (1890–1911)" [Foreign experts and educators in Hubei (1890–1911)], *Zhonghua wenhua fuxing yuekan* 8 (April 1975): 51–52; Su Yunfeng, *Zhongguo xiandaihua*, 423.

2. Zhang Zhidong, *Zhang Wenxianggong quanji* [The complete works of Zhang Zhidong; hereafter abbreviated *ZW*], 6 vols, 229 juan (Taibei, 1963), 99:8–8b.

3. *ZW* 99:8b–9.

4. *ZW* 99:25–25b.

5. *ZW* 99:26–29b.

6. *ZW* 99:33b–34.

7. William Ayers, *Chang Chih-tung and Educational Reform in China* (Cambridge, Mass.: Harvard University Press, 1971), 130–131.

8. *ZW* 151:19b–20.

9. Ayers, *Chang Chih-tung*, 131.

10. *ZW* 153:13.

11. Partridge to Honorable President of Cornell University, 15 March 1897, 14 June 1897, Brill Papers, Cornell University (hereafter abbreviated CU).

12. Ibid. Emphasis in the original.

13. Brill to Partridge, 19 April 1897, CU; Merle Curti and Kendall Birr, *Prelude to Point Four: American Technical Missions Overseas, 1838–1938* (Madison: University of Wisconsin Press, 1954), 29.

14. Curti and Birr, *Prelude to Point Four,* 29.

15. Partridge to Schurman, 14 June 1897, Brill Papers, CU.

16. Curti and Birr, *Prelude to Point Four,* 29; D. M. Osborne and Company to Roberts, 3 August 1897, Brill Papers, CU.

17. Su Yunfeng, *Zhongguo xiandaihua,* 418. Su drew upon the Chinese-language version of Brill's report that appeared in the *Nongxuebao.* Without the English-language original, which remains undiscovered, no analysis can be made of how well Brill's original words were rendered into Chinese.

18. Ibid., 418–419.

19. Ibid., 419.

20. Brill to His Excellency Chang Chi Teng, 5 October 1899, Brill Papers, CU.

21. Ayers, *Chang Chih-tung,* 149–150.

22. ZW 203:30–30b.

23. ZW 203:30b.

24. ZW 203:30b; Jian Bozan et al., ed., *Wuxu bianfa,* 4:554; Y. C. Wang, *Chinese Intellectuals and the West, 1872–1949* (Chapel Hill: University of North Carolina Press, 1966), 53.

25. Curti and Birr, *Prelude to Point Four,* 30.

26. ZW 47:9b–10; 121:2b.

27. Curti and Birr, *Prelude to Point Four,* 29–30.

28. Jian Bozan, et al., ed., *Wuxu bianfa,* 2:250.

29. Ayers, *Chang Chih-tung,* 178.

30. Su Yunfeng, "Hubei nongwu xuetang—jindai Zhongguo nongye jiaoyu de xianqu" [The Hubei Agricultural College—A pioneer in modern China's agricultural education], *Xinzhi zazhi* 4 (December 1974): 45–47; Su Yunfeng, *Zhongguo xiandaihua,* 417; Curti and Birr, *Prelude to Point Four,* 32.

31. ZW 47:10, 121:2b; Brill to His Excellency Chang Chi Teng, 5 October 1899, Brill Papers, CU.

32. Brill to His Excellency Chang Chi Teng, 5 October 1899; Brill to Dodge, 30 January 1899; Brill to Dodge, 5 March 1899, Brill Papers, CU.

33. Brill to His Excellency Chang Chi Teng, 5 October 1899, Brill Papers, CU; Curti and Birr, *Prelude to Point Four,* 32.

34. Brill to His Excellency Chang Chi Teng, 5 October 1899, Brill Papers, CU.

35. Ibid.; Curti and Birr, *Prelude to Point Four,* 31.

36. Curti and Birr, *Prelude to Point Four,* 32.

37. Brill to His Excellency Chang Chi Teng, 5 October 1899, Brill Papers, CU.

38. Brill to Aunt Statia [Dodge], 15 December 1899, Brill Papers, CU.

39. Su Yunfeng, "Waiguo zhuanjia," 55–56; Su Yunfeng, *Zhongguo xiandaihua,* 417–421; T. H. Shen [Shen Zonghan], *Shen Zonghan zishu* [The autobiography of Shen Zonghan; hereafter abbreviated SZH] (Taibei, 1975), 3:85.

40. Gerow D. Brill, "Chinese Incubators," in U.S. Department of Agriculture, *Seventeenth Annual Report of the Bureau of Animal Industry for the year 1900* (Washington, D.C.: Government Printing Office, 1901), 247–253.

41. "Notes on Americans as Teachers in Chinese Government Schools," 9 February 1910, NA 893.42/19.

42. Zhang Yufa, "Ershi shiji chuqi de Zhongguo nongye gailiang (1901–1916): Yanhai yanjiang shisange shengqu de bijiao yanjiu" [Chinese agricultural improvement in the early twentieth century, 1901–1916: A comparative study of thirteen coastal and riverine provinces and districts], *Shixue pinglun*, no. 1 (July 1979): 138; *SZH*, 3:85.

43. Arthur W. Hummel, ed., *Eminent Chinese of the Ch'ing Period* (Washington, D.C.: Government Printing Office, 1943 and 1944), 1:136–137, 2:232–234; Xu Shichang, *Dongsansheng zhenglue* [A brief account of administering the Three Eastern Provinces] (Taibei: Wenhai, 1965, reprint of 1911 ed.), juan 11, Fengtian, 2.

44. Ibid.

45. Henry C. Taylor and Anne Dewees Taylor, *The Story of Agricultural Economics in the United States, 1840–1932* (Ames: Iowa State College Press, 1952), 394–400; Edward C. Parker, "Farming as a Business Enterprise," *Review of Reviews* 33 (January 1906): 62–67.

46. Edward C. Parker, "The Future Wheat Supply of the United States," *Century Magazine* 76 (September 1908): 736–746.

47. Ibid., 746; Hunt, *Frontier Defense*, 249.

48. Edward C. Parker, "Commercial Manchuria," *Review of Reviews* 40 (December 1909): 713.

49. Ibid., 713–715.

50. Ibid., 714–715.

51. Ibid., 717–719.

52. Ibid., 718–719; Edward C. Parker, "Manchuria and World's Wheat Supply," *Northwestern Miller* 82 (4 May 1910): 280.

53. Edward C. Parker, "Outline of a Plan for Assisting the Agricultural Development of Manchuria," in *Outline and Comments on the Agricultural Development of Manchuria*, ed. The Bureau of Agriculture, Industry, and Commerce (Moukden [Mukden], 1908), 1–8; "Agriculture in Manchuria," U.S. Department of Commerce and Labor, *Daily Consular and Trade Reports*, no. 3430 (16 March 1909): 7.

54. Parker, "Commercial Manchuria," 716–717.

55. Parker, "Outline of a Plan," 4; "Agriculture in Manchuria," 7.

56. Parker, "Outline of a Plan," 5.

57. Ibid., 5–7.

58. Couchman to Heid, 19 February 1909, International Harvester Archives (hereafter abbreviated IHA).

59. Cyrus McCormick, *The Century of The Reaper* (Boston: Houghton Mifflin, 1931), 121–122; Fred V. Cartensen, *American Enterprise in Foreign Markets: Studies of Singer and International Harvester in Imperial Russia* (Chapel Hill: University of North Carolina Press, 1984). 206; Couchman to International Harvester Company, Vladivostok, 5 April 1909, IHA.

60. Couchman to International Harvester Company, Vladivostok, 5 April 1909; "1909 Sales by Governments and Divisions," IHA.

61. Heid to Couchman, 10 April 1909, IHA.

62. Parker to His Excellency Ching Te Chuen [Cheng Dequan], 17 August 1909. Uncataloged carbon copy of letter found, unbound, in the inside cover of Bureau of Agriculture, Industry, and Commerce, *Outline and Comments on the Agricultural Development of Manchuria* (Moukden [Mukden], 1908), at Claremont College, Claremont, California.

63. Ibid.

64. Huffman to Cloud, 28 May 1910, NA 893.61311.

65. Parker to Huffman, 10 July 1910, NA 893.61311.

66. Ibid.

67. Ibid.

68. *London and China Telegram*, 26 June 1911, in NA 893.61/1; NA 893.01/1.

69. Heid to Kosters, 3 March 1911; Heid to Kosters, 17 June 1911, IHA.

70. Parker to Far Eastern Division, Department of State, 28 December 1911, NA 893.61/1.

71. Bancroft to Knox, 15 August 1911, NA 893.01A/1; Heid to Kosters, 1 July 1911, IHA; [Illegible] to AmLegation, 30 September 1911, cable, NA 893.01A/3.

72. Parker to Commissioner Hsiung Hsi Ling, 4 January 1912, NA 893.61/4.

73. Edward C. Parker, *Field Management and Crop Rotation* (St. Paul, Minn.: Webb Publishing, 1915), 388–391.

74. Mukden consul report, 19 July 1921, NA 893.61/22; "Mechanical Farming in Manchuria," *Contemporary Manchuria* 3 (October 1939): 43–50; Heid to Kosters, 31 December 1911; Heid to Maynard, 20 September 1912; Heid to Kosters, 16 September 1913, 18 September 1913, 13 November 1913; "Notes on the China Trade" (n.d.), IHA; Cartensen, *American Enterprise*, 222.

75. Samuel C. Chu, *Reformer in Modern China: Chang Chien, 1853–1926* (New York: Columbia University Press, 1965), 148; Charles Davis Jameson, "River, Lake and Land Conservancy in Portions of the Provinces of Anhui and Kiangsu, North of the Yangtze River," *Far Eastern Review* 9 (November 1912): 247–251.

76. Mabel Thorp Boardman, *Under the Red Cross Flag at Home and Abroad*, 2d ed. (Philadelphia: J. B. Lippincott, 1915), 205; translation of "Peking Gazette," dated 17 February 1914, in NA 893.811/115.

77. Davis to Secretary of State, 10 June 1911, with Jameson's résumé attached, NA 893.811/50.

78. *North China Daily News*, 31 October 1911, in NA 893.811/67.

79. Ibid.

80. Jameson to Davis, 30 July 1912; Jameson to Calhoun, 30 July 1912, NA 893.811/75.

81. Jameson to Davis, 30 July 1912, NA 893.811/75; Jameson, "River, Lake and Land Conservancy," 256–263.

82. Zhang Qian, *Zhang Jizi jiulu* [The collected works of Zhang Qian] (Shanghai, 1931), 9:1–3b; *Conservancy Work in China: Being a Series of Documents and Reports by Chang Chien* (Shanghai: National Review, 1912), preface, 2.

83. Chu, *Reformer in Modern China*, 150–152.

84. Jameson to Boardman, 20 August 1912, NA 893.811/75.

85. Jameson to Davis, 19 August 1912, NA 893.811/75.

86. Boardman to President [Taft], 14 October 1912; Wilson to President [Taft], 25 October, 1912; Wilson to AmLegation, 25 October 1912, cable, NA 893.811/75; Calhoun to Secretary of State [Wilson], 4 November 1912, cable; Wilson to AmLegation, 8 November 1912, cable, NA 893.811/76.

87. Jameson to Boardman, 20 August 1912, NA 893.811/75.

88. Williams to Lou [Lu], 10 May 1913, NA 893.811/86.

89. Minister of Foreign Affairs [Lu] to Williams, 14 June 1913; Williams to Secretary of State, 20 June 1913, NA 893.811/88.

90. Davis to Secretary of State, 9 July 1913, NA 893.811/89.

91. Telegram from Peking Legation, 19 December [1913], NA 893.811/98; telegram from Peking Legation, 14 January 1914, NA 893.811/102; Reinsch to Secretary of State, 23 January 1914, NA 893.811/109.

92. "The Hwai River Conservancy," *Far Eastern Review* 10 (May 1914): 469; "The Hwai River Conservancy Commission," *Far Eastern Review* 11 (June 1914): 14.

93. "Huai River Conservancy Project," *Far Eastern Review* 11 (April 1915): 415–424.

94. Chang Chien to Chinese Minister, 1 October 1914, telegram, NA 893.811/154.

95. John R. Freeman, "Flood Problems in China," *Transactions of the American Society of Civil Engineers* 85 (1922): 1405–1460; Chu, *Reformer in Modern China*, 157–160.

CHAPTER 3: ZEAL

1. Joseph Bailie, "A Letter from Mr. Joseph Bailie, Head and Organizer of Agriculture and Forestry at the University of Nanking, to the China Press," *The University of Nanking Magazine* 6 (June 1914): 207.

2. Victoria W. Bailie, *Bailie's Activities in China* (Palo Alto, Calif.: Pacific Books, 1964), 22.

3. John H. Reisner, interview by Gould Colman, 8 November 1962, transcript, CU.

4. Joseph Bailie, "Famine and Afforestation in China," *International Review of Missions* 6 (July 1917): 451.

5. Undated typescript by Joseph Bailie, appended to Wells to Sample, 20 January 1938, YUDS 198/3399.

6. Ibid.

7. Ibid.

8. Ibid.

9. "Colonizing the Chinese," *North China Daily News*, 19 April 1912, YUDS 200/3423.

10. "Professor Bailie's Plan for the Famine Refugees," *The University of Nanking Magazine* 2 (September 1911): 4.

11. Joseph Bailie, "Magna Charta of China's Forestry Work," *American Forestry* 22 (May 1916): 268.

12. Joseph Bailie, "Conserve Life Through Reclamation of Waste Lands," *The University of Nanking Magazine* 6 (March 1915): 400–401. Emphasis in the original.

13. "Colonizing the Chinese."

14. Bailie, "Conserve Life," 399.

15. Ibid.

16. Bailie to Bowen, 6 January 1913, YUDS 203/3472.

17. Bailie, "Conserve Life," 398–399; Bailie to Williams, 5 May 1912, YUDS 203/3472.

18. Bailie to Williams, 5 May 1912, YUDS 203/3472; Central China Famine Relief Committee, *Report and Accounts 1910–1911* and *Report and Accounts from October 1, 1911 to June 30, 1912* (Shanghai, 1912).

19. Bailie, "Magna Charta," 268–269.

20. Bailie to Williams, 5 May 1912, YUDS 203/3472.

21. Ibid.

22. Bailie to Williams, 16 October 1912, YUDS 203/3472.

23. "Constitution of the Colonization Association of the Republic of China," *The University of Nanking Magazine* 6 (June 1914): 214–215.

24. Bailie to Williams, 16 October 1912, YUDS 203/3472.

25. Ibid.

26. Ibid.

27. Ibid.; Joseph Bailie, "The Nanking Land Colony Scheme," *North China Daily News*, n.d., YUDS 200/3423.

28. "The Nanking Colony," *North China Daily News*, 5 September 1912, YUDS 200/3423.

29. Bailie to Bowen, 6 January 1913, YUDS 203/3472.

30. Bailie to Bowen, 8 January 1913, YUDS 203/3472.

31. Bailie to Williams, 16 March 1913, YUDS 203/3472.

32. Ibid.

33. Ibid.

34. Bailie to Williams, 4 April 1913, YUDS 203/3472.

35. Bailie to Bowen, 8 June 1913, YUDS 203/3472.

36. Ibid.

37. "Nanking Colony," YUDS 200/3423; Bailie to Williams, 26 May 1913, YUDS 203/3472.

38. Bailie to Williams, 9 June 1913, YUDS 203/3472.

39. Ibid.

40. Bailie to Bowen, 11 June 1913; Bailie to Clear, 13 June 1913, YUDS 203/3472.

41. Bailie to Bowen, 12 July 1913, YUDS 204/3473.

42. Bailie to Bowen, 3 August 1913, YUDS 204/3473.

43. Bailie to Bowen, 15 August 1913, YUDS 204/3473.

44. Ibid.

45. Bailie to Bowen, 10 September 1913, YUDS 204/3473.

46. Ibid.

47. Bailie to Bowen, 31 October 1913, YUDS 204/3473.

48. Bailie to Bowen, 15 November 1913, YUDS 204/3473.

49. Bailie to Bowen, 24 October 1913, YUDS 204/3473.

50. Bailie [open letter], 14 December 1913, YUDS 204/3473.

51. "Colonization: The Organization of the Nanking Branch Association," University of Nanking, Agricultural Department Bulletin no. 2 (n.d.): 5–12.

52. Joseph Bailie, "Chinese Arbor Day," 1, undated ms., YUDS 198/3399.

53. Ibid., 1–2.

54. Ibid., 2.

55. Ibid., 2–3.

56. Chinese Forestry Association, "Arbor Day for China," pamphlet, 1918, YUDS 198/3399.

57. "Colonization," 3, 5.

58. Bailie to Williams, 11 May 1912, YUDS 203/3472.

59. Bailie to Williams, 16 October 1912, YUDS 203/3472.

60. Zhang Yufa, "Ershi shiji chuqi," 138, 142–143; Guoli Nanjing gaodeng shifan xuexiao nongye yanjiu hui [Nanjing Teachers' College, Agricultural Studies Committee], *Nongye jiaoyu* [Agricultural Education] (1919): 177–178.

61. John Reisner, "Agricultural Education in China," *World Agriculture* 2 (Spring/Summer 1921): 97; Bailie, "A Letter from Mr. Joseph Bailie," 206.

62. Ibid.

63. University of Nanking, *Bulletin 1914–1915*, Agricultural Development, 4.

64. Reisner interview, transcript 1–2, CU.

65. Ibid., 2, 9–10.

66. Ibid., 5.

67. Bailie, "A Letter from Mr. Joseph Bailie," 206; University of Nanking, *Bulletin 1914–1915*, Agriculture Department, 1.

68. Bailie to Reinsch, 19 June 1915, NA 893.6171/3.

69. Ibid.

70. Bailie to Reinsch, 19 June 1915; Reinsch to Bureau of Forestry, 2 September 1915; Department of State to AmLegation, Peking, telegram, 13 October 1915, NA 893.6171/3.

71. Joseph Bailie, "Letter to Dr. Fong F. Sec.," *The University of Nanking Magazine* 6 (June 1915): 414.

72. Bailie, "Letter to Dr. Fong F. Sec.," 415.

73. Bailie, "Magna Charta," 272.

74. Victoria W. Bailie, *Bailie's Activities in China*, 80–81.

75. Ibid., 81–83.

76. Ibid., 117, 120.

77. Ibid., 120.

78. Ibid., 120–121.

79. Ibid., 121.

80. Ibid., 125.

81. Woodworth to Bailie, n.d., YUDS 319/4873.

82. Chen Hanseng, "Gung Ho! The Story of the Chinese Cooperatives," Institute of Pacific Relations, pamphlet no. 24 (1947): 50–55.

CHAPTER 4: MISSION

1. Helen S. Nevius, *The Life of John Livingston Nevius* (New York: Fleming H. Revell Company, 1895), 431.

2. Benjamin H. Hunnicutt and William Watkins Reid, *The Story of Agricultural Missions* (New York: Missionary Education Movement of the United States and Canada, 1931), 16–18; Valentin H. Rabe, "Evangelical Logistics: Mission Support and Resources to 1920," and Clifton J. Phillips, "The Student Volunteer Movement and Its Role in China

Missions, 1886–1920," both in *The Missionary Enterprise in China and America*, ed. John K. Fairbank (Cambridge, Mass.: Harvard University Press, 1974), 56–109.

3. G. W. Groff, "Agricultural Education for China under Missionary Influence," *Chinese Recorder* 45 (March 1914): 160.

4. Groff, "Agricultural Education," 159–160.

5. Ibid., 160–161.

6. Ibid., 164.

7. "Minutes of the Directing Committee of the Pennsylvania State College Mission to China," Pennsylvania State University (hereafter abbreviated PSU).

8. Groff to Fagan, 17 December 1913, PSU.

9. Ibid.

10. Attachment to Fagan to Graybill letter, 17 March 1915, PSU.

11. Fagan to Groff, 2 November 1915, PSU.

12. Ibid.

13. "Penn State in China," pamphlet, circa 1921, PSU.

14. Groff to Penn State Friend, 29 December 1924, PSU.

15. Ibid.

16. Ibid.

17. Groff to Edmunds, 16 June 1918, PSU.

18. Canton Christian College, *Report of the President, 1919–1924* (New York: Trustees of the Canton Christian College, n.d.), 38–45.

19. Lingnan University, College of Arts and Sciences, Lingnan Agricultural College, *Catalogue 1926–27*, 34–37. Canton Christian College was renamed Lingnan University in 1926.

20. John Reisner, "Practical Agriculture and Missions in China," *Millard's Review* 6 (2 November 1918): 372.

21. "Inter-Society Debate Between Arts and Agricultural-Forestry Literary Societies," *The University of Nanking Magazine* 10 (February 1919): 13–23.

22. John Reisner, "Agriculture in the Program of Christian Education," *Educational Review* 18 (October 1926): 549.

23. *China Mission Year Book, 1919* (Shanghai: Kwang Hsueh Publishing House, 1920), 154–155.

24. Ibid., 155–156.

25. Ibid., 156–157.

26. "The American E. F. Farmer's Club," *World Agriculture* 1 (October/December 1919): 1; "The World Agriculture Society," *World Agriculture* 1 (June 1920): 7.

27. John H. Reisner, "Recent Agricultural Missionary Developments," *World Agriculture* 2 (Summer 1922): 196.

28. Kenyon L. Butterfield, "The Far East and World Agriculture," *World Agriculture* 2 (Winter/Spring 1922): 163.

29. "Objectives of the China National Branch," *World Agriculture* 2 (Summer 1922): 193.

30. "Nanking Chapter Report," *World Agriculture* 2 (Summer 1922): 193.

31. "Cornell International Agricultural Society," *World Agriculture* 3 (June 1923): 255.

32. William Overholt, interview by Jane Baker Coons, 14 March 1980, transcript, 26–27, Midwest China Center, Oral History and Archives Collection.

33. John Reisner, "Foreign Missions and Agriculture," *Chinese Recorder* 51 (October 1920): 697–698.

34. Ibid., 699.

35. Ibid., 698–699.

36. *The Chinese Church as Revealed in The National Christian Conference* (Shanghai: The Oriental Press, 1922), 324–328.

37. Milton T. Stauffer, ed., *The Christian Occupation of China* (Shanghai: China Continuation Committee, 1922), 421.

38. Ibid.

39. "China's First Agricultural Institute," *The [China] Weekly Review* 24 (12 May 1923): 380–382.

40. "Our Rural Symposium," *Chinese Recorder* 55 (December 1924): 761–762, and inset.

41. John H. Reisner, "The Church and China's Rural Population," *Chinese Recorder* 50 (December 1924): 762–765.

42. G. W. Groff, "The Rural Church," *Chinese Recorder* 50 (December 1924): 775–782.

43. Ibid., 777.

44. Reisner, "The Church," 763.

45. "Report of the Conference of Christian Rural Leaders" and "Report of the Conference on Agricultural Education," University of Nanking, College of Agriculture and Forestry Bulletin no. 12 (1926).

46. Hunnicutt, *The Story*, 18.

47. Lowdermilk to Speer, 30 January 1922, YUDS 215/3655.

48. Walter Lowdermilk, "Forestry and Erosion in China, 1922–1927," *Forest History* 16 (April 1972): 5.

49. Reisner to Lowdermilk, 14 February 1922, YUDS 215/3655.

50. Lowdermilk to Reisner, 20 February 1922, YUDS 215/3655.

51. Reisner to Lowdermilk, 28 February 1922, YUDS 215/3655.

52. Ibid.

53. Ibid.

54. Marks to Reisner, 13 June 1922, YUDS 215/3655.

55. Ibid.

56. Reisner to Marks, 22 June 1922, YUDS 215/3655.

57. Lowdermilk to Reisner, 15 June 1922, YUDS 215/3655.

58. Reisner to Lowdermilk, 22 June 1922, YUDS 215/3655.

59. Lowdermilk to Reisner, 22 June 1922, YUDS 215/3655.

60. Reisner to Lowdermilk, 14 July 1922, YUDS 215/3655.

61. Ibid.

62. John Lossing Buck, interview by Gould Colman, 21 September 1962, transcript, 1–6, CU; Nora Stirling, *Pearl Buck: A Woman in Conflict* (Piscataway, N.J.: New Century Publishers, 1983), 35–36.

63. Stirling, *Pearl Buck*, 36–37.

64. Ibid., 36–42.

65. Ibid., 40.

66. J. Lossing Buck, "Missionaries Begin Agricultural Education in China," *Millard's Review* 6 (14 September 1918): 78.

67. Ibid.; Alfred Charles True, *A History of Agricultural Education in the United States, 1785–1925* (Washington, D.C.: U.S. Government Printing Office, 1929), 283–284.

68. Buck, "Missionaries," 78.

69. Ibid., 79.

70. Buck interview, transcript 53–54, CU.

71. Ibid., 9–10.

72. Stirling, *Pearl Buck*, 47. Also see photograph of Buck, standing beside bike, surrounded by a huge crowd, described as "A Gang of 1,000, Which Stopped Work to See a Foreigner and His Bicycle," in J. Lossing Buck, "River Conservancy in Northern Anhwei," *Far Eastern Review* 13 (December 1917): 774.

73. J. Lossing Buck, "Agricultural Work of the American Presbyterian Mission at Nanhsuchow, Anhwei, China, 1919," *Chinese Recorder* 51 (June 1920): 412.

74. Ibid., 414.

75. Ibid., 418.

76. Ibid., 417–418.

77. Ibid., 416; J. Lossing Buck, "Practical Plans for the Introduction of Agriculture into Our Middle and Primary Schools," *Chinese Recorder* 50 (May 1919): 314; Stirling, *Pearl Buck*, 49.

78. Buck, "Agricultural Work," 413; Stirling, *Pearl Buck*, 47.

CHAPTER 5: COMPETITION

1. Meng Zhou, "Nongye gexin" [The reform of agriculture], *Nongmin*, no. 1 (November 1928): 1–19.

2. "Lun Zhongguo yi caiyong Meiguo zhongnong zhengce" [China should adopt the American policy of promoting agriculture], *Jiangning shiye zazhi*, no. 8 (20 February 1911): 55–59.

3. Peng Jiayuan, "Meiguo yanjiu nongshi zhi yiban" [A glance at American research in agriculture], *Zhonghua nongxue huibao*, no. 45 (February 1924): 74–75.

4. Hu Shih, in *Living Philosophies* (New York: Simon and Schuster, 1931), 251–252.

5. Hu Shih, "The Personal Reminiscences of Dr. Hu Shih," interview, edited transcript, 43–44, Chinese Oral History Project, East Asian Institute, Columbia University, 1959.

6. Y. C. Wang, *Chinese Intellectuals*, 510–511; D. Hoe Lee, "The Chinese Student of American Agriculture," *The Chinese Students' Monthly* 13 (April 1918): 333.

7. Ibid., 334, 336.

8. Ibid.; Chang Fu Liang [Zhang Fuliang], "Agricultural Education and Country Life," *Educational Review* 22 (April 1930): 188–189; "Nali hui you quchang buduan de lijie he nengli" [Where is the understanding and capability for learning from others to offset our own shortcomings?], *Nongye zhoubao*, no. 7 (1 December 1929): 170–171; Deng

Zhiyi, "Zhong Mei nongye zhi bijiao" [A comparison between Chinese and American agriculture], *Nonglin jikan* 1 (December 1923): 7–8.

9. John Reisner, "School Nurseries," University of Nanking Agriculture and Forestry Series, vol. 1, no. 1 (February 1920; rev. January 1924): 3.

10. "What the College of Agriculture and Forestry Can Do for You!" University of Nanking, pamphlet, n.d., 1–4.

11. John Reisner, "The Farm Implement Market of China," *The China Weekly Review* 17 (6 August 1921): 490.

12. John Reisner, "Modern Commercial Fertilizers in China," *American Fertilizer* 54 (7 May 1921): 54.

13. Ibid., 55.

14. Ibid., 55–56.

15. "Nanking University Introduces New Methods in Sericulture," *Millard's Review* 14 (6 November 1920): 508–509.

16. Ibid.

17. "Sericulture in Nanking," *Chinese Economic Monthly* 2 (August 1925): 10.

18. "Silkworm Raising by Old Methods," *Chinese Economic Bulletin*, no. 223 (30 May 1925): 305–306.

19. Ibid.

20. J. B. Griffing, "Report of Three Years' Cotton Improvement Work," n.d., n.p., 2–3, held at the National Agricultural Library, Beltsville, Maryland.

21. John Reisner, "Report on Cotton Experiment 1919," typescript, 1–2, YUDS 199/3416.

22. Ibid., 3–4.

23. Ibid., 6–7.

24. J. B. Griffing, "Cotton Culture," University of Nanking, Agriculture and Forestry Series, vol. 1, no. 3 (December 1920): 2–3.

25. Griffing, "Report of Three Years," 2, 4.

26. Ibid., 5.

27. J. B. Griffing, "Roguing of Cotton," University of Nanking, Agriculture and Forestry Series, vol. 1, no. 2 (August 1920): 1.

28. Ibid., 2.

29. Ibid., 3.

30. Ibid., 4.

31. Ibid., 6–7.

32. Ibid., 1, 7–8.

33. Griffing, "Report of Three Years," 6–7.

34. John Reisner, "Dangers and Control of Cotton Seed Importation and Distribution in China," *Millard's Review* 15 (29 January 1921): 473.

35. Ibid.

36. J. B. Griffing, "Possibilities in American Cotton Introduction in China," *Millard's Review* 13 (12 June 1920): 101.

37. Ibid.

38. Griffing, "Report of Three Years," 8–9.

39. Ibid., 9–10.

40. Ibid., 13.

41. Ibid.; Julean Arnold, "Agriculture in the Economic Life of the New China," *The China Weekly Review* 25 (30 June 1923): 144.

42. Griffing, "Report of Three Years," 13.

43. J. B. Griffing, "Economic Aspects of the Cotton Industry," *The University of Nanking Magazine* 12 (November 1922): 9.

44. Griffing, "Report of Three Years," 8, 13.

45. Ibid., 13–14, 20a.

46. "Improving China's Cotton," *The China Weekly Review* 27 (22 December 1923): 128; "China's First Agricultural Institute," *The [China] Weekly Review* 24 (12 May 1923): 380–382.

47. Griffing, "Report of Three Years," 14–15.

48. Ibid., 20.

49. Ibid.

50. Ibid., 21–23.

51. Ibid., 18.

52. Ibid., 15.

53. Ibid., 15–16.

54. Ibid., 16–17.

55. Griffing to Williams, 20 May 1923, YUDS 213/3626.

56. John Davis, "Southeastern University for Nanking," 25 May 1921, NA 893.42/133.

57. National Southeastern University, "A Brief Statement of the College of Agriculture," Information Bulletin no. 1 (August 1921): 1–2, 10–13.

58. Ibid., 2–5.

59. "Guoli Dongnan daxue nongke jiaoxue wenti" [Instructional problems in the Department of Agriculture at National Southeastern University], n.d., *Di er dang'an guan* [Number Two Historical Archives], Nanjing, China, file 648/389.

60. Ibid.

61. Ibid.

62. P. W. Tsou, "Working for More and Better Cotton in China," *The China Weekly Review* 28 (8 March 1924): 44–45.

63. Ye Yuanding, "Qingnian zhimian jingjin tuan zhi chengji" [Achievements of the Young People's Cotton Improvement Clubs], Dongnan daxue [Southeastern University], 1925.

64. Zhou Qing, "Jiangpu mianchang mianzuo tuiguang shishi zhi jingguo ji qi chengxiao" [The facts about cotton extension in Jiangpu and extension results], *Nongxue zazhi*, no. 1 (September 1928): 89–90.

65. Zhu Chunyuan, "Jiangpu shixing tuiguang Meimian baogao ji jianglai jinxing zhi shangque" [A report on experimental extension of American cotton in Jiangpu and a discussion of future implementation], *Nongxue* 1 (May 1924): 34.

66. Ibid., 37.

67. Ibid., 35–36.

68. Ibid., 36.

69. Ibid., 37.

70. Ibid.

71. "Sericulture in Nanking," 11.

72. John K. Davis, "Higher Education and Politics in the Nanking District," 16 March 1925, NA 893.42/209.

73. For a sample of Southeastern's promotionalism-by-numbers, see T. F. Tung, "Does Agricultural Improvement Pay?" *Far Eastern Review* 21 (January 1925): 40.

74. National Southeastern University, "A Brief Statement," 7–9; National Southeastern University, The College of Agriculture, "A Six-Year Review: 1917–1923," June 1923, 3–8.

75. Davis, "Higher Education," 16 March 1925, NA 893.42/209.

76. P. W. Tsou [Zou Bingwen], "Jiangsu shixing xinxuezhihou zhi nongye jiaoyu banfa" [Methods of agricultural education since implementation of the new educational system of Jiangsu], *Nongxue* 1 (15 June 1923): lunzhu 29–35.

77. Andrew Nathan, *A History of the China International Famine Relief Commission* (Cambridge, Mass.: East Asian Research Center, Harvard University, 1965), 6; "China Famine Fund Concludes Session," *The China Weekly Review* 27 (23 February 1924): 4.

78. "Famine Prevention Program of the College of Agriculture and Forestry," University of Nanking, Agriculture and Forestry Series, vol. 1, no. 9 (May 1924): 2.

79. "Third Annual Meeting of the Association," *World Agriculture* 2 (Winter-Spring, 1923): 168.

80. "Famine Prevention Program," 2.

81. Ibid., 5.

82. Ibid., 8.

83. Ibid., 7–8.

84. Ibid., 12–13.

85. Ibid., 13–15.

86. Ibid., 14.

CHAPTER 6: TIMIDITY

1. George W. Gray, *Education on an International Scale: A History of the International Education Board, 1923–1938* (Westport, Conn.: Greenwood Press, 1941), 3–7.

2. Ibid., 9–10.

3. Ibid., 8–9.

4. Rose to Farrand, 9 October 1923; Farrand to Rose, 10 October 1923; Rose to Mann, 17 October 1923; Rose's trip notes, 25 October 1923; Rose to Mann, 26 October 1923; Mann to Rose, 27 October 1923, Rockefeller Foundation Archives/International Education Board (hereafter abbreviated RFA/IEB) 19/285.

5. Reisner to Love, 4 February 1924, in H. H. Love and John H. Reisner, *The Cornell-Nanking Story*, Cornell International Agricultural Development Bulletin no. 4 (April 1964): 6.

6. Love and Reisner, *Cornell-Nanking*, 7; "Proposed Project to be Conducted Cooperatively by Nanking University, International Education Board and Cornell University,

for the Reorganization and Conducting of Plant Breeding Work at Nanking University, Nanking, China," RFA/IEB 27/386.

7. "Proposed Project," 2–4.

8. Gray, *Education*, 11–13.

9. "Synopsis of Course of Procedure to Follow in Educational Survey of Far East," RFA/IEB 22/327.

10. Ibid.; Rose to Trowbridge, 22 September 1925, and Rose to Mann, 22 September 1925, RFA/IEB 22/327.

11. H. L. Russell, Log Two, China and Philippines, 7, RFA/IEB.

12. Ibid., 7–8.

13. Ibid., 10–11.

14. Kuo to Rose, 29 December 1924; Rose to Kuo, 21 January 1925, RFA/IEB 27/384.

15. Tsou to Russell, 31 December 1925, attachment to Russell Log, 45s–45cc, RFA/IEB.

16. Russell Log, 69, RFA/IEB. Emphasis in the original.

17. Barry Keenan, *The Dewey Experiment in China: Educational Reform and Political Power in the Early Republic* (Cambridge, Mass.: Council on East Asian Studies, Harvard University, 1977), 113–115.

18. Davis, "Higher Education," 16 March 1926, NA 983.42/209.

19. Russell Log, 61–62, RFA/IEB.

20. Ibid., 43–45.

21. Ibid., 41–43.

22. Ibid., 46–47.

23. Ibid., 48x–48z.

24. Ibid., 49–52.

25. Ibid., 52.

26. Ibid., 26–27.

27. Ibid., 27.

28. Rose to Mann, 29 January 1926; Mann to Love, 19 January 1926, RFA/IEB 27/387.

29. Russell to Rose, 27 January 1926, RFA/IEB 27/384.

30. Rose to Russell, 9 March 1926, RFA/IEB 27/384.

31. Gray, *Education*, 13, 92–93.

32. Porter to Love and Myers, 9 April 1927, R. H. Porter Papers, CU.

33. Love and Reisner, *Cornell-Nanking*, 14–24.

34. Ibid., 11–15.

35. C. H. Myers, "Final Report of the Plant Improvement Project Conducted by the University of Nanking, Cornell University, and the International Education Board," n.d., 44, YUDS 201/3433.

36. Love and Reisner, *Cornell-Nanking*, 19.

37. Ibid., 33–34.

38. Ibid., 35.

39. Ibid., 37–42, 46.

40. Myers to Love, 10 April 1926, C. H. Myers Papers, CU.

41. Reisner to Love, 24 April 1926, J. H. Reisner Papers, CU.

42. Reisner to Love, 24 June 1926, Reisner Papers, CU; Myers to Love, 24 July 1926, Myers Papers, CU.

43. Myers to Love, 24 July 1926, Myers Papers, CU.

44. Myers, "Final Report," 3, YUDS 201/3433.

CHAPTER 7: MYOPIA

1. Buck to John [Reisner], 16 October 1920, YUDS 208/3537.

2. Stanley W. Warren, interview by Gould Colman, 8 August 1962, transcript 17, CU; Stirling, *Pearl Buck*, 57.

3. Stirling, *Pearl Buck*, 56–57, 65.

4. Taylor and Taylor, *Story of Agricultural Economics*, 91.

5. Ibid., 358–360; Buck to John [Reisner], 16 October 1920, YUDS 208/3537.

6. George F. Warren, *Farm Management* (New York: Macmillan Company, 1913), 2, 15–16.

7. Ibid., 30–31, 144–145, 242.

8. Ibid., 242–245, 263.

9. Ibid., 145.

10. Ibid., 264; Buck interview, transcript 14–15, CU.

11. J. Lossing Buck, *An Economic and Social Survey of 102 Farms Near Wuhu, China*, University of Nanking, Agriculture and Forestry Series, vol. 1, no. 7 (1923): 4–5.

12. Ibid., 6–8.

13. Ibid., 3, 7.

14. Ibid., 10–11, 14–15, 19.

15. Ibid., 2.

16. Ibid., 19; J. Lossing Buck, *Development of Agricultural Economics at the University of Nanking, Nanking, China, 1926–1946*, Cornell International Agricultural Development Bulletin no. 25 (September 1973): 15, 17.

17. J. Lossing Buck, "The Chinese Church and Country Life," *Chinese Recorder* 54 (June 1923): 319–320.

18. Ibid., 321.

19. Ibid., 321–322.

20. Ibid., 322–323.

21. Ibid., 323.

22. Buck, *Development of Agricultural Economics*, 16; Myron T. Herrick, *Rural Credits: Land and Cooperative* (New York: D. Appleton and Company, 1919), 281–295; Buck, "The Chinese Church," 323–325.

23. Xu Guodong, "Nanjing chengbei Fengrun nongcun xinyong hezuoshe canguan ji" [A visit to the Fengrun Rural Credit Cooperative in north Nanjing], *Nongxue* 3 (June 1926): 2; Buck, *Development of Agricultural Economics*, 17–18.

24. Buck, *Development of Agricultural Economics*, 18; Xu Guodong, "Nanjing chengbei," 7.

25. Paul C. Hsu, "Rural Cooperatives in China," *Pacific Affairs* 1 (October 1929): 613–615; Buck, *Development of Agricultural Economics*, 20.

26. Hsu, "Rural Cooperatives," 615–616.

27. Ibid., 617, 624.

28. Ibid., 616–617, 619.

29. Stirling, *Pearl Buck*, 70, 75.

30. Ibid., 71; Buck interview, transcript 61, CU.

31. J. Lossing Buck, "The Self-Supporting Church," reprint from *The China Council Bulletin*, no. 123 (n.d.): 1–5.

32. J. Lossing Buck, "The Building of a Rural Church," *Chinese Recorder* 58 (July 1927): 404.

33. Ibid., 406.

34. Ibid., 407.

35. Ibid., 413–415.

36. Ibid., 409–410.

37. Stirling, *Pearl Buck*, 78–80; Buck, *Development of Agricultural Economics*, 28–29.

38. Stirling, *Pearl Buck*, 79–80; Buck, *Development of Agricultural Economics*, 29.

39. Pearl Buck to Friends, 13 April 1927; J. Lossing Buck to Shen, 16 April 1927, H. H. Love Papers, CU.

40. J. Lossing Buck, "Peasant Movements," in *The China Christian Year Book*, ed. Frank Rawlinson (Shanghai: Christian Literature Society, 1928), 273.

41. Ibid., 274–278.

42. Ibid., 277, 280–281.

43. J. Lossing Buck, *Farm Ownership and Tenancy in China* (Shanghai: National Christian Council, 1927), 1.

44. Ibid., 2–3, 30.

45. Ibid., 15, 18–25.

46. Ibid., 12–13, 25–27.

47. Buck to Friends, 17 September 1928, H. H. Love Papers, CU.

48. Buck to Love, 11 December 1928, H. H. Love Papers, CU; J. Lossing Buck, "The Big Swords and the Little Swords Clash," *The China Weekly Review* 46 (13 October 1928): 213.

49. Buck, "The Big Swords," 213.

50. J. Lossing Buck [J. L. B.], "A Farmer's Pitful [*Sic*] Tale about Bandits," *The China Weekly Review* 47 (8 December 1928): 73.

51. Buck to Love, 11 December 1928, H. H. Love Papers, CU; Buck, "The Big Swords," 214.

52. Stirling, *Pearl Buck*, 90; J. Lossing Buck, *Chinese Farm Economy: A Study of 2866 Farms in Seventeen Localities and Seven Provinces in China* (Chicago: University of Chicago Press, 1930), 426.

53. Buck, *Chinese Farm Economy*, 1, 6–7, 130.

54. Ibid., 23–28.

55. Ibid., 20, 81–97, 105.

56. Ibid., 116, 132–134, 424.

57. Ibid., 314–315.

58. Ibid., 357–358, 364–365.

59. Ibid., 409–411, 415–416.

60. Alfred Kaiming Chiu, "Recent Statistical Surveys of Chinese Rural Economy, 1912–1932," Ph.D. dissertation, Harvard University, 1933, 166.

61. Buck, *Chinese Farm Economy*, 401.

62. Ibid., 145, 159–166.

63. Charles Josiah Galpin, *Rural Social Problems* (New York: Century, 1924), 76–92; "Loan Books for Rural Workers," University of Nanking, College of Agriculture and Forestry Bulletin no. 16 (December 1926): 6–7.

64. Chiu, "Recent Statistical Surveys," 213–214.

65. Albert Z. Guttenberg, "The Land Utilization Movement of the 1920s," *Agricultural History* 50 (July 1976): 477–491; David Weeks, "Scope and Methods of Research in Land Utilization," *Journal of Farm Economics* 11 (October 1929): 597.

66. O. E. Baker, "Land Utilization in China," in *Problems of the Pacific: Proceedings of the Second Conference of the Institute of Pacific Relations, Honolulu, Hawaii, July 15 to 29, 1927*, ed J. B. Condliffe (Chicago: University of Chicago Press, 1928), 324–338.

67. Ibid., 329–330.

68. Ibid., 335.

69. Ibid., 325; Stirling, *Pearl Buck*, 90; Buck, *Development of Agricultural Economics*, 30.

70. Buck, *Development of Agricultural Economics*, 30, 32–35; "Visiting Specialists for China Land Utilization and Population Project," chart, YUDS 208/3538.

71. Warren interview, transcript 18, CU.

72. Buck, *Department of Agricultural Economics*, 40–41.

73. Warren interview, transcript 6, CU; Buck to Friends, 3 December 1930, YUDS 208/3539.

74. Ibid.; Buck, *Development of Agricultural Economics*, 41–42.

75. J. Lossing Buck, "The Meaning of Agricultural Improvement," *The China Critic* 4 (25 June 1931): 608–609, 632–633.

76. J. Lossing Buck, "Agricultural Extension Methods," *The China Weekly Review* 61 (18 June 1932): 94–95.

77. J. Lossing Buck, "Possible Contributions of Agricultural Economics to Rural Improvement in China," *The China Weekly Review* 59, Reconstruction Supplement (19 December 1931): 22.

78. Stirling, *Pearl Buck*, 145; Buck, *Development of Agricultural Economics*, 37–38.

79. J. Lossing Buck, *Land Utilization in China* (Nanking: University of Nanking, 1937); vol. 2, *Atlas*; vol. 3 *Statistics*.

80. Buck, *Development of Agricultural Economics*, 30; Buck, *Land Utilization*, 1:x.

81. Buck, *Land Utilization*, 1:ix.

82. Ibid., 1:vii, 26.

83. Ibid., 1:169–179.

84. Ibid., 1:1.

85. Ibid., 1:20.

86. Ibid., 1:21, 178–179, 202–203.

87. Ibid., 1:9, 20–21, 196, 285.

88. Ibid., 1:243.

Chapter 8: DEFEAT

1. Shen's autobiography consists of three volumes, which were eventually collected together and republished as Shen Zhonghan, *Shen Zonghan zishu* (Taibei: Chuanji wenxue chubanshe, 1975). Its three components are *Kenan kuxue ji* [A record of diligent study and conquered obstacles]; *Zhongnian zishu* [My middle years]; and *Wannian zishu* [My late years]; each component has separate pagination and will be abbreviated hereafter as *SZH* 1, 2, and 3, respectively. Shen also published a condensed version in English, *Autobiography of a Chinese Farmers' Servant* (Taibei: Linking Publishing Company, 1981), which omits much but occasionally contains an anecdote missing from the Chinese work. For an example of Shen's interest in inspiring others with the virtues of hard work and dedication, see *SZH* 1, *zixu* (preface): 2.

2. *SZH* 1:1–26.

3. *SZH* 1:27–30; Shen, *Autobiography*, 51.

4. *SZH* 1:31–48.

5. *SZH* 1:49.

6. *SZH* 1:52–53, 63–64.

7. *SZH* 1:67–72.

8. T. H. Shen [Shen Tsung-han/Zonghan], "How Can America Best Help China?" *Millard's Review of the Far East* 13 (3 July 1920): 268–270.

9. Ibid.

10. *SZH* 1:72–75; Shen, *Autobiography*, 102; Sherman Cochran, *Big Business in China: Sino-Foreign Rivalry in the Cigarette Industry, 1890–1930* (Cambridge, Mass.: Harvard University Press, 1980), 22–27, 75.

11. *SZH* 1:75–78.

12. *SZH* 1:78–79.

13. Shen, *Autobiography*, 107; *SZH* 1:78–79; T. H. Shen, *Shen Zonghan wannian wenlu* [Writings from Shen Zonghan's later years] (Taibei: Chuanji wenxue chubanshe, 1979), "Zhongguo nongye kexuehua de chuqi" [The early period in the emergence of scientific agriculture in China], 86.

14. Shen, *Autobiography*, 107–108; *SZH* 1:79.

15. Shen, *Autobiography*, 108–109; *SZH* 1:79–80.

16. *SZH* 1:80.

17. *SZH* 1:80–81.

18. *SZH* 1:81–82; Shen, *Autobiography*, 110.

19. *SZH* 1:77, 82.

20. *SZH* 1:83–84.

21. *SZH* 1:83–84, 91; Shen, *Autobiography*, 115.

22. Reisner to Love, 10 September 1926, Reisner Papers, CU.

23. *SZH* 1:87.

24. *SZH* 1:89.

25. *SZH* 2:1, 4–6, 8–9.

26. *SZH* 2:6–7.

27. *SZH* 2:11–24.

28. *SZH* 2:40.

29. *SZH* 2:30.

30. Shen, *Autobiography*, 140; *SZH* 2:40–41.

31. *SZH* 2:41.

32. *SZH* 2:42.

33. *SZH* 2:43, 55.

34. National Agricultural Research Bureau (of China; hereafter abbreviated NARB), *History and Scope of Work (July 1933–December 1934)*, Miscellaneous Publication no. 4 (April 1935): 3; *SZH* 2:29.

35. NARB, *History*, 4–16.

36. Ibid., 13–14.

37. *SZH* 2:44; National Agricultural Research Bureau and the National Rice and Wheat Improvement Institute, *Report for the Year 1936*, Miscellaneous Publication no. 7 (Chongqing, 1937), 4. The English version of the story differs slightly—Shen says that the NARB paid for salaries as well as travel expenses—but the discrepancy appears to be a translation error. See Shen, *Autobiography*, 143.

38. *SZH* 2:44–46.

39. *SZH* 2:47–48.

40. Shen, *Shen Zhonghan wannian wenlu*, 92; *SZH* 2:56, 61–62.

41. Mary Brown Bullock, *An American Transplant: The Rockefeller Foundation and Peking Union Medical College* (Berkeley, Los Angeles, London: University of California Press, 1980), 5–6; "Report of the Committee on Appraisal and Plan," RFA 3/22/170.

42. James C. Thomson, Jr., *While China Faced West: American Reformers in Nationalist China, 1928–1937* (Cambridge, Mass.: Harvard University Press, 1969), 125.

43. Selskar M. Gunn, "Report on Visit to China," RFA 12/129.

44. Ibid.

45. Ibid.

46. Selskar M. Gunn, "China and the Rockefeller Foundation," 23 January 1934, typescript, 40, RFA 12/130.

47. Ibid., 32–34.

48. Ibid., 36–37, 61.

49. "Report of the Committee on Appraisal and Plan," 29, RFA 3/22/170.

50. Ibid., 45–46, 105.

51. Ibid., 106–108.

52. RF Board Minutes, 21 December 1934, 34488; "Report of the Committee on Appraisal and Plan," 24, RFA 3/22/170.

53. Gunn to Mason, 29 March 1935, RFA 14/143.

54. Ibid.

55. Ibid.

56. RF *Annual Report 1935*, 321–323.

57. "China Program: Preliminary Interim Statement," October 1935, 12–13, RFA 12/130.

58. Selskar M. Gunn, "China Program: Progress Report for the Period July 1, 1935–February 15, 1937," 2, 6, 12, RFA 12/130.

59. NARB, "Biennial Report of Insect Control Work," Special Publication no. 20 (November 1938).

60. RF, *Annual Report 1935*, 324, 341.

61. NARB, "Biennial Report"; "China Program" (1937), RFA 14/146; RF, *Annual Report 1936*, 313.

62. Buck, *Land Utilization*, 1:4.

63. Huang Hao, "Jiangning zizhi shiyanxian tianfu zhi guoqu xianzai yu jianglai" [The past, present, and future of land taxes in the Jiangning Self-government Experimental County], *Jingjixue jikan* 4 (September 1933): 53.

64. Zhang Jubo, "Jiangsusheng huangchong wenti" [Jiangsu's locust control problems], in *Jiangsusheng nongzheng huiyi huibian* [Proceedings of the Jiangsu Conference on Agricultural Administration] (Shanghai, 1929), 90–93.

65. Ibid., 92.

66. Wang Chaoran, "Jiangningxian caizheng gaikuang ji qi piping" [The general situation of Jiangning County finances and some criticism], *Zhengzhi yuekan* 12 (15 October 1934): 130; "Jiangning qian zhi" [Jiangning's change in administration], *Suheng* 1 (June 1935): 5.

67. Bao Shangxian, "Nikan zenme ban" [Look, what can be done?], *Nonglin xinbao* 7 (11 November 1930): 476.

68. Li Zude, "Nanjingshi Hepingxiang zhi minsu" [Folk customs of the Heping District, Nanjing], Graduation thesis, Jinling University, 1937, 121a; Jiang Jie, *Jingjiao nongcun shehui diaocha* [A social survey of villages in Nanjing's suburbs] (Nanjing, 1937), 46; Zhang Jubo, "Jiangsusheng huangchong," 92.

69. "Jiangning zizhi shiyanxian xianzhengfu dishiwu ci zizhi zhidao weiyuanhui jilu" [Minutes of the fifteenth meeting of the County Government Guidance Committee of the Jiangning Self-government Experimental County], *Jiangning xianzheng gongbao*, no. 24 (30 December 1935): 3.

70. Chuan Shengfa, "Shoudu fujin tuiguang caichong yaoji wenti" [Problems with extension of insecticide for vegetable pests in the capital's suburbs], *Nongye tuiguang*, no. 12 (September 1936): 13.

71. Xu Shuojun, "Dongji zhiming qianshuo" [Simple instructions on how to control winter rice-stem borers], *Nongbao* 2 (30 October 1935): 1040.

72. Ibid., 1040–1041.

73. Cai Banghua, "Zuijin jixiang zhiming gongzuo zhi jiantao" [Self-criticism of work on several recent rice-stem borer control programs], *Nongbao* 3 (30 August 1936): 1251.

74. Lü Jinluo, "Minguo ershiwunian Jiangsu Wujiang zhiming jishi" [The real record concerning the 1936 rice-stem borer control program in Jiangsu's Wujiang], *Nongbao* 4 (30 March 1937): 449–450.

75. Wu Fuzhen, "Zhiming xingzheng wenti" [Problems in the administration of rice-stem borer control], *Nongbao* 3 (10 October 1936): 1445–1446.

76. Lü Jinluo, "Minguo ershiwunian Jiangsu Wujiang," 450.

77. SZH 2:61–62.

78. Gunn to Fosdick, 17 August 1937, RFA 14/146; "Effects of Sino-Japanese Conflict on Work of the Rockefeller Foundation in the Far East," 12 September 1939, RFA 14/148.

79. Gunn to Ray [Raymond Fosdick], 23 February 1937, RFA 14/146.

80. Ibid.

Epilogue

1. T. H. Shen, *The Sino-American Joint Commission on Rural Reconstruction: Twenty Years of Cooperation for Agricultural Development* (Ithaca, N.Y.: Cornell University Press, 1970), 9–14, 257–260.

2. Kenneth L. Turk, *The Cornell–Los Banos Story* (Ithaca: New York State College of Agriculture and Life Sciences, 1974), vii–xi, 8–13.

3. Shen, *The Sino-American Joint Commission,* 12–13.

4. Wayne G. Broehl, Jr., *John Deere's Company: A History of Deere & Company and Its Times* (Garden City, N.Y.: Doubleday, 1984), 716.

BIBLIOGRAPHY

CHINESE-LANGUAGE SOURCES

The bibliography that follows lists only those sources that are cited in the text. Reflecting the book's focus on Americans in China, its coverage of Chinese sources is limited to those works that happen to refer to Americans. Thus it does not provide a very satisfactory survey of the many other useful primary materials related to modern Chinese agricultural history—namely, periodicals that do not happen to refer to Americans which I discovered in the libraries of the People's Republic and used for my doctoral dissertation, a local study of agricultural change in Republican China's Jiangsu Province. Most of these sources necessarily went unmentioned in this book. Because few historians outside of China have used many of these materials, annotation of some of the more important kinds of Chinese-language sources that provided background for this study may nevertheless be of interest to future researchers.

Agricultural societies, formed by professional Chinese agriculturalists, issued journals and newsletters for their memberships that today offer an excellent point of entry into the agricultural literature. Luo Zhenyu's *Wunonghi* 務農會 issued the pioneering agricultural "newspaper," the *Nongxuebao* 農學報, which appeared two or three times a month between 1897 and 1906 (this was the paper for which Zhang Zhidong ordered multiple subscriptions, as mentioned in chap. 2). A total of 315 issues was published, many filled with translations of foreign articles on agriculture; today, the *Nongxuebao* provides an invaluably early record of Chinese sifting and filtering of contemporary agricultural knowledge in the world. The most important professional society that emerged in the prewar period, the *Zhonghua nongxuehui* 中華農學會, began publication in 1918 of its journal, the *Zhonghua nongxue huibao* 中華農學會報, which was published regularly until 1937, when the war with Japan intruded. Occasionally, provincial-level societies also attempted to issue a regular journal; for example, the *Jiangsusheng nonghui zazhi* 江蘇省農會雜誌 put out one issue in 1917, but the journal then disappeared from view. Another important professional journal from the late 1910s is *Nongxue zazhi* 農學雜誌, a quarterly published by Commercial Press in Shanghai (and not to be confused with another journal of the same name published later by Southeastern University).

During the 1920s, important new independent journals appeared, written by and for professional agriculturalists, and contributors began to address nontechnical topics that pertained to agricultural policies. *Xinnongye jikan* 新農業季刊, for example, published five issues in 1924 and 1925 and is interesting for its anti-imperialist tone. In 1929, the *Nongye zhoubao* 農業週報 began its ambitious schedule of weekly publication; it lasted only two years, but its 80 issues are one of the best sources of lively editorials and of truthful reports about agricultural administration for the entire Republican period. In 1931, a new publisher assumed its Chinese name and continued publication through 1937, but the frequency of insightful articles seems to have dropped off abruptly.

Agricultural colleges and schools published various journals, papers, reports to trustees, and course catalogues, which form another large body of valuable material. One of the earliest sets of college publications was put out by the National College of Agriculture in Beijing. Appearing in the late 1910s under the name *Guoli Beijing nongye zhuanmen xuexiao zazhi* 國立北京農業專門學校雜誌, the early issues were thin and sporadic, but a new series, called *Xin nongye* 新農業, was published in 1922 and 1923 and ran progressive and controversial articles about the needed reform of Chinese agriculture in general and of Chinese agricultural education in particular. The college also published another journal, *Xin nongmin* 新農民, in 1931 and 1932.

In accord with its status as the largest college of agriculture in prewar China, the College of Agriculture and Forestry at the University of Nanking published the largest number and variety of publications, most of which were concerned primarily with matters related to the institution: technical articles contributed by the faculty, progress reports on extension programs, personnel news. Perhaps the single most useful publication was *Nonglin xinbao* 農林新報, a newsletter issued two or three times a month beginning in 1918. It ran continuously through the college's evacuation from Nanjing in 1937, thus constituting a rare continuous prewar run of a single agricultural journal over a period of twenty years.

Nanking's neighboring rival, Southeastern (Dongnan, later Zhongyang) University, also put out a considerable number of publications, such as *Nongxue zazhi* 農學雜誌, a technical journal issued during the 1920s which reported the results of faculty research. The university's agricultural newsletters—*Nongxueyuan xunkan* 農學院旬刊, issued in the late 1920s, and *Zhongda nongxun* 中大農訊, issued in the mid-1930s—are filled with short items about institutional plans, alumni news, and reports of improbably successful research and extension programs.

Another notable run, perhaps second in importance only to Nanking's *Nonglin xinbao*, is the remarkable string of 211 issues of *Nong sheng* 農聲, produced between 1919 and 1937 by the extension department of the College of Agriculture at Zhongshan University, in Guangzhou. The newsletter contains college and professional association news, recent speeches, research reports, and translations of articles from foreign sources.

Other smaller agricultural colleges—in Shanxi, Zhejiang, and Fujian, to mention a few locations—published newsletters, some for runs of several years, others for only several issues. Some agricultural high schools also attempted to produce a regular periodical—for example, *Xin Sunong* 新蘇農, published quarterly in late 1928 and early 1929 by the *Suzhou nongye xuexiao* 蘇州農業學校.

Administrators and teachers in rural education programs generated a large literature about their professional speciality and usually included agricultural improvement in their agenda of changes needed in the countryside. A magazine such as *Jiaoyu yu nongcun* 教育與農村, which was published in Zhenjiang, Jiangsu, in the early 1930s, was typical of many similar periodicals in its inclusion of articles that dispense advice about agricultural improvement.

The final major source of periodicals is the Chinese government at various levels, from national ministries responsible for agriculture to county and, in some areas, subcounty experiment stations and extension programs. For official pronouncements of agricultural policies, many different series of national and provincial gazettes are available. The NARB published numerous technical papers that would be of interest to a historian of science. It also published two series that were not agronomical. Its bimonthly newsletter, *Nong bao* 農報, which began publication in 1934, is a miscellany of agricultural news and reports, not always restricted to NARB projects or to the officially sanguine perspective that tends to inform many of its other publications. The NARB also was responsible for collecting and publishing crop reports gathered from around the country: *Nongqing baogao* 農情報告 began publication in 1934.

One of the best publications that reported on agricultural extension activities is *Nongye tuiguang* 農業推廣, published in Nanjing from 1930 to 1937 by the National Extension Committee. This periodical was directed toward agricultural-extension staff members throughout the country and contains both lengthy accounts of extension plans still on the drawing board and reports of extension projects already in progress. The plans may seem dreamy now, but the reports of attempted extension projects ring with verisimilitude. General or anecdotal articles about agriculture are also found at the front of each issue.

A number of government agencies, colleges, and schools also attempted to produce an agricultural literature that would be understandable to Chinese farmers who had only a minimal education. One of the earliest such series of publications was *Nong hua* 農話, produced in the mid-1920s by the Number One Agricultural School of Jiangsu. Each short issue provides practical advice on one specific subject, such as fertilizers, sericulture, or afforestation. The NARB and many other institutions put out similar pamphlet series, often called *qianshuo* 淺說.

In the late 1920s and 1930s, the periodical literature that reported on the countryside swelled with publications issued by rural reconstruction offices, public and private; by new rural schools and cooperatives; by banks that specialized in rural credit programs; and by sociology departments at colleges and universities. All of these agencies and programs took some interest in agricultural production. The rural reconstruction literature, however, must be used with some skepticism, because it tends to be long on plans and short on credible reports of actual programs in progress.

The major newspapers, such as *Zhongyang ribao* 中央日報 and *Shenbao* 申報, may appear at first glance to be too urban-oriented to offer much to the student of early twentieth-century Chinese agriculture. On the pages of the typical edition, the countryside remains largely invisible, except for the routine notice that is taken of a severe natural disaster, a tax protest ending in violence, or an armed gang of marauders kidnapping a rural notable for ransom (Republican-period newspapers should be credited with outstanding reporting of crimes of any and all description). But patient combing of the small, stray story related to agriculture can yield important discoveries. For example, a little item that appeared in a 1935 issue of the *Zhongyang ribao* reported that the Jiangsu government was eliminating the entire province's network of agricultural extension posts to "achieve large savings in the annual budget"; this was surprising and valuable information, and not to be found in regular agricultural newsletters.

In closing this brief survey, I would like to encourage the researcher to cast her or his net as widely as possible when trolling for material. One of my own favorite sources is an unlikely one, *Dongfang zazhi* 東方雜誌, whose general-interest stories do not touch upon agriculture very regularly. But the magazine is a good record of what was topical at any given time in Shanghai and the other cities. Occasionally agriculture was a topic of conversation or the subject of articles (often written in a sensational style), and in one instance almost an entire issue was devoted to it. By looking at such general magazines, or at the short stories and novels of China's gifted writers who were so prolific before the war with Japan, we can trace the process through which urban, literate China became increasingly aware and concerned with rural, illiterate China. In an important sense, the history of modern Chinese agriculture is in part the story of gaining visibility in its own country.

MANUSCRIPT AND ARCHIVAL COLLECTIONS

Bancroft Library. University of California. Berkeley, California.

Columbia University. East Asian Institute. Chinese Oral History Project. New York, New York.

Cornell University Libraries (CU). Department of Manuscripts and University Archives. Ithaca, New York.

Di er dang'an guan 第二挡案馆 [Number Two Historical Archives]. Nanjing, China.

International Harvester Archives (IHA). International Harvester Company. Chicago, Illinois.

Midwest China Center. Oral History and Archives Collection. St. Paul, Minnesota.

National Archives (NA). Records of the Department of State Relating to Internal Affairs of China, 1910–1929. Record Group 59. Washington, D.C.

Pennsylvania State University Libraries (PSU). Penn State Room. University Park, Pennsylvania.

Rockefeller Foundation Archives (RFA). Rockefeller Archive Center. Pocantico Hills, North Tarrytown, New York.

Yale University Divinity School (YUDS). Day Missions Library. China Records Project. Record Group 11. New Haven, Connecticut.

BOOKS AND ARTICLES

"Agriculture at Yale College," *Scientific American*, new series, vol. 2, no. 7 (11 February 1860): 100.

"Agriculture in Manchuria." U.S. Department of Commerce and Labor. *Daily Consular and Trade Reports*, no. 3430 (16 March 1909): 1–8.

Agriculture of the United States in 1860 (Eighth Census). Washington, D.C.: Government Printing Office, 1864.

"The American E. F. Farmer's Club." *World Agriculture* 1 (October/December 1919): 1.

Anderson, George. "Agricultural Implements in China." U.S. Department of Commerce and Labor. Bureau of Statistics. *Monthly Consular Reports*, no. 291 (December 1904): 52–53.

Arnold, Julean. "Agriculture in the Economic Life of the New China." *The China Weekly Review* 25 (30 June 1923): 141–146.

Ayers, William. *Chang Chih-tung and Educational Reform in China*. Cambridge, Mass.: Harvard University Press, 1971.

Bailey, Joseph C. *Seaman A. Knapp: Schoolmaster of American Agriculture*. New York: Columbia University Press, 1945.

Bailie, Joseph. "Conserve Life Through Reclamation of Waste Lands." *The University of Nanking Magazine* 6 (March 1915): 398–403.

———. "Famine and Afforestation in China." *International Review of Missions* 6 (July 1917): 450–456.

———. "A Letter from Mr. Joseph Bailie, Head and Organizer of Agriculture and Forestry at the University of Nanking, to the China Press." *The University of Nanking Magazine* 6 (June 1914): 206–207.

————. "Letter to Dr. Fong F. Sec." *The University of Nanking Magazine* 6 (June 1915): 414–417.

————. "Magna Charta of China's Forestry Work." *American Forestry* 22 (May 1916): 268–272.

Bailie, Victoria W. *Bailie's Activities in China.* Palo Alto, Calif.: Pacific Books, 1964.

Baker, O. E. "Land Utilization in China." In *Problems of the Pacific: Proceedings of the Second Conference of the Institute of Pacific Relations, Honolulu, Hawaii, July 15 to 29, 1927.* Ed. by J. B. Condliffe. Chicago: University of Chicago Press, 1928.

Bao Shangxian 鮑尙賢. "Nikan zenme ban" 你看怎麼辦 [Look, what can be done?]. *Nonglin xinbao* 農林新報 7 (11 November 1930): 473–478.

Bentley, W. P. *Guojia zhuanshe nongbu yi* 國家專設農部議 [A suggestion for a national department of agriculture]. Shanghai: Commercial Press, 1903.

Boardman, Mabel Thorp. *Under the Red Cross Flag at Home and Abroad.* 2d ed. Philadelphia: J. B. Lippincott, 1915.

Bray, Francesca. "The Chinese Contribution to Europe's Agricultural Revolution: A Technology Transformed." In *Explorations in the History of Science and Technology in China.* Ed. by Li Guohao et al. Shanghai: Shanghai Chinese Classics Publishing House, 1982.

Brill, Gerow D. "Chinese Incubators." In *Seventeenth Annual Report of the Bureau of Animal Industry for the Year 1900.* U.S. Department of Agriculture. Washington, D.C.: Government Printing Office, 1901.

Broehl, Wayne G., Jr. *John Deere's Company: A History of Deere & Company and Its Times.* Garden City, N.Y.: Doubleday, 1984.

Bronfenbrenner, Martin. *Academic Encounter: The American University in Japan and Korea.* New York: The Free Press, 1961.

Bryce, James. *The American Commonwealth.* 2 vols. New York: Macmillan, 1889.

Buck, J. Lossing. "Agricultural Extension Methods." *The China Weekly Review* 61 (18 June 1932): 94–95.

————. "Agricultural Work of the American Presbyterian Mission at Nanhsuchow, Anhwei, China, 1919." *Chinese Recorder* 51 (June 1920): 412–419.

————. "The Big Swords and the Little Swords Clash." *The China Weekly Review* 46 (13 October 1928): 213–214.

————. "The Building of a Rural Church." *Chinese Recorder* 58 (July 1927): 403–416.

————. "The Chinese Church and Country Life." *Chinese Recorder* 54 (June 1923): 319–326.

————. *Chinese Farm Economy: A Study of 2866 Farms in Seventeen Localities and Seven Provinces in China.* Chicago: University of Chicago Press, 1930.

————. "Contributions to Western Agriculture." In *There Is Another China: Essays and Articles for Chang Poling.* New York: King's Crown Press, 1948, 108–115.

————. *Development of Agricultural Economics at the University of Nanking, Nanking, China, 1926–1946.* Cornell International Agricultural Development Bulletin no. 25, September 1973.

————. *An Economic and Social Survey of 102 Farms Near Wuhu, China.* University of Nanking. Agriculture and Forestry Series, vol. 1, no. 2, 1923.

————. *Farm Ownership and Tenancy in China.* Shanghai: National Christian Council, 1927.

————. "A Farmer's Pitful [*sic*] Tale about Bandits." *The China Weekly Review* 47 (8 December 1928): 73.

————. *Land Utilization in China.* 3 vols. Nanking: University of Nanking, 1937.

————. "The Meaning of Agricultural Improvement." *The China Critic* 4 (25 June 1931): 608–609, 632–633.

————. "Missionaries Begin Agricultural Education in China." *Millard's Review* 6 (14 September 1918): 78–79.

————. "Peasant Movements." In *The China Christian Year Book.* Ed. by Frank Rawlinson. Shanghai: Christian Literature Society, 1928.

————. "Possible Contributions of Agricultural Economics to Rural Improvement in China." *The China Weekly Review* 59, Reconstruction Supplement (19 December 1931): 22, 25, 34.

————. "Practical Plans for the Introduction of Agriculture into Our Middle and Primary Schools." *Chinese Recorder* 50 (May 1919): 307–319.

————. "River Conservancy in Northern Anhwei." *Far Eastern Review* 13 (December 1917): 772–774.

————. "The Self-Supporting Church." Reprint from *The China Council Bulletin*, no. 123, n.d.

Bullock, Mary Brown. *An American Transplant: The Rockefeller Foundation and Peking Union Medical College.* Berkeley, Los Angeles, London: University of California Press, 1980.

Bureau of Agriculture, Industry, and Commerce. *Outline and Comments on the Agricultural Development of Manchuria.* Moukden [Mukden], 1908.

Butterfield, Kenyon L. "The Far East and World Agriculture." *World Agriculture* 2 (Winter/Spring 1922): 163.

Cai Banghua 蔡邦華. "Zuijin jixiang zhiming gongzuo zhi jiantao" 最近幾項治螟工作之檢討 [Self-criticism of work on several recent rice-stem borer control programs]. *Nongbao* 農報 3 (30 August 1936): 1245–1255.

Canton Christian College. *Report of the President, 1919–1924.* New York: Trustees of the Canton Christian College, n.d.

Carstensen, Vernon. "An Overview of American Agricultural History." In *Farmers, Bureaucrats, and Middlemen: Historical Perspectives on American Agriculture.* Ed. by Trudy Huskamp Peterson. Washington, D.C.: Howard University Press, 1980.

Cartensen, Fred V. *American Enterprise in Foreign Markets: Studies of Singer and International Harvester in Imperial Russia.* Chapel Hill: University of North Carolina Press, 1984.

Central China Famine Relief Committee. *Report and Accounts 1910–1911.* Shanghai, 1912.

————. *Report and Accounts from October 1, 1911 to June 30, 1912.* Shanghai, 1912.

Chang Fu Liang [Zhang Fuliang 張福良]. "Agricultural Education and Country Life." *Educational Review* 22 (April 1930): 188–193.

Chen Hanseng. "Gung Ho! The Story of the Chinese Cooperatives." Institute of Pacific Relations Pamphlet no. 24, 1947.

"China Famine Fund Concludes Session." *The China Weekly Review* 27 (23 February 1924): 4.

China Mission Year Book, 1919. Shanghai: Kwang Hsueh Publishing House, 1920.

"China's First Agricultural Institute." *The [China] Weekly Review* 24 (12 May 1923): 380–382.

The Chinese Church as Revealed in the National Christian Conference. Shanghai: The Oriental Press, 1922.

Chiu, Alfred Kaiming. "Recent Statistical Surveys of Chinese Rural Economy, 1912–1932." Ph.D. diss., Harvard University, 1933.

Chu, Samuel C. *Reformer in Modern China: Chang Chien, 1853–1926*. New York: Columbia University Press, 1965.

Chuan Shengfa 傅勝發. "Shoudu fujin tuiguang caichong yaoji wenti" 首都附近推廣菜蟲藥劑問題 [Problems with extension of insecticide for vegetable pests in the capital's suburbs]. *Nongye tuiguang* 農業推廣, no. 12 (September 1936): 8–20.

Cochran, Sherman. *Big Business in China: Sino-Foreign Rivalry in the Cigarette Industry, 1890–1930*. Cambridge, Mass.: Harvard University Press, 1980.

"Colonization: The Organization of the Nanking Branch Association." University of Nanking. Agricultural Department Bulletin no. 2, n.d.

"Colonizing the Chinese." *North China Daily News*, 19 April 1912.

Conservancy Work in China: Being a Series of Documents and Reports by Chang Chien. Shanghai: National Review, 1912.

"Constitution of the Colonization Association of the Republic of China." *The University of Nanking Magazine* 6 (June 1914): 214–215.

"Cornell International Agricultural Society." *World Agriculture* 3 (June 1923): 255.

Crawford, R. P. "World Crops for America." *Scientific American* 126 (April 1922): 226–227.

Cunningham, Isabel Shipley. *Frank N. Meyer: Plant Hunter in Asia*. Ames: Iowa State University Press, 1984.

Curti, Merle, and Kendall Birr. *Prelude to Point Four: American Technical Missions Overseas, 1838–1938*. Madison: University of Wisconsin Press, 1954.

Denby, Charles. "Agriculture in China." *Forum* 32 (November 1901): 328–340.

———. "Among the Plants: In Garden, Field and Forest." *Current Literature* 27 (March 1900): 258–259.

———. *China and Her People*. Boston: L. C. Page and Company, 1905.

Deng Zhiyi 鄧植儀. "Zhong Mei nongye zhi bijiao" 中美農業之比較 [A comparison between Chinese and American agriculture]. *Nonglin jikan* 農林季刊 1 (December 1923): 1–8.

Donald, W. H. "China as a Most Promising Field for Plant Exploration." *Far Eastern Review* 12 (July 1915): 41–48.

Douglas, Margery Stoneman. "The Most Unforgettable Character I've Met." *Reader's Digest* 53 (November 1948): 67–71.

Edwards, Everett E., comp. *Washington, Jefferson, Lincoln, and Agriculture*. Washington, D.C.: U.S. Department of Agriculture, 1937.

Elvin, Mark. *The Pattern of the Chinese Past*. Stanford, Calif.: Stanford University Press, 1973.

Fairchild, David. "An Agricultural Explorer in China." *Asia* 21 (January 1921): 7–13.

———. "A New Exploration of the World." *Youth's Companion* 83 (6 May 1909): 219–220.

———. *Letters on Agriculture in the West Indies, Spain, and the Orient*. U.S. Department of Agriculture. Bureau of Plant Industry Bulletin no. 27. Washington, D. C.: Government Printing Office, 1902.

———. "Two Unknown Modern Languages." *The Outlook* 93 (4 September 1909): 43–44.

———. *The World Was My Garden: Travels of a Plant Explorer*. New York: Charles Scribner's Sons, 1945.

Fairchild, David, and Walter T. Swingle. "China's Contributions to the World's Food." *World Agriculture* 2 (Spring and Summer 1921): 102–103.

"Famine Prevention Program of the College of Agriculture and Forestry." University of Nanking. Agriculture and Forestry Series, vol. 1, no. 9, May 1924.

Farrer, Reginald. "Mr. Reginald Farrer's Explorations in China." *Gardener's Chronicle*, series 3, 58 (1915): 1.

Feng Guifen 馮桂芬. *Jiaobin lu kangyi* 校邠廬抗議 [Protest from the Jiaobin Studio]. Taibei: Wenhai, 1971, reproduction of 1898 edition.

Franklin, Benjamin. *The Papers of Benjamin Franklin.* 24 vols. Ed. by William B. Willcox. New Haven, Conn.: Yale University Press, 1959–1984.

Freeman, John. "Flood Problems in China." *Transactions of the American Society of Civil Engineers* 85 (1922): 1405–1460.

Galpin, Charles Josiah. *Rural Social Problems.* New York: Century, 1924.

Gray, George W. *Education on an International Scale: A History of the International Education Board, 1923–1938.* Westport, Conn.: Greenwood Press, 1941.

Griffing, J. B. "Cotton Culture." University of Nanking. Agriculture and Forestry Series, vol. 1, no. 3 (December 1920).

———. "Economic Aspects of the Cotton Industry." *The University of Nanking Magazine* 12 (November 1922): 9–10.

———. "Possibilities in American Cotton Introduction in China." *Millard's Review* 13 (12 June 1920): 98–102.

———. "Report of Three Years' Cotton Improvement Work." N.d., n.p. Held at the National Agricultural Library, Beltsville, Maryland.

———. "Roguing of Cotton." University of Nanking. Agriculture and Forestry Series, vol. 1, no. 2 (August 1920).

Groff, G. W. "Agricultural Education for China under Missionary Influence." *Chinese Recorder* 45 (March 1914): 158–164.

———. "The Rural Church." *Chinese Recorder* 50 (December 1924): 775–782.

Guoli Nanjing gaodeng shifan xuexiao nongye yanjiu hui 國立南京高等師範學校農業研究會 [Nanjing Teachers' College, Agricultural Studies Committee], *Nongye jiaoyu* 農業教育 [Agricultural Education] n.p. (1919).

Guttenberg, Albert Z. "The Land Utilization Movement of the 1920s." *Agricultural History* 50 (July 1976): 477–491.

Harrison, John A. "The Capron Mission and the Colonization of Hokkaido, 1868–1875." *Agricultural History* 25 (May 1951): 135–142.

Herrick, Myron T. *Rural Credits: Land and Cooperative.* New York: D. Appleton and Company, 1919.

Ho Ping-ti. *Studies on the Population of China, 1368–1953.* Cambridge, Mass.: Harvard University Press, 1959.

Hsiao Kung-chuan. *A Modern China and a New World: K'ang Yu-wei, Reformer and Utopian, 1858–1927.* Seattle: University of Washington Press, 1975.

Hsu, Paul C. "Rural Cooperatives in China." *Pacific Affairs* 1 (October 1929): 611–634.

Hu Shih. In *Living Philosophies.* New York: Simon and Schuster, 1931.

"Huai River Conservancy Project." *Far Eastern Review* 11 (April 1915): 415–424.

Huang Hao 黃豪. "Jiangning zizhi shiyanxian tianfu zhi guoqu xianzai yu jianglai" 江寧自治實驗縣田賦之過去現在與將來 [The past, present, and future of land taxes in the Jiangning Self-government Experimental County]. *Jingjixue jikan* 經濟學季刊 4 (September 1933): 33–86.

Hummel, Arthur W. *Eminent Chinese of the Ch'ing Period.* 2 vols. Washington, D.C.: Government Printing Office, 1943 and 1944.

Hunnicutt, Benjamin H., and William Watkins Reid. *The Story of Agricultural Missions.* New York: Missionary Education Movement of the United States and Canada, 1931.

Hunt, Michael H. *Frontier Defense and the Open Door: Manchuria in Chinese-American Relations, 1895–1911.* New Haven, Conn.: Yale University Press, 1973.

"The Hwai River Conservancy." *Far Eastern Review* 10 (May 1914): 469.

"The Hwai River Conservancy Commission." *Far Eastern Review* 11 (June 1914): 14.

"Improving China's Cotton." *The China Weekly Review* 27 (22 December 1923): 126–128.

"Inter-Society Debate Between Arts and Agricultural-Forestry Literary Societies." *The University of Nanking Magazine* 10 (February 1919): 13–23.

Jameson, Charles Davis. "River, Lake and Land Conservancy in Portions of the Provinces of Anhui and Kiangsu, North of the Yangtsze River." *Far Eastern Review* 9 (November 1912): 247–263.

Jefferson, Thomas. *The Papers of Thomas Jefferson.* 20 vols. Ed. by Julian P. Boyd. Princeton, N.J.: Princeton University Press, 1950–1982.

Jian Bozan 翦伯贊, et al., ed. *Wuxu bianfa* 戊戌變法 [The Reforms of 1898]. 4 vols. Shanghai: Shanghai renmin chubanshe, 1961.

Jiang Jie 蔣傑. *Jingjiao nongcun shehui diaocha* 京郊農村社會調查 [A social survey of villages in Nanjing's suburbs]. Nanjing, 1937.

"Jiangning qian zhi" 江寧遷治 [Jiangning's change in administration]. *Suheng* 蘇衡 1 (June 1935): 5.

"Jiangning zizhi shiyanxian xianzhengfu dishiwu ci zizhi zhidao weiyuanhui jilu" 江寧自治實驗縣縣政府第十五次自治指導委員會紀錄 [Minutes of the fifteenth meeting of the County Government Guidance Committee of the Jiangning Self-government Experimental County]. *Jiangning xianzheng gongbao* 江寧縣政公報, no. 24 (30 December 1935): 1–5.

Kahn, E. J., Jr. *The Staffs of Life.* Boston: Little, Brown, 1985.

Kahn, Harold L. *Monarchy in the Emperor's Eyes: Image and Reality in the Ch'ien-lung Reign.* Cambridge, Mass.: Harvard University Press, 1971.

Keenan, Barry. *The Dewey Experiment in China: Educational Reform and Political Power in the Early Republic.* Cambridge, Mass.: Council on East Asian Studies, Harvard University, 1977.

King, F. H. *Farmers of Forty Centuries.* Madison, Wis.: Democrat Printing Company, 1911.

Knapp, Seaman A. *Recent Foreign Explorations, As Bearing on the Agricultural Development of the Southern States.* U.S. Department of Agriculture. Bureau of Plant Industry Bulletin no. 35. Washington, D.C.: Government Printing Office, 1903.

La Fargue, Thomas E. *China's First Hundred.* Pullman: State College of Washington, 1942.

LaFeber, Walter. *The New Empire: An Interpretation of American Expansion, 1860–1898.* Ithaca, N.Y.: Cornell University Press, 1963.

Lee, D. Hoe. "The Chinese Student of American Agriculture." *The Chinese Students' Monthly* 13 (April 1918): 333–340.

Li Zude 李祖德. "Nanjingshi Hepingxiang zhi minsu" 南京市和平鄉之民俗 [Folk customs of the Heping District, Nanjing]. Graduation thesis, Jinling University, 1937.

Lingnan University. College of Arts and Sciences. Lingnan Agricultural College. *Catalogue, 1926–27,* Canton [Guangzhou].

Liu Boji 劉伯驥. *Meiguo huaqiao shi* 美國華僑史 [The history of overseas Chinese in America]. Taibei: Xingzhengyuan qiaowu weiyuanhui, 1976.

"Loan Books for Rural Workers." University of Nanking. College of Agriculture and Forestry Bulletin no. 16, December 1926.

Love, H. H., and John H. Reisner. *The Cornell-Nanking Story*. Cornell International Agricultural Development Bulletin no. 4, April 1964.

Lowdermilk, Walter. "Forestry and Erosion in China, 1922–1927." *Forest History* 16 (April 1972): 4–15.

Lü Jinluo 呂金羅. "Minguo ershiwunian Jiangsu Wujiang zhiming jishi" 民國二十五年江蘇吳江治螟紀實 [The real record concerning the 1936 rice-stem borer control program in Jiangsu's Wujiang]. *Nongbao* 農報 4 (30 March 1937): 445–450.

"Lun Zhongguo yi caiyong Meiguo zhongnong zhengce" 論中國宜採用美國重農政策 [China should adopt the American policy of promoting agriculture]. *Jiangning shiye zazhi* 江寧實業雜誌, no. 8 (20 February 1911): 55–59.

Martin, William. "Agricultural Implements in China." U.S. House of Representatives. *Consular Reports* 62 (June 1900): 202–203.

McCormick, Cyrus. *The Century of the Reaper*. Boston: Houghton Mifflin, 1931.

McCormick, Thomas J. *China Market: America's Quest for Informal Empire, 1893–1901.* Chicago: Quadrangle Books, 1967.

McCullough, David. *The Path Between the Seas: The Creation of the Panama Canal, 1870–1914.* New York: Simon and Schuster, 1977.

"Mechanical Farming in Manchuria." *Contemporary Manchuria* 3 (October 1939): 42–62.

Meng Zhou 孟周. "Nongye gexin" 農業革新 [The reform of agriculture]. *Nongmin* 農民, no. 1 (November 1928): 1–19.

Meyer, Frank N. "China a Fruitful Field for Plant Exploration." In *Yearbook of the United States Department of Agriculture—1915*. Washington, D.C.: Government Printing Office, 1916.

―――. "Economic Botanical Explorations in China." *Transactions of the Massachusetts Horticultural Society*, part 1 (1916): 125–130.

Miller, Henry B. "American Fruit in China." U.S. House of Representatives. *Consular Reports* 65 (January 1901): 40–42.

"Nali hui you quchang buduan de lijie he nengli" 哪里會有取長補短的理解和能力 [Where is the understanding and capability for learning from others to offset our own shortcomings?]. *Nongye zhoubao* 農業週報, no. 7 (1 December 1929): 170–171.

"Nanking Chapter Report." *World Agriculture* 2 (Summer 1922): 193.

"Nanking University Introduces New Methods in Sericulture." *Millard's Review* 14 (6 November 1920): 507–509.

Nathan, Andrew. *A History of the China International Famine Relief Commission*. Cambridge, Mass.: East Asian Research Center, Harvard University, 1965.

National Agricultural Research Bureau [of China; NARB]. "Biennial Report of Insect Control Work," Special Publication no. 20, November 1938.

―――. *History and Scope of Work (July 1933–December 1934)*. Miscellaneous Publication no,. 4, April 1935.

National Agricultural Research Bureau and the National Rice and Wheat Improvement Institute. *Report for the Year 1936*. Miscellaneous Publication no. 7, 1937.

National Southeastern University. "A Brief Statement of the College of Agriculture." Information Bulletin no. 1, August 1921.

————. College of Agriculture. "A Six-Year Review: 1917–1923." June 1923.

Nevius, Helen S. *The Life of John Livingston Nevius.* New York: Fleming H. Revell Company, 1895.

"Objectives of the China National Branch." *World Agriculture* 2 (Summer 1922): 193.

Oliver, John W. *History of American Technology.* New York: Ronald Press Company, 1956.

"Our Rural Symposium." *Chinese Recorder* 55 (December 1924): 761–762.

Parker, Edward C. "Commercial Manchuria." *Review of Reviews* 40 (December 1909): 713–719.

————. "Farming as a Business Enterprise." *Review of Reviews* 33 (January 1906): 62–67.

————. *Field Management and Crop Rotation.* St. Paul, Minn.: Webb Publishing, 1915.

————. "The Future Wheat Supply of the United States." *Century Magazine* 76 (September 1908): 736–746.

————. "Manchuria and World's Wheat Supply." *Northwestern Miller* 82 (4 May 1910): 279–280, 298–299.

————. "Outline of a Plan for Assisting the Agricultural Development of Manchuria." In *Outline and Comments on the Agricultural Development of Manchuria.* Ed. by The Bureau of Agriculture, Industry, and Commerce. Moukden [Mukden], 1908.

Peng Jiayuan 彭家元. "Meiguo yanjiu nongshi zhi yiban" 美國研究農事之一斑 [A glance at American research in agriculture]. *Zhonghua nongxue huibao* 中華農學會報, no. 45 (February 1924): 69–75.

"The People Who Stand for Plus." *Outing* 53 (October 1908): 69–76.

Perkins, Dwight H. *Agricultural Development in China, 1369–1968.* Chicago: Aldine, 1969.

Phillips, Clifton J. "The Student Volunteer Movement and Its Role in China Missions, 1886–1920." In *The Missionary Enterprise in China and America.* Ed. by John K. Fairbank. Cambridge, Mass.: Harvard University Press, 1974.

"Plants from China." *Wallace's Farmer* 41 (11 February 1916): 235.

"Professor Bailie's Plan for the Famine Refugees." *The University of Nanking Magazine* 2 (September 1911): 4.

Rabe, Valentin H. "Evangelical Logistics: Mission Support and Resources to 1920." In *The Missionary Enterprise in China and America.* Ed. by John K. Fairbank. Cambridge, Mass.: Harvard University Press, 1974.

Rasmussen, Wayne D., and Gladys L. Baker. *The Department of Agriculture.* New York: Praeger, 1972.

Reisner, John. "Agricultural Education in China." *World Agriculture* 2 (Spring/Summer 1921): 97–98.

————. "Agriculture in the Program of Christian Education." *Educational Review* 18 (October 1926): 546–549.

————. "The Church and China's Rural Population." *Chinese Recorder* 50 (December 1924): 762–765.

————. "Dangers and Control of Cotton Seed Importation and Distribution in China." *Millard's Review* 15 (29 January 1921): 473–474.

————. "The Farm Implement Market of China." *The China Weekly Review* 17 (6 August 1921): 489–491.

————. "Foreign Missions and Agriculture." *Chinese Recorder* 51 (October 1920): 696–700.

————. "Modern Commercial Fertilizers in China." *American Fertilizer* 54 (7 May 1921): 54–57.

————. "Practical Agriculture and Missions in China." *Millard's Review* 6 (2 November 1918): 370–372.

————. "Recent Agricultural Missionary Developments." *World Agriculture* 2 (Summer 1922): 196.

————. "School Nurseries." University of Nanking. Agriculture and Forestry Series, vol. 1, no. 1 (February 1920; rev. January 1924).

Report of the Commissioner of Agriculture, 1862, 1863, 1864. Washington, D.C.: Government Printing Office, 1863–1865.

Report of the Commissioner of Patents, 1837. Washington, D.C.: Government Printing Office, 1838.

"Report of the Conference of Christian Rural Leaders" and "Report of the Conference on Agricultural Education." University of Nanking. College of Agriculture and Forestry Bulletin no. 12, 1926.

Schlebecker, John T. *Whereby We Thrive: A History of American Farming, 1607–1972.* Ames: Iowa State University Press, 1975.

Schwantes, Robert S. *Japanese and Americans: A Century of Cultural Relations.* New York: Council on Foreign Relations, 1955.

"Sericulture in Nanking." *Chinese Economic Monthly* 2 (August 1925): 8–14.

Shen, T. H. [Shen Zonghan 沈宗瀚]. *Autobiography of a Chinese Farmers' Servant.* Taibei: Linking Publishing Company, 1981.

————. "How Can America Best Help China?" *Millard's Review of the Far East* 13 (3 July 1920): 268–270.

————. *Shen Zonghan wannian wenlu* 沈宗瀚晚年文錄 [Writings from Shen Zonghan's later years]. Taibei: Chuanji wenxue chubanshe, 1979.

————. *Shen Zonghan zishu* 沈宗瀚自述 [The autobiography of Shen Zonghan]. 3 vols. Taibei: Chuanji wenxue chubanshe, 1975.

————. *The Sino-American Joint Commission on Rural Reconstruction: Twenty Years of Cooperation for Agricultural Development.* Ithaca, N.Y.: Cornell University Press, 1970.

"Silkworm Raising by Old Methods." *Chinese Economic Bulletin*, no. 223 (30 May 1925): 305–306.

Stauffer, Milton T., ed. *The Christian Occupation of China.* Shanghai: China Continuation Committee, 1922.

Stirling, Nora. *Pearl Buck: A Woman in Conflict.* Piscataway, N.J.: New Century Publishers, 1983.

Su Yunfeng 蘇雲峯. "Hubei nongwu xuetang—jindai Zhongguo nongye jiaoyu de xianqu" 湖北農務學堂─近代中國農業教育的先驅 [The Hubei Agricultural College—A pioneer in modern China's agricultural education]. *Xinzhi zazhi* 新知雜誌 4 (December 1974): 45–55.

————. "Waiguo zhuanjia xuezhe zai Hubei (1890–1911)" 外國專家學者在湖北 [Foreign experts and educators in Hubei (1890–1911)]. *Zhonghua wenhua fuxing yuekan* 中華文化復興月刊 8 (April 1975): 51–64.

————. *Zhongguo xiandaihua de quyu yanjiu: Hubeisheng* 中國現代化的區域研究：湖北省

[A regional study of Chinese modernization: Hubei Province]. Taibei: Academia Sinica, 1981.

Sutton, Stephanne B. *In China's Border Provinces: The Turbulent Career of Joseph Rock, Botanist-Explorer*. New York: Hastings House, 1974.

Taylor, Henry C., and Anne Dewees Taylor. *The Story of Agricultural Economics in the United States, 1840–1932*. Ames: Iowa State College Press, 1952.

"Third Annual Meeting of the Association." *World Agriculture* 2 (Winter-Spring 1923): 168.

Thomson, James C., Jr. *While China Faced West: American Reformers in Nationalist China, 1928–1937*. Cambridge, Mass.: Harvard University Press, 1969.

True, Alfred Charles. *A History of Agricultural Education in the United States, 1785–1925*. Washington, D.C.: Government Printing Office, 1929.

Tsou, P. W. [Zou Bingwen 鄒秉文]. "Jiangsu shixing xinxuezhihou zhi nongye jiaoyu banfa" 江蘇實行新學制後之農業教育辦法 [Methods of agricultural education since implementation of the new educational system of Jiangsu]. *Nongxue* 農學 1 (15 June 1923): lunzhu 論著 27–38.

———. "Working for More and Better Cotton in China." *The China Weekly Review* 28 (8 March 1924): 44–45.

Tung, T. F. "Does Agricultural Improvement Pay?" *Far Eastern Review* 21 (January 1925): 40.

Turk, Kenneth L. *The Cornell–Los Banos Story*. Ithaca: New York State College of Agriculture and Life Sciences, 1974.

Turner, Frederick Jackson. *The Early Writings of Frederick Jackson Turner*. Ed. by Everett E. Edwards. Madison: University of Wisconsin Press, 1938.

U.S. Patent Office. *Annual Report—1837*. Washington, D.C.: Government Printing Office, 1837.

University of Nanking. *Bulletin 1914–1915*.

Wakeman, Frederic, Jr. *The Fall of Imperial China*. New York: The Free Press, 1975.

Wang Chaoran 汪綽然. "Jiangningxian caizheng gaikuang ji qi piping" 江寧縣財政概況及其批評 [The general situation of Jiangning County finances and some criticism]. *Zhengzhi yuekan* 政治月刊 12 (15 October 1934): 124–132.

Wang, Y. C. *Chinese Intellectuals and the West, 1872–1949*. Chapel Hill: University of North Carolina Press, 1966.

Warren, George F. *Farm Management*. New York: Macmillan Company, 1913.

Weeks, David. "Scope and Methods of Research in Land Utilization." *Journal of Farm Economics* 11 (October 1929): 597–608.

"What the College of Agriculture and Forestry Can Do for You!" University of Nanking. Pamphlet, n.d. (1922?).

Wildman, Rounsevelle. "Chinese Agriculture and American Machinery." U.S. House of Representatives. *Consular Reports* 66 (May 1901): 121–122.

Wills, Garry. *Cincinnatus: George Washington and the Enlightenment*. Garden City, N.Y.: Doubleday, 1984.

"Woman Off to China as Government Agent to Study Soy Bean," *New York Times*, 10 June 1917, section VI, 9.

"The World Agriculture Society." *World Agriculture* 1 (June 1920): 7.

Wu Fuzhen 吳福楨. "Zhiming xingzheng wenti" 治螟行政問題 [Problems in the administration of rice-stem borer control]. *Nongbao* 農報 3 (10 October 1936): 1443–1447.

Xu Guodong 徐國棟. "Nanjing chengbei Fengrun nongcun xinyong hezuoshe canguan ji" 南京城北豐潤農村信用合作社參觀記 [A visit to the Fengrun Rural Credit Cooperative in north Nanjing]. *Nongxue* 農學 3 (June 1926): 9 pp.

Xu Shichang 徐世昌. *Dongsansheng zhenglue* 東三省正略 [A brief account of administering the Three Eastern Provinces]. Taibei: Wenhai, 1965, reprint of 1911 edition.

Xu Shuojun 徐碩俊. "Dongji zhiming qianshuo" 冬季治螟淺說 [Simple instructions on how to control winter rice-stem borers]. *Nongbao* 農報 2 (30 October 1935): 1039–1041.

Ye Yuanding 葉元鼎. "Qingnian zhimian jingjin tuan zhi chengji" 青年植棉競進團之成績 [Achievements of the Young People's Cotton Improvement Clubs]. Dongnan daxue 東南大學 [Southeastern University], 1925.

Zhang Jubo 張巨伯. "Jiangsusheng huangchong wenti" 江蘇省蝗蟲問題 [Jiangsu's locust control problems]. In *Jiangsusheng nongzheng huiyi huibian* 江蘇省農政會議彙編 [Proceedings of the Jiangsu Conference on Agricultural Administration]. Shanghai, 1929.

Zhang Qian 張謇. *Zhang Jizi jiulu* 張季子九錄 [The collected works of Zhang Qian]. 80 juan. Shanghai, 1931.

Zhang Yufa 張玉法. "Ershi shiji chuqi de Zhongguo nongye gailiang (1901–1916): Yanhai yanjiang shisange shengqu de bijiao yanjiu" 二十世紀初期的中國農業改良 (1901–1916): 沿海沿江十三個省區的比較研究 [Chinese agricultural improvement in the early twentieth century, 1901–1916: A comparative study of thirteen coastal and riverine provinces and districts]. *Shixue pinglun* 史學評論, no. 1 (July 1979): 119–159.

Zhang Zhidong 張之洞. *Zhang Wenxianggong quanji* 張文襄公全集 [The complete works of Zhang Zhidong]. 6 vols, 229 zhuan. Taibei, 1963.

Zhou Qing 周清. "Jiangpu mianchang mianzuo tuiguang shishi zhi jingguo ji qi chengxiao" 江浦棉場棉作推廣事實之經過及其成效 [The facts about cotton extension in Jiangpu and extension results]. *Nongxue zazhi* 農學雜誌, no. 1 (September 1928): 85–90.

Zhu Chunyuan 朱春元. "Jiangpu shixing tuiguang Meimian baogao ji jianglai jinxing zhi shangque" 江浦試行推廣美棉報告及將來進行之商榷 [A report on experimental extension of American cotton in Jiangpu and a discussion of future implementation]. *Nongxue* 農學 1 (May 1924): 32–37.

INDEX

Designer: Linda Robertson
Compositor: Asco Trade Typesetting Ltd.
Text: 10/12 Palatino
Display: Palatino
Printer: Braun-Brumfield, Inc.
Binder: Braun-Brumfield, Inc.